The Crisis of the Constitution

The Crisis of

the Constitution

An essay in constitutional and

political thought in England

1603–1645

By

Margaret Atwood Judson

Foreword by J. H. Hexter

Rutgers University Press

New Brunswick and London

First paperback printing, 1988

Library of Congress Cataloging-in-Publication Data

Judson, Margaret Atwood, 1899–
    The crisis of the constitution : an essay in constitutional and
political thought in England, 1603–1645 / by Margaret Atwood Judson.
— 1st paperback ed.
        p.   cm.
    Includes bibliographical references and index.
    ISBN 0-8135-1316-2 : ISBN 0-8135-1307-3 (pbk.)
        1. Great Britain—Constitutional history.   2. Great Britain—
Politics and government—1603–1645. 3. Political science—Great
Britain—History—17th century.   I. Title.
JN193.J8 1988
320.942—dc19   87-32406
                                                          CIP

British Cataloguing-in-Publication information available

ACKNOWLEDGMENT is made to the following publishers for permissions granted
to use quotations from books published by them. Each quotation used is cited
fully in a note:

American Philosophical Society	Huntington Library
Cambridge University Press	Law Quarterly Review
Jonathan Cape	Longmans Green & Co.
Columbia University Press	The Macmillan Co.
Cornell University Press	University of Minnesota Press
Harper & Brothers	Northwestern University Studies
Harvard Law Review	Oxford University Press
Harvard University Press	Speculum

Yale University Press

FOREWORD

"'WHY in the world,' a reader may well ask, 'should you, a retired professor, 84 years old, write your professional autobiography as a woman professor, historian, and educator in the years before the women's movement?'" Such is the first sentence of the memoir Margaret A. Judson wrote in 1984. In the plain elegance of its fit it was a beginning worthy of the woman who wrote it. It is the simple, sensible, and uncluttered question of an uncluttered mind examining itself. And the answer is as cogent and clear as the question. In her retirement years Margaret Judson had become "interested in women's history." Feminists urged her to tell her story as one more chapter in the unending chronicle of the injustices inflicted on her sex. "This story," she went on, however, "will surprise some of those urging me to write it. Of course it will include frustrations and inequities, but only in part. For it tells of many opportunities and satisfactions, and I believe, some successes along the way."[1] Indeed her story tells of successes, all well earned. And why should it not? Just last year, as if merely stating the obvious, a young English historian, Johann Sommerville, wrote, in his *Politics and Ideology in England, 1603–1640*, "The best general account of political thinking in early Stuart England is M. A. Judson, *The Crisis of the Constitution*." Of course he is right.

Judson's work appeared thirty-eight years ago. Until Sommerville published his study no historian of political thinking in

---

[1] Margaret A. Judson, *Breaking the Barrier* (Rutgers University Press, New Brunswick, N.J., 1984), 3.

v

England in early modern times had produced a work which, in depth of scholarship, clarity of exposition, and meticulous sizing up of meaning, came within a country mile of Judson's. Dr. Sommerville's study did come a good bit nearer than a country mile but did not overtake *The Crisis of the Constitution.* Partly this was because Margaret Judson had surveyed most of the ground so thoroughly, so skillfully, and so justly that to go over it again with any purpose but to confirm and verify it by replication at a half-dozen checkpoints would be a waste of time. Partly it was because no scholar, however acute and energetic, could cover in a single decade the ground that Professor Judson had taken nearly thirty years of tenacious study and patient reflection to traverse.

Moreover, no historian since Judson has displayed a sense as acute as hers of the waxing ambivalence of the Englishmen who, early in the seventeenth century, exalted the monarch to the very skies in one breath, and before they even breathed again, firmly placed him under the law. During the first quarter of that century, the voices of the age, which we still can hear, held to these two contradictory positions resonantly and with apparent but diminishing ease. In 1949 Professor Judson, who listened long and closely to those voices, showed us beyond doubt that throughout that time span this ambivalence penetrated all social strata. With or without intention to do so, subsequent studies which intersected with hers have verified that penetration.

Nearly four decades ago, therefore, relying on surviving evidence and reasoned inference, Margaret Judson caught, better than anyone has since, the consciousness and consciences of the people of England in the first quarter of the seventeenth century in the matters of political obligation and the rights of the rulers of England and their subjects. This is no small achievement. Nor was it a small achievement (at least in one sense of the word *small*) for British historians of Stuart England to have overlooked for so many years so large an achievement and thus to have missed its implications, for all the world like a dotty, nearsighted Oxford don who, having forgotten his spectacles, somehow misses the Bodleian. How *did* they do it?

Was it a certain condescension in those days among the scholars of Great Britain toward colonials, even toward de-fected colonials, who vaingloriously ventured opinions and judgments as to what in the past had been going on in the mother country?[2] Or was it a certain condescension of those scholars to American academics not visibly bearing the stig-mata of one of a small cluster of American universities deemed "U" or OK?[3] Or, despite Professor Judson's denial that she suffered significantly from the discrimination against women pervasive in academia in the United States in the 1940s and 1950s, were the English silent about *The Crisis of the Constitution* because it was the work of a quasi-colonial woman from a non-U academic institution? Recalling with some queasiness the time long ago when I qualified as an academic male chauvinist pig, I find the injection of a "gender factor" here rather more persuasive than Professor Judson might.

In the United States, Professor Judson's book was reviewed with deep appreciation at all the Right Addresses—*The Ameri-can Historical Review, The American Political Science Review, The Political Science Quarterly*—except the *Journal of the History of Ideas*. Though not a regular reviewer, that journal should have given *The Crisis of the Constitution* the attention it de-served. It was surely worth a review article.

What happened in England was this. In 1951 the *English Historical Review* printed a succinct, intelligent, and laudatory short notice of *The Crisis of the Constitution*. No more reviews

---

[2] Actually, I think not. I have been doing that sort of thing now for more than half a century. Although my work has rarely been of the consistently high quality of Professor Judson's, I have published more often. I have been overtly condescended to, however, only twice in fifty years. The effects in the final outcome were comical rather than considerable.

[3] Again this was not my experience during my twenty-five years at Queens College and then Washington University, 1939–1964.

after that. Three empathic footnotes, though belated, did something to redress a gross professional solecism. Christopher Hill wrote, "Professor Judson . . . produced a powerful case for seeing consistent policies in the House of Commons in defence of property against the prerogative" (1981). And Conrad Russell in footnotes twice did Judson's work the justice she had so well earned. Her book, he said, "is by far the best general account of constitutional ideas in the early seventeenth century." And describing the work of another historian as "a brave attempt to tackle a number of difficult questions," Russell added that "it will not offer a serious challenge to the work of Margaret Judson. . . . For the sheer factual accuracy with which she reported what she read, she deserves her reputation as the Gardiner of political ideas." Here Russell shows the true generosity that is fairness.

Nevertheless, there was only one short review in an English journal, and that review was written by Godfrey Davies. Davies had been a lecturer at Oxford University. When he wrote the review, however, he was a member of the staff of the Huntington Library, San Marino, California. He was also probably the only English-born academic historian living in those days who was culturally capable of recognizing the quality and scope of Professor Judson's achievement. By that time the best of those historians were well launched on an odd intellectual venture, which has gone on up to now and has seriously impaired their ability to make anything of or to take seriously what Professor Judson was talking about. What she was talking about was what articulate Englishmen, still audible today in the sources, were actually saying between 1603 and 1645 about governance and authority in communities, societies, and states and about their relation to (among other matters) law, reason, duties, rights, God, religion, and justice.

Among articulate Englishmen, Professor Judson concerned herself with seventeenth-century equivalents of those we today call opinion makers. In the early seventeenth century they were the king and his officials in both government and household, the clergy, the lawyers, and the sorts of people who attended parliaments. Historians attentive to the way people saw the world, alert to what it was once chic to call *mentalité*, had long kept their ears open to major royal officials and kings because such folk were important in their day, and to the clergy because historically they had a long lead over all other social orders in the habit of resort to the intruments of public communication and exhortation, both oral and written: not for nothing were they called ministers of the Word.

Professor Judson did not feel impelled to concern herself with one particular kind of opinion maker, the kind to which today we would apply the words "creative" and "literary"— the poets and the playwright. There are good reasons why as a historian of opinion, ideas, and theory she might well hesitate to use as direct evidence of current opinion works literary or creative in intent. In addition to all the corrections of course that one ordinarily needs to make during a run through any document in order to be sure one has put it in just relation to the context in which it was uttered, for literary documents— poems, plays and other forms of fictive utterance—she would have also had to consider the literary conventions current in the era she was writing about. And she would have had to decide to what extent the words of a particular poem or play say what they say in order to reflect the author's sense of the matter, and to what extent and in what ways they represent the writer's acquiescence to a formal convention current among literary folk. If she felt constrained to neglect one mode of discourse, she surely chose the sensible one to neglect.

For the shortfall of references to belles lettres, Professor Judson more than compensated her readers. In her dogged pursuit of what articulate Englishmen had to say, she pressed through a most formidable undergrowth and infiltrated the *mentalité* of early seventeenth-century lawyers and judges. The labor, surely Herculean for her, was richly rewarding to her readers. Though she was without formal training in the law, she was, nevertheless, able to sift from the dross of the grim mountain deposited by the law reporters of that age—Brownlow, Croke, Godbolt, Hobart, Jenkins, Noy, even the well-nigh impenetrable Coke—small but invaluable traces of gold, reflecting the political perceptions and judgments of common lawyers during what Professor Milsom has called the second great era of the making of the common law. Beyond the common law courts, Professor Judson pursued legal opinion in Chancery through Lord Ellesmere and Francis Bacon and on into the Star Chamber, where, during the reign of James I, most of the luminaries of the bench and the bar shone. Besides listening closely to courtiers, clergymen and lawyers, Professor Judson listened more intently and more extensively than anyone ever had before to what the sorts of people who came to Parliament in those days had to say about the subjects that they, and therefore she, were engaged with. She listened through the records and accounts of what such men said—casual reports, ocasional remarks in occasional pamphlets, and correspondence. Mainly, however, she listened to the sorts of people who came to Parliament in the place where records were made of what they had to say and of what they actually did about the matters of greatest interest to her. That place, of course, was Parliament itself, especially the House of Commons; the matters people talked about there and sometimes acted on were the governance of the commonwealth and the grievances of the subjects, matters presumed to be of interest not only to Professor Judson but to the members of Parliament themselves from 1603 to 1645.

Professor Judson chose the right listening post. The easiest places to find what the sorts of men who came to Parliament talked about were the two houses of Parliament. Of course, one could have found rather similar sorts of men in Parliament from at least 1400 on. In parliament after parliament from then on one could have listened intently while the members went about doing things rather like what they did from 1603 to 1640—through taxes, supplying their ruler with part of the money to run the commonwealth and amuse himself and considering the means, often statutory, for redressing the grievances of the community of the realm and those of the particular communities they served in Parliament. One could have listened intently all that time and heard almost nothing of what men said in Parliament beyond the reading of the bills that became statutes. Of *how* a bill happened to become a statute in those days—under whose impulsion, with what intention, and out of what motives—we know little for sure beyond what the statute itself may tell us, which is often very little indeed. Once in a great while, quite casually and intermittently, a brief, but clear and sharp, burst of audible discourse cuts into the pervasive silence like a fragment of conversation about matters of consequence that a microphone in a rarely used lavatory off the boardroom happened to pick up.

For the House of Commons this situation began to change in 1571, about a quarter of a century after the Commons got its own clerk. During three weeks of that parliament a private member of the House of Commons kept full notes on the debates, which he later worked up into a coherent account. By 1604 the clerk himself, apparently as the spirit moved him, was recording bits of debate as well as the actual *doings* of the House of Commons in its journal. From 1601 to 1641, the surviving accounts of debate in the House of Commons vary from meager (1604) to excessive (1624). Professor Judson made it her business, as no historian who has published his or her research since has done, to follow the accounts of the proceedings in every parliament from 1601 to 1642 that actually did anything that a parliament was supposed to do. Without the access which Professor Wallace Notestein graciously afforded her, and which she graciously acknowledged, to his transcriptions of private diaries of parliaments from 1621 to 1642, Professor Judson could hardly have done what she so superbly did. As it was, however, through her good offices the voice of the people, as the Commons deemed itself and as James I said he deemed it, for the first time could be heard by scholars, not merely in the illusory massed chorus of statute, but also in the varied, sometimes divergent, sometimes concordant, and occasionally dissonant solo voices of particular speakers.

The Crisis of the Constitution, then, was a heroic scholarly effort enormously illuminating to those who paid attention to it. It was hardly Professor Judson's fault that so few who should have paid attention did so. With rare exceptions, until recently, as far as its use by university scholars born, trained, and practicing their craft in England goes, she might as well not have written her book at all. In the country that it was all about, the work was seed sown in barren ground. It was the ground that was barren, not the seed that was sterile. Nor, indeed, during the past forty years was that native ground itself sterile in historical studies linked to the era to which Professor Judson gave her attention. The first third of the century was indeed a period of fallow in research, publication, and controversy about the years from the accession of James I to the restoration of his elder grandson, Charles II, to the English throne. From the early 1940s on, however, such activities flourished like amber waves of grain (or perhaps grew like swamp grass). Still, about the matters that Professor Judson had so fruitfully examined, English-born historians from then to just a little while ago have been quite inattentive.

Why this should have been so is no great mystery. A giant figure who during the era between the world wars dominated the writing of English history from the accession of Elizabeth I to the restoration of Charles II had built high fences around the area of Professor Judson's special concern and had sown it not with seed but with salt. That figure was R. H. Tawney. Tawney—not perhaps wholly conscious of what he was doing—accepted "the whig interpretation of history" whole cloth, wholer cloth, perhaps, than any whig historian had ever woven. He was sure that in constitutional matters the whig historians had everything right, that the history of the transformation of the structures of English governance was just what they had limned it as, only more so. Therefore the interesting thing for a historian to do was not to redescribe the demonstrated (ultra-whig) pattern of political development from absolute divine right monarchy to the dominion of the Whig republican oligarchs of the eighteenth century, which of course "led to" the triumph of the middle class in the nineteenth century, and to democracy soon thereafter. The new task of historians would be to trace those underlying socioeconomic forces, invisible on the surface of history as it had so far been written, that nevertheless ineluctably impressed the whig pattern on that surface. The underlying forces, sharp and clear on close inspection, when viewed from the correct angle, turned out to be—surprise, surprise!—dialectical: the movement of the middle class or bourgeoisie through class struggle toward the victory of capitalism over the prostrate body of the feudal order in decline. On the tercentenary of the English Revolution in 1940 this particular way of construing such evidence as one chose to construe was initiated with great vigor and learning (and somewhat less prudence) by an extraordinarily bright and erudite young scholar, Christopher Hill. In the next two years Tawney published his two thoughtful, pioneering studies, "The Rise of the Gentry, 1558–1640" (1941) and *Harrington's Interpretation of His Age* (1942). Without serious exaggeration, one may ascribe to the flexibilities that Tawney introduced into the rigid, orthodox Marxist scheme propounded by Hill the salvation of that scheme from the earliest storms that it encountered and from a rigor close to being *mortis*.

The highly intelligent, highly motivated generation of English-born historians of the late forties and fifties who became proponents of this view or of modified versions of it had made their effective entry into the profession after a delay imposed by the Second World War. Their personal memories were black-dyed by their earlier awareness of unemployment, the dole, and "appeasement" at home and by their narrow escape from the world triumph of nazism, grace to the heroic resistance of the Soviet Union. In the light of much of their experience, a Marxist or quasi-Marxist approach to the English Age of Revolutions made sense: find the explanation of the surface, the superstructural, "political" events, by way of their connection with the deep, underlying socioeconomic currents. Paradoxically, the Marxist and quasi-Marxist English-born historians who stood center stage in these decades fixed their eyes on the connections, not on the socioeconomic base and the superstructural everything-else that the connections were assumed to connect. In the meantime, however, professional economic historians with no assumptions about the superstructure, and indeed with not much interest in it, had undertaken detailed, specific studies of the actual economy and society of Britain. The effect of their work had been so to erode the Marxist preconceptions of the character of that base as to leave it no safe mooring for the superstructure—a superstructure on which the Marxists happily reclined, scarcely aware that they had drifted out to sea on it and were about to be caught by severe squalls most jeopardous indeed to the weatherworthiness of their bark.

The results of subsequent intensive research in social, economic, and political history, however, had the odd effect of creating bundles of well-wrought "connections," but, paradoxically, at the same time eroding the terminals both in "the economic base" and in "the superstructure" that they had been supposed to connect—*both* feudalism and capitalism. Or, putting it another way, this supposedly scientific theory of historical motion called for so many epicycles to account for observed deviations from it in seventeenth-century England that in the interest of sanity the sensible thing to do was to abandon a framework of thought which had become stifling rather than emancipating, as the Copernicians had once abandoned the Ptolemaic version of the cosmos. Meantime, during the era of ascendancy of these Ptolemaic historians over research in early modern history, they naturally paid little attention to the work of Professor Judson. She had wasted none of her valuable time whittling her findings to fit the then-current socio-Marxist categories. A good thing, too, since such shaping would have deprived those findings of the pristine purity they convey, the sense of their being what is actually out there, *wie es ist eigentlich gewesen.*

The erasure of the whig interpretation of history had also begun in the interwar years with two truly seminal works by men of deeply differing background and experience: *The Whig Interpretation of History* (1931), by Methodist lay preacher Herbert Butterfield, and *The Structure of Politics at the Accession of George III* (1929), by naturalized Polish Jew Lewis Namier. Butterfield's message was that to see England as a place where seventeenth-century men like Sir Edward Coke and Sir John Eliot were doing the Right Thing by purposefully seeking to create the free Liberal England of the mid-nineteenth century was to see earlier times badly askew. In general, to see history that way was both a historical mistake (anachronism) and a moral error (spiritual pride). In Namier's view, politics in a broad sense, and therefore political history, was always the story of the acquisition, tenure, and loss of power and of the pleasures, riches, and other goodies appurtenant thereto. "Always" necessarily includes the early seventeenth century. Among the historians of that era, the sequelae of Namier, known as revisionists, have largely committed themselves to the view not only that the struggle for place or power was the pressing concern of the ruling elite, which, of course, it always is, but also that, whatever they may have *said*, place and power were all that they *really* cared about. What men engaged in politics said or wrote in those bygone days, therefore, should be referred not to the manifest meaning of their utterances but to the hidden agenda of

the politician, that is, to ways of shinnying up the greasy
pole of office, of hanging on for dear life, and of laying and
keeping hands on all the perks that are in reach of those
who get to the top.

And so for nearly forty years after the publication of *The
Crisis of the Constitution* the course of historical writing by
English-born historians did not bring them up against that
formidable obstacle to historiographic foolishness but de-
toured them around it. During those years there have been
plenty of questions to ask about early Stuart England, and
those questions ostensibly have not required investigators to
confront the tightly packed mass of evidence that Professor
Judson's labors had piled up and to find their way through
it. To those who traverse the road near its base when its
slopes are concealed by fog, Mount Shasta is "not there."
The Crisis of the Constitution is "not there" if an investigator
assumes that the language of contemporaries which it exhibits
was mere "superstructure" to be explained away. One school
of historians, as we have seen, assumed that it was just that.
Another and more recent school mainly treats that language
as a sham, a mere smoke screen thrown up to conceal the
hanky-panky going on behind it. There the *real* actors in
the *real* political comedy pursued their nefarious little plans.
The words of contemporaries—a mere cover to conceal
the underlying reality—do not command or deserve an attention which would better be devoted to baring that reality.
So much for the wraithlike "substance" of *The Crisis of the
Constitution*.

Except—except . . . ! A little attention, please, to what
these early Stuart people are talking about, to what forty
years ago Professor Judson tried to teach us they were talking
about. Most of them most of the time were not just talking
about ideology, or ideas of sovereignty, or the nature of
justice, or even the best forms of government or the state
according to Hobbes or Locke. Nor were they just engaged
in the hyperinflation of some old theologicopolitical no-

tions, though a number of clerics of varying persuasions were, as usual, up to that. Until the penultimate moment before the Civil War, many of the people Professor Judson listened to were talking about quite mundane matters when she was listening: monopolies, informers, rip-offs by the royal family and its hired help, illicit search and seizure, drunkenness and bastardy, arbitrary taking of property, forced free quartering of soldiers and their excessive tendency to roll in the hay with (will she, nill she) the daughter of their reluctant host, and the bland readiness of many clerics to allege that these were the sorts of things that good subjects should be thankful for or at least put up with thankfully and quietly, given the blessing of being ruled by James Stuart or by George Villiers, Duke of Buckingham, with the proxy and the connivance of Charles Stuart. What the subjects of Charles I were talking about in general by 1628 were the unpleasant consequences of being deprived of all the protections which in their view the law of England gave to property—that is to life, liberty, and estate—which also in their view the unrestrained rulers of the great Popish monarchies, France and Spain, did not.

It is indeed possible to write about class conflict in early Stuart England without paying much attention to what the people Professor Judson wrote about had to say on such matters, without even noticing that, despite its occasional glitches for which the natural sinfulness of both the lower orders and the upper was held morally responsible, "status differentiation" was deemed by its immediate beneficiaries in early modern England to be part of the law not of history but of nature.

It is also possible to overlook or little heed an increasing readiness of Stuart rulers to find ways of raising money by taking the property of their subjects without the due consent of their elected representative, possible to treat the unbailable imprisonment of those subjects who refused to pay up under the threat of such imprisonment as a side issue, and, disregarding such grubby matters, to center one's attention on the game of high politics as played at court—sucking up to the momentary powers that be and fiddling with the patronage and pull levers—a game of which any politically ambitious man had to learn the rudiments at least. This is indeed possible, so much so that both courses have been pursued by historians, one for almost fifty years, the other for more than a decade, both with loud trumpetings of their superior wisdom and sophistication.

The difficulty is that with decency and regard for the standards of their vocation they could not do such things if they gave serious attention to the evidence that Margaret Judson put in front of them almost forty years ago. The time has come not just to pause and reconsider; *the time has come to stop and pay attention.* What now demands the attention that English-born historians did not give four decades ago is the reissue of a great book, *The Crisis of the Constitution,* a work to which up to now those historians have paid small heed. And, colleagues, should you perchance now belatedly look at this book, please, when you do so, keep forward in your mind the anguished cry of one of the greatest of English men of the seventeenth century—I paraphrase Oliver Cromwell with minor modifications—"Gentlemen and ladies, in the bowels of Christ, think that you may have been wrong!"

J. H. Hexter
Washington University,
St. Louis, Missouri

PREFACE

FOR the past three hundred years distinguished historians have told and retold the story of England's constitutional and political struggle in the seventeenth century. Nevertheless, the student and teacher of English history in this period still comes upon certain questions which send him to the sources to try to discover his own answers. Fortunately for his investigations, there exist not only the law reports and treatises, state and family papers, and printed tracts and sermons of the period, but also the newly available parliamentary diaries edited in recent years by Wallace Notestein, Hartley Simpson, Frances Relf, David Willson, and Willson Coates. The wealth of ideas revealed in these diaries convinced me that it was time for a reevaluation and interpretation of English constitutional and political thought in the first half of the seventeenth century.

There are many to whom my thanks are due. Professors Notestein and Simpson of Yale University generously allowed me to use their transcripts of the unpublished diaries for the parliaments of 1624, 1626, and 1628. Professor McIlwain of Harvard, to whom, with the late Professor Neilson of Mount Holyoke, I owe my interest in constitutional problems and ideas, has read the work in manuscript, given me good advice, and always encouraged and inspired my undertaking. His interpretations of the medieval period and of the seventeenth century have helped to focus and guide my own studies. I am also grateful to my colleagues and friends who have read all or parts of the work in manuscript and given me valuable criticisms and suggestions.

For the use of their manuscripts or early printed books, tracts, and sermons, acknowledgment is due the officials of the British Museum, the Public Record Office, the Library of Lincoln's Inn, the Huntington Library, the Harvard Law Library, the Union Theological Seminary, and the libraries of Harvard, Yale, Princeton, and Rutgers Universities. I am grateful to the staffs of all of these libraries for the assistance given me in my research.

To Mount Holyoke College I am indebted for a fellowship which helped me to begin the research for this book in 1938. Above all, I wish to express my sincere thanks and deep appreciation to Rutgers University. The preparation and publication of the book was made possible by two generous grants of the Rutgers Research Council and by two leaves of absence given me for this work by the New Jersey College for Women.

M. A. J.
New Brunswick,
July 1949

CONTENTS

ABBREVIATIONS

Bor. Borlase (Stowe MSS 366). This manuscript account of the 1628 parliament was probably a daily newsletter. It was once owned by William Borlase.

Bowyer. D. H. Willson ed., *The Parliamentary Diary of Robert Bowyer, 1606–1607,* (University of Minnesota Press, Minneapolis, 1931).

Brownlow. Richard Brownlow, *Reports,* (London, 1652).

Cal.St.P. *Calendar of State Papers.* Domestic and Venetian series.

C.J. *Journals of the House of Commons.*

Coke, *Institutes*. Sir Edward Coke, *The Institutes of the Laws of England.* First part (London, 1684), second part (London, 1669).

Coke, *Reports*. Sir Edward Coke, *Reports,* 7 vols., (Dublin, 1793).

***Commons Debates 1621*.** W. Notestein, F. H. Relf, and H. Simpson eds., *Commons Debates 1621,* 7 vols., (Yale University Press, New Haven, 1935).

***Commons Debates in 1625*.** S. R. Gardiner ed., *Debates in the House of Commons in 1625,* (Camden Society, London, 1873).

***Commons Debates for 1629*.** W. Notestein and F. H. Relf, eds., *Commons Debates for 1629,* (University of Minnesota Press, Minneapolis, 1921).

Croke. Sir George Croke, *Reports,* 3 vols., (London, 1683).

D'Ewes (Elizabeth). Sir Simonds D'Ewes, *The Journals of All the Parliaments during the Reign of Queen Elizabeth,* (London, 1682).

D'Ewes. Diary of Sir Simonds D'Ewes for the parliament of 1624. Harleian MSS 159.

D'Ewes (Long Parl.) **ed. W. Notestein.** W. Notestein ed., *The Journal of Sir Simonds D'Ewes,* (Yale University Press, New Haven, 1923).

xxiii

D'Ewes (Long Parl.) ed. W. Coates. W. Coates ed., *The Journal of Sir Simonds D'Ewes* (Yale University Press, New Haven, 1942).

Erle. Diary of Sir Walter Erle for the parliament of 1624. Additional MSS 18597.

Gardiner. S. R. Gardiner, *History of England from the Accession of James I to the Outbreak of the Civil War,* 10 vols., (Longmans, Green, London, 1883–84).

Godbolt. John Godbolt, *Reports,* (London, 1653).

Gros. Diary of Sir Richard Grosvenor for the parliaments of 1626 and 1628. Library of Trinity College, Dublin, MS 611.

Gurney. An anonymous diary for the parliament of 1624. Gurney MS, (at Keswick Hall, near Norwich).

H. M. C. *Publications of the Historical Manuscripts Commission.*

Harl. Harleian MSS 2313 and 5324. This diary for the parliament of 1628 may have been written by Denzil Holles.

Hawarde. John Hawarde, *Les Reportes del Cases in Camera Stellata, 1593 to 1609,* ed. W. P. Baildon, 1894.

Hobart. Sir Henry Hobart, *Reports,* (London, 1678).

Holdsworth. W. S. Holdsworth, *A History of English Law,* 12 vols. (Little, Brown and Co., Boston, 1909–38).

Jenkins. David Jenkins, *Eight Centuries of Reports . . . ,* (London, 1734).

L. J. *Journals of the House of Lords.*

Lords Debates in 1628. F. H. Relf ed., *Notes of the Debates in the House of Lords . . .* 1621, 1625, 1628, (London, 1929).

Mass. This manuscript account of the 1628 parliament in the Massachusetts Historical Society Library is one of the surviving copies of "The True Relation," a daily newsletter.

Nalson. John Nalson, *An Impartiall Collection of the Great Affairs of State from . . . 1639 to the Murther of King Charles I . . . ,* 2 vols. (London, 1682–83).

Nicholas P. and D. Edward Nicholas, *Proceedings and Debates in the House of Commons in 1620 and 1621,* 2 vols., (Oxford, 1766).

Nich. Diary of Sir Edward Nicholas for the parliaments of 1624 and 1628. St. P. Domestic 14/166 and 16/97.

Noy. William Noy, *Reports and Cases . . . ,* (London, 1656).

Parl. Debates in 1610. S. R. Gardiner ed., *Parliamentary Debates in 1610,* (Camden Society, London, 1862).

Pym. Diary of John Pym for the parliament of 1624. Manuscript is in the possession of the Earl of Winchilsea.

Rich. Diary of Sir Nathaniel Rich for the parliaments of 1624 and 1626. Manuscript is in the possession of the Duke of Manchester.

Rushworth. John Rushworth, *Historical Collections,* 8 vols., (London, 1721).

S. T. William Cobbett, *A complete collection of state trials . . . ,* 21 vols., (London, 1809–1814).

Spedding. James Spedding, *The Letters and Life of Francis Bacon,* 7 vols., (London, 1861–74).

S. P. Domestic. State Papers Domestic, Public Record Office.

Whit. Diary of Sir Bulstrode Whitelocke for the parliament of 1626. Cambridge University Library MS D.D. 12, 20–22.

EXPLANATION

For all the manuscript diaries of parliament listed in the abbreviations, I have used the typewritten copies of Professor Notestein at Yale. In citing a reference, I have given the diary, the month, the day, and the year. For example, a citation from the Grosvenor diary for May 20, 1628 is given in this form: Gros. 5/20/28.

INTRODUCTION

DURING the sixteenth century, Tudor rulers transformed a feudal land into a national state. When Elizabeth died, she left England a more integrated and unified country than any European nation had ever been before. Never again did feudal lords, special regions, or the church seriously challenge the central political authority of this state whose political supremacy over all competing jurisdictions had become so firmly established under strong Tudor rule. And yet forty years after the death of the last Tudor monarch, Englishmen who agreed upon the political pre-eminence of the state were fighting a civil war to determine who should govern that state. Such a conflict could not have taken place if the Tudors had not done their work of state building so well. On the other hand, if those monarchs had completed their task, the war might never have come about. The Tudors built well, but they failed to clarify, to integrate, and to bring up-to-date the constitutional arrangements of the different parts of the government which served their immediate purposes; and thus, even before James became king, Englishmen, who had learned some of the art of governing from their Tudor sovereigns, began to argue and debate the constitutional foundations of their government.

To understand those arguments it is necessary first to survey the great political work the Tudors did achieve. These monarchs did their work at a time when building a state in England required much of its rulers. They must, above all, devise and carry out governmental policies and actions in relation to the interests and problems of their people, and this was no easy task in the sixteenth century when Englishmen were developing wider public interests than ever before. Although the Reformation in England was essentially an "act of State," [1] by the middle of the century controversial religious issues had come to be of vital concern to many men and might easily have led here, as they did on the continent, to internal chaos, civil war, and foreign intervention. During that same century Englishmen were engaging in new and diversified economic enterprises. They were busy acquiring landed property and were using it in new ways—farming more capitalistically, enclosing their holdings to raise sheep for the expanding woolen trade, and sinking mines to meet the new demands and opportunities in industry. English merchants were freeing their land from its dependence on Italian and Hanse merchants, and were pushing their way into the Baltic, the Mediterranean, and even to the New World and to India. As their economic interests and activities expanded, their social problems increased also. The question of enclosures, of the poor, of apprentices, could no longer be handled locally but required national policies and actions. In an era of rapidly expanding economic activities and growing social problems, governments often fail to take action commensurate with their responsibilities. That charge, however, can not be made against the Tudors. They were keenly aware of all matters of concern to their people and initiated and fashioned their policies to meet the needs of government and the desires and interests of their subjects.

Their success is the history of England in the sixteenth century. In doing their work they of course benefited by some things not of their own creation. They were helped by geography—by the fact that the English Channel and North Sea, which were never barriers to new ideas and afforded open roads to English merchants, presented serious obstacles to foreign invasion. They benefited by the work which earlier kings from William the Conqueror to Edward III had done in devel-

---

[1] F. M. Powicke, *The Reformation in England*, (Oxford University Press, London, 1941), p. 1.

oping institutions which survived for Henry VII to strengthen. They were fortunate that after the feudal anarchy of the fifteenth century most Englishmen welcomed law and order and supported the strong government which brought internal peace, even though at times the government acted despotically. The Tudors also profited from the bad timing of their most dangerous enemies at home and abroad. The greatest internal rebellion of the century, the Pilgrimage of Grace, took place when Henry VIII and not the boy Edward occupied the throne, and when France and Spain were fighting each other and therefore unable to unite to try to bring England back to Catholicism. Another serious internal rebellion, the Rising of the Earls, took place in 1569, nineteen years before Spain was aroused and ready to send the Armada against England.

To recapitulate the fortunate circumstances which helped the Tudors is not to minimize the greatness of their work for which credit properly belongs to them. Their strong rule brought an end to the feudal anarchy which the country had experienced for a hundred years before Henry VII and was welcomed by all classes except the great feudal lords. Under Tudor leadership England, which at the accession of Henry VII had been only a fourth-rate European state, became by the end of Elizabeth's reign a power of the second magnitude. The government reached out to protect and encourage native commerce and industry, thereby assisting the merchants and budding industrial capitalists. By the Statute of Wills it made the transfer of land easier for the land-hungry gentry. The peasant and artisan might well feel that they were neglected by the government at a time when many of them were suffering from economic dislocations; but Tudor monarchs never forgot that the welfare of every class was necessary for the health of the whole body politic, and passed Enclosure Acts and Poor Laws recognizing the responsibility of the government towards the poorer classes in society. The most drastic and most far-reaching action which was taken by the Tudors was their complete break from Rome and the establishment of the Anglican church. In initiating and in carrying out such a momentous change, both Henry VIII and Elizabeth demonstrated their high qualities of leadership. They discovered and used the right techniques. They knew when to move ahead, when to slow the pace, whom to associate with them, how much opposition they could withstand.

None of their work, even the break from Rome, was done single-handed or by a few paid administrators and court favorites, but each important task they undertook became a co-operative enterprise of Englishmen who counted politically and economically in the sixteenth century. The work of the Tudors was done not only with the support of the influential people, but also with the co-operation of all parts of the government. Tudor kings in privy council, star chamber, and parliament, and in common law courts and quarter sessions of the justices of the peace, built sixteenth-century England into a commonwealth more compact and integrated than she had been before.

In building the state, the Tudors developed governmental machinery adequate to administer the greater tasks which government now undertook. Whenever possible, each of the Tudors used whatever existing machinery could be made to serve his need. Henry VII strengthened the common law courts, freeing them in some measure from the dominance of the great feudal lords, and later Tudors never abolished these courts, whose practices and precedents reached back to the twelfth century. The Tudors inherited parliament and used it to achieve law and order under Henry VII, to break from Rome under Henry VIII, to establish a common English religion under Edward, to return to Rome under Mary, to re-establish the Anglican church under Elizabeth, and to pass a series of great statutes on economic and social matters. The Tudors found the justices of the peace already busy with duties in the fifteenth century, but they increased the burden and work of these amateur local administrators in almost every statute enacted during the sixteenth century. The Tudors needed a strong executive, and transformed the medieval council into a body competent to guide and control the whole machinery of government. They needed courts and commissions to deal with over-mighty subjects, with poor men's causes, with special areas, and with religious conformity; and they developed or created the star chamber, the court of requests, the council of the north, and the high commission to handle these problems. As England became more important and more active in foreign affairs, officials of government who once had been clerks became secretaries of state responsible for international affairs. The Tudors, like all their great medieval predecessors, beginning with William the Conqueror, were able to find or create governmental machinery adequate for the job at hand.

Under the Tudors all parts of the government, the old and the new, functioned together with remarkable harmony. Through the privy council and star chamber, so close to the monarch, and through parliament, so skillfully guided by the ministers of the crown, a unified public policy suited to the needs of the state was achieved in the sixteenth century.

This commonwealth built by the Tudors remains their greatest achievement, for it lasted through the constitutional controversies and revolutions of the seventeenth century, through the aristocratic rule of the eighteenth century, and through the upheavals which came with the industrial revolution and growing democracy of the nineteenth century. When in June, 1940, England was left as the one country resisting German might, the state was able to carry on the war for one year alone partly because Englishmen of all types were united in their determination to save England or to perish together. England's unity has been seriously threatened from within and from without many times since the sixteenth century, but it has never yet been broken.

The sharp divisions among Englishmen, apparent even before Elizabeth was in her grave, grew in intensity during the seventeenth century, resulting in civil war and culminating in the revolution of 1688; but the controversy was debated and fought out by men on both sides who did not question the necessity of a strong and unified government. Neither the royalists nor the parliamentarians [2] wanted to break down the unity of England and restore the semi-independence of feudal lords over certain geographical areas. Nor did they desire to restore the independence of the church from state control. Both the royalists and parliamentarians, including probably the majority of the leading Puritans, were staunch Erastians. In the realm of political ideas, also, both groups during most of the century were largely unconcerned with theories of the state in which men existed in a state of nature without organized government. The greatest political thinker in England and perhaps in Europe in the seventeenth century, Thomas Hobbes, brought mankind very quickly out of a state of nature, and John Locke's state of nature was one where at least the rudiments of government prevailed.

The Tudors had taught their countrymen the value of a unified state and of strong government and had achieved a public policy suited to the needs of the age. The harmony among all parts of the government was due, however, mainly to the personal qualities of leadership of the Tudor monarchs, to their wise use and adaptation of traditional laws and institutions, and to the support their strong government and policies received from influential parts of the population. It did not depend on unified and integrated constitutional procedures and machinery.

It is possible for a united nation to go forward for a time without smoothly integrated governmental machinery, but in

[2] Since in the first part of the seventeenth century organized political parties did not exist, the terms royalist and parliamentarian have been arbitrarily chosen to designate those supporting, respectively, the claims of the king and of parliament. Neither term is satisfactory, for, as will be shown in chapters I, II, and III, many supporters of the king were not only members of parliament, but were also believers in the institution. Likewise, most parliamentarians were believers in monarchy. Moreover, both groups were shifting and not stable, and both included men of moderate and extreme views.

the long run the structure and relationship of the different parts of the government can not be too confused and unco-ordinated without causing serious constitutional difficulties. In a unified state it is particularly necessary that the final authority on public questions be clearly known and generally accepted. Because of the rapid development of governmental action and machinery during the sixteenth century, it was inevitable that sooner or later the question be asked of the relation of privy council and its proclamations to parliament and its statutes, of star chamber and its decrees to common law courts and their judgments. Answers to such questions could not be postponed indefinitely, whether a Tudor or a Stuart monarch sat on the throne. Skillful and tactful as Elizabeth was in evading or transcending unpleasant problems, she did not die in time to avoid embarrassing constitutional questions and issues. She died, however, with those questions unanswered and those issues unresolved. Because she never brought the constitutional arrangements of the government into line with its actual functioning, she bequeathed to her successors the great constitutional problem of the seventeenth century.

That problem we now realize was this: Where was the final legal authority in government? Was it in the king-in-parliament or in the king alone? If it was in the king alone, then England's government was an absolute monarchy. If the supreme legal authority lay in the king-in-parliament, then England possessed a mixed monarchy. In such a government when king, lords, and commons agreed to enact a statute, that law was the supreme law of the land, legally binding upon all men and all institutions of government. If, however, they could not agree, there was no constitutional or legal way by which their disagreement could be resolved. The problem then transcended the law and constitution and became political. The issue now was which of the three—king, lords, or commons—was really supreme. In the last analysis that political problem could be solved only by civil war or a return to a state of nature. There was no legal constitutional answer to the

question of supremacy in a mixed monarchy if the legally
recognized partners in the mixture could not agree. The
analysis just given is not mine, but Philip Hunton's.[3] Because
of his profound insight and brilliant analysis, we are better
able to see the complexity of the issue and to realize that it
involved both the question of legal supremacy in the government and also the question of ultimate political supremacy.
Hunton's analysis is not simple, but it is, in my judgment, absolutely clear and correct. Unfortunately, however, it was not
set forth until 1643 when his *Treatise of Monarchie* was first
published.

For forty years prior to the publication of that book, which
still does not receive the credit properly due it,[4] Englishmen
argued and debated their constitutional and political issues
without understanding the essential nature of these issues as
clearly as Hunton did. As we read their arguments and try to
grasp their basic ideas, we often wonder whether they were
living in the seventeenth century or in the thirteenth. Their
most important convictions and most ardent pleas frequently
seem unsuited and unrelated to the actual problems they were
facing. Living in a unified state and confronted with the
problem of recognizing and accepting the final governmental
authority within it, they seem to wander back in their ideas
along many bypaths to the Middle Ages and to employ medieval ideas in the solution of their seventeenth-century problems,
ignoring the fact that those older ideas had developed at
a time when the state hardly existed and the question of
the final authority in its government was not a vital problem.

Perhaps the most striking and outstanding fact in the history
of the first part of the seventeenth century, when momentous
political issues were at stake, is the poverty of the political

[3] Philip Hunton, *A Treatise of Monarchie,* (London, 1643).
[4] See chapter X for a fuller discussion of Hunton and for references to
scholars who in recent years discussed his ideas.

thinking of men participating in the great controversy between king and parliament. The meagerness of their political thought is even more remarkable in view of the fact that beginning in 1642, when the civil war broke out, there began an outpouring of political thought more extensive and more profound than England had ever experienced before. The great and the less important political theorists, Hobbes and Harrington, Filmer and Milton, Hunton and Parker, Ferne and Lilburne—to name but a few who wrote between 1642 and 1660—won for their country by their writings during these years the pre-eminent position in which English political thought of the seventeenth century is held today. In 1603, however, when James ascended the English throne, Thomas Hooker was the only great political thinker, and among those who can even be labelled political theorists at all, there were few who seem to have grasped the full meaning and import of the developments in political thought which had taken place during the sixteenth century on the continent. Englishmen who disagreed and debated for forty years on constitutional and political, religious and economic matters, and eventually fought a civil war, do not reveal in their writings and speeches that their political ideas and theories were in line with recent developments in their own history or with up-to-date theories in European thought.

Although the sixteenth century was a time when England became a more united state than any other in Europe and her government successfully established its supremacy over the older rival authorities of feudal lords and church, no Englishman appeared in either the sixteenth or early seventeenth century to grasp the full significance, as Bodin did in France, of the emergence of the sovereign state and the legal sovereignty of its government. By the beginning of the seventeenth century Bodin had been translated into English and read by many Englishmen, as their references to him testify; but most of them before the civil war seem to have been more interested in and influenced by his ideas on the limitations of monarchy, than in his ideas on its legislative sovereignty.[5]

During the sixteenth century also the doctrine of the divine right of kings had been proclaimed and preached by supporters of Tudor monarchs to justify the unprecedented sway those rulers claimed and exercised over "all men and all causes." Because the English monarch became the head of an Anglican church entirely independent of Rome, whereas the French and Spanish monarchs never had such complete power over the church within their countries, the doctrine of the divine right of kings to be above and free from all earthly sanctions, and responsible immediately and only to God, was perhaps stated more often and more forcefully in England than elsewhere in western Europe in the sixteenth century.[6] Nevertheless, the doctrine in its more extreme form was not the platform or belief of a great number of Englishmen taking part in the constitutional struggles of the first half of the seventeenth century.[7]

A third contemporary political doctrine, that of popular sovereignty, by which resistance to kings could be justified, was a theory with medieval origins which had taken on new meaning and vitality in the great religious controversies of the sixteenth century, and had been set forth most clearly in France by the author of the *Vindiciae Contra Tyrannos*. Two English writers in the sixteenth century, John Ponet[8] and

[5] See, for example, Judge Crawley's remarks in the ship-money case (S. T., III, 1081). Crawley quotes Bodin's statement that English subjects are protected by statutes from charges laid upon them by the king without consent of parliament.

[6] On this subject see particularly J. W. Allen, *A History of Political Thought in the Sixteenth Century*, (The Dial Press, New York, 1928); F. V. Baumer, *The Early Tudor Theory of Kingship*, (Yale University Press, New Haven, 1940); and C. H. McIlwain, *The Political Works of James I*, (Harvard University Press, Cambridge, Mass., 1918), Introduction.

[7] See chapters IV and V.

[8] A *Shorte Treatise of Politicke Power*, (1556). Reprinted by W. S. Hudson in *John Ponet, Advocate of Limited Monarchy*, (The University of Chicago Press, Chicago, 1942).

Christopher Goodman,[9] had proclaimed that the people were the basic and final authority in government and had championed the right of resistance to kings. In the growing opposition to Stuart kings in the first four decades of the seventeenth century, the ideas of popular sovereignty and of resistance to kings played their subtle part,[10] but no John Locke fashioned these concepts into a theory of government to serve as a philosophical justification for the parliamentary case.

Active politicians and preachers, rather than political theorists, furnished the ideas with which men battled or supported the crown, and those ideas with which Englishmen carried on their political and constitutional struggles in the period before the civil war were for a number of years more in line with medieval constitutionalism than with up-to-date developments in sixteenth-century European constitutional and political thought. Englishmen believed firmly and sincerely in certain fundamentals in their government, but few before the civil war put their ideas together in any complete or systematic way. Leaders like Bacon or Pym who spoke and wrote most forcibly and fully on some phases of government failed to develop their ideas to the logical conclusions implicit in them.

Even in the realm of constitutional thinking there were no great writers on the English constitution. There had not been in England in the sixteenth century [11] a succession of writers upon the constitution as there had been in France, beginning with Seyssel and ending with Loyseau.[12] By the seventeenth century there were in England important legal writers like Coke, and antiquarians like Selden, but until Ferne, Hunton, and Twysden wrote during the civil war, there were no great

[9] *How Superior Powers Ought to Be Obeyed* . . . , (Geneva, 1558).
[10] See chapters VII, VIII, and IX.
[11] The *De Republica Anglorum* by Sir Thomas Smith, L. Alston, ed., (Cambridge University Press, Cambridge, 1906) is the most important book upon the English government written by a sixteenth-century Englishman.
[12] See W. F. Church, *Constitutional Thought in Sixteenth-century France,* (Harvard University Press, Cambridge, Mass., 1941); and also J. W. Allen, *op. cit.*

constitutionalists setting forth in their writings a well-rounded analysis of the constitution to defend which many men eventually died.

The basic beliefs of leaders in the constitutional struggle must be reconstructed from scattered and incomplete remarks in law reports, legal treatises, sermons, pamphlets, letters, and parliamentary speeches. It is difficult to define during the earlier years of the controversy either a distinct royalist or a definite parliamentary theory of the constitution. Historians have often pointed out that the civil war was unnatural—that brother fought brother and squire fought squire—that moderate Anglican fought moderate Puritan—that although there were some extremists in both camps, there were more men of moderate views. If the line of division between Cavalier and Roundhead is hard to draw when men were fighting and dying on the field of battle, it is infinitely harder to draw during the forty years preceding the actual strife. The clashes of words and of ideas during the earlier period of controversy were clashes between men whose thinking agreed on many essentials. Leaders in both groups came from the same social background and inherited many of the same basic assumptions concerning the nature of their polity.

It is of course true that there were extremists on both sides whose ideas played an important part in the history of these years, but more men in both groups were moderate than extreme; and it is the ideas of the moderates, rather than those of the extremists, which best reveal the full meaning of the struggle over the constitution at this time. The moderates were often so close to each other in their constitutional ideas that only a thin line divided many of them in 1610, in 1621, 1628, 1637, and even in 1642. Bacon was a good parliamentarian in many respects, and Coke a staunch monarchist. Men of moderate views like Wentworth and Noy, who turned from the support of parliament to the support of the king, shifted over to his side, for one reason, in order to preserve the integrity of their own constitutional views, which, according to the evidence, remained substantially the same between 1621 and 1641. Likewise in the last months of 1641 and in the early months of 1642, many moderates, like Hyde and Falkland, who had supported the earlier measures of the Long Parliament, now sincerely and justifiably believed that the constitution, as they interpreted it, could best be preserved by the king. At times in the struggle of these years there was a direct clash between "despotic will and law," as, for example, when James insisted that the privileges of the commons came from him, and the commons replied that they rested on law; or later when the commons, exercising the sovereign will of a small minority of the nation, brought Charles to trial, and Charles correctly refused to accept the jurisdiction of the court, for there was no English law by which he could be tried. More often, however, the clash was not between law and will, but between law and law. The strongest and most successful claims made by the royalists did not rest on divine right or sovereign will, but were based on the law and constitution.[13] On the parliamentary side, the more political and less constitutional arguments and claims of parliament proved eventually to be the most effective,[14] but parliament also made a great stand upon the law and constitution.[15] Both royalists and parliamentarians looked to the law to justify their claims and positions, and both drew their strength and nourishment from the same medieval constitution.

The nature and significance of both the constitutional and political ideas, and the part they played in the history of these critical years in England, can best be approached by starting with the views most Englishmen held in common in the first decades of the seventeenth century. Despite the growing divergence of the ideas of men supporting the claims of the king and those supporting parliament's position, there existed a common denominator of constitutional and political thought from

[13] See chapter IV.
[14] See chapter VII.
[15] See chapter VI.

which each side drew and advanced its own views. In many, although not all respects, most royalists and parliamentarians agreed in their ideas of the king's position and the subjects' rights. They both loved the law and their balanced polity. They both believed in parliament and its place in the English commonwealth. Only when the concepts and beliefs on which men agreed are understood is it possible fully to appreciate the way in which they came to disagree in their ideas. Moreover, their common agreement on so much is an important reason, from the ideological point of view, why men argued and debated for forty years before drawing their swords to attempt to resolve the issue.

During the same years when Englishmen agreed on so much in their constitutional and political thinking, they were also coming to disagree sharply on some points. The king's supporters, his councillors, judges, and clergy, pushed his claims and exalted his position, drawing upon both legal-constitutional and political concepts to support and advance their case. Their parliamentary and Puritan opponents also turned to the law and constitution and to political thought to defend their position and to justify their aggressive claims. In law court and parliament, in pulpit and press, the debate was carried on for forty years with neither side presenting an entirely straightforward and decisive case for itself. Not until war finally came did some few pamphleteers and writers grasp and present clearly and unequivocally the constitutional and political issues in this great crisis in English history.[16]

[16] See chapter X.

THE CRISIS OF THE CONSTITUTION

CHAPTER I

ENGLISHMEN VIEW THE KING'S
POSITION AND THE SUBJECTS'
RIGHTS

IN THE EARLY PART of the seventeenth century, men agreed that the king was God's anointed, His vicar or lieutenant on earth, responsible for administering divine justice to man. This belief was proclaimed most often and most eloquently by Anglican preachers, but it was also set forth by lawyers and by leaders of the parliamentary opposition. The judge Sir Henry Finch, in his *Law, or a Discourse Thereof*, wrote as follows: "The king is the head of the commonwealth, *immediate under God*. And therefore carrying God's stamp and mark among men, and being as one may say, a God upon earth, as God is a king in heaven, hath a shadow of the excellencies that are in God, in a similitudinary sort given him." [1] Lambard, in the *Archeion*, said that the king "is within his owne *Kingdome* the *Vice-roy* of God." [2] Another lawyer, giving a charge to the assizes held at Norwich, August 4, 1606, said that James "is over us the Lords annointed, and in these his Realms and Dominions, in all Causes, and over all Persons, as well Ecclesiasticall as Civile, next under Christ Jesus our supreme Gouvernour." [3] Twenty-two years later in parliament the same lawyer expressed a similar sentiment concerning Charles when he remarked that "trust in him is all the confidence wee have under god, hee is gods leiuetenant." [4] The lawyer, referring to both

[1] London, 1759, p. 81.
[2] W. Lambard, *Archeion, or, A Discourse Upon the High Courts of Justice in England,* (London, 1635), p. 97.
[3] Law Tracts 1596–1664. *The Lord Coke His Speech and Charges . . . ,* (London, 1607), p. 2.
[4] Mass., 5/6/28.

James and Charles as God's lieutenant, was Sir Edward Coke.
Coke was not the only parliamentary opponent of the king's
policies who believed that the king was God's agent on earth.
John Pym, in 1621, acknowledged that "as the Image of God's
Power is expressed in your royal Dignity, so is the Image of his
[God's] Goodness by your Lenity and Clemency." [5] In the debates leading up to the Petition of Right, Dudley Digges referred to the king as the "image of G[od]," [6] and Coryton,
another leader of the parliamentary opposition, said he knew
"the King hath the power of God." [7]

Puritan preachers also expressed similar sentiments. Robert
Bolton, who became a zealous Puritan in 1610, denounced the
statement of Bellarmine "That the power of Kings, Princes
and Magistrates, is not ordained by the divine Law of God, but
an humane ordinance." [8] To strengthen his own case against
Bellarmine he quoted with approval [9] the *Answer to Perron* [10]
written by James himself in defense of the divine right of kings.
Even after the Long Parliament began its sessions, the prominent Puritan divine, Stephen Marshall, preaching before the
house of commons, referred to the king as "the Lord's annoynted, who is the *breath of the nostrils*," and called for God's
immediate punishment upon any "that had lift up his hand
against him." [11]

Both the royalists and the leaders of the parliamentary opposition also viewed monarchy as the most natural and best form
of government. Sir Edward Coke said in the Owen alias Collins

[5] Nicholas, *P. and D.*, II, 234.

[6] Harl., 4/22/28. Digges continued: "to whome we are tyed by obedience, who hath as absolute power as any King, yet the Common law
provide for all."

[7] Mass., 5/2/28.

[8] R. Bolton, *Two Sermons Preached at Northhampton at Two Severall
Assisses There* . . . 1621 . . . 1629, (London, 1635), pp. 14–15.

[9] *Ibid.*, p. 31.

[10] *A Remonstrance for the Right of Kings, . . . against an Oration or
the Most illustrious Card: of Perron,* in C. H. McIlwain, *The Political
Works of James I*, pp. 177–268.

[11] S. Marshall, *A Sermon Preached before the Honourable House of
Commons* . . . Nov. 7, 1640, (London, 1641), p. 18.

case, "That in point of Allegiance none must serve the King with *Ifs* and *Ands*." [12] During the stormy and controversial sessions of the 1621 parliament, Pym spoke of "The State of Monarchy" as "the perfectest State of Government," [13] and Sandys, pleading for the freedom of each man to speak according to his conscience, added that "noe man can have any conscience to speake against the Kinge." [14] In 1628 leaders of the parliamentary opposition were still at heart good monarchists. Phelips, for example, spoke eloquently for liberty but reminded the commons that subjection was also necessary.[15] This able leader also said: "And I beseech you take away that blott of Antymonarchicall. Our late King saied, were hee to chuze a lawe, hee would chuze our Common lawe, and I say were wee to chuze a government, it should bee that of Englande." [16] When the king threatened to end the session of parliament before the opposition could finish its business, it was Phelips who cried out, "If it be a cryme to have loved his Majestie to well: we are criminous." [17]

Right up to the moment when the civil war broke out, the leaders of the parliamentary opposition and Puritan preachers joined with royalist supporters and Anglican clergy in proclaiming the divine origin and sanction of kingly authority and the superiority of the monarchical form of government to all other forms. The parliamentary opposition did not talk of resistance until 1642, and at that late date they insisted they were not resisting the person of the king.

This acceptance of the exalted position of a king is not at all surprising in view of the long history of the idea. The general concept that kings received their authority from God, the giver

[12] Godbolt, p. 264.
[13] Nicholas, *P. and D.*, II, 238.
[14] *Commons Debates 1621*, IV, 38. See also vol. II, 104. Sir James Perrot said: "I confess we owe active obedience unto his Majesty in all lawfull things and passive obedience in all things unlawful."
[15] Rushworth, I, 504.
[16] Bor., 4/12/28.
[17] Gros., 6/5/28.

of all authority, reached back at least to the early Middle Ages, when kingship began in England. The divine origin and sanction of kingly authority was accepted in medieval England as it was in all western Europe during those centuries when the king's actual authority was limited in many ways, and doctrines of resistance to kings who became tyrants were not uncommon. As the Tudors strengthened the position and power of the king in the sixteenth century, their supporters and admirers raised to new exalted heights the concept of divine right. When James wrote and talked of the divine right of kings, he was not introducing an entirely new concept, even though he interpreted and extended it in ways many Englishmen came to doubt and distrust. It is quite probable that some of James' subjects were surprised, not at their sovereign's ideas, but at his constant preaching of them. Many men, including some of his parliamentary opponents, wished that, since he was God's lieutenant on earth, he would measure up to such a standard and act like a true king. Tudor kings had acted and had left to their admirers the humbler task of talking and writing.

It is essential in understanding the constitutional and political thinking of Englishmen in the early seventeenth century to realize that most of them believed in the divine origin and right of kingly authority; but it is equally necessary to understand that the great majority of them also believed that the king's authority was limited in many ways by the law, the constitution, and the consent of man. To believe in both the divine right of kingly authority and at the same time in its limited nature was perfectly natural and consistent for many excellent seventeenth-century minds.

A second concept concerning the king's authority which almost all men agreed upon at this time was the belief that God, who ordained and established a king, bestowed upon him grace sufficient for his task. To govern was not essentially to wield naked or veiled power, but to practice an art for which a king was peculiarly and uniquely endowed by God. Samuel Daniel wrote of James:

But God, that rais'd thee up to act this parte,
Hath given thee all those powers of worthines,
Fit for so great a worke, and fram'd thy heart
Discernable of all apparences;
Taught thee to know the world, and this great Art
Of ord'ring man, *Knowledge of Knowledges*;
That from thee men might reckon how this State
Became restor'd, and was made fortunate.[18]

Lawyers as well as poets expressed this same belief in the peculiar art of kingship. In the law case of *Anne Needler* v. *the
Bishop of Winchester,* the plaintiff claimed an advowson on
the basis of grants made by Henry VIII. Although these grants
contained technical flaws, such flaws should not invalidate
them, according to Hobart, who argued as follows:

> And the same reason that supplies the King's ignorance of
> matters in fact, will also excuse his want of knowledge even
> of the Laws in the subtilties of it. For, he studies a greater
> Art, sc. *Arcanum regni*, the Art of Regiment, which is *Ars
> Artium*, and contains all Arts, as the Commonwealth in-
> cludes all private societies.[19]

This belief that a king possessed in the highest degree the art
of governing entered into the arguments used by men on both
sides of the struggle. James, for example, once remarked that
he wished all his subjects were kings, because only then could
they truly understand the difficult and kingly art of managing
foreign affairs.[20] On the other hand, the parliamentary opposition made use of the belief in their attack in the 1621 parliament upon monopolists, arguing that the king could not grant
to anyone else certain rights, as for example, the right to dis-

[18] S. Daniel, "A Panegyrike Congratulatorie To the Kings most excellent *Majestie*" in *The Complete Workes . . . of Samuel Daniel,* ed. A. B.
Grosart, 4 vols., (London, 1885), I, 165.

[19] Hobart, p. 224. See also the remark of Maurice Griffyn to Ellesmere
(Ellesmere MSS, 2029, Hunt. Lib.). "To governe is the arte of all artes for
it hath greatest difficulties." See also Godbolt, p. 295. Hobart remarks in
this case: "The Law amplifies everything which is for the Kings benefit . . .
because the King cannot so nearly look to his particular, because he is
intended to consider *ardua regni pro bono publico*."

[20] L. J., III, 213.

pense with a penal law, a privilege given to some holders of monopolies. This power of dispensing, when wielded by a king, was legal, benefiting all, but when exercised by a person not endowed with the kingly art of governing harmed all people. In the words of Sandys, "this regall power ought not to be putt into the hand of a person that hath not a Regall minde." [21]

Because men believed that God had ordained kings and endowed them with the art of ruling, they also believed that kings were responsible for doing God's will in the land—for ruling with justice and also with mercy. The king's commands "ought to be just," the speaker said in parliament in 1604, "for he sitteth in the Judgment Seat of the absolute King of Justice." [22] The queen's duty, the lord keeper declared, is "perpetuatly to administer judgment and justice to her subjects, without which they would not be governed, but [would be] apt for rebellion, insurrection, and all disorder." [23] Her "greateste care" is that she may administer justice to all—that *"shee wyll have her wyndinge sheete unspotted."* [24] These sentiments of Queen Elizabeth were proclaimed by the lord keeper and by the attorney general, not in the common law courts, but in star chamber, a court which some men later came to associate with great injustice. According to Prynne, "The Kings of England by their vary Kingship, and Office are next under God within their Realmes, the fountains both of Right, and Justice as well mercy, upon which account they have been always Sworne, and obliged at their Coronations . . ." [25] Samuel Daniel expressed the idea in these words: "powre may have our knees, but Justice hath our harts." [26] Patricke Scot in his *Table Booke for Princes* discoursed at length upon the same question:

> The Princely distribution of justice is nothing else but *suum cuique tribuere,* is the helme of government, the hap-

[21] *Commons Debates 1621,* V, 54.

[22] C. J., I, 254.

[23] Hawarde, p. 66.

[24] *Ibid.,* p. 122.

[25] Hargrave MSS., 98 f. 32, Prynne, 1661, Brit. Mus., pp. 38 r-v.

[26] S. Daniel, *op. cit.,* verse 26.

pinesse of kings and people. From Justice ariseth religion, peace, truth, innocency and true friendship: in it Princes are to bee noble, judicious, grave, severe, inexorable, powerfull, and full of majestie; neither enclining to the right or the left hand, to the rich or poore, but determining all matters under their censure, as they looke to bee judged by that supreame Judge whose Lieutenants they are.[27]

The unanimity of opinion among Englishmen on the greatness and divine responsibility of their king was not confined to general statements upon the nature of his authority, but also prevailed in considerable measure whenever the question of his particular prerogatives arose. In view of the key role which the prerogatives of the king played in the constitutional controversies of the first half of the seventeenth century, it would be natural to hope that a contemporary treatise upon the subject might provide at least an introduction to an understanding of it. Since, as far as this writer knows, no full and systematic treatment exists,[28] it has been necessary to rely upon the incomplete and scattered statements which were made by men in referring to such prerogatives in law treatises, or in discussing and debating them in law courts, privy, council, or parliament.

For purposes of the discussion in this chapter, it is helpful to divide the king's prerogatives in the early seventeenth century into three categories: (*1*) the special privileges accorded the king in the law courts; (*2*) his prerogatives as chief feudal lord in the kingdom; (*3*) his prerogatives as head of the government of the commonwealth.

Protagonists in the seventeenth-century constitutional struggles were not concerned with prerogatives in the first category. No one seems to have questioned these legal privileges, which had been quite fully treated by Staunford in his treatise on the prerogative, the most important Tudor work on that subject.[29]

[27] P. Scot, *A Table-Booke for Princes*, (London, 1621), p. 113.
[28] See p. 112 for a discussion of the short manuscript treatise by Sir John Doderidge.
[29] Staunford, *An exposition of the Kinges Prerogative, collected out of the great Abridgement of Justice Fitzherbert*, (London, 1577).

Illustrative of such prerogatives was the important one that the property rights of the king could not be prejudiced in the law courts by the mistake of a subordinate official or by the oversight of a clerk.[30] Neither was the king tied to time. Prescription did not run against him. There was valid reason why the law favored the king, granting him these special privileges. According to Sir Edward Coke,[31] the king possessed some of his prerogatives because his time and energy were spent on important public business, and according to Hobart,[32] because he studied the art of ruling, the greatest of all arts, and was "intended to consider *ardua regni pro bono publico.*"

A second group of prerogatives of the king consisted of his feudal rights and those obligations due him as the chief feudal lord in the kingdom. Although Tudor kings had cut deep into the feudal rights of important subjects, they had clung tenaciously to their own feudal rights. In the face of rising expenses and reduced revenues neither James nor Charles had any intention of parting, except for a significant consideration, with any of the feudal rights which had long provided part of the revenue of the English king. By the seventeenth century these feudal prerogatives had become extremely annoying and burdensome to the king's subjects, but desirous as many members of parliament were of getting rid of them, in the debates on the question in 1610 they accepted the fact that these feudal rights belonged to the king, and that their freedom from them could only be obtained by a Great Contract with him.

The most extensive and controversial prerogatives of the king were those connected with his position as head of the state. In that capacity he made the important appointments to the council, the law courts, other departments of government, and to the church. As head of the state he summoned and dismissed parliament at his pleasure. Prerogatives of this sort were seldom mentioned in the law courts and, when they were,

[30] Croke, III, 349.
[31] Coke, *Institutes*, vol. I. lib. II, ch. 5., sect. 125, p. 90v.
[32] Godbolt, p. 295.

never denied. They came to be discussed and eventually questioned and challenged in parliament, but they were not directly attacked there until 1641 and 1642. When at that time some members of parliament worked to take away these particular prerogatives from the king and transfer them to parliament, the civil war soon broke out.

In the years leading up to that war, men agreed also that the king as head of the state was peculiarly competent and solely responsible in certain realms they called government. Here he was most particularly the head of the state, practicing the art of governing, a craft possessed only by kings. Within these realms his authority was accepted as absolute. It must be, they believed, or else he would be unable to carry on his craft as a true artist. These realms of government within which his authority was accepted as absolute included foreign policy, questions of war and peace, the coinage, and the control of industries and supplies necessary for the defense of the realm. These matters had been included within the realm called government in the Middle Ages, and had been regarded as peculiarly the king's concern and responsibility. His actions within this special realm had been accepted as absolute, but nevertheless it was believed that such actions could not and did not affect the realm of property within which subjects as well as kings had an interest. In the loosely organized state of the Middle Ages it had often been possible for the king to administer these public matters as his own private concern without the property or welfare of the subject being seriously affected by his administration of them. Naturally this situation no longer prevailed in the more compact and integrated state which England had become by the seventeenth century, but even at that late date the older medieval idea still prevailed. In the parliamentary debates of 1610, for example, Hedley, one of the most ardent opponents of the king, admitted that the king possessed the prerogatives of war and peace, but he explained that these matters concerned the king more than they did the subjects.[33]

[33] *Parl. Debates in 1610*, p. 74.

As the constitutional difficulties sharpened in the seventeenth century, each of these spheres formerly accepted as coming under the king's absolute authority as head of the state became a disputed issue between loyal supporters of the king and his parliamentary opponents. It is very striking, however, that most of the leaders in the struggle against the king accepted for a surprisingly long time the absolute power of the king within certain realms. As late as 1621 Coke said: "I will not meddle with the King's prerogative, which is twofold: 1, absolute, as to make war, coin money, etc.; 2, or in things that concern *meum et tuum,* and this may be disputed of in courts of parliament." [34] In the great debate taking place on foreign affairs in the 1621 parliament, the secretary presented a typical view of the king's prerogative in foreign affairs. "Methinks it's a very strange thing for a king to consult with his subjects what war he means to undertake. This were the means for his enemies to know what he intends to do." [35] "I meant not what to do but how to maintain that which he intends to do," Phelips replied,[36] revealing, in spite of his boldness, that he recognized the subject was encroaching upon the sphere of the king. Phelips was a leader in advancing the claim of parliament to discuss foreign affairs, but he proceeded carefully, either by means of petitioning the king or by invoking the money-granting power of parliament.

Other bold spirits were equally cautious and confined their demands within regular channels of procedure. Crew argued in the following way. "To make war and peace, to coin, to marry the prince, they are all prerogatives royal; yet in the marriage of the king's sone we have all an interest yet we claim no right in it, but only petition for it." [37] In one of the arguments, Delbridge said, "Let us petition and petition again as we usually do to God and without ceasing till he hear us." [38]

[34] *Commons Debates 1621,* II, 193.
[35] *Ibid.,* II, 88–9.
[36] *Ibid.,* 89.
[37] *Ibid.,* II, 494.
[38] *Ibid.,* 500.

In a debate on foreign affairs in the 1624 parliament Alford remarked, "Whatsoever we do the King is free . . ."[39] In the 1628 parliament, Sherland, one of the most zealous supporters of the parliament's cause, said: "The Kinge may make warr, may make peace, call parliaments, and dissolve them, these are of the highest nature, for there the Kinge is the lex loquens."[40] Even Oliver St. John, who defended Hampden in the ship-money case, paid lip service to the concept that the king's power was absolute within certain realms; "in this business of defence," he said, "the *suprema potestas* is inherent in his majesty, as part of his crown and kingly dignity."[41] When finally in 1642, in the debates over the militia bill, parliament openly claimed control of the defense of the kingdom, this denial of a prerogative long associated with the king helped to precipitate the civil war.

There was still another way in which the king possessed a great prerogative as head of the state. He was responsible for its general well-being, for the "preservation of the whole."[42] According to Staunford, the king was "the preserver, nourisher, and defender of all the people; . . . by his great travels, study, and labors, they enjoy not onely their lives, landes and goodes, but all that ever they have besides, in rest, peace, and quietnes, . . ."[43] Salisbury explained in parliament in 1610 that "the true [scale] of the King's prerogative was when it had concurrances with the public good."[44] To Sir Julius Caesar, the king was the "generall father," and all his subjects were "his children,"[45] while a speaker in parliament referred to him as *"Parens Patriae."*[46] The preacher John Stoughton compared the king to a fountain. "The Ancients," Stoughton wrote,

[39] Nich., 3/19/24.
[40] Bor., 3/29/28.
[41] S. T., III, 860–61.
[42] Ellesmere MSS. 170, Roger Owen to Ellesmere, 22 Sept. 1606, Hunt. Lib.
[43] Staunford, *op. cit.*, p. 5.
[44] *Parl. Debates in 1610*, p. 8.
[45] St. P. Domestic, 16/8: 77.
[46] Rich., 5/12/26. Mr. Wild speaking.

"were wont to place the Statues of their Kings by Fountaines, intimating they were the Fountaines of good or ill in the Common-wealth, as indeed they are." [47] Mr. Browne said in the commons in 1628 that "the King is our Soveraigne and that his power is for our good without which wee cannot live a godly life." [48] In the ship-money case, it was Oliver St. John, the lawyer defending Hampden, and not one of the king's judges, who remarked: "His majesty is concerned in the way and manner of execution of the highest and greatest trust which the law hath reposed in him, the Safety and Preservation of the Kingdom." [49]

The king's prerogative of pardoning was regarded as existing for the public good. "Justice is tyed to Rules," an anonymous person wrote, "and runs in known and certain Channels, his Mercy hath no other bounds or Limits but those of his good pleasure. This is a Prerogative left in the Crown not for the Crown's sake but for the Peoples and t'is one Essential part of our Liberties that the King should be invested with a fullness of power to show Mercy." [50]

Men agreed in these years of controversy that the king was responsible for the general welfare of all, although they came to disagree on the means or channels through which he could exercise that responsibility. This general-welfare power of English kings had grown up with the development of kingship in England, but its importance had greatly increased during the sixteenth century, when Tudor monarchs raised the state up above the feudal lords and the church, and extended

[47] J. Stoughton, *Choice Sermons* . . . , (London, 1640), Sermon 4, *The Magistrates Commission*, p. 9.

[48] Mass., 5/22/28.

[49] S. T., III, 864. See also Spedding, IV, 271. Bacon said that some offences "concern the King's people, and are capital; which nevertheless the law terms offences against the crown, in respect of the protection that the King hath of his people, and the interest he hath in them and their welfare; for touch them, touch the king."

[50] Harleian MSS. 6209, Brit. Mus., p. 110. This tract deals with the king's pardoning power, and was probably written in connection with Danby's pardon.

its care for the general welfare into realms which had not normally in earlier ages been the concern of government. Under
Tudor rulers the state became integrated and strong, and its
welfare carefully guarded by institutions of prerogative government. Both the state and the king grew mighty in the sixteenth
century, but they developed together and still remained close
together in the early seventeenth century. By that time men
were more conscious of the state than ever before, but they still
looked to the king, as its head, to guard and guide its welfare.

They also believed that the king could not truly discharge
his great responsibilities unless at times he used his discretion
for the welfare of all. That the king needed discretionary
power was clearly explained by Lambard:

> As in the government of all *Common-weales,* sundry things
> doe fall out both in *Peace* and *Warre,* that doe require
> an extraordinarie helpe, and cannot awaite the usuall cure
> of common *Rule* and setled *Justice,* the which is not per-
> formed, but altogether after one sort, and that not without
> delay of helpe, and dispense of time: So, albeit here within
> this Realme of *England,* the most part of *Causes* in com-
> plaint are and ought to bee referred to the ordinarie pro-
> cesse and solemne handling of *Common Law,* and singular
> distribution of *Justice;* yet have there alwayes arisen, and
> there will continually, from time to time, grow some rare
> matters meet (for just reason) to be reserved to a higher
> hand, and to be left to the aide of absolute *Power,* and
> irregular Authoritie.[51]

Such "irregular authority" did not harm the subject, Lambard
believed. On the contrary, it existed for his welfare—to enable
the king to render justice to all his people. Without it "the in-
juriously afflicted [subject would] be deprived of that helpe
and remedie, which both the *Ordinance* of *God,* the *Dutie* of a
Kingly Judge, and the *common Law* of *Nature* and *Reason* doe
afford unto him." [52]

Chancellor Ellesmere presented penetrating reasons why
only the king could safely be trusted with discretionary power.

[51] W. Lambard, *Archeion,* pp. 78–9.
[52] *Ibid.,* 119.

The king, but no lower official, Ellesmere argued,[53] could be fair and objective to all, because only he was so unconcerned with private interests that he could view the whole dispassionately, free from the private desires which sometimes swayed and clouded the judgments of less exalted men. The king's interests were "public and general"; he was not concerned with "private gain." [54] ". . . the King in that he is the Substitute of God (ymediatelie); the father of his people; and the head of the Commonwealth hath by participation with God and with his (Sovereignity) a discretion of Judgmnt and feeling of love towarde those over whome he raigneth and proper to himselfe and his place and person . . ." [55] Because of his office only the king and no lesser person was "capable of generall discretion." [56]

Neither James nor Charles lived up to the high concept of kingship set forth by Ellesmere. Too often they used their discretionary power for their own private interests or those of their personal favorites, with little consideration for the general welfare of all. Nevertheless, Ellesmere, in his remarks, touched upon a fundamental need in government for which no completely satisfactory solution has ever been found—the need for placing discretionary power, without which no government can function effectively, in hands which will use that power for the public good of all. For Ellesmere and most of his countrymen to believe at this time that a king was the safest wielder of such power was natural. In the first place, a king came closest of all men to God, who was perfect justice; and in the second place, it can be argued on valid psychological and sociological grounds that one raised up by virtue of his office as high above others as a king might have greater consideration for the public welfare than one among equals.

[53] Ellesmere MSS., dated 1628. "A coppie of a written discourse by the Lord Chaunccellor Ellesmere concerning the Royall Prerogative . . . ," Treasure Room, Harvard Law School Library.

[54] *Ibid.*, p. 7. (The paging is my own.)

[55] *Ibid.*, pp. 4–5.

[56] *Ibid.*, p. 9.

As the difficulties between king and subject intensified in the early decades of the seventeenth century, some Englishmen wanted to increase the discretionary power of the king and to use it in new ways and realms, while others worked to reduce it and confine it within such narrow limits that the best king would have found it hard, if not impossible, to provide for the general welfare. When James ascended the English throne, however, most of his subjects probably would have subscribed to the views of Lambard and Ellesmere on the discretionary power.

In connection with the king's prerogative as head of the state, the term "act" or "matter of state" was frequently used in the first forty years of the seventeenth century. Sometimes this term was used for his special power in certain realms, such as foreign affairs, sometimes for his general-welfare power, and sometimes in reference to his discretionary power. In the departments of government closest to the king, such as privy council and star chamber, the phrase, "act" or "matter of state" came to be more and more used for actions and decrees of the government. Such actions and decrees were eventually attacked by the parliamentary opposition, but at times the term "act of state" was used in parliament with no disapproval of it implied. When, for example, in 1625 Sir Robert Cotton discussed the government's foreign policy, he said that in the reign of James "For matters of state, the Council Table held up the fit and ancient dignity." [57] When leaders of the parliamentary opposition insisted upon discussing certain matters of state which the king tried to prevent their considering, many of those leaders freely admitted that a matter of state was not for them to question. "Lett's not with too much curiosity enter into theis things," Wentworth said in 1621. "If it were for matter of State,

[57] W. Cobbett (ed.), *Parliamentary History of England*, 36 vols., (London, 1806–1820), II, 14. In Sir Edward Coke's case, the justices said "that an Oath . . . may be well injoined by the King and order of State without Parliament; and it may be well imposed upon the Sheriff to take, being for publique benefit and execution of the Laws." Croke, III, 26. See also Bowyer, p. 211.

lett us not question *archana imperii*. And not like the Burgundians before Paris thinke so many thistles so many lawnces, but goe on to owr business and not be diverted." [58]

It is well known that, in the 1621 parliament, Sir Edward Coke argued in favor of the king's possessing the power to commit persons on grounds of state without the reason being given. According to Coke, it was "against the Books of the Law, that the Privy Council should be restrained: . . . That it will hinder the finding out of divers Mischiefs both of State and Commonwealth, if the *Mittimus* must contain the Cause of every Man's Committment." [59] In the debate which followed, Alford, as staunch a parliamentarian as Coke, agreed that he was willing to leave out from the bill "such Matters as concern the Weal of the State." [60] The question of commitment by the king for reasons of state came up again in parliament in 1624 in connection with the first reading of a bill "for the better securing of the subject from wrongful imprisonment." A proviso was attached that any penalty provided in the bill for wrongful imprisonment "shall not extend to any commitment made by his Majesty, or 6 of the Privy Council." [61]

By 1628 many parliamentary opponents of the king had become alarmed at the extent to which the privy council was employing acts of state in the regular administration of government and was imprisoning men who refused to comply with such acts. Coke now declared that the opinion he had expressed in 1621 was mistaken. He and a large group of parliament men agreed that the discretionary power of the king in "matters of state" must be restricted, and in the parliament of 1628 they refused to consent either to a statute or a petition of right which included any mention or saving of the discretionary

[58] *Commons Debates 1621*, III, 437.
[59] Nicholas, *P. and D.*, II, 109.
[60] *Ibid.* Alford continued, "but, if Patents and Monopolies and the like be accounted Matter of State, and that that should be excepted out of this Bill, then *pereat* Respublica."
[61] Nicholas, 2/25/24.

power.[62] It must not be forgotten, however, that until 1628 most Englishmen, including the leaders of the parliamentary opposition, seem to have believed that the king's discretionary power to act for the general welfare was both legal and necessary.

Despite some disagreements on the extent and scope of the king's prerogatives, they were still regarded as so inherently a part of kingship that a ruler, even if he would, could not dissociate them from himself. His prerogatives were inseparably annexed to his office. This doctrine of an inseparable prerogative and the legal practices in accord with it had come down from the Middle Ages and the Tudor period.[63] Just exactly which prerogatives were inseparable and which were separable is a difficult and obscure subject which cannot be fully treated here. Although writers did not theorize upon the subject, it is clear that many of the most important prerogatives were regarded as inseparable because without them the king could not truly perform the functions associated with kingship. Those special spheres of government, such as foreign affairs "which concern Government in an high degree," [64] wherein the king's power was absolute were accepted as inseparable. So also was the dispensation of mercy—that quality above and beyond justice. This doctrine of the inseparable prerogative was accepted and used in the seventeenth century both by lawyers in court decisions and law treatises and by parliamentary opponents of the king. In the attacks in the 1621 parliament upon monopolists, it was one of the important arguments used by Coke, Sandys, and other leaders. The king, they argued time and time again, could not transfer to anyone else certain rights, as, for

[62] See chapter VI. Even in 1628 the parliamentary opposition recognized that the king should possess some discretionary power, but did not want such power written into the law of the land.

[63] See P. Birdsall, *"Non Obstante*—A study of the Dispensing Power of English Kings," in *Essays in History and Political Theory in Honor of Charles H. McIlwain,* (Harvard University Press, Cambridge, Mass., 1936).

[64] Jenkins, p. 79.

example, the right to dispense with a penal law. Such power
wielded by a king was legal and beneficial, but when exercised
by another not possessing a "regal mind" was illegal and malicious.[65]

The prerogatives of the English king set forth in this chapter
were those upon which men generally agreed in the early seventeenth century. Those prerogatives were very extensive, giving him great authority in the government. Because he was
king, he was privileged in the law courts; because he was head
of the feudal system, he possessed certain rights; because he
was endowed above other men with the art of ruling, he practiced his kingly craft with absolute power in certain definite
fields of government; and because he was head of the state, he
was responsible for its welfare and must use his discretion when
necessary to guard that welfare. These prerogatives were part
of the law and constitution in the sense that judges, privy councillors, other officials, and even the lawmakers of that age recognized and accepted them without serious controversy, working out their legal decisions and fashioning their laws with due
respect for them. A king with such prerogatives possessed great
authority by the law of the land. Because his generally recognized prerogatives were so great, he did not need the doctrine
of divine right to enable him to rule his people, if he respected
their rights and secured their co-operation.

The king "hath a prerogative in all things that are not in-
jurious to the subject." [66] As kings possessed prerogatives, so
subjects possessed rights; and those rights, like the king's prerogatives, were part of the law and basic in the constitution.
Only when the nature and extent of the subjects' rights are
understood is it possible to present some aspects of the preroga-

[65] See, for example, C. J., I, 564, and chapter I, note 21.

[66] Finch, *op. cit.*, p. 84. Finch also wrote: "But in them all it must be
remembered, that the king's prerogative stretcheth not to the doing of
any wrong: for it groweth wholly from the reason of the common law . . .
you shall find it to be law almost in every case of the king that is law in
no case of a subject." *Ibid.*, p. 85.

tive and some controversies concerning it which have not been discussed up to this point.

The most important of these rights were property rights. To protect them was the principal concern of the common law. It was also the main concern of great English subjects in the sixteenth and early seventeenth centuries.[67] According to the evidence revealed by the law reports and family papers of this time, men in the upper social classes were adding to their landed holdings. In their acquisition of property, parliament helped them by measures, like the Statute of Uses, which made the transfer of property easier than it had been before. The crown helped them also by its sale of the confiscated monastic lands. The great mistake of the Tudors if they wished to be despots (as Harrington clearly pointed out in his *Oceana* in 1656) was their encouragement of such measures. It was a mistake from the point of view of the king's position, because, at the same time as the king's authority was increasing in the sixteenth century and the concept of the divine right of kings was rising to new exalted heights, the amount of property possessed by influential subjects was also increasing and thereby strengthening the old medieval concept that property was a right belonging to subjects. Among the many reasons why the growing absolutism of the Tudors did not become complete absolutism under the Stuarts is the fact that the medieval concept of the inviolability of a man's property did not disappear or become weaker in the sixteenth or early seventeenth centuries. Tudor and Stuart noblemen, gentry, and merchants who were acquiring property did not forget that although "government belonged to kings, property belonged to subjects."

Men looked to the common law courts to protect their property, and those courts did not fail them. During the same period when the decisions in Bate's case and the ship-money case in favor of the king's prerogative against the subjects' property were rendered, many decisions were handed down and remarks

[67] R. H. Tawney, "The Rise of the Gentry 1558–1640," *The Economic History Review* XI, (1941), pp. 1–38.

made in the common law courts in favor of the subjects' property—even against a private prerogative or right of the king. In the case of the Duke of Lennox, for example, it was said that the king could not pardon an offender who had not repaired a bridge because the subjects had an "interest" in that bridge which could not be taken away by the king's pardon.[68] Likewise, in the case of *The King* v. *Boreston and Adams* it was implied that although the king's mercy could pardon a person who had been attainted, his pardoning power could not restore the right to land of such a person because that right was another's and not the king's.[69] Extensive as the king's prerogative was admitted to be for the defense of the realm, it was declared by all the justices in the case of the prerogative of the king in saltpeter that, although the king's officials might dig for saltpeter, they were "bound to leave the inheritance of the subject in so good plight as they found it."[70] Another illustration of similar care for the subjects' property occurs in the case of lands acquired by the crown which were subject to certain obligations, as for example, tithes. "It would not be permitted to the Crown to refuse Payment [of such obligations] if, by so doing the obligation would be thrown on the other persons."[71]

Respect for the property right of the subject was shown at times in proclamations issued by the king and in star chamber. In a proclamation of April 25, 1606, for example, James declared that certain inferior officers responsible for securing the king's right of purveyance had been punished in star chamber because they had taken "Timber trees growing (which being parcel of our Subjects inheritance were never intended by us to be taken) without the good will and full contentment of the Owners."[72]

Along with property rights strictly defined were other impor-

[68] Brownlow, p. 303.
[69] Noy, p. 168.
[70] Coke, *Reports*, vol. VII, pt. XII, p. 12.
[71] W. W. Lucas, "Exemption of the Crown from charges in respect of land," *Law Quarterly Review*, XXVIII, (1912), pp. 378–79.
[72] Proclamation April 25, 1606, Brit. Mus., 506, h., 10.

tant rights of the subject which in a general way could also be
called property rights. One of the most important of these was
the right which a man had in his craftsmanship and skill. It
was a well-known precept of the common law that beasts of
the plow, essential for the livelihood of man, could not be
distrained.[73] As God gave kings the authority to rule, so likewise He gave men the right to work, and both rights were
fundamental. As Fuller said in the famous case of *D'Arcy* v.
Allen, "But arts, and skill of manual occupations rise not from
the King, but from the labour and industry of men, and by the
gifts of God to them . . ." [74] Supporters of Stuart kings expressed the same belief. The royalist Doderidge said in the
parliamentary debate in 1610, "The Kinge cannot take away
the meanes of any Man's living nor graunt that one Man shall
have the sole trade of an occupation to the overthrowe of
others." [75] Another lawyer, Finch, remarked that "the grant of
an office to an ignorant man that hath no skill at all is merely
void." [76] Corresponding then to the prerogatives of the king
were certain rights of the subject, which belonged particularly
to him and could not legally be taken from him, because they
were essential to his existence as a man. Such rights were legally
inseparable from the subject as certain prerogatives were inseparable from the king.

To protect these inherent rights the courts recognized and
accepted certain rules, procedures, and maxims. The body of a
freeman is so important that it "can not be made subject to
distresse or imprisonment by Contract, but only by judgement." [77] An English subject "is not to be impeached in his life
lands or goods by flying rumours, or wandering fames and

[73] Coke, *Institutes,* vol. I, lib. 1, ch. 7, sect. 58, p. 47. Coke wrote:
"Beasts belonging to the Plow, *averia carucae* shall not be distreined
(which is the Ancient common law of England, for no man shall be
distreined by the Utensils or Instruments of his Trade or Profession, as
the Axe of the carpenter, or the books of a scholar) . . ."
[74] Noy, p. 181.
[75] Cotton MSS., Titus F IV, Brit. Mus., 244 v.
[76] Finch, *op. cit.,* p. 162.
[77] Hobart, p. 61.

reports, or secret and privy inquisitions; but by the oath and presentment of men of honest condition, in the face of justice." [78] Although there was little talk of liberty in the abstract, at least before 1628, there was great concern for specific forms and rules which guarded the liberty as well as the property of the subject. No formal bill of rights protected the English subject in the early seventeenth century, but the law courts recognized his rights and followed definite and basic forms of action affording him considerable protection. Such protection was not unimportant nor hollow in this age which put greater emphasis than we do today on form and procedure as a means of protecting rights.

The concept that in general the king's prerogatives stopped at the point where the subjects' rights began was firmly established and frequently mentioned by legal writers. Staunford in his discussion of the king's power to pardon says that "the pardon doth not restore him but to the law. For though the king would pardon him with words of restitution, yet his grace could not thereby restore him to the lands holden of other." [79] Typical of the attitude of lawyers are the following remarks found in a lawyer's commonplace book now in manuscript in Lincoln's Inn:

> The King's prerogative cannot prejudice the property of the
> Subject
> that the King cannot grant power to any person to act contrary to common or statute law
> That the King's prerogative shall not be extended to the Injury of any subject [80]

[78] Spedding, IV, 265. This remark was made by Bacon, not by Coke. Bacon also wrote: "The benignitie of the law is such, as when to preserve the principles and grounds of law it depriveth a man of his remedie without his own fault, it will rather put him in a better degree and condition than in a worse." F. Bacon, *A Collection of some principal Rules and Maxims of the common Lawes of England*, (London, 1639), p. 34. When the proposed union of England and Scotland was under discussion, Bacon proposed that "one Great Charter" of the liberties of both nations be drawn up and confirmed. Spedding, III, 234.

[79] Staunford, *op. cit.*, p. 50.

[80] Commonplace Book found among the Papers of Sir W. Lee, Lincoln Inn MSS., pp. 242 r-v.

In keeping with such beliefs was the doctrine that the king could not legally take a subject's property away from him. Parliamentary taxes were voluntary grants—gifts of the subject from his own property to the king.[81] There was almost complete agreement on this important principle. James and Charles, as well as Tudor and medieval monarchs, had to ask their subjects for grants of money. Leaders of the parliamentary opposition naturally found this doctrine a strong bulwark in their stand against the king, but it is important to realize that most of the leading royalists never denied it.

Salisbury, Bacon, and Ellesmere, the three most important supporters of the crown in the first part of James's reign, all believed that property belonged to the subject. Salisbury remarked to a group of the lords and commons that the king "accompteth himself but your steward of whatsoever you give him," [82] and it was probably Salisbury who advised James to suppress the first edition of Cowell's *Interpreter,* in which the author attributed the power of direct taxation to the king.[83] In Bate's case, the judges arguing for the king never claimed that he could levy direct taxes without parliament. On the contrary, they carefully explained that the issue was not one of direct taxation. Judge Fleming, whose views on the king's absolute prerogative went too far to be accepted by some Englishmen, explained that the currants upon which an imposition had been levied were not the goods or property of a subject

[81] In this connection it is interesting to note that the statute confirming the dissolution of the monasteries and their lands referred to the free and voluntary gift of such property. K. Pickthorn, *Early Tudor Government,* 2 vols., (Cambridge University Press, Cambridge, 1934), II, 375. In the courts also, reference was made to the gift of monastic lands. See Hobart, p. 308, and Sir John Bridgman, *Reports . . . ,* (London, 1659), p. 34. See also H. Townshend, *Historical Collections . . . ,* (London, 1680), p. 49, where the following statement is recorded: "*Nota* here, to the Subsidy-bill, because it is the meer gift of the Subject, the Queen's consent is not required for the passing of it, but as it is joyned with her thankful acceptance; nor to the Bill of Pardon, because it is originally her free gift, no other circumstance is required, than that the thankful acceptance by the Lords and Commons be likewise expressed."

[82] Bowyer, pp. 41–42.

[83] Holdsworth, VI, 23.

within the land.[84] In the great parliamentary debate of 1610 on the question of these impositions, at least two of the leading supporters of the king, Doderidge and Montague, took pains to point out that actual taxes could be granted only by parliament.[85]

In the debates in the 1628 parliament, leading royalists also proclaimed that property belonged to the subject. The second proposition drawn up by the lords as a suggested basis for agreement with the commons proposed that the king should declare that "every Free Subject of this Realm hath a Fundamental Propriety in his Goods, and a Fundamental Liberty of his Person." [86] There is very interesting evidence that Laud accepted this principle. In rambling historical notes jotted down by him, now in the Public Record Office, he made the following remarks. "Tonnage and poundage *given* to the kinge for his life, . . . nothing passed or *given* this session . . . The Com[mons] *gave* the kinge two subsidyes." [87] Another revelation of Laud's views occurs in a long statement seemingly coming from Charles but probably drawn up by Laud in about 1629, which is now among the Stowe Papers in the Huntington Library. It is unfortunate that Charles never issued the statement because, although its tone is firm, the point of view is moderate and the temper reasonable. At one point in it the following remark occurs: "We never denyed them Propriety in their Goods. Nay We knowe that wthout those two be maynteyned, Liberty and Propriety, no care, courage, or Industry will be found among any people." [88]

In the months before parliament met in 1629 Charles tried to take tonnage and poundage without waiting for parliamentary sanction. He attempted to justify himself in the eyes of parliament in the following way: This action of mine would

[84] S. T., II, 389–390. See chapter IV for a fuller discussion of the views of Fleming.

[85] *Parl. Debates in 1610*, pp. 62 and 98. Bacon agreed, (*Ibid.*, p. 66).

[86] L. J., III, 769.

[87] St. P., Domestic, 16/96:31. Italics are mine.

[88] Stowe MSS., Parliamentary Papers, Box I, C. 84. Hunt. Lib.

not be objected to "if my words and actions be rightly understood, . . . if men had not imagined that I have taken these duties as appertaining to my hereditary prerogative in which they are much deceived; for it ever was and still is my meaning, by the gift of my people to enjoy it; and my intention in my speech at the ending of the last Session concerning this point was not to challenge Tonnage and Poundage as of right, but *de bene esse;* showing you the necessity, not the right by which I was to take it, until you had granted it to me." [89]

During the years between 1630 and 1640 the principle that property belonged to the subject was never directly attacked, even though parliament was never in session to guard it. Royalist judges in the ship-money case still accepted in principle the property rights of the subject. The remarks of these men, staunchly upholding the correctness of ship money yet insisting that it was not a tax, are very revealing. Littleton said: "Again, it is not in question, whether the subject hath a property in his goods, or can lose them without consent in Parliament. I shall shew that his property shall remain unto him not withstanding this assess." [90] Banks remarked that "This writ denieth not the property to be in the subject." [91] Berkeley showed that although this government is monarchical, yet subjects "have in their goods a property a peciliar interest, a 'meum and Tuum' ";[92] while Trevor said of the sum assessed, "the subjects are not prejudiced by it, either in their dignities, or properties in their goods."[93]

Most Englishmen not only admitted the sanctity of property but liked to point out that a monarchy respecting the subjects' rights was the highest and truest form of monarchy.[94] England, they were proud to proclaim, was most fortunate in its gov-

[89] *Commons Debates for 1629,* p. 11.

[90] S. T., III, 924.

[91] *Ibid.,* p. 1059.

[92] *Ibid.,* p. 1090.

[93] *Ibid.,* p. 1127.

[94] See Hawarde, p. 33 where it is recorded that Essex said that Elizabeth "regards more the love of her subjects and their good estate than her own honour and revenues."

ernment. "This Iland," Richard Martin of the Middle Temple told James, "shall never feare the mischiefes and misgovernments, which other countries and other times have felt. Oppression shall not be here the badge of authoritie, nor insolence the marke of greatnesse. The people shall every one sit under his owne Olive tree, and anoynt himselfe with the fat thereof, his face not grinded with extorted sutes, nor his marrow suckt with most odious and unjust Monopolies." [95]

A monarch was regarded as a true monarch if he ruled over free people who showed their love and gratitude to him by voluntary gifts of their own. "It was the greatest Honour of the king to govern Subjects moderately free." [96] The speaker of the commons in 1624 explained that James was under God "a sole and entire Monarch," yet nevertheless parliamentary grants were free.[97] In the words of Archbishop Abbot, "There is a *Meum* and a *Tuum* in Christian Common-wealths, and according to Laws and Customs, Princes may dispose of it, that saying being true *Ad Reges potestas omnium pertinet, ad singulos proprietas."* [98] A monarch whose authority did not include the right to take his subjects' property was royal, as Bodin had once said. Such a monarch possessed something greater than the mere material wealth of his people—he possessed their love. With their love he did not need to own their property, for they would freely grant it to him for his legitimate needs. A monarch of this type most truly reflected the divinity and justice of God, who had ordained and exalted the king and given him many prerogatives, but who had also given property to the greatest of his subjects and manual skill to the lowliest, and had provided that neither the subject's property nor his manual skill fell within the realm of the king's authority.

During all the years of controversy leading up to the civil

[95] A Speach Delivered, to the Kings Most Excellent Majestie . . . by Maister Richard Martin of the Middle Temple, (London, 1603), Fol. B.
[96] C. J., I, 153.
[97] Rushworth, I, 118.
[98] *Ibid.,* 443.

war, the belief that the subject possessed property which was truly his own and could not be taken from him without his consent, played a major part in shaping men's beliefs and in determining their policies and actions. When the king and his supporters encroached too much upon that basic principle, as they did in 1626, 1627, and again in the thirties, the parliamentary opposition grew strong. Men of moderate views joined with the leaders of the parliamentary opposition in 1628 to enact the Petition of Right and in 1640–1 to pass the statutes abolishing the instruments of prerogative government. These moderates agreed with the aggressive leaders that drastic measures must be taken to preserve the subjects' rights.

Most royalists agreed that the subject had rights, even though they tried in council, star chamber, law court, and parliament to circumvent them.[99] When the civil war finally came in 1642, the king, following the wise advice of Clarendon, made himself the guardian of the subjects' rights and property. Now many moderates cast their lot with the king, believing that their property rights and their traditional form of government were better maintained under the king than under parliament, which by 1642 was claiming complete control over the subjects' rights and taxing their property with little regard for their consent.

[99] See chapter IV.

CHAPTER II

ENGLISHMEN LOVE THE LAW
AND A BALANCED
POLITY

ENGLISHMEN entered into the constitutional controversies of
the seventeenth century with a profound belief in the importance of law. To them law was not primarily a decree
enacted by a sovereign legislature to deal with a particular
problem of the moment. Law was normally regarded as
more than human, as the reflection of eternal principles of
justice. When men considered it in relation to their own
England, they looked upon it as a binding, cohesive force in
their polity without which there would be no commonwealth,
no government, no rights, and no justice.

They believed that the law was impartial—serving well both
the king and the subject, enabling the king to fulfill his divine
mission of governing with justice and protecting the subject
in his God-given rights. To the seventeenth-century mind, rule
by the king and rule by law were harmonious and not competing concepts. As the king's authority gave sanction to the
law, so the law gave strength to the king's rule. To Yelverton,
a faithful servant of Queen Elizabeth, "to live without government is hellish and to governe without lawes is brutish." [1]
James himself remarked that both king and parliament have
a "union of interest" "in the lawes of the Kingdome, without
which as the Prerogative cannot subsist, soe without that the
Lawe cannot be maynteyned." [2]

[1] *The Farewell address of Sir Christopher Yelverton to the Hon. Society of Gray's Inn 1589,* (1882), p. 16.
[2] *Parl. Debates in 1610,* p. 23. Salisbury is reporting James's judgment
of Cowell's *Interpreter.*

Eulogies of law were common. In 1609 Ferdinando Pulton wrote the following poetic tribute to law:

These lawes bee as his [the king's] Privie Counsellours, incessantly respecting the preservation of his person, peace, Crowne, and dignitie: These be as his Gentlemen Pentioners, attending daily in his presence, to do him all princely honor and service: These bee as the Yeomen of his guard, waiting day and night to protect his person in peace, from all forcible assaults, and other perils: These bee as his great and goodly Shippes, which lye hovering on the Seas, and his strong castles and forts of defence, which stand firmly upon the land, wherewith he doth prevent forrein hostilitie, represse inward tumults, and so keep himself and his people in peace: These be as the Judges, Justices, Sherifes, Constables, and other Officers, watching everie houre and moment in all the Shires, places, corners, and creekes of the Realme, to represse outrages, and to maintain his peace: And lastly, these be to him as his mynt, by which he doth coyn gold and silver to defend himselfe and his people in the time of warre, and to support his honour and royall estate in the time of peace. And also by the protection of these lawes everie good member of the whole kingdome doth receive the like benefit of peace: for in feare of them each person doth enjoy his life and limmes in peace, and is defended from the bloudie minded murderer, and manqueller, and the rage of the furious quareller and fighter: And in feare of them the housekeeper resteth in peace, with his wife and family under his owne roof, without being assaulted by burglers: And in feare of them the traveller journieth in peace from one country to another, without being spoiled by robbers: And in feare of them the Grasiers cattell do feed quietly in his pasture, without being stolne by theeves.[3]

Francis Bacon was another Englishman who frequently praised the laws. In a letter offering advice to the young Buckingham in 1616, he wrote:

Next touching the Laws (wherein I mean the Common Laws of England) . . . if they be rightly administered they are the best, the equallest in the world between the Prince

[3] F. Pulton, *De Pace Regis et Regni,* (London, 1609), Preface.

and People; by which the King hath the justest Prerogative, and the People the best liberty. . . .[4]

In the Laws we have a native interest, it is our Birth-right and our Inheritance, and I think the whole Kingdom will always continue that mind which once the two Houses of Parliament publicly professed, *Nolumus Legem Angliae mutare;* under a Law we must live, and under a known Law, and not under an arbitrary Law is our happiness that we do live.[5]

. . . As far as it may lie in you, let no arbitrary power be introduced. The people of this kingdom love the laws thereof, and nothing will oblige them more than an assurance of enjoying them. . . .[6]

It is well known that the parliamentarians based much of their case against the king on the law,[7] but it is sometimes forgotten that the royalists also looked to the law to sanction the great authority they claimed for the monarch.[8] In the long period of controversy between 1603 and 1642, both royalists and parliamentarians turned to the law to justify their actions, and both believed that the law was on their side. Even after the civil war broke out with its appeal to force, both groups strove to prove the legality of their actions, and only a few men admitted that the law had failed them. During the war, however, some men on both sides came to see that law could not be supreme. Henry Parker was one who led the way in recognizing that sovereign power must be above law, but Parker clearly saw that men of his own age found it difficult to accept the concept, for they had so long believed that law was supreme. "To place a superior above a supreme, was held unnatural . . ."[9] These words of Parker, written by the clearest

[4] Spedding, VI, 18.

[5] *Ibid.,* p. 19.

[6] *Ibid.,* p. 33.

[7] See chapter VI.

[8] See chapter IV.

[9] Henry Parker, *Observations upon some of his Majesties late Answers and Expresses,* July 2, 1642, p. 13. This tract is reprinted in W. Haller, *Tracts on Liberty in the Puritan Revolution,* 3 vols., (Columbia University

and most realistic parliamentary thinker during the civil war period, serve to remind us that the medieval belief in the supremacy of law remained firm and strong in men's minds throughout the period of Tudor "absolutism" and Stuart "divine right."

It is important, therefore, to consider the historical reasons why this medieval concept survived to play a vital part in the constitutional controversies of the seventeenth century. It could live on because of the unique nature of Tudor rule. Absolute and despotic as the Tudors often were, they carried on and strengthened the rule of law inherited from their medieval predecessors. Henry VII brought back the supremacy of the law of the land over powerful feudal lords and factions, and no later Tudor ruler undid his work. At the end of the sixteenth century no administrative bureaucracy had been created in England, but officials of the government still carried on their duties under the law, as they had in the Middle Ages. The common law courts still played a most vital and necessary part in governing the country, notwithstanding the increasing importance of star chamber and other prerogative courts; and their survival kept alive medieval ideas of the supremacy of law respecting the subjects' rights as well as the king's prerogative, and thereby providing a great "barrier against absolutism." [10]

The Stuarts inherited governmental machinery geared to legal forms and constitutional ideas premised upon the supremacy of law and not of power in human affairs. They also inherited advisers and councillors trained in the Elizabethan way of acting and thinking. The rule of James I and Charles I was conditioned by this inheritance. They talked divine right but carried on much of the routine work of governing the

Press, New York, 1934), II, 167–213. See chapter X for a discussion of Parker.

[10] On this subject see C. H. McIlwain, "The English Common Law, Barrier against Absolutism," *American Historical Review* XLIX, (1943), 23–31. See also W. Holdsworth, *Some Makers of English Law*, (Cambridge University Press, Cambridge, 1938), p. 82.

country with proper respect for traditional legal forms and beliefs. Moreover, their most serious and most successful attempt to become more absolute was not based on divine right but on an interpretation of English law advanced by royalist judges and councillors. This attempt will be the subject of chapter IV, but in this context it is necessary to examine the limitations upon royal authority.

From the description and analysis of the English polity presented up to this point it is clear that the king was absolute in some realms and that in many ways his authority was limited. He was limited in the first place by the rights of his subjects. During the Tudor period the number of means or remedies available for the subject to use in securing justice against the crown did not diminish but increased in number. Many statutes passed in the sixteenth century included new or improved remedies for the subjects' use. For example, the statute of 1541–2 creating the court of surveyors gave "extended powers to the Court of Augmentations to settle claims by or against the Crown in respect of property which was placed under the jurisdiction of that Court." [11] Throughout the century, common law, equity, and statute provided concrete ways and means to assist the subject to secure his proper rights. After a century of strong Tudor rule, the monarch still governed as a king limited in some respects by the rights of his subjects.

Under the Stuarts, as in earlier periods, the courts rendered decisions against the king's prerogatives. Significant as were the great decisions rendered in Bate's case and ship money in favor of the public prerogative, the fact that judges still followed traditional legal forms and rules in handling his private prerogatives helped to keep alive the idea that the king's authority was limited in some realms. Suits were brought and decisions given against officials of the king who transgressed the law defining their authority. Noy, for example, reports a case in which Popham fined a deputy purveyor for his

[11] W. S. Holdsworth, "The History of Remedies against the Crown," *Law Quarterly Review* XXXVIII, (1922), 28.

misdemeanors and delivered "the opinion of all the Justices of England in these three points [:] 1. That no Purveyor or his Deputy may take anything, without shewing of his Commission. 2. That they cannot take wood or trees growing, without the consent of the owners; Because they belong to the Freehold. 3. That no Purveyor may take that which a man hath provided for his own provision: but of that which is to be sold, the King shall have the buying at reasonable prices . . ." [12]

A second important way in which the king's authority was limited may be called procedural. Officials in the different departments of government—in privy council, star chamber, chancery, common law court, and parliament—acted through carefully defined and recognized forms, which afforded considerable protection to the subject and distinctly confined some of the king's authority within the proper procedural channel. The king was the fountain of justice, but in cases of treason and felony where he was a party, he could not "sit in judgement," for his justice must be carried out by his "Justices, or Commissioners." [13] The king was the greatest landlord in the kingdom, yet "a Freehold cannot pass from the King, but by patent under the great Seal." [14] The king could issue proclamations on many matters, but "a proclamation binds not unless it be under the Great Seal." [15] Although the highest duke could be brought low before the king's council and star chamber, the decisions of those bodies were not supposed to touch the freehold of even the lowliest subject.

When James and Charles refused to recognize this principle and began to deal with the subjects' property in council and star chamber, men began to distrust and hate these prerogative courts. There is evidence that at least two supporters of the king did not believe that the privy council should deal with questions involving property. Bacon advised Buckingham in 1616 that "the entertaining of private causes of *meum* and

[12] Noy, p. 101.
[13] M. Dalton, *The Country Justice*, (London, 1727), p. 1.
[14] Croke, III, 513.
[15] *Ibid.*, p. 180.

tuum" was "not fit for that board," that these causes "should be left to the ordinary course and courts of justice." [16] A very interesting opinion on this same question was expressed by Sir Robert Heath, who championed the king's prerogative in the Five Knights case. When in 1641 parliament passed the act abolishing star chamber and restricting the power of the privy council, Heath approved of some parts of this measure. In his own copy of Staunford's *Plees del Coron* [17] Heath scribbled:

> I did willingly subscribe to that pt of the act. For the regulatinge of the privye Counsell: havinge Long been of opinion: that the privie Counsell, and that honorable board the Counsell table, should not have meddled with questions of meum and tuum. and therefore in that point, it did deserve a Regulation.[18]

James and Charles could never completely ignore established ways of acting. During their reigns the dead weight of administrative procedure still afforded considerable protection to the subject.

So also did the long-established procedural principle that parliament was necessary for many of the king's actions. It was necessary for the making of laws. The attempts of James and Charles to legislate in council by proclamation, rather than in parliament by statute, were bitterly contested; and their attempts to bypass the money-granting power of parliament never completely succeeded. In the making of laws and in the securing of direct taxes, parliament still had a voice in seventeenth-century England. In these respects the king's authority was very definitely limited.

Stuart kings themselves sometimes found it very helpful to be limited by the proper procedure. In 1606, for example, the Venetian ambassador was trying to secure James's permission to have grain exported to Venice. The king told the ambassador

[16] Spedding, VI, 41.
[17] 1567 edition. In the Treasure Room, Harvard Law School Library.
[18] Heath continued: "But for that pt. which concernes the Court of Star Chamber, I did wish it had been but a Regulation also, and not a totall taking away thereof."

he was sorry he could not come to the assistance of Venice with English grain, but "This question of grain was one wherein he had only a limited authority; it belonged to the law, the constitution, the Parliament, which ought not to be contravened in a matter of such moment as the people's bread." [19]

A third important way in which the king's authority and that of his officials was limited was by oath. For centuries oaths had played a vital role in the English government [20] and still did in the early seventeenth century. An office of government was one of trust whose duties were entered into only after a solemn oath, which men in the seventeenth century did not take lightly. Coke was insulted that anyone should think he did not believe in and respect the king's prerogative, for he had "binne twice sworne to it." [21] There was a great difference between the words and advice of judges given in courts of justice when "they have an Oath to tie them" and when "they are but Assistants to the Lords in Parliament." [22] In judgment a judge "speaketh Sworne, and the best Subject is to stand before him uncovered, but elsewhere he is an other Kinde of man." [23]

Oaths were regarded as so necessary in government that some men wondered whether civil government could function at all without them:

> The sacred, the soveraigne instrument of justice among men, what is it, what can it bee in this world but an oath, being the strongest bond of Conscience? [24]

> . . . the Lawe and civill policy of England, being chiefly founded uppon Religion and the feare of God, doth use the religious Ceremonie of an oath, not onely in legall proceedinge but in other transactions and affaires of most Importance in the commonwealth; esteeming oath, not onely as the best

[19] *Cal. St. P., Venetian* X, 1606, pp. 439-40.
[20] See P. E. Schramm, *A History of the English Coronation Oath*, trans. by L. G. W. Legg, (Clarendon Press, Oxford, 1937).
[21] Bor., 3/25/28.
[22] Bowyer, p. 218. Sandys speaking.
[23] *Ibid.*, p. 121. Fuller speaking.
[24] E. Sandys, *Europae Speculum, Or, A View or Survey of the State of Religion in the Westerne parts of the World*, (Hagae-Comitis, 1629), p. 45.

Touchstone of Truste in matters of controversie, But as the safest knott of Civill societie, and the firmest band to tie all men to the performance of their severall duties.[25]

In this government "the safety of the King himselfe," and "every mans estate in particular, and the state of the realme in generall doth depend upon the truth and sincerity of mens oathes." [26] When men attached such importance to oaths as these statements indicate, they naturally regarded the oath taken by the king at his coronation as especially significant.[27] This promise to his people to keep their lawes and customes was a solemn pledge given before God, limiting his authority in the most binding way the seventeenth-century mind could imagine.

In the first part of the seventeenth century, then, the monarch still carried on the work of government with a considerable number of practical limitations to his freedom of action. Consequently, it was natural for men still to believe in the idea of limited authority. Most royalists agreed with the parliamentary opposition that the king was limited in some respects. The royalists, however, believed he was limited too much, whereas the parliamentary opposition believed his limitations were too few and too ineffectual. The one, primarily interested in strong and effective government, strove to circumvent or abolish some of the traditional legal restrictions upon the king's power, while the other, concerned with the protection of its own rights, worked to increase those legal restraints. The parliamentarians also set out to find a solution for the great constitutional problem which had never been resolved in the Middle Ages or in the Tudor period: the problem of controlling a king whose authority was legally limited but who could not be coerced by legal means. This great constitutional

[25] Ellesmere MSS. vol. 30, no. 2191, 7 Paschal 11 Jacobi in the Castle Chamber, The Case of concealment or mentall reservation, Hunt. Lib., p. 6.

[26] *Ibid.,* p. 7.

[27] See Rushworth, I, 200, for the coronation oath taken by Charles I.

problem was unsolved when James became king of England and constituted one of the great difficulties the parliamentary opposition faced. Their efforts to limit and control the king took two forms—the constitutional and the political—each of which will be discussed in subsequent chapters.

In dealing with the ideas of law and limited authority agreed upon by most Englishmen, two important questions quite naturally arise. The first concerns the kind of law Englishmen praised and the kind of law they believed limited the king. To modern thinkers, concerned with analytical distinctions between different kinds of law, the question is very real. To most seventeenth-century Englishmen fine distinctions between kinds and types of law played a small part in their thinking, particularly before 1628. The concept of law itself was primary and distinctions secondary. It was the harmony and not the discrepancies between types of law which Englishmen stressed in these years of controversy. To seventeenth-century men, divine and natural law were not far away but close at hand to strengthen and to give added sanction to certain basic laws of the land. Yelverton could not "sufficiently nor amply enough magnifie the majestie and the dignitie of the lawe, for it is the divine gifte and invention of God." [28] "The common Law," Edward Phelips, speaker of the house, said in 1604, was "grounded or drawn from the Law of God, the Law of Reason, and the Law of Nations." [29] George Saltern, a legal writer, gave the following account of the relation of English and divine law:

> Now I take in hand to speake of our auncient Lawes, and God is the beginning and end of my worke. . . . For whether we consider our Statutes enacted since the *Norman,* wee shall finde them grounded upon moste just and prudent intentions: or the remnants of our Actes made by the *Saxons,* we shal see them ful of Godly & devout admonitions, or the secret footesteps of the auncient British constitutions,

[28] *The Farewell address of Sir Christopher Yelverton,* p. 12.
[29] C. J., I, 254.

appering yet in the bodie of our common Lawes, the principles thereof will appear to be the verie Lawes of the eternal God, written in the two immortal tables of nature & Scripture.[30]

Chancellor Ellesmere expressed the same point of view in the case of the Post-Nati, when he said: "The common law of England is grounded upon the law of God, and extends itselfe to the originall law of nature, and the universall lawe of nations."[31] Again Ellesmere, arguing in the Earl of Oxford's case on behalf of property, pointed out that "By the Law of God, He that builds a House ought to dwell in it."[32] So closely knit together were the law of God and the law of the land that judges were admonished by one writer to "Take heede what ye doe: for ye execute not the judgments of man, but of the Lord; and he will be with you, in the cause and judgment."[33]

References such as these to divine and natural law were made simply and naturally by men starting with certain basic laws and reaching upward and outward to higher authorities. These higher laws were not invoked to expound a philosophy but to drive home a particular point in a court of law,[34] in a parliamentary debate,[35] or in a popular pamphlet. Nor were appeals to them the monopoly of either side. By 1628 the parliamentary party had come to be suspicious of and to condemn

[30] George Saltern, *Of the Antient Lawes of Great Britaine*, (London, 1605), Sig. B2 r-v.

[31] S. T., II, 670.

[32] *Reports in Chancery, Taken and adjudged in the Court of Chancery* . . . , (London, 1736), p. 3.

[33] *The Argument of Master Nicholas Fuller in the case of Thomas Lad, and Richard Maunsell, his Clients* . . . , (1607), Title page.

[34] See, for example, Noy, p. 160. The reason for our law of inheritance is said to be "grounded upon the Law of Nature, and the Law of God."

[35] See *Commons Debates 1621*, V, 465. Brooke remarked in a debate on a "Bill touching the Restraint of the great vast of Gold and Silver in Apparrell . . . that Costliness of Apparell was both against the Law of Nature and of God, that God did not attire our first Parents with Excrements of Worms, . . . but did apparell them with Skins . . ."

arguments advanced by royalist clergy which claimed that divine and natural law justified kings in taking taxes from their people. As early as 1614, however, Ellesmere advised the lords against meeting with the commons because the commons' leaders would be fortified with arguments drawn from divine and natural law, and he doubted whether the lords were adequately prepared to meet such arguments. Ellesmere was not denying the validity of those arguments, only admitting the greater skill with which the commons' leaders used them.[36] During the whole period from 1603 to 1642 it is apparent that both parties in the growing controversy turned to natural and divine laws whenever they thought that their case would thereby be strengthened.

A second question relevant to the part that ideas of law played in the thinking of this period concerns the interpretation of the term "fundamental law." Although the ways in which judges and lawyers viewed statute laws in reference to the fundamental laws and principles of the constitution is discussed later in this volume (chap. III), it is necessary here to consider briefly the general use of the term in the period between 1603 and 1640. Since Englishmen of this period did not draw any sharp and clear distinctions between laws which were fundamental and laws which were not, no definitive conclusions are possible. An examination of the available material appears to substantiate the following conclusions:

During the entire period from 1603 to 1640, Englishmen used both the term "fundamental law" and "fundamental laws." They used these terms in various places—occasionally in common law court and in legal treatise, but also in star chamber. They used them in parliament and also in letters, pamphlets, and poems. Hakewill, Coke, and Pym, leaders of the parlia-

---

[36] Hastings MSS., Parliamentary Papers 1614, A booke of remembrances of those thinge that doe happen . . . in the higher house of Parliament begunne the fyfe daie of Aprill 1614 . . . May 25, 1614, Hunt. Lib.

mentary opposition, spoke of fundamental laws, but so did Bacon,[37] Samuel Daniel,[38] and even James,[39] and Charles.[40] For the most part speakers and writers used the words simply without attaching special meaning to the adjective "fundamental." Laws labelled as fundamental were important, but so were many laws not so designated; and there is no clear or conclusive evidence that a law to which the adjective "fundamental" was attached was regarded as more basic or in a different category from a law without the adjective. The term "fundamental" was used at times in reference to important prerogatives of the king and also in reference to important rights of the subject; but, basic as these were, the value attached to those prerogatives or those rights cannot be evaluated in terms of the use or omission of the word "fundamental." It is true that as the differences sharpened between the royalists and the parliamentarians, each side maintained that it was the guardian and defender of the laws, and consequently each side used the word "fundamental" freely. In 1628 and in the early months of the Long Parliament, the parliamentary opposition used the phrase more often and more effectively than the royalists did, while in the latter part of 1641 and in 1642 the royalists used it more often and more tellingly. At neither of these times, however, was it the monopoly of one party. That would have been impossible since the law served both the king and the subject.

The importance attached to law by Englishmen of differing beliefs illuminates many aspects of the history and thought of this period. Above all, it explains why some men believing in the law supported the king, and why others with an equally firm belief in law cast in their lot with parliament. There were

[37] F. Bacon, *A Collection of some principal Rules and Maximes of the Common Lawes of England,* Epistle Dedicatory.

[38] S. Daniel, *A Panegyrike Congratulatorie,* p. 153. In the 1601 folio edition, verse 30 reads: "Thou will not touch the fundamentall frame of their Estate thy ancestors did forme."

[39] C. H. McIlwain, *The Political Works of James I,* p. 54.

[40] Rushworth, I, 268, and *D'Ewes, (Long, Parl.),* ed. W. Notestein, p. 280.

moderates on both sides, and those moderates looked to the law to resolve their differences and difficulties. Because of their great faith in the law's competence to do this, they often seemed blind to the fact that laws coming down from medieval times might not always be adequate to meet all the problems of their own age. During the whole first half of the seventeenth century very few men—moderate, radical, or conservative—faced up squarely to the fact that the issue was more one of power than of law. Theories of government based on power and not on law never became popular with any group in this period. If today many people rate Hobbes as the greatest political thinker of his age, he was not so regarded by his English contemporaries, who spared no time and effort to condemn his Godless and lawless *Leviathan*. They approached the crisis of their constitution with an attitude towards law which we today must understand in order truly to grasp the meaning and significance of the arguments they employed.

The thinking of Englishmen during the troubled years of controversy cannot be understood without a knowledge of their attitude towards law. Nor can it be grasped without understanding their belief in a balanced polity. Faith in a government well poised and properly balanced did much to shape and color the point of view of both royalists and parliamentarians.

They could believe in a balanced polity because adjustment played such an important part in the actual functioning of the English government in the early seventeenth century. To adjust the king's prerogative to the subjects' rights was a regular and normal task of officials of the government. Kings, councillors, and royalist judges in this period were primarily concerned with exalting the king's prerogative, but they were under oath to respect the rights of Englishmen and the law of the land. They could not legally ignore the fact that any adjustment of the prerogative desired by them must not completely ignore the rights of the subject. When Stuart kings encroached upon those rights, they consulted with their judges, explained their actions to their people, or tried to secure favorable legal judgments, because they or their advisers knew that by the law of the land their prerogatives must be so adjusted. Whenever their actions, however correct in form, actually failed to make a proper adjustment, the opposition to their rule increased, and the more moderate royalists urged caution.

The task of adjustment constantly confronted the lawyers and judges in the common law courts, as any reading of the law cases in this period clearly reveals. To make adjustments was also a normal task of parliament, and from one point of view parliament was well constituted to perform this function, for in parliament both king and subject were present to see that any proposed measure did not harm either the king's prerogative or the subjects' rights. Before any bill could become law, it must be accepted by king, lords, and commons, and the acceptance of a bill by each signified that the adjustment had been properly made.[41] At times, however, it was hard to achieve such an adjustment in parliament, for leaders of the opposition, in their efforts to strengthen and protect the subjects' rights, found it difficult to do this without encroaching too much upon the prerogative. Nevertheless, they could not and did not completely ignore the fact that some adjustment of their rights with the law and constitution must be made. If they encroached too much, they carefully explained that they were not really encroaching, but only guarding the subjects' rights. At times when their encroachment failed to achieve a respectable adjustment, the more moderate members

---

[41] On this subject Dudley Digges wrote in 1642: "But now (contrary to the use of inferiour Courts) the parties in Parliament (in those things that concern the publique) meddle not as meere Judges, but as Parties interessed, with things that concerne every of their own Rights, in which case it is neither Law nor Reason, that some of the Parties should determine of that that concernes all their mutuall interests, *invita altera parte*, against the will of anyone of the parties. But that all parties concurre or else their mutuall interest to remain in the same condition it was before." [Dudley Digges], *A Review of the Observations upon some of his Majesties late Answers and Expresses*, (Oxford, 1643), p. 12.

of the commons urged caution. If the opposition persisted in its course of action, some moderates went over to the support of the king.

The fact that the government functioned in the first half of the seventeenth century with due respect for both the king's prerogative and the subjects' rights can clearly be seen by examining an important procedure geared to such adjustment. Because the king was the supreme head of the state to whom all owed obedience, the subject must humbly petition him for redress of grievances, but there existed for his use a petition of right and a petition of grace. In a petition of right the subject was petitioning for what was his own, and a king who was true to his office, high calling, and his coronation oath had no choice but to grant a real right to the subject. In a petition of grace, however, the subject was asking the king to grant that which belonged to the king, which admittedly he had every legal right to refuse, but which the subject humbly petitioned him of his grace to grant.

A second illustration of the fact that adjustment was a normal function of government can be seen in connection with the way the dispensing power of the king operated in the seventeenth century. Professor Birdsall [42] has shown that the courts in that period still drew a sharp line, as they had earlier in the Middle Ages, between statutes involving the administrative realm of the king, and those concerned with the subjects' rights and means for their protection. The king, so the courts held, might dispense *non obstante* with the first kind of statute because within the realm of government he was absolute, but he might not dispense with the second type because the subjects' rights were legally beyond the range of his authority. Notwithstanding the fact that in the seventeenth century more and more statutes dealt with public matters of concern to both king and subject, judges in the courts continued to apply to such public statutes the old medieval distinction. They judged some statutes to be within the realm of the

[42] P. Birdsall, *op. cit.*, pp. 51–68.

king's government and so capable of being dispensed with, since within that realm "the subject individually or collectively has no interest," [43] and others dealing directly or indirectly with the subjects' rights they agreed must not be dispensed with.

Such distinctions were made both in the courts and in parliament in the first half of the seventeenth century. The debates over the bill against monopolies in 1621 reveal very interestingly that leaders of the parliamentary opposition did not yet venture to attack directly the king's dispensing power. Sandys carefully explained in one debate "That this Act meddles not with the King's Dispensation of Penal Laws; but this extends only to the Grievance, which is, that it shall not be in the Power of a Subject to dispense with a Penal Law." [44] The statute of monopolies finally passed parliament in 1624 and constituted, according to Professor McIlwain, "the first statutory invasion of the royal prerogative." [45] Nevertheless, materials necessary for the defense of the realm were expressly exempted from the provisions of the statute,[46] quite probably because leaders in the commons knew and agreed that any provision on that subject could be dispensed with by the king.

Coke's views on the dispensing power, expressed in a number of law cases, could be profitably supplemented and further clarified by his views on the subject set forth in the commons. In the parliament of 1621, for example, he gave very definite reasons why only the king might dispense with statutes. Since "no Law can fit every Country" the king who is "pater patriae" will like a father be most impartial to all his subjects.[47] The realm trusts the king "when they will not trust a private man." [48]

[43] *Ibid.*, p. 63.
[44] Nicholas, *P. and D.*, I, 200.
[45] C. H. McIlwain, *Constitutionalism Ancient and Modern*, (Cornell University Press, Ithaca, 1940), p. 138.
[46] Statutes of the Realm, 21 Jac. I., c. 3.
[47] C. J., I, 553. See also Coke's opinion in the case of *Non Obstante*, as cited by Birdsall, *op. cit.*, p. 51.
[48] *Commons Debates 1621*, II, 228.

In 1628 the parliamentary opposition made its most determined attempt to curb the prerogative of the king and
thereby protect the liberty of the subject, but the leaders of
that opposition still accepted a distinction between statutes
with which the king might dispense and those with which he
could not. As Glanville said before a committee of both houses,
"When statutes are made to prohibit things not *mala in se,* but
only *mala quia prohibita* . . . the commons must and ever
will acknowledge a regal and sovereign prerogative in the king,
touching such statutes, that it is in his majesty's absolute and
undoubted power, to grant dispensations to particular persons
with clauses of *non obstante,* to do as they might have done
before those statutes, wherein his majesty, conferring grace
and favour upon some, doth not do wrong to others." [49]

It seems quite clear that in the first part of the seventeenth
century councillors, lawyers, judges, and members of parliament recognized, as they carried on the work of government
in council, court, and parliament, that an adjustment must
often be made between the king's prerogative and the subjects'
rights. To them such adjustment was not a medieval survival
but a living reality—an indispensable means of preserving the
prerogative of the king and the rights of the subjects they held
so dear.

As adjustment was a live and necessary part of the functioning of government, so the ideal of balance was one of the
most cherished and strongest beliefs Englishmen agreed upon
between 1603 and 1640. Late in Elizabeth's reign James Morice
gave a picture of the happy balance between king and subject
prevailing in England:

> Behold with us the Sovereigne Aucthoritie of one, an
> absolute Prince, Greate in Majestie, rulinge and reigninge,
> yet guyded and directed by Principles and precepts of
> Reason, which wee terme the lawe. No Spartane Kinge, or

[49] S. T., III, 206. On the question of the dispensing power, see E. F.
Churchhill, "The Dispensing Power and the Defence of the Realm," *Law
Quarterly Review,* XXXVII, (1921), 412–42.

Venetian Duke, but free from accompt and cohercion of anye, eyther equall or Superiour; yet firmilie bound to the Comon wealth by the faithfull Oathe of a Christian Prince, bearinge alone the sharpe sworde of Justice and Correction, yet tempered with mercy and compassion; requiringe Taxe and Tribute of the people, yet not causelesse, nor without commen assent.

Wee agayne the Subjects of this Kingdome are borne and brought upp in due obedience, butt farre from Servitude and bondage, subject to lawfull aucthoritye and commaundement, but freed from licentious will and tyrannie; enjoyinge by lymitts of lawe and Justice oure liefs, lands, goods, and liberties in greate peace and security. . . .[50]

This Elizabethan ideal of a balanced government lived on to play an important part in the thinking of men in the early seventeenth century. In their Apology of June 1604 the commons, accepting the prerogatives of princes but recognizing that such prerogatives "may easily and do daily grow," drew up for James the rights and liberties of his new English subjects which were their due inheritance. When these prevail, they told their king, "an harmonical and stable state is framed, each member under the head enjoying that right, and performing that duty, which for the honour of the head and the happiness of the whole is requisite." [51]

Time and time again in his writings and speeches, Bacon talked of harmony and balance in government. To him the king's prerogative, the subjects' liberty, and the laws existed side by side, each one complementing and strengthening the others, and all working together to produce a delicately poised and beautifully balanced harmony:

The King's Sovereignty and the Liberty of Parliament . . . do not cross or destroy the one the other, but they strengthen and maintain the one the other. Take away liberty of

[50] James Morice, A Remembrance of Certeine Matters concerning the Clergie and theire jurisdiction; 1593, M^m, 1. 51, (Baker MSS. vol. 40) pp. 105–134, Cambridge University Library as quoted by M. Hume, *History of the Oath ex officio in England*, Doctoral dissertation, Radcliffe, p. 286.

[51] C. Stephenson and F. G. Marcham, *Sources of English Constitutional History*, (Harper & Brothers, New York, 1937), p. 421.

Parliament, the griefs of the subject will bleed inwards: . . . On the other side, if the King's sovereignty receive diminution or any degree of contempt with us that are born under an hereditary monarchy . . . it must follow that we shall be a *meteor* or *corpus imperfecte mistum;* which kind of bodies come speedily to confusion and dissolution.[52]

And let no man weakly conceive that just laws and true policy have any antipathy; for they are like the spirits and sinews that one moves with the other.[53]

These words are, I believe, the keystone of Bacon's constitutional thinking. His views on the king's prerogative and sovereignty, the subjects' rights and liberty, and the importance of laws must always be interpreted in relation to his Renaissance faith in the ultimate harmony of all.

This great faith in harmony during an age torn by bitter conflict did not die with Bacon and the other Elizabethans to whom it was so real, but lived on into the years of even more acute controversy in the sixteen-twenties. The leading royalists in the 1628 parliament turned to the concept of a balanced government in their efforts to withstand the attempts of the parliamentary opposition to reduce the king's prerogative within very narrow limits. Attorney General Heath worked hard and long to find a formula which would maintain a balance not tipped too much against the prerogative.[54] Sir Francis Nethersole reminded the commons that "There is not any government in the world like ours, neyther in practise nor right. The kings prerogative sutch as it were not good for the Subject to have it lesse nor the kinge to have it bigger. So the liberty of the Subject sutch as it were not fitt to have it lesse and dangerouse to make it bigger. This on both sydes both kinge and people I thincke desire to make good." [55]

[52] Spedding, IV, 177.

[53] J. Spedding, R. L. Ellis, and D. D. Heath, *The Works of Francis Bacon* . . . , 15 vols., (Boston, 1861–63), XII, 270.

[54] St. P. Domestic, 16/105: 95. Three suggested Royall Answers to the Petition of Rt.

[55] Bor., 3/25/28.

Leaders of the parliamentary opposition also thought and talked of a balanced government. To them as to the royalists it still remained an ideal. Eliot remarked in 1624, "If there were not false glasses between us and the King, our privileges and his prerogative would stand well together." [56] In 1626 Wilde said, "The prerogative of the King and the libertye of the people must have a reciprocall relation and respecte" [57]; and Browne remarked, "The prerogative of the King and privileges of the Subject are equall. bothe great: a reciprocall relacion betwixt the King and us." [58] By 1628 the parliamentary party had reached the conclusion that the king, royalist ministers, judges, and clergy had tipped the scale too much in favor of the prerogative. To restore a proper balance according to the subject his rightful place in the polity became the task to which they bent all their energies. At times in their zeal for the subjects' rights they tended to forget prerogative, but even in the midst of bitter controversy many of these ardent leaders working for rights expressed the belief that both prerogative and liberty were necessary and that a balanced polity was best. Coke, for example, said that "It was a Wonder for him to hear that the Liberty of the Subject should be thought incompatible with the Regality of the King." [59] Wentworth also believed in a balance where there was a "just Symetry, which maketh a sweet harmony of the whole." [60] The fact that Wentworth came to believe that parliament had upset "the sweet harmony of the whole" was an important reason for joining the ranks of the royalists. To the end of his life, however, he still believed in a balanced polity. In one of his speeches defending himself before the lords in 1641, he expressed the same belief he had held in 1628. "All the Strings of this Government and Monarchy," he said, "have been so perfectly tuned through the skill and attention of our Fore-Fathers, that if you wind any of them

[56] Pym, 2/27/24.
[57] Whit, 5/17/26.
[58] Gros., 5/17/26.
[59] L. J., III, 761.
[60] Rushworth, I, 500.

higher, or let them lower, you shall infallibly interrupt the
sweet accord, that ought to be entertained of King and People." [61] He hoped that prerogative and liberty "may be kept at
that Agreement and perfect Harmony one with another, that
they may each watch for, and not any way watch over the
other." [62]

Finch in his opening speech of the Long Parliament asked,
"Where was there a Common-wealth so free, and the ballance
so equally held, as here." [63] He recognized, however, the difficulty of keeping the delicate balance, remarking on this point:
"And certainly so long as the beam is so held, it cannot be
otherwise, in right *Angles,* if you turn the line never so little
it groweth quickly acute or obtuse; and so in States the least
deviation makes a great change." [64] He thought that with the
king's great wisdom and goodness the "pole of Security" would
be preserved.[65] During the first months of the Long Parliament, moderate men like Falkland and Hyde supported the
parliamentary cause, partly because they thought that the king
and his ministers had tipped the balance too much against the
subject; but the grasping and aggressive actions of parliament
at the end of 1641 and in the early months of 1642 upset completely any sweet harmony and accord between king and people
and played a significant part in driving many moderate men
into the royalist camp. From now on the idea of a balanced
polity became a cornerstone of royalist thought. Hyde believed,
so he tells us, that the constitution of government was "so
equally poised, that if the least branch of the prerogative was
torn off, or parted with, the subject suffered by it, and that his
right was impaired: and he was as much troubled when the
crown exceeded its just limits, and thought its prerogative hurt
by it." [66]

[61] Rushworth, VIII, 640.
[62] *Ibid.*, p. 182.
[63] Nalson, I, 483.
[64] *Ibid.*
[65] *Ibid.*
[66] *Life of Edward Earl of Clarendon, written by himself,* 2 vols., (Ox-

By the latter months of 1641 and during the years of civil war it was hard for parliament to continue to talk of a balanced government, for by that time its encroachments upon the prerogative had so disturbed the equilibrium that parliament itself was acting as sovereign and not as one partner in a balanced government. Yet the idea that parliamentary leaders had stood and worked for a proper balance was still expressed. In a poem appearing after his death Pym was praised because

> He knew the bounds and everything
> Betwixt the people and the King;
> He could the just Proportions draw
> Betwixt Prerogative and Law.[67]

The extent to which many men on both sides believed in a balanced polity is rather remarkable in view of the fact that they recognized how difficult it was to maintain one. As Mr. John Coke said in the debates of 1628, we "have to cutt a haire betwixt the Kings sovereignty and the liberty of the subject." [68] Over that hair-like line of demarcation arose many of the constitutional problems and issues of the period, and because it proved impossible to work out a constitutional solution acceptable to both parties, a civil war occurred. Men fought and died in that war on both sides because they believed in a balanced government. Forty years of controversy over the proper adjustment between the king's prerogative and the subjects' rights had not shaken their faith in that ideal.

Even after the death of the king, the ideal of a balance lived on. Implicit in much of Harrington's political thinking was the ideal of balance which his countrymen had long associated with their government. To fashion a properly

ford, 1857), I, 89. I cannot agree with B. H. G. Wormald, who holds that Clarendon did not believe in a balanced constitution, and that such a theory did not prevail in his age and earlier. B. H. G. Wormald, "How Hyde became a Royalist," *The Cambridge Historical Journal,* VIII (1944–46), pp. 69–70.

[67] I have lost the exact reference. The poem is in the Thomason Tracts in the British Museum for the year 1644.

[68] Gros., 4/28/28.

balanced polity was the main purpose of his *Oceana*. Since he recognized that the old law and constitution had been unable to achieve a correct balance, he looked to the economic facts behind the law and strove to achieve a proper balance among the owners of land. The ideal of a balance survived to play a very important part in Restoration history and thought. A reader in the Middle Temple, delivering a formal speech in 1663, said of the English polity: "For it so harmoniously intermixes the rights of Soveraignty with the liberty of the Subject, that the one balances the other, nay, the least jarr in the one, makes a loud discord in the *other*." [69] Englishmen, however, failed again after the Restoration to achieve legally a balanced government. Under Charles II and James II they could not agree on a proper adjustment between their rights and the king's prerogative. Because of their failure the Revolution of 1688 came about; essentially that revolution marks an end of the efforts to maintain a government poised between the king's prerogative and the subjects' rights. By that revolution the balance was upset politically in favor of the subjects' rights, and remained permanently so adjusted in their favor that any earlier balance was effectively destroyed. With this victory of the subjects, the ideal of a balanced government grew more nebulous and further away from reality. Montesquieu was almost a century too late in picturing the English government as balanced. He also erred, as Professor McIlwain has pointed out,[70] in thinking of the balance as a political concept--as a separation of powers. Montesquieu's interpretation of the English constitution, however, possesses at least some truth, for the balance he attributed to the English government had once been both a reality in the functioning of government and an ideal cherished by Englishmen.

[69] *The Readers Speech of the Middle Temple at the Entrance into his Reading Feb. 29, 1663/4 upon the Statute of Magna Charta, cap. 29,* (London, 1664), p. 5.

[70] C. H. McIlwain, *Constitutionalism Ancient and Modern,* p. 145.

CHAPTER III

ENGLISHMEN BELIEVE IN
PARLIAMENT

ENGLISHMEN who agreed upon so much in their polity also held many views in common upon the nature of parliament. Because the Stuarts seldom got along with their parliaments or the parliamentary opposition with their rulers, and because in each session of parliament between 1603 and 1642 some conflict occurred, it is all too easy to assume that men in the first half of the seventeenth century held fundamentally divergent views upon the nature of parliament and its part in their government. Such an assumption is incorrect, as any serious student of this period well knows. Most Englishmen, whether they were royalists or parliamentarians, accepted parliament without question and agreed in some measure upon its true nature and place in the English polity.

This agreement is perfectly natural in view of the indispensable role which parliament had for so long played in the government. For centuries statutes had been passed upon vital matters. No department of government could carry on its work without these statutes, and in the first half of the seventeenth century no department of government made any attempt to do so. Although the privy council and star chamber used and exalted the king's prerogative, much of their work would have been impossible without statute. The councillors often told the justices of the peace that statutes had been broken, and many decisions in star chamber were based upon statute. Royalist judges also cited statutes when they endeavored in the common law courts to increase the range and effectiveness of the king's prerogative.

James did not understand parliament and came to distrust

and dislike this institution, but he called four during his reign of twenty-two years, as many on the average as his predecessors had called, while Charles called three during the first four years of his reign. Early in Charles's reign the rumor began to go around that the king might try to rule without parliament, but prior to that time parliament seems to have been generally accepted as a necessary and important part of the government. When men in the years between 1626 and 1628 began to fear that Charles might find ways and means of governing alone, the opposition to him quickly increased, for many moderates now joined with the leaders of the opposition to preserve their rights and their parliaments. If ever James had tried to dispense permanently with parliament, he would have had little or no support from most of his councillors. In a discussion held by the lords of the council on September 24, 1615, the councillors present agreed that a parliament should be held, partly because it was the best way of "supplying the king" and of bringing him and his people together.[1]

Most Englishmen accepted parliament as a necessary part of their government, looking upon it as an institution which typified or fulfilled many of their cherished ideals. To Bacon, Ellesmere, and Wentworth, as well as to Coke, Sandys, and Phelips, parliament was the place where the king and his subjects, lords and commons, came together in a common council to discuss and act upon matters common to all. It was the highest council and court of the king, and also of the realm. In it the king was most absolute, and by it the subjects' rights were best maintained and strengthened. Here the king and his subjects adjusted and balanced their respective rights, sometimes driving hard bargains each with the other, and sometimes co-operating harmoniously to enact statutes for the general welfare of all.

[1] Spedding, V, 194–207. D. H. Willson, *The Privy Councillors in the House of Commons 1604–1629*, (University of Minnesota Press, Minneapolis, 1940), p. 52, writes: "The council's judgment was surprisingly constant that parliaments were essential and must be conciliated, summoned frequently, and not dissolved in anger."

In these years speakers and writers stressed the fact that parliament was a common council of both king and subject for matters common to both. Coke wrote in his *Institutes* that "The King of England is armed with divers Councels, one whereof is called *Commune Councilum,* and that is the Court of Parliament." [2] Lambard described it in the following terms:

The generall Assembly in *Parliament,* is termed in our old *Writs, Commune Consilium Regni Angliae,* the Common Councell of the Realme of *England,* called to gether by the *King,* for advice in matters concerning the whole Realme.[3]

To Bacon parliament was "the great Council of the King, the great Council of the Kingdom, to advise his Majesty of those things of weight and difficulty which concern both the King and kingdom." [4] St. John called parliament " 'Commune Concilium Regni,' in respect that the whole kingdom is representatively there; and secondly, that the whole kingdom have access thither in all things that concern them, . . . and thirdly, in respect that the whole kingdom is interested in, and receive benefit by the laws and things there passed." [5]

In any consideration of the nature of parliament, it must never be forgotten that the king was a vital component part of it. By the exercise of his absolute power he called and dissolved it, and when it was in session, he was present as a real partner of lords and commons. His assent was necessary for laws. When the commons showed little respect for the king in the bitter sessions of the 1629 parliament, Sir John Coke reminded them that "The King is a Parl [iament] man

---

[2] E. Coke, *Institutes,* vol. 1, lib. II, ch. 10, sect. 164, p. 110r.

[3] W. Lambard, *Archeion,* p. 102.

[4] Spedding, VI, 38.

[5] S. T., III, 862. Doderidge said in 1610 that escuage was assessed in parliament because "It concernes the whole realme, *mesne* lords as well as the Kinge." *Parl. Debates in 1610,* p. 102. Fuller remarked in the same parliament: "That the Parliament consisting of theise 3 estates was the armamentary or storehouse whearin theise things were safely reposed and preserved, as well the lawes of the land as the rights and proprieties of the subjects to theyre lands and goods. " *Ibid.,* p. 37.

as well as we are," and cautioned them, "not soe to advance our priviledge as to justle with the King." [6]

The king was a member of parliament but so was the subject, and while parliament was in session, each of the component parts was an indispensable part of the whole. Here the subject could present his grievances to the king, and here the king could graciously remedy them and pardon offences. Here the king could ask for grants of money, and here the subject could graciously supply him of his own. By parliament the king was "established" [7] and the subject protected, in parliament "common wrongs not holpen in other Courts, are there amended and heard, and difficult causes are there ended." [8] Errors are corrected and judgments amended or reversed, doubtful points of the common law are made clear, and "new springing mischiefs standing remediless by the elder customs" [9] are there considered and remedy found. Parliament deals with the "Grandia Regni," [10] the "publick businesses of the commonwealth." [11] "What consent is given there, is given by everyman of the kingdom, by the power of the voice which they gave in chusing the knights of the shires and burgesses." [12] Since consent given there to laws is the "consent of the whole

[6] *Commons Debates for 1629*, p. 230.

[7] T. Hearne, *A collection of curious Discourses* . . . 2 vols. (London, 1775), I, 287.

[8] Ellesmere, *Certaine Observations concerning the office of the Lord Chancellor*, (London, 1651), p. 23. Holdsworth states (V, 272–3) that *Certaine Observations* was probably not written by Ellesmere.

[9] T. Hearne, *op. cit.*, I, 282.

[10] *Ibid.*, 287.

[11] *Ibid.*, 291.

[12] S. T., III, 1130. For penetrating discussions of the earlier history of the idea that parliament was not only the council of the king, but the representative body of the kingdom, see S. B. Chrimes, *English Constitutional Ideas in the Fifteenth Century* (Cambridge University Press, Cambridge, 1936), ch. II; G. L. Haskins, *The Growth of English Representative Government*, (University of Pennsylvania Press, Philadelphia, 1948); and F. M. Powicke, *King Henry III and the Lord Edward: The Community of the Realm in the Thirteenth Century*, 2 vols., (Clarendon Press, Oxford, 1947). For a discussion of this subject in the seventeenth century, see chapter VII of this book.

Realm," laws made there must necessarily "procure the Weale of the whole Realme." [13]

This brief summary of some of the matters with which parliament dealt indicates the dual nature of its business. Here the king and his subjects could bargain with each other, and here they could co-operate. Some of the Stuart parliaments began their sessions with co-operation and harmony prevailing, but as the sessions developed, bargaining and competition became the prevailing note. The privy councillors were thinking how many "crumbs of the prerogative" could be dropped without weakening the royal authority in order to get the necessary parliamentary grants; while the commons, in return for the scanty grants they did vote, were driving harder and harder bargains which encroached seriously on the king's prerogative. Such attitudes and tactics, when employed to the exclusion of co-operative effort, helped to weaken parliament as an effective governmental institution capable of decisive action on common problems.

Bargaining and competitive methods, however, were inherent in the nature of parliament, for there the king was present with his prerogative and the subject with his rights. Whenever the king needed money, as he always did in the seventeenth century, he had to bargain with his subjects. He whose authority was recognized as absolute in the realm of war and peace had to ask parliament for money to wage a war occasioned by his kingly guidance of foreign affairs; while the subject, possessing absolute control of his property, could either grant or refuse to grant money for the war, or, as parliament had long ago learned to do, grant it under certain conditions. Chaworth explained the situation in exact mathematical terms when he said, "and if we give the King but a

[13] *The Priviledges and Practice of Parliaments in England* . . . 1628, p. 14. In Melton's case the following remark is made. "Note, an Act of Parliament hath every mans consent as well to come, as present, and so he is here an Author of his own hurt, and also he must hold it as the Act gives it, having power to bind every mans right; either finally or *sub modo*, . . ." Hobart, p. 256.

third part of his demand, we must expect from him but a third of our desires." [14] Parliament men actually referred to such arrangements between the king and his subjects as contracts. In 1608, when the disputed question of purveyance was being discussed, Bowyer referred to a "treaty touching Purveiors." [15] When the question of support for the king was being debated in 1610, John Tey remarked:

> If wee shall fynde ourselves able to give more [than] one hundred thowsand pounds per ann. then he wisht that wee might buy out a general statute of explanation of the King's Prerogative, so farre as it might tend to the right and liberty of the subjecte in his body, lands, or goods. [16]

In 1621 when the king was asking parliament for money for war and the commons were demanding redress of grievances, Wentworth suggested "That there be a covenant between the King and his seed and us and our Seed." [17] By 1624 the parliamentary opposition had become so skilled in its bargaining tactics that Glanville asked in a debate on foreign affairs whether "the King be taken to be so weak as that he cannot undertake a war without contracting with his subjects?" [18] The efforts of the commons in 1628 to find a means to protect better the subjects' rights were regarded by some men as involving a contract between king and people. Wentworth made it clear that "we care not to make a new contract," [19] while Noy said "that we desire noe new thing or contract betwixt the King and his people: but to establish the old." [20]

[14] Pym, 3/19/24.

[15] Bowyer, p. 33.

[16] *Parl. Debates in 1610*, p. 47.

[17] *Commons Debates 1621*, II, 454.

[18] Pym, 3/5/24. In this same parliament the lord keeper said: "But it is true, *lex est communis sua sponsie*. It is a contract between the king and his people and between the people amongst themselves, in which there must be a mutual consent, as was Exodus, 24:3. Now for the royal assent, it is proper only to the king as Genesis, 49:10." D'Ewes 5/29/24. The contract here is a double one as in the *Vindiciae Contra Tyrannos*.

[19] Gros., 4/26/28.

[20] *Ibid.*

Selden wrote in his *Table Talk*, "Every law is a Contract between the king and the people, and therefore to bee kept." [21]

These men did not erect their ideas of contract into a theory of government, but their views of parliamentary legislation and parliamentary grants as contracts between king and people are extremely significant. They indicate, for one thing, that the contract theory of government did not spring full blown from the brain of Lilburne, Hobbes, or Locke. Such a theory of government had a goodly medieval, and perhaps classical heritage, as historians of political thought have long pointed out. Those historians, however, do not seem to have given sufficient attention to institutions of government in which the idea of contract became a functioning reality. In England in the Middle Ages and later, kings met with the estates of the realm and made contracts with their subjects within the structure of the government. What, for example, was the Reformation in England but a great contract between Tudor rulers and their influential lay subjects? The fact that in the early decades of the seventeenth century men in parliament so naturally referred to agreements between the king and subject as contracts suggests that the idea of contract was deeply embedded in English thought and in the actual functioning of the English parliament, where for many centuries king and subject had met together. Scholars have recognized that medieval ideas of law, limited authority, and rights survived to play a vital part in shaping modern constitutional ideas and institutions. They have also known that in England where these ideas were firmly woven into institutions of government they did not weaken and disappear in the sixteenth, seventeenth, and eighteenth centuries, when absolute monarchs were generally overriding and overthrowing them. The fact that the medieval idea of contract was woven into the business of parliament in England must surely be one reason why that particular concept came down to modern times to play its great part in fashioning our western world.

[21] John Selden, *The Table Talk*, ed. D. Irving, (Edinburgh, 1854), p. 102.

Englishmen in parliament in the early seventeenth century were familiar with bargains and contracts and not afraid of them, but they did not propound or support theories of government based only on contract. They all recognized, even in the midst of their bargaining tactics, that co-operation as well as competition was necessary if parliament was to continue to play its historic role in their balanced government. Despite the stormy sessions of most Stuart parliaments, the co-operative nature of parliament remained an ideal which was never forgotten. Common action and agreement arising from the king's love of his people and from the subjects' for their king was still recognized as the truest and best form of parliamentary action. The royalists knew that James and Charles must not just bargain with their subjects in parliament if they were to secure there the co-operation and consent so necessary for the adequate functioning of the government. Bacon advised James in 1613 to "put off the person of a merchant and contractor, and rest upon the person of a King." [22] In 1620 Bacon and two chief justices agreed that the government should be ready with "some commonwealth bills, that may add respect to the King's government . . . ; not wooing bills to make the King and his graces cheap; but good matter to set the Parliament on works, that an empty stomach do not feed upon humour." [23]

Sir John Davies, attorney general in Ireland, whose views on the royal prerogative were more extreme than those of most royalists, presented a glowing picture of parliament as a place and means for achieving harmony between king and people. According to Davies:

> Such Common Councils or Assemblies of States are usual in all States and Commonwealths . . . under the English Monarchy and the French, which are the two best temper'd Monarchies in the World, they are called Parliaments. These Parliaments though they consist of three different Estates, the King, the Nobility, and the Commons, Yet as in Musick,

[22] Spedding, IV, 371.
[23] *Ibid.*, VII, 116.

distinct and severall Notes do make a perfect Harmony, so these Councils compounded of divers States and Degrees, beeing well ordered and *Tuned,* do make a perfect Concord in a Commonwealth . . . And this Concord and Harmony doth ever produce the Safety and Security of the People.[24] [England and France] which have been ruled by the Parliaments are . . . withall two of the most flourishing Common-Wealths, that are to be seen upon the Face of the Earth.[25]

Parliamentary leaders, like the king's supporters, looked to parliament as a place where co-operation and harmony should prevail. These men were driving hard bargains during the twenties; but they recognized, even as they were perfecting their bargaining tactics, that such methods were sordid and, if followed to too great extremes, the government and the common weal would suffer. Wentworth remarked in 1621 that he hoped bills of grace might go with the subsidy "not by way of merchandise, but as the subsidies came free from us so these bills of grace might freely come from his Majesty." [26] On the twentieth of March, 1624, a discussion took place on the money grant under consideration and the many grievances still rankling in their minds. Some members wanted to tie the two together, "But it was thought by others that our grant would savor too much of a bargain if we should mingle with it any matters of demand." [27] In parliament the realm met, and such meetings should take place with love and harmony prevailing. The complete breakdown of agreement between the commons and the king in June, 1628, when Charles threatened to dissolve parliament before giving a satisfactory answer to the Petition of Right, and without letting them finish important business, caused many of the parliamentary leaders to weep. Quite possibly their tears

[24] Two speeches by Sir John Davies . . . 1613, before the Lords Deputy of Ireland; Sir Thomas Clarke and Lord Alvanley's MSS., Lincoln's Inn, p. 6.
[25] *Ibid.*
[26] *Commons Debates 1621,* II, 163.
[27] Pym, 3/20/24. In February, 1605, Martin said, "Not to buy Laws, nor to indent but freely." C. J., I, 266.

expressed their genuine sorrow that the king's failure to agree to those fundamentals which they regarded as their minimum rights meant the end of co-operative effort. Perhaps unconsciously these hardened politicians realized that a balanced government, in which each part fulfilled its own function and worked harmoniously with the other parts on common problems, had broken down with little hope that such a co-operative enterprise would ever be restored. D'Ewes lamented the fact that in this parliament "some acts or statutes were passed; but nothing effected to the full and perfect uniting of the hearts of Prince and people." [28] To him, apparently, harmony between king and people was more fundamental than a Petition of Right, which set forth the subjects' rights, but did not truly bring king and people together.

This great faith of both the royalists and parliamentarians in parliament as a place of harmony and co-operation, at a time when almost every session of parliament demonstrated that men could not agree, becomes more understandable when the nature of statute is examined. Statute represented an agreement among king, lords, and commons. It was the legal embodiment of their harmony. By that harmony expressed in statute, and only by it, many important matters could be handled. Statute was regarded as benefiting all, the king, the subject, the law, and the whole commonwealth. Although statute might restrain in some measure the king's prerogative in administrative realms, it could also enlarge his power in relation to the property rights of the subject. An interesting case of this sort is reported by Croke. In the case of *Cornwallis* v. *Spurling* the question arose of whether land which once had belonged to the Templars free of tithes remained free when the king took over the priories. All the judges agreed that "by the Common Law a Lay-person was not capable of such a Privilege; and if such Lands had come to the King by the Relinquishment or Dissolution of any Monastery, the

[28] *The Autobiography and Correspondence of Sir Simonds D'Ewes,* ed. J. O. Halliwell, 2 vols., (London, 1845), I, 377.

King should not have had the benefit of that Privilege, untill the Statute of 31H8." [29] Statute benefited the king in other ways. Monarchy, according to James "is the stronger and the surer built" "by the advice and assistance of Parliament," [30] while Bacon said that "when the King sits in Parliament, and his Prelates, Peers, and Commons attend him, he is in the exaltation of his orb." [31]

The matters handled by statute were very important—so important that parliament, where all the realm met and each part of the realm guarded its own rights and respected the rights of the other, was regarded as the proper place for action involving these basic matters. There are many illustrations in the seventeenth-century law cases of this attitude toward statute. Only in parliament could certain types of actions affecting property be made. For example, "a Will cannot alter the Law, or make a new form of an Estate, which is not allowed by the Rules of Law as an Act of Parliament is" [32] allowed to do. An act of parliament was necessary to restore blood which was attainted. [33] The extent to which monopolies might restrain free trade was a controversial question, although in the Clothworkers of Ipswich case [34] the power of parliament to do so was recognized as greater than that of the king. Custom and common law could, according to the statements of lawyers, be changed only in parliament, and "it is holden that the Pope, nor any other person can change the common Law, without a Parliament." [35] ". . . Custome of the Realme cannot be taken away but by act of Parliament." [36] Both the moderate

[29] Croke, II, 58.
[30] Spedding, VII, 177. Bacon made this remark in reference to James's speech in 1624.
[31] *Ibid.* Bacon here quoted the speaker of the commons.
[32] Bridgman, *op. cit.*, p. 135.
[33] See, for example, F. Bacon, *The Use of the Law*, (London, 1639), p. 42.
[34] Godbolt, p. 254.
[35] Godbolt, p. 201.
[36] Brownlow, p. 38.

Archbishop Abbot [37] and the hot-headed Buckingham agreed that parliament was necessary for an act of toleration.[38]

The clearest statement I have discovered concerning the nature of parliament's actions in relation to the rights of king and subject was made by Dudley Digges, a supporter of the king, after the civil war began, when men on both sides analyzed the nature of their polity as they never had before. In parliament, according to Digges, king, lord and commons all have a voice. There "(contrary to the use of inferiour Courts) the parties in Parliament (in those things that concerne the publique) meddle not as meere Judges, but as Parties interessed, with things that concern every of their own Rights, in which case it is neither Law nor Reason that some of the Parties should determine of that that concernes all their mutuall interests, *invita altera parte,* against the will of anyone of the parties. But that all parties concur, or else their mutuall interest to remain in the Same condition it was before." [39] This analysis of the situation would, I believe, have been generally accepted by Englishmen in the years prior to 1640.

It is clear that men regarded parliament as a meeting place of king and subject—a place where each must agree to any change in their respective rights, to any change in the law upholding their rights, and to any new adjustment between their different rights. It is also clear that when king and subject could reach agreement, the statute embodying their mutual consent was regarded as very significant and binding. By statute the king's position was ennobled, either by an enlargement of his prerogative or by an agreement with his people. By statute the subject's rights were fortified, either by some improved remedy for their protection or by some agreement reached with the king on controversial questions. By statute the law of the land was strengthened and the

[37] Rushworth, I, 85.

[38] Nich., 2/24/24.

[39] [Dudley Digges], *A Review of the Observations upon some of his Majesties late Answers and Expresses,* (Oxford, 1643), p. 12.

balanced government more surely poised. By statute the commonwealth benefited, for all parts of the realm had mutually agreed upon the measures necessary for the general welfare. When most Englishmen in the early seventeenth century thought of statute, they viewed it in relation to these fundamentals in their polity. They did not think of it as a master over the king, the subject, the law, or the commonwealth, but as the trusty servant and helper of each—as strengthening the king, protecting the subject, clarifying the law, and working for the general welfare. Their views of statute harmonized with their ideas on other important parts of their polity.

Up to this point in the discussion the question of the legislative supremacy of statute and the legal sovereignty of parliament, where statutes were passed, has not been raised, because most Englishmen in the early seventeenth century viewed parliament and statute in the manner already presented. The majority of them were much less concerned than we are today with statute as legislation or with parliament as sovereign. Nevertheless, it has been maintained that some Englishmen must have come to accept parliament as sovereign by the end of the sixteenth century.

The first and strongest argument in support of this belief rests on the fact that Tudor parliaments functioned as true sovereigns, passing a series of great legislative acts. In the legal field, statute in the sixteenth century dealt with questions of private rights, naturalization, improved means of transferring property, attainder, and treason. In the economic and social fields, statute handled problems connected with expanding trade and industry and with enclosures and the poor. By statute the king, the lay lords, and the commons joined in a common attack upon the church, severing all ties with Rome and bringing the church under the control of the state.[40] The

40 See K. Pickthorn, *Early Tudor Government*, (Cambridge University Press, Cambridge, 1934), p. 276 and p. 375, where material is cited suggesting that in the dissolution of the monasteries the fiction was maintained that the monks "voluntarily gave" the monastic property to the crown. See also A. von Mehren, "The Judicial Conception of

Act of Appeals and of Supremacy were truly acts of a sovereign legislature. So also were the Acts of Uniformity by which a religion common for all was established by statutory action. Never before in England had legislation dealt with such a wide range of subjects or effected such profound changes in the body politic. The sixteenth century on the continent was a time of violent and revolutionary upheaval, involving civil strife and bloodshed. In England it was a century of comparative peace and stability when problems of the new age were not solved by civil wars but by the common action in parliament of all the realm. In England alone of the important European countries, a medieval parliament not only survived into the first century of the modern world but also shared in the building of the first national state. Tudor rulers in parliament, as well as in privy council and star chamber, built England into a commonwealth more compact and integrated than she had been in 1485. By 1603 parliament had for so long acted as sovereign on some matters that it is perfectly natural and logical to assume that Englishmen must have come to accept it as the final all-controlling authority in government. These historical arguments in favor of an acceptance of a belief in parliamentary sovereignty carry considerable weight.

Before they can be accepted, however, other facts in Tudor history must be reviewed. Although important statutes increasing the scope of parliament's authority were passed in the sixteenth century, a great increase in the power of the monarch outside parliament also took place at that time. Old institutions of prerogative government were strengthened and new ones created to extend the king's authority from the north to

Legislation in Tudor England," in *Interpretations of Modern Legal Philosophies*, (Oxford University Press, New York, 1947), pp. 751–66.
Mr. von Mehren points out that "The Statute of Uses, which introduced what were in fact new rules as to the holding of property, was not looked upon by the court [in 1550] as a legislative act but was considered only the occasion for, and a recognition of, a series of private grants" (p. 752).

the south, from east to west, and from the highest duke to the lowliest beggar. The spheres of government recognized as within the absolute jurisdiction of the king, such as foreign affairs, the army, the navy, the coinage, became more extensive and important in the Tudor period. Within these fields the monarch acted as absolute, not sharing his authority with parliament and successfully preventing it from encroaching upon them. The Stuarts did not create but inherited institutions of prerogative government and spheres of action in which their kingly authority was generally accepted as absolute.

While these spheres and agencies of government belonging to the king expanded in the sixteenth century, the sphere of property and rights belonging to the subject, particularly to the great subjects present in parliament, also increased as Tudor lords, gentry, and merchants built up their landed holdings, buying church and crown property whenever it was available in the market, enclosing common and villein land, and putting strip next to strip to make their holdings more compact. Naturally these gentlemen with increased amounts of property clung tenaciously to all legal and constitutional concepts hallowed by theory and practice which recognized that their property was their own and that the rights by which it was held were fundamental.

The constitutional ideas of Englishmen must be interpreted in relation to these facts. Parliamentary authority had expanded to a great extent in the sixteenth century, but it had not by the end of the century absorbed or taken over ultimate control of either the spheres of government belonging absolutely to the king or the property rights belonging absolutely to the subject, since both the government of the king and the property of the subject had also increased at the same time. The joint action of the king and subject which had taken place in parliament in the sixteenth century had been possible because of Tudor skill and appreciation of fundamental beliefs and policies, and also because the members of parliament were still content to let the king handle many governmental matters alone, provided he furnished them the opportunity to acquire landed property. When all these facts are taken into account, the argument, that because Tudor parliaments often passed sovereign laws men must therefore have accepted parliament as the sovereign authority in the government, becomes less convincing.

A second argument often put forward as support for a belief in the sovereignty of parliament is based upon two statements made in the sixteenth century. The first is the famous remark, attributed to Henry VIII, that "the judges have informed us, that we at no time stand so high in our estate royal as in the time of parl.; when we as head, and you as members, are conjoined and knit together into one body politic;" [41] Henry VIII, whom Pollard calls the "greatest Parliamentarian" who ever sat on the English throne, might well have made this statement and meant it. He meant, in my opinion, that the king's estate or government could act in the highest and most sweeping manner in parliament where the king was knit most closely to the rest of the realm; but he certainly did not mean that the king could not function through other important channels over which parliament as yet had no authority. If Henry really believed in parliamentary sovereignty, he would have had to believe that all his authority as king was ultimately subject to the supremacy of the king-in-parliament, and such control could hardly be accepted by this Tudor ruler.

The second familiar statement occurs in *De Republica Anglorum,* by Sir Thomas Smith:

> The most high and absolute power of the realme of Englande, consisteth in the Parliament. For as in warre where the king himselfe in person, the nobilitie, the rest of the gentilitie, and the yoemanrie are, is the force and power of Englande: so in peace and consultation where the Prince is to give life, and the last and highest commaundement, the Baronie for the nobilitie and higher, the knightes, esquires, gentlemen and commons for the lower part of the commonwealth, the bishoppes for the clergie bee present to advertise,

[41] Ferrer's case, W. Cobbett (ed.) *Parliamentary History,* I, 555.

consult and shew what is good and necessarie for the common wealth, and to consult together, and upon mature deliberation everie bill or lawe being thrise reade and disputed uppon in either house the other two partes first each a part, and after the Prince himselfe in presence of both the parties doeth consent unto and alloweth. That is the Princes and whole realmes deede: whereupon justlie no man can complaine, but must accommodate himselfe to finde it good and obey it.[42]

Mr. Alston, the editor of *De Republica Anglorum,* has pointed out in his introduction the reasons why he does not believe Smith attributes complete sovereignty to parliament.[43] His interpretation can be supplemented in several ways. In the first place, whereas Smith attributes absolute power to parliament in Chapter One of the second book, in Chapter Three he attributes absolute power to the king alone. Moreover, Smith calls parliament sovereign only in peace, not in war. He also speaks of changing and of defining rights, not of abrogating them. It is remarkable that Smith chooses most of his illustrations of the great authority of parliament, not from the major legislative acts of the Tudor period, but from examples of the long-established authority of parliament in regard to private rights. It is also significant that Smith speaks of parliament as the most absolute power *of* the realm not

[42] Ed. L. Alston, (Cambridge University Press, Cambridge, 1906), p. 48.

[43] See also, G. L. Mosse, "Change and Continuity in the Tudor Constitution," *Speculum* XXII, 1947, pp. 18–28. Mosse maintains that Smith, in contrast to Fortescue, asserted that parliament "has the power to dispose of the rights and possessions of private men," and that such a belief "is a momentous step towards the doctrine of Parliamentary sovereignty" (p. 24). I agree with Mosse that Smith conceived of parliament's authority as more nearly sovereign than Fortescue ever did, but doubt whether Smith's statement on parliament's power over property is quite as sweeping as Mosse suggests. Smith wrote (*De Republica Anglorum*, p. 49) that parliament "abrogeteth olde lawes"; but when in the same paragraph he discussed parliament's power concerning rights, he wrote that parliament "changeth rightes, and possessions of private men, . . . defineth of doubtfull rightes. . . ." He did not use the words abrogate, abolish, or dispose. A. von Mehren does not believe that the judges in the courts in Tudor England looked upon parliament as sovereign. *The Judicial Conception of Legislation in Tudor England,* pp. 760–63.

in the realm. The realm included all those who met and treated together in parliament. For action of that joint entity, the realm, parliament was the most high and absolute power. Such absolutism, however, would not necessarily mean that the king, in the sphere of government belonging to him, was not also absolute, or that many fundamental rights of the subject were not still accepted as outside the range of parliament's authority.

There appears to be no conclusive evidence that Tudor thinkers conceived of parliament as the final all-controlling authority in the English government. On the other hand, it is quite probable that, had parliaments continued to pass great constructive statutes between 1603 and 1642, the belief in parliamentary sovereignty would have rapidly become a commonplace. The parliaments of James I and Charles I, however, had other matters than legislation to deal with. Because of the widening breach between the king and some of his subjects in parliament, the amount of legislation on matters common to both ruler and subjects decreased sharply. As the king and royalists went their prerogative way, strengthening the government outside parliament, leaders in the commons concentrated more and more of their efforts not on legislation, but on guarding their rights and trying to check and control the king. The fact that the great development of legislation in the Tudor period slowed down under the first Stuarts helps to explain why the concept of parliamentary sovereignty, which had certainly been developing in the sixteenth century, does not seem to play too significant a part in the thinking of men on both sides of the controversy in the first forty years of the seventeenth century.

It is of course true that during these years men agreed in attributing great competence to statute. Bacon claimed that "it is in the power of a parliament to extinguish or transferre their own authority, but not whilst the authority remains entire to restraine the functions and exercises of the same authority." [44]

[44] F. Bacon, *A Collection of some Principal Rules and Maximes*, p. 69.

At least three of the royalist judges who decided in favor of the king against Hampden in ship money admitted in a subsequent case that parliament could reverse its decision. After the judgment in ship money had been rendered, Lord Say brought a case to recover his oxen which had been assessed by the sheriff of Lincoln to collect £3 5s. worth of ship money. Holbourne wanted to argue the case again, but Bramston, Jones, and Berkeley said "That a Judgment ought to stand, until it were reversed in Parliament." [45]

Leaders of the parliamentary opposition were in agreement that parliament's authority was very extensive, but for a number of years few of them tried to base the case for parliament on its legislative supremacy. James Whitelocke is the outstanding exception. In 1610 he presented the clearest and most unequivocal statement of parliament's supremacy made prior to 1641:

> . . . it will be admitted for a rule, and ground of state, that in every commonwealth and government there be some rights of sovereignty, *jura majestatis,* which regularly and of common right doe belong to the sovereign power of that state; unless custome, or the provisional ordinance of that state, doe otherwise dispose of them: which soveraigne power is *potestas suprema,* a power that can controule all other powers, and cannot be controuled but by itself. It will not be denied, that the power of imposing hath so great a trust in it, by reason of the mischiefes may grow to the common-wealth by the abuses of it, that it hath ever been ranked among those rights of soveraign power. Then is there no further question to be made, but to examine where the soveraigne power is in this kingdome; for there is the right of imposition. The soveraigne power is agreed to be in the king: but in the king is a two-fold power, the one in parliament, as he is assisted with the consent of the whole state; the other out of parliament, as he is sole, and singular, guided merely by his own will. And if of these two powers in the king one is greater than the other, and can direct and controule the other; that is *suprema potestas,* the soveraigne power, and the other is *subordinata.* It will

[45] Croke, III, 524.

then be easily proved, that the power of the king in parliament is greater than his power out of parliament; and doth rule and controule it; for if the king make a grant by his letters patent out of parliament, it bindeth him and his successors: he cannot revoke it, nor any of his successors; but by his power in parliament he may defeat and avoyd it; and therefore that is the greater power.[46]

In these words Whitelocke stated the issue clearly. Because of his insight, the parliamentary opposition possessed as early as 1610 a powerful legal argument which could be squarely met only if the royalists would assert and could prove that the king was greater out of parliament than in it. Fortunately for their cause the royalists did not have to rest their case on such a contention, which, since it would have been hard or impossible to prove legally, could never have secured for them a large number of adherents. They were able for the most part to bypass the issue put forward so clearly by Whitelocke, because the parliamentary opposition either failed to grasp the significance of his remarks or was too conservative to agree that parliament could control the king in all realms. This failure of the parliamentary opposition generally to argue as Whitelocke did, is an important reason supporting the conviction I have come to hold that men in the early decades of the seventeenth century did not yet view parliament as sovereign.

Additional evidence for that thesis can be found by examining the ideas men expressed in parliament in the process of preparing parliamentary legislation. Parliament, which more than any other part of the government could rightly claim to be the final authority, proceeded with great caution when it was considering possible statutes. Debates on bills frequently sound like arguments in a law court, with law and precedent, rather than policy and expediency, determining the decisions of the lawmakers. Proposed bills encroaching too much upon the rights of king or subject seem often to have been thrown out before they reached final form. Tenacious and stubborn

---

[46] S. T., II, 482–83. The speech is by J. Whitelocke, and not by Yelverton, who is credited with it in *State Trials*.

as the parliamentary opposition was in upholding the subjects' rights and in checkmating the king's, and aggressive as it was in nibbling away at the king's prerogative, one of the most striking facts about its stand in these years was that it seldom denied or directly attacked the king's prerogative in most realms. In 1624, for example, in a discussion of a bill touching carts and carriages used in purveyance, it was Sir Edward Coke who said, "It appears by Magna Carta that the king hath right." [47] In the bitter controversy over patents and monopolies, one important argument was not that the king should have no control over them, but that he had granted to the subject certain rights inseparable from himself. In the midst of a discussion in 1624 on the question of certain customs levied in James's reign, Sir Robert Phelips asked that "the King['s] Council may have a time allowed them to prove the legality of them." [48] Another equally aggressive spirit, John Pym, argued against a proposed bill in the parliament of 1621 because the action under consideration could legally be done by the king without parliament, and "it is not good to have that done by an extraordinary Means which may be done by an ordinary Course from his Majesty." [49] Noy concurred with this opinion since "that which is to be granted is in the King's Power to grant, without an Act of Parliament." [50] When the Long Parliament met, the leaders pushed ahead relentlessly their program against the king's ministers and his prerogative government. The Triennial Bill was not passed, however, without opposition, on the ground that the bill deprived the king of his prerogative of summoning parliament.[51] Digby, who supported the bill, spun out fine arguments to show that its passage would not detract from the king's prerogative.[52] In December, 1641, a bill to take away some of the king's power

[47] Erle, 3/13/24.
[48] Gurney, 4/13/24.
[49] Nich., *P. and D.*, I, 344.
[50] *Ibid.*
[51] *D'Ewes, (Long Parliament)*, ed. W. Notestein, pp. 263–64.
[52] Nalson, I, 732.

over the militia was under discussion, and arguments were advanced against it that the bill encroached too much upon the prerogative.[53] When the vote was taken, D'Ewes records that "ther weere manye IIs but moore Noes." [54] Not until the spring of 1642 did the two houses boldly claim control over many prerogatives of the king.

Parliament also showed some respect for the rights of the church in this period, even though its claims to control religion were mounting. For example, a bill was proposed in 1621 for freeing the fishers of Newfoundland from tithes on fish, on the ground that the tithes were too high for poor fishermen to pay. Against the proposed bill, however, it was argued that the tithes this bill suggested abolishing were not theirs to dispose of, and that "this Act would violate the Right of the Church; That they should be as carefull to preserve the Rights thereof as of any private Person." [55] The same respect for the rights of the church as beyond the authority of parliament can be seen in the discussion in 1628 over "An Act to prevent and restraine disorders that or may bee in the ministers of gods word." Marten argued against the bill, reminding the commons that the clergy had helped to secure Magna Carta, and "shall wee at one blow take away Magna Charta from the Cleargie." [56] Sir John Eliot was not one to admit many limitations to parliament's competence; but in 1629, when he was pressing charges against the Arminian bishops and clergy, he admitted that "it is not in the Parliament to make a new Religion." [57] ". . . The Truth that we profess is not mans but Gods, and God forbid that man should be made a judge of that Truth." [58]

By 1641 the hue and cry against bishops had become very loud and insistent, and the parliamentary opposition had

[53] *D'Ewes, (Long Parliament)*, ed. W. Coates, p. 245.

[54] *Ibid.*, p. 248.

[55] *Commons Debates 1621*, V, 490.

[56] Mass., 5/16/28. Selden and Wentworth also argued against the bill. Gros., 5/16/28.

[57] *Commons Debates for 1629*, p. 25.

[58] *Ibid.*, pp. 26–7. This remark is made with the implication that the bishops and other clergy should not change the established religion.

demonstrated its strength by successfully passing a series of great statutes curbing the king's ministers and institutions of prerogative government. Nevertheless, it was difficult to secure the necessary votes to eject bishops from parliament. Any notion that the majority in both houses had power to legislate out of parliament any one part of the realm was hotly debated. Charles expressed a sentiment shared by many when he declared that he could not assent to depriving bishops of votes in parliament because "their right is grounded upon the fundamental Law of the Kingdom, and constitution of Parliament." [59] The opponents of bishops had to use interesting arguments to advance their case. Pierrepont reported from a committee "That bishops ought not to have Votes in Parliament . . . Because they are but for their Lives; and therefore are not fit to have Legislative Power over the Honours, Inheritances, Persons, and Liberties of others." [60] Probably he meant that legislative power, which inevitably affects property and liberty, should not be exercised by those who do not personally possess property. Pym argued against bishops having votes in parliament "Because they have no such inherent Vote, Right, nor Liberty of being there, as the Lords Temporal, and Peers of the Realm have; for they are not Representative of any body else, not of the Clergy; for then they were twice represented, by Them in the Lords House, and by Those in the Convocation-house." [61] A similar point of view was expressed by a pamphleteer at a later date when he said, "The Bishops right in Parliament is of another nature then that of the Noble Peers, for that of the Peers is inherent and hereditary; but the Bishops theirs is onely *durante bene placito,* during the Kings pleasure, or so long as they shall please him." [62] Arguments placing bishops in a different category from other members of parliament and denying that they had an

[59] *His Majesties Answer to the Petition which accompanied the Declaration of the House of Commons,* [Dec. 1], 1641, p. 5.
[60] C. J., II, 167.
[61] *Ibid.,* p. 296.
[62] T. Robinson, *The Petitioners Vindication* . . . , [May] 1642, p. 9.

inherent right to sit there were presumably put forward because of the strength of the belief that the bishops' place in parliament rested upon law and right beyond the competence of parliament to annihilate by any statute not agreed to by the bishops.

If Stuart parliaments showed considerable respect for the rights of king and church, they also demonstrated great concern for the property rights of the subject and the legal forms and procedures protecting such rights. Arguments were often put forward that a proposed bill should be rejected because it abolished or too greatly affected the right of the subject. Phelips argued against a private bill proposing a change in a certain legal procedure, for "what a floud gate would this sett open in mens estates if we showed graunte this bill passage that such things be reversed by Act of Parliament." [63] Another private bill involving a change in legal procedure where freehold land was involved brought forth bitter protests. In this bill, Jones said, "You vyolate posterity, nay you go against the resolution of the howse in the cause of propriety of goods so mutch stood uppon." [64] Littleton pointed out that "that Bill is agaynst a fundamentall ground of Justice, which is to give everyone his owne." [65]

Parliament also showed concern for legal forms and procedures dear to the common lawyers. An exception was taken to one bill to improve legal procedure, because the proposed change would mean that "In some cases the same will be both judge and party." [66] An act "to avoid all trial by battle" evoked the following comment from Selden, "An ancient fundamental law and not to be taken away with a breath without commitment." [67] An act concerning petty larcenies was objected to on the ground that "it alters the fundamentall lawe," [68] and

[63] *Commons Debates 1621*, III, 241–42.
[64] Bor., 6/2/28.
[65] Gros. 6/10/28.
[66] Pym, 4/21/24.
[67] Pym, 3/22/24.
[68] *Commons Debates in 1625*, p. 90.

a third act proposing legal reform was "rejected at the third reading because it taketh away a fundamental law of the realm, which is that actions transitory may be laid where the plaintiff pleaseth the same." [69]

Perhaps most surprising of all is the respect which for about a year the Long Parliament showed for law and right. In view of the fact that this parliament had inherited a working technique enabling it to be a real legislature, that its members were determined that it should accomplish positive and lasting results, and that its leaders were politicians who had carefully planned their actions, it is the restraint, not the extent of its claims and arguments, which strikes the modern reader of the debates in 1640 and 1641. The one hundred and six years which had elapsed since a sovereign parliament had legislated away the age-old ties with Rome, and had decreed that the church in England should have a temporal and not a spiritual head, were not a long-enough span of time for a parliamentary majority to come to think and to debate in terms of parliamentary sovereignty. When members of parliament considered proposed legislation in the years between 1603 and 1642, they still viewed it in relation to the whole balanced polity. Before statutes were passed, these legislators, not wishing to override by statute the basic rights of king or subject, passed upon the constitutionality of the statutes.

Once, however, statutes had been enacted by king, lords, and commons, were they not viewed as final, all-embracing, and all-controlling decrees of a sovereign legislature? The answer to that question involves an examination of the way lawyers and judges in their court decisions and legal writings viewed statute in the first decades of the seventeenth century.[70] The

[69] Nich., 5/3/24.

[70] The most illuminating treatment of the subject for the sixteenth century is, in my judgment, the article by A. von Mehren, "The Judicial Conception of Legislation in Tudor England." According to Professor von Mehren, in the Tudor period "a precarious balance was attained and even preserved among three elements: a conception of fundamental law; reason and unity; and an increasing Parliamentary activity in the

whole question of the interpretation of statutes is a difficult and extremely controversial subject upon which historians and lawyers hold widely divergent views. Professor Thorne has pointed out in his introduction to *A Discourse upon the Exposicion and Understandinge of Statutes*[71] that, as legislation increased in the sixteenth century, lawyers and judges worked out more general rules for the interpretation of statutes than had existed in the medieval period, when few such rules prevailed. In the sixteenth century they began to "treat statute on a public—rather than a private—law level," [72] and they enlarged their concept of equity in interpreting particular statutes. Such developments were moving towards an interpretation of statute as sovereign; but, as Professor Thorne has also shown, lawyers and judges in the sixteenth and early seventeenth centuries still viewed statute in relation to certain fundamental concepts of law, justice, and right. They did not yet consider the statute as a decree in the interpretation of which they as judges had no latitude or discretion.[73] They were concerned that statutes truly establish law and justice, and their idea of justice included respect for and preservation of the king's prerogative and the subjects' rights. Statute by itself was not viewed by them as all-sufficient, but as a law establishing justice which must be interpreted in relation to basic common law principles.

Although the research on which this volume is based was not primarily concerned with the interpretation of statutes in the first half of the seventeenth century, the pertinent material which was examined appears, in general, to substantiate Thorne's conclusions. It seems quite clear that the principles and rules regarding the interpretation of statutes cannot be truly understood unless they are studied in relation to the

making of law itself. These three elements, at least in their extreme ramifications, were perhaps logically irreconcilable. Judicial theory during the Tudor period, made its bow to all these elements" (p. 752).

[71] Huntington Library, San Marino, Calif., 1942.

[72] *Ibid.*, p. 54.

[73] *Ibid.*, pp. 55–68.

94   *The Crisis of the Constitution*

general ideas of government and law prevailing at that time. It also seems apparent that those principles, rules, and practices fit in consistently with the contemporary concepts of government and law presented in the earlier chapters of this book.

All the law cases which have been examined indicate that, in the first part of the seventeenth century, lawyers and judges did not accept statute as final and binding just because it was statute. It was never passed over lightly, its sanction was accepted as great, and its authority often recognized as binding; yet statutes were frequently, not just occasionally, examined in reference to their nature and in relation to other fundamentals in the constitution—in relation, for example, to the absolute power of the king, the property rights of the subject, and the most fundamental principles of the common law. The rules followed when the question of the relation of a statute to these fundamentals was involved were not mere technicalities, but represented realities which were necessary to achieve an equitable and harmonious adjustment between statute and other fundamentals of the constitution.

Lawyers often said that statutes must be examined very carefully—that "the meaning of an Act of Parliament ought to be expounded by an examination of the intention of the makers thereof, collected out of all the causes thes therein, so that there be no repugnancy, but a concordancy in all parts thereof." [74] ". . . where the Reason of the Law differs from the Letter of the Law, the Judges follow and ought to follow the Intention of the Legislature." [75] It was Ellesmere, not Coke, who said "And the Judges themselves do play the Chancellors Part upon Statutes, making Construction of them according to Equity, varying from the Rules and Grounds of Law, and enlarging them *pro bono publico* against the Letter and Intent of the Makers, whereof our Books have many Hundred of Cases . . ." [76] Lawyers believed that the makers of a

[74] Richard Lane, *Reports in the Court of Exchequer*, (London, 1657), p. 118.
[75] Jenkins, p. 70.
[76] *Reports in Chancery, op. cit.*, p. 7.

statute would never presume to encroach upon the king's prerogative or the subjects' rights without express words to that effect.

It was still recognized in the seventeenth century that the king might dispense with statutes affecting his action in the sphere of governmental administration. In other words, statute did not bind the king if he did not wish to be bound within those realms still accepted as belonging to his absolute power. On the other hand, it was equally well recognized that the king might not dispense with a statute in which the right of the subject was involved.[77]

Statutes were interpreted very strictly when the property right of the subject might be affected. Two interesting cases illustrate this type of interpretation. The first case, reported by Coke, concerned a statute made in 34.H.8. in which the king had been given some authority to make laws for Wales. The judges in Hil.5.Jacobi. decided that the statute was intended to apply only to Henry VIII and not to his successors. His successors were not specifically mentioned in the statute, and it was never the intention of the act to give kings in the future the power to alter laws in Wales "so that none of that country could be certain of his life, land, goods, or liberty, or any thing which he hath."[78] Another interesting case was reported by Owen.[79] Two men had been committed for recusancy and their lands seized in order that the recusancy fine might be secured. Since some of their lands were held by copyhold tenure, the question arose of whether "Copy hold lands were within the said Statute of the 29 Eliz." dealing with recusants. Considerable division of opinion prevailed, Popham holding that "If Copyhold lands are not within the Statute, some persons shall be free; . . . But after great debate it was adjudged, that Copyhold lands are not within the Statute by reason of the prejudice that may come thereby to the Lord, who hath

[77] P. Birdsall, "Non Obstante," p. 57.
[78] Coke, *Reports*, vol. VII, pt. XII, p. 49.
[79] Thomas Owen, *Reports*, (London, 1656), p. 37. See also Brownlow, p. 45.

not committed any Offence, and therefore shall not loose his Customes and Services." [80]

When the king's prerogative or the subject's property was involved, statutes were interpreted very strictly, the decision frequently being given against the words and apparent intent of the statute in favor of prerogative or property. The same strict interpretation prevailed when statutes and common law clashed. Hobart said that "Statutes that are made in imitation or supply of Common law, shall be expounded according to the law"; [81] while Jenkins, discussing a case involving a statute, interpreted it strictly *"quae legi communi derogant stricte interpretantur."* [82] Coke expressed more far-reaching views on this subject, saying in the 1621 parliament "That there is no Act of Parliament that takes away a main point of the Common Law, but an infinite number of Inconveniencies follow." [83] For statute to be tender of the king's government, the subjects' property, or the principles of the common law was accepted practice.

Occasionally in the first part of the seventeenth century, judges interpreted statutes very strictly, even asserting that a statute was or might be void if it conflicted too directly with the law of God or of nature, with equity, the king's government, the subjects' property, or the principles of the common law. Finch wrote in 1627: "Therefore Lawes positive, which are directly contrary to the former [the law of reason] lose their force, and are no Laws at all. As those which are contrary to the law of Nature. Such is that of the Egyptians, to turne women to merchandize and commonwealth affaires and men to keepe within dores." [84]

Acts of parliament were declared void if they encroached too much on the inseparable prerogatives of the king. In the ship-

[80] *Ibid.*
[81] Hobart, pp. 97–98.
[82] Jenkins, p. 29.
[83] Nich., *P. and D.*, I, 193.
[84] Finch, *Law*, 1636, B. I., ch. 6, as quoted in R. Pound, "Common Law and Legislation," *Harvard Law Review*, XXI (1908), pp. 391–92.

money case, two of the judges rendering verdict against the king and in favor of Hampden were Hutton and Davenport. These judges, who can hardly be called subservient royalists, asserted that an act of parliament against the king's prerogative might be void. Hutton held that there were some prerogatives so inseparable from the king that even parliament could not sever them from him.[85] Davenport insisted that in case of real necessity the king had the right to compel aid in order to prevent real danger; "And if an act of parliament should be made to restrain such a charge on the subjects in case of necessity it would be *Felo de se,* and so void; for it would destroy that *regale ius.*" [86] These statements of Hutton and Davenport actually declare that an act of parliament might be void.

As judges opposing the extreme royalist claims made statements that acts of parliament encroaching too much on the king's prerogative might be void, so, on the other hand, Ellesmere, a faithful servant of James, rendered a decision based on the principle that acts of parliament, encroaching too much on the property of the subject, might be declared void. In the famous case of Magdalen College the court had decided for the defendant, the decision being based on a statute which the court claimed bound the queen. The whole case came up again in chancery as the Earl of Oxford's case,[87] the plaintiff claiming that he had already built many houses on the property taken from him by the decision in the Magdalen College case. Ellesmere supported the property rights of the plaintiff, and in the report of the case, it seems to be Ellesmere who made the following remarks:

1. The Law of God speaks for the Plaintiff. Deut. 28. 2. And Equity and good Conscience speak wholly for him. 3. Nor does the Law of the Land speak against him. But that and Equity ought to join Hand in Hand, in moderating and restraining all Extremities and Hardships. By the Law of

[85] S. T., III, 1194.
[86] *Ibid.,* p. 1216.
[87] *Reports in Chancery, op. cit.*

God, He that builds a House ought to dwell in it; and he that plants a Vineyard ought to gather the Grapes thereof; and it was a Curse upon the Wicked, that *they should build Houses and not dwell in them, and plant Vineyards and not gather the Grapes Thereof. Deut. 28. V. 30.*[88]

According to the previous decision, the doctor would possess a house he had not built. Such a situation would be wrong, Ellesmere argued. ". . . Chancellors have always corrected such and corrupt consciences and caused them to render *quid pro quo;* for the Common Law itself will admit no Contract to be good without *quid pro quo,* and therefore Equity must see that a proportionable Satisfaction be made in this Case . . . And Equity speaks as the Law of God speaks." [89]

The decision in the Magdalen College case had been based upon a statute, but Ellesmere did not believe that statute always prevailed, for

It has ever been the Endeavour of all Parliaments to meet with the corrupt Consciences of Men as much as might be, and to supply the Defects of the Law therein, and if this Cause were exhibited to the Parliament it would soon be ordered and determined by Equity; and the Lord Chancellor is, by his Place under his Majesty, to supply that Power until it may be had, in all matters of *Meum* and *Tuum,* between Party and Party; and the Lord Chancellor doth not except to the Statute of the Law, (Judgment) upon the Statute, but taketh himself bound to obey that Statute according to 8 Ed. 4. and the Judgment thereupon may be just, and the College in this Case may have a good title in Law, and the Judgment yet standeth in Force. It seemeth by the Lord Coke's *Report,* fol. *118* in Doctor Bonham's case, that Statutes are not so sacred as that the Equity of them may not be examined. For he saith, That in many Cases the Common Law hath such a Prerogative, as that it can controul Acts of Parliament, and adjudge them void; as if they are against Common Right, or Reason, or Repugnant, or impossible to be performed. . . .[90]

[88] *Ibid.,* p. 3.
[89] *Ibid.*
[90] *Ibid.,* p. 6.

It is important to note that Ellesmere insisted upon two points: one, that a statute might be declared void if a decision based upon it overrode property belonging to a man by the law of God; and two, that it was the chancellor's responsibility to see that justice conformable to God's law be done, even if statute should be overridden.

The right of property was undoubtedly the most important right belonging to the subject, but other rights were recognized as his also. Among these other rights discussed in Chapter One was the fundamental right of a man to live by the labor of his hands or mind. God gave man the right to work as he gave a king the authority to rule, and both rights were fundamental. In the famous case of *Darcy* v. *Allen* the right of a man to live by his labor was pronounced so fundamental that it stood against the monopoly granted by the patent of the queen, and even against statute. In the words of Fuller, "But arts, and skills of manual occupations rise not from the King, but from the labour and industry of men, and by the gifts of God to them." [91] "Now therefore," Fuller also said, "it is unlawful to prohibit a man not to live by the Labour of his own trade, wherein he was brought up as an Apprentice, and was lawfully used, as to prohibit him not to live by Labour, which if it were by act of Parliament it were a void act: for an act of Parliament against the Law of God, directly is void, as is expressed in the book of Doctor and Student, much more Letters Patents against the Law of God are void." [92]

As protection for some of the most fundamental rights of the subject, certain basic principles had long been recognized in common law. One of the most important of these maxims was that a man could not be judge in his own case. In the first part of the seventeenth century two famous cases occurred where this maxim protecting the right of the subject was invoked against statute. In the case of *Day* v. *Savage* the following statement was made, perhaps by Hobart: "Even an Act of

[91] Noy, p. 181.
[92] *Ibid.*, p. 180.

Parliament, made against natural equity, as to make a man judge in his own case, is void in itself, for *Jura naturae sunt immutabilia,* and they are *leges legum."* [93] This principle was only stated in the case of *Day* v. *Savage.* In the more famous case of Dr. Bonham it was basic in the decision, prevailing even against statute. Because so much disagreement and controversy have arisen over this case, it will be discussed here more fully than the other cases cited. Dr. Bonham, a physician who had practiced medicine in London, brought action of false imprisonment against the Royal College of Physicians. The college alleged that their action against Bonham was correct since such power had been granted them by a patent of 10 Hen. 8, twice confirmed by statute. The judges decided for Bonham, thus overriding the two statutes confirming the patent on which the college had justified its right of imprisoning him. Coke's argument supporting Bonham contains the following statement basic in the decision:

> The censors can not be judges, ministers, and parties; judges to give sentence or judgment; ministers to make summons; and parties to have the moiety of the forfeiture, *quia aliquis non debet esse Judex in propria causa, . . .* And it appears in our books that in many cases the common law will controul acts of Parliament, and sometimes adjudge them to be utterly void: for when an act of Parliament is against common right and reason, or repugnant, or impossible to be performed, the common law will controule it, and adjudge such an act to be void. [94]

This statement should be interpreted as simply as possible. Coke said that it is a fundamental principle of the common law that a man cannot be judge in his own case. He did not explain the reason for that principle because he assumed that to the seventeenth-century mind the reason was obvious. He might have added, however, for our edification, that such a principle was necessary in order that every man might have a just remedy for any action against him, and that the remedy could hardly

[93] Hobart, p. 87.
[94] Coke, *Reports,* vol. IV, pt. VIII, p. 234.

be just, giving both plaintiff and defendant his due, if the party were a judge as well as a participant in the case. Without just remedy, there was no security for the property and liberty of a man. Basic rights were at stake in this particular case—the property and liberty of a man, recognized as fundamental, and an important principle by which they might be assured— namely, that no man can be a judge in his own case. Since the makers of a statute would never intend to deny such fundamental rights, particularly unless there were express words to that effect, statute must be interpreted in conformity with, and not counter to, such fundamental principles. In this case, as in many similar ones, acts of parliament must be interpreted according to basic principles of the common law. In this case, therefore, those basic principles prevail, and a statute pleaded against them is void because the makers would never have wanted it interpreted in any subsequent case to deny such basic principles.[95]

If this interpretation of Coke's reasoning is correct, his argument is not startling or incongruous to readers conversant with seventeenth-century legal and constitutional thinking. From the legal point of view it is similar to a number of other statements made in the courts in the seventeenth century. In all of those cases where statute was declared void, something recognized as fundamental was at stake—either the government belonging to the king, the property or means of livelihood belonging to the subject, or the remedies provided by the common law for the protection of such fundamentals. In interpreting statutes in the early seventeenth century, judges and lawyers were extremely respectful of the king's government and the subjects' property. Some judges went so far as to declare a particular statute void because it denied fundamentals pre-

[95] For recent discussions of this case, see T. F. T. Plucknett, "Bonham's Case and Judicial Review," *Harvard Law Review*, XL (1926), 30–70; and S. E. Thorne, "Dr. Bonham's Case," *Law Quarterly Review*, LIV (1938), 543–52. Thorne also discusses this case in *A Discourse upon the Exposicion and Understandinge of Statutes*, pp. 85–90. I find myself most in agreement with Thorne.

sumably accepted by all. The opinion expressed by Coke in Bonham's case was similar to other views expressed in this age and should not be isolated and studied apart from the constitutional ideas men held in the early seventeenth century.

From the constitutional point of view, the ideas of Coke in this case coincide with the generally prevailing ideas of the constitution already presented in the first part of this book. Men believed that the constitution should be balanced between the government of the king and the rights of the subject, and that the balance was achieved through the law. Statute was important and very necessary; but since statute was the joint work of king, lords, and commons, each of whom desired and intended to perpetuate their respective rights (certainly not to change them without definitely expressed words to that effect), statute must be properly interpreted. It must be viewed in such a fashion that the rights of all, and the fundamental principles of common law by which those rights were preserved, must not be overridden or denied. In some cases, therefore, in order to preserve the fundamentals, a particular statute might be declared void. Coke explicitly said that in some (not all) cases, common law will control. In his reasoning in Bonham's case, Coke, like Ellesmere in the Earl of Oxford's case, followed the generally accepted rules of statutory interpretation. When those rules are viewed from the legal point of view, as Professor Thorne has done, "There is no conscious constitutional problem raised here, but only one of statutory construction." [96]

And yet those rules are of great constitutional significance, for they represented ways and means by which the common lawyers made an adjustment between the parts of the constitution. Technical and obscure at points as those rules were, they aimed, when put into practice, to take everything into account —the king's rights and the subjects', the basic principles of common law, as well as statute. In an age when formal constitutions were not put together in one document, and when

[96] *Law Quarterly Review*, LIV, p. 549.

the rights of kings and of subjects were not listed in formal fashion, such forms and seeming technicalities afforded some guarantee that acts of government and decisions in courts would be constitutional, that is, in accord with principles, beliefs, and ways of acting generally accepted by all. When Coke in his dictum in Bonham's case followed the "ordinary common law rules of statutory interpretation," [97] he was using one of the important means evolved by this time in the history of the English constitution to guarantee a balanced government respecting the king's rights, protecting the subjects' rights, and interpreting statute in reference to the whole constitution and commonwealth, not just in reference to the parliament enacting it.

One more pertinent question in relation to the problem of whether lawyers and judges accepted statute as the act of a sovereign legislature must be raised. How did these men interpret those statutes supposedly aiming at the general welfare and yet inevitably operating in some cases to hurt the subjects' rights, the king's prerogative, or the common law? Was there a generally accepted doctrine and practice among lawyers by the seventeenth century that the general welfare came first, even when its primacy meant the denial of the rights of king or subject? Although I have not attempted to make any thorough investigation of this problem, I have not discovered in the law cases examined that any such doctrine had been clearly developed and generally accepted by the early seventeenth century. Lawyers and judges faced a very delicate and difficult question when they were forced to weigh the respective merits of the general welfare, the king's prerogative, and the subjects' rights.

The problem may perhaps be stated in this form: Since king, lords, and commons in making a statute were supposedly always aware of their respective rights, no one of the three would agree to change or redefine them unless it were advantageous.

[97] *Ibid.*

The general interest of the commonwealth, however, required that laws for its benefit, perhaps affecting the rights of the different parts of the body politic, should be passed. Those statutes, if they did not conflict too patently with the king's prerogative or the subjects' rights, were interpreted liberally, with the result that in such cases the general welfare prevailed. If, however, a conflict was involved between the general welfare and the king's prerogative or subjects' rights, the interpretation became very difficult, and the judges often disagreed. What seemed to happen in such a situation is this: A lawyer or judge might argue that a statute operated on behalf of the general welfare. The pleader in his arguments, however, talked about general welfare, but failed to come to grips with the real issue, namely, what decision should be reached if the general welfare and the king's rights, or the general welfare and the subjects' rights, were diametrically opposed. He evaded the problem, hoping perhaps, we may surmise, by talk of general welfare to convince the court of its importance. His opponent did exactly the reverse. He talked of the king's prerogative, the subjects' right, or the importance of a principle of common law, pleading for it as basic and as determining in the particular case under discussion. He seldom suggested that the particular right should be considered, not in a vacuum, but in relation to the general welfare; or, if he did, he assumed or stated that the general welfare could only be truly the general welfare if property was given due respect and its full rights, or if the king's prerogative, necessary for the general welfare, was preserved. Neither the supporter of rights nor his opponent, the advocate of general welfare, met squarely the real issue. Each jockeyed for position, striving so to state the issue and to argue the case, that his own point of view would prevail. Neither admitted frankly the dilemma and attempted to work out a truly equitable solution. The arguments of one ran parallel to, not counter to, the arguments of the other. The same situation which existed in the arguments in parliament prevailed. There each side started from its own vantage point, in one case government, and in the other property, and built up its case from its own starting point without admitting the point of conflict or the real dilemma.[98]

Why did such a situation prevail in the law courts? A tentative answer may be suggested although this subject must be thoroughly investigated before a definitive answer can be given. The sixteenth century had seen statute do more than it had ever done before. Although the common lawyers did not ignore that great development of statute, they were conservative by nature and training. In the sixteenth century they stood their ground against developments in prerogative government and law, proceeding cautiously and slowly—accepting statute but still interpreting it in reference to rights. For them to believe that the general welfare could be benefited by a statute encroaching too much upon the subjects' rights or the king's prerogative would be a striking deviation from their general philosophy and training. Quite understandably they failed to keep pace with the rapidly changing situation in the sixteenth century, and did not evolve a doctrine of general welfare to correspond with the realities of the great sixteenth-century statutes passed for the benefit of the commonweal. Lawyers and judges uttered many remarks concerning general welfare but failed to see that in the integrated state evolving in the Tudor period they must clearly define the relation of the general welfare to the traditional rights of king and subject.

Because of the conservatism of their predecessors, seventeenth-century lawyers found no developed and accepted doctrine of general welfare at hand for them to use. There may have been some development of such a doctrine in that century, but in the legal material examined there is little evidence of it. It would certainly be surprising to discover any such development, for the bigger issue in parliament and nation would tend to prevent its growth. It would be strange to find Coke, who stood for property and other rights in parliament, talking general welfare at the expense of the subjects' rights, and it

[98] See chapters IV and VI.

would be unusual to discover royalist judges admitting the dilemma in ordinary law when they were not facing it in the wider sphere of government.

Contributing therefore to the complexity of constitutional thinking in the seventeenth century was the fact that in the law courts there existed no developed and generally accepted doctrine of general welfare to act as a guide in the great state trials of the period or in the controversial issues of every Stuart parliament. Such a doctrine might have developed had the Tudors reigned another fifty years, and had they been able to achieve without too much parliamentary opposition the difficult task of integrating the realm more completely than they had already done. If such a doctrine had developed, it would naturally have worked to hasten the acceptance of a concept of parliamentary sovereignty.

From many points of view the weight of evidence substantiates the thesis presented in this chapter: that Englishmen in the first forty years of the seventeenth century did not possess a clear and firm belief in a doctrine of parliamentary sovereignty. Their failure to grasp the concept before the civil war increases immensely the difficulty of interpreting and analyzing the arguments upon which the parliamentary opposition built up its case against the king and royalists. Instead of resting their case simply and squarely upon the supremacy of the king-in-parliament over the king-out-of-parliament, they talked of law, rights, and the responsibility of parliament to the nation at large—arguments which the modern reader of their debates may lightly dismiss as confused and unrealistic. On the other hand, the failure of the parliamentary opposition to use to the utmost the strongest legal weapon in its armory made the task of the royalists infinitely easier, for their case, built around the supremacy of the king-out-of-parliament, could be put forward without a constant challenge from the opposition that the king was supreme only in parliament.

CHAPTER IV

ROYALIST COUNCILLORS AND JUDGES EXALT THE ABSOLUTE POWER OF THE KING

THE IDEAS of royalist councillors and judges are primarily significant because they were the ideas of men who governed England between 1603 and 1641. During those years of growing tension government went on, and that government was royal and not parliamentary. The privy council of the king still administered the English government, not as effectively as under Elizabeth, but still with a firm hand, showing a general responsibility for the nation's welfare and carrying out diplomatic, administrative, economic, and religious policies often more national and less local, more progressive and less traditional, than those advocated by the parliamentary opposition.

Government was royal during the first four decades of the seventeenth century, but for the most part it cannot be called tyrannical or arbitrary. There were no secret police, no intendants, no Bastille, and no *Lettres de Cachet*. James and Charles raised the divine right of kings to new exalted heights of absolutism in their speeches and treatises, but these kings were more humble and conventional, more legal and circumscribed, in their actions than in their words. Many of the important officials actually carrying on the work of administration under them in court and council and parliament were not lip servants or executors of divine-right theories.

Nor were they mere hirelings or court favorites of the king. To be sure, there were court favorites willing to do or say almost anything in order to receive a royal plum or a crumb of the kingly prerogative, and there were also some writers, mostly clerical, who endeavored to match or even out-do the divine-right theories of James.[1] These writers and court favorites, particularly Buckingham, who ruled England for several critical years, played an important part in the history of this period. Because of their favors and fawnings, their incompetencies and pretentions, they aroused great resentment and distrust, which weakened the monarchy and strengthened the parliamentary opposition.

On the other hand, they did not furnish the support which sustained monarchy during those decades of growing conflict. Had James and Charles been supported only by their court favorites and the divine-right theorists, it is possible that, barring foreign intervention, the parliamentary opposition might have secured in the twenties without a civil war effective control of the most important parts of the government. The controversy between king and parliament went on for forty years before the civil war broke out, because, for one important reason, during much of that time James and Charles administered royal government, not through court favorites, but through men of the caliber and with the views of Cecil, Ellesmere, and Bacon, Fleming and Heath, Cranfield and Weston, Banks and Wentworth. These men and others like them carried on government in England between 1603 and 1641, and their support of monarchy gave the crown its most legal and therefore its most sure foundation, enabling it to stand fairly firm at times against the parliamentary opposition.

Officers in the government received favors and lucrative positions from the king, and such benefits undoubtedly influenced their actions and words; but it must not be forgotten that many of these supporters of monarchy, like many of their parliamentary opponents, were men of principle and of conscience.[2] Devotion to conscience and principle was not a Puritan mo-

---

[1] See chapter V.

[2] Jones remarked in the ship-money case: "Brother we sit one next another, antient judges, though different in opinion. I speake out of my conscience, as you have spoken out of yours; so though there be variety of opinions, yet conscience is the same." S. T., III, 1186.

nopoly. Since many of the royalists were lawyers, much of the kingly absolutism they advocated and administered rested on the firm foundation of law. Except for Bacon, they were men of action, not philosophers, viewing government in council, court, and parliament as a job to be done, not an idea to be theorized about. They admired the work Tudor monarchs had done in the previous century, for then England had become strong and united, law and order had come to prevail throughout the land, and the government had met the new problems of the rapidly changing age by initiating and carrying out progressive measures and policies. They knew that England in the seventeenth century was a more secure and happy land for men to dwell in than it had been in the fifteenth because of the work of Tudor rulers. They knew also that some of that work had been done in parliament, but much of it in council and star chamber, and all of it, whether in or out of parliament, by rulers who were powerful.

Kings were still needed to hold the reins of government in the seventeenth century if orderly and efficient administration and progressive policies were to prevail. Although the Tudors had curbed the power of feudal lords, riot and disorder still broke out in the land, and star chamber was kept busy handling such problems. Councillors and administrators close to the king knew better than most members of parliament that orderly and efficient government could be achieved only by preserving, using, and perhaps increasing the monarch's power. They also realized that strong kingly rule was absolutely necessary if government was to continue the Tudor policy of working for the welfare of all parts of the body politic.

There was still in the seventeenth century great need for the guiding and controlling hand of government, for the death of Elizabeth did not stop the economic and social changes which were transforming feudal England into a more modern state. Stuart as well as Tudor gentry and merchants were land hungry. Profit-minded Tudor merchants had extended English trade in Europe, but Stuart merchants traded in far distant lands all over the world, bringing back to England new goods and undreamed of profits. The "first industrial revolution" [3] began under the Tudors and continued in the first half of the seventeenth century. With so many new fields of endeavor and opportunity opening up before them, it is no wonder that men desired to get rich quickly by some new device or venture. It was the responsibility of government, and primarily of the king through his councillors, to see that these new opportunities and ventures did not harm the commonweal. Government must not only be strong, but also progressive and enlightened to handle the pressing problems connected with these economic and social changes. As recent historians have pointed out, many advocates of strong prerogative government in the time of James and Charles had some desire to use the prerogative for the general welfare of all against the selfish interests of the few. They wanted the "Crown as head of the nation to cope with the selfishness of powerful individuals and classes. They wished, in short, to give the government the sort of rights conferred on a foreign executive by the principles of administrative law." [4] Enclosure laws must be enforced, wage laws must not be disregarded by budding industrial capitalists, and commerce must be regulated in the national interest. Government must keep pace with changing conditions by effecting needed reforms in antiquated laws and law courts. Many royalist councillors did not show such unselfish concern for the public welfare as these remarks suggest, but some did, and on the whole the record of the privy council in curbing private selfish interests and in carrying out policies beneficial to the general public was a good one, particularly in comparison with the individual self interest displayed by some members of the parliamentary opposition. Through the work of the privy council, and not of parliament, considerable governmental

[3] J. U. Nef, *Industry and Government in France and England, 1540–1640,* (American Philosophical Society, Philadelphia, 1940), p. 1.

[4] A. V. Dicey, *Introduction to the Study of the Law of the Constitution,* (The Macmillan Company, London, 1931), p. 366. Used with permission of the Macmillan Company.

control and guidance of the public weal was maintained between 1603 and 1640. Royalist councillors under James and Charles said relatively little about the divine right of kings, for they desired that kings should be powerful enough to maintain an efficient and progressive government working for the welfare of all.

Men holding such views in the seventeenth century should not be condemned as reactionary or even conservative, for in Europe at large at this time absolutism was the alternative, not to democracy, but to feudalism and localism. The great European states which maintained peace and order within their borders and initiated progressive policies in keeping with the expanding field of economic enterprise were ruled by monarchs whose power became more absolute during the century. Englishmen desiring stability and orderly progress could look admiringly across the channel at their neighbor France, or back into their own history of the two previous centuries, and find ample justification for their belief that the way of absolutism was the way of order and progress.

To realize their beliefs, royalist councillors and judges needed only to turn to the institutions of strong government and the ideas of absolute power which were their heritage. In privy council and star chamber, in high commission and numerous special courts and councils, they possessed prerogative institutions of government which had served the Tudors well. In the realm of ideas also, the royalists did not have to convince most Englishmen in the early seventeenth century that the king's authority came from God, that he was charged with the responsibility for the general welfare of all, and that in certain important realms of government his power was absolute. These concepts were accepted and proclaimed for a number of years by moderates and members of the parliamentary opposition.[5]

This absolute power of the king so generally accepted by Englishmen was not a new thing. As Professor McIlwain has

[5] See chapter I.

demonstrated, it "was nothing more nor less than the old familiar *gubernaculum* of Bracton." [6] It was the regal power in Fortescue's *Regimen politicum et regale*. It was also the power of government so freely used by the Tudors, concerning which the Venetian ambassador had said in 1551, "the King of England exercises two powers, . . . the one royal and absolute, the other ordinary and legal." [7] Sometime late in Elizabeth's reign, Judge Doderidge sketched an outline for a *Treatise on the King's Prerogative*.[8] The monarch's power, he wrote, is double, "absolute and ordinate," [9] and he promised to treat of both. Concerning the "fullnesse and plenartie" of the absolute power, he would show "whearin it doth consist and in what causes in discourse wheareof ar detearmined at large manie notable questions of most high importaunce touching the dignitie Roiall and the estate of the Realme, by the Lawes, Statutes, and publick Recordes of this Realme." [10] Unfortunately, Doderidge did not, as far as I can discover, carry out his promise and fill in the outline he sketched. His outline reveals, however, that the concept of the king's absolute power to be used for the general welfare of all was a subject upon which lawyers were beginning to speculate and theorize in the late sixteenth century.

In the seventeenth century, royalist councillors and judges upholding and advancing the claims of the king needed only to repeat with emphasis and clarity the views of their predecessors and contemporaries. This they proceeded to do. The clearest and fullest statement of the royalist position during

[6] C. H. McIlwain, *Constitutionalism Ancient and Modern*, p. 128.

[7] *Cal. St. P., Venetian*, V, 341, as quoted in C. H. McIlwain, *Constitutionalism Ancient and Modern*, p. 126. In his report in 1607 to the government of Venice, Molins wrote: ". . . all justice, both civil and criminal, is in the hands of special officers; but all that concerns the State is absolutely in the King's discretion; he, like his ancestors, is absolute lord and master." *Cal. St. P., Venetian*, X, 508.

[8] Sir J. Doderidge, "Treatise on the King's Prerogative Dedicated to Lord of Buckhurste . . . ," Harleian MS. 5220, Brit. Mus.

[9] *Ibid.*, p. 9v.

[10] *Ibid.*

the whole period of controversy was made in 1606 by Sir Thomas Fleming [11] in Bate's case:

> And first, for the person of the King, '*omnis potestas a Deo, et non est potestas nisi pro bono.*' To the King is committed the government of the realm and his people; and Bracton saith, that for his discharge of his office, God had given to him power, the act of government, and the power to govern. The king's power is double, ordinary and absolute, and they have several lawes and ends. That of the ordinary is for the profit of particular subjects, for the execution of civil justice, and the determining of *meum;* and this is exercised by equitie and justice in ordinary courts, and by civillians is nominated *jus privatum* and with us, common law; and these laws cannot be changed, without parliament; and although that their form and course may be changed and interrupted, yet they can never be changed in substance. The absolute power of the King is not that which is converted or executed to private use, to the benefit of any particular person, but is only that which is applied to the general benefit of the people, and is *salus populi;* as the people is the body, and the king the head; and this power is guided by the rules, which direct only at the common law, and is most properly named *Pollicy and Government;* and as the constitution of this body varieth with the time, so varieth this absolute law, according to the wisdome of the king, for the common good; and these being general rules and true as they are, all things done within these rules are lawful.[12]

Fleming's distinction between the absolute and the ordinary power of the king was repeated time and time again by the royalists. Sir John Davies, in his treatise on impositions,

---

[11] In 1599, Fleming, then Recorder of London, set forth his political views in a speech presenting the lord mayor to the barons of the exchequer. Fleming said: "A citty is a society of men congregated into one place, not only by mutual helps to live to-gether, but to live well and godlie to-gether; but can they live without order and government? and what order and government can there be where there is not one to commaund, others to obey, one to rule, and others that submit themselves?" J. Nichols, *The Progresses and Public Processions of Queen Elizabeth,* 3 vols., (London, 1823), III, 255.

[12] S. T., II, 389.

wrote: "By the positive Law the King himself was pleased to limit and stint his absolute power, and to tye himself to the ordinary rules of the Law, in common and ordinary cases," [13] but nevertheless in many realms his power was absolute. Sir Robert Heath, attorney general for the king, who defended the royalist position in Darnel's case in 1627 and in parliament in 1628, pointed out that "there is a great difference between those legal commands and that *absoluta potestas* that a sovereign hath, by which a king commands." [14] The attorney general in 1637, Sir John Banks, said that the great question of ship money "concerneth the king both in his ordinary and absolute power." [15]

Frequently this absolute power was called by another name. Fleming said that it was most "properly named Pollicy and Government," and Sir John Doderidge, who not only sketched the outline of a treatise on the prerogative but also defended the prerogative in parliament, referred to it in 1610 as *ius publica*.[16] Banks also called it *ius majestatis*,[17] and Sir Francis Crawley, another royalist judge in the ship-money case, called it regal [18]—a term used by Fortescue. According to the lords in 1628, it was the prerogative "intrinsical" to the king's sovereignty.[19] When the king employed such power, he was acting for reasons of state, and the affairs handled by such power were called "matters of state."

There is meaning and significance in each of the terms employed. This power was absolute and not ordinary because it was not tied to, nor limited by, ordinary rules of procedure or by forms of action. It was regal or royal because it belonged most peculiarly and most intimately to the king. It was in

[13] Sir John Davies, *The Question concerning impositions, tonnage, poundage . . . fully stated and argued from Reason, Law and Policy,* (London, 1656), p. 30. Davies was attorney general for Ireland.

[14] S. T., III, 37.

[15] S. T., III, 1016.

[16] Cotton MSS. Tit. Fv. fol. 244, Brit. Mus., Doderidge's speech, p. 246.

[17] S. T., III, 1016.

[18] *Ibid.,* 1083.

[19] Gardiner, VI, 260.

fact inseparable from him and intrinsic to his sovereignty
because without it there could be no royal government and no
kingly sovereignty at all. It handled matters of state because
only the king possessed the art and wisdom to deal with those
affairs so integrally a part of his "estate." It was public and not
private because it existed in order to enable the king to provide for the general and public welfare of all.

The royalists found the general-welfare power of the king
a strong bulwark for their claims. Doderidge in the skeleton
manuscript already referred to, said "That the Saulftie of the
Commonwealth of England moste dependeth upon the Princlie
Care of the Monarche of the same." [20] This is the power, Fleming claimed "which is applied to the general benefit of the
people." [21] Judge Clarke, arguing on behalf of the king in
Bate's case, stated that the king is the "preserver, nourisher,
and defender of the people; and true it is, that the weal of
the king is the public weal of the people." [22] In 1628, in the
course of one of his arguments in parliament, Heath pointed
out that "God hath trusted the King with governing the
whole." [23] A paper in the Public Record Office in the handwriting of Secretary Coke discusses the "component parts of the
Privy Council and the mode of their proceeding in the trans-
action of business." In this paper "Matters of state" are said
to be such "as concerne the whole of the Kingdome, the safety,
honor, and dignitye of the sacred person of the King, the
Queen, and the Prince, Peace, plentye, military discipline,
reformation of disorders, upholding of government, Execution
of Lawes, or what else hath relation to the *esse* or *bene esse* of
the State and are of infinite latitude, and extent." [24]

The royalist contention that the king possessed absolute
power to be used, not for his personal aggrandizement or pleasure, but for the general welfare and safety of the whole realm

[20] Sir J. Doderidge, *op. cit.*, p. 11v.
[21] S. T., II, 389.
[22] *Ibid.*, II, 383–84.
[23] L. J., III, 757.
[24] St. P. Domestic, 16/8:78.

was a concept justified by past precedents and present needs. Certainly "the English constitution included such a sovereign power," [25] and the need for a definitely recognized final authority with over-all responsibility had increased in the sixteenth century as the Tudor state became more integrated and close-knit. In fact, this kingly authority was so firmly recognized and accepted that the parliamentary opposition challenged it very slowly and hesitatingly. Even in 1628 they did not deny that such authority existed and should exist; they were determined only that it should not be written into the law of the land.[26]

The Tudors had wisely been content to accept the absolute power of the king as "government," knowing that most Englishmen were glad such power existed. At times they had used such power in an arbitrary and high-handed fashion, but they did not explain such actions to their subjects nor did they attempt to justify them legally. James and some of his councillors made statements indicating that there were times when they also viewed such power as outside or beside the law. James once said of the absolute prerogative of the crown: "that is no Subject for the tongue of a Lawyer, nor is lawfull to be disputed." [27] His sovereignty "ought not to be disputed or handled in vulgar argument." [28] It was, according to Bacon, a "matter of government and not of law," and therefore "must be left to his managing by his Council of State," and not "censured" by any judge.[29] The king's absolute power, Fleming insisted, "is most properly called *Pollicy and Government,*" and is "guided by the rules, which direct only (i.e., do not control) at the common law." [30]

[25] C. H. McIlwain, *Constitutionalism Ancient and Modern*, p. 130.
[26] See chapter VI.
[27] C. H. McIlwain, *The Political Works of James I,* p. 333.
[28] Spedding, V, 363.
[29] *Ibid.,* III, 37. Spedding (p. 368) remarks that it was probably Bacon who wrote these words.
[30] S. T., II, 389. The part in parentheses is my insertion.

Notwithstanding such statements, the Stuarts and their supporters were unwilling or unable consistently to accept this
"absolute" power as policy and government without attempting to write it into law. In contrast to the Tudors, who quite
clearly maintained the distinction between the absolute and
ordinary power of the crown, the Stuarts followed less consistent policies. At times their supporters insisted that the absolute power was so apart from the ordinary that common
lawyers and parliament should not encroach upon it, but at
other times they deliberately set out to demonstrate the complete legality of this "absolute power." When James or Charles
and their officials departed from ordinary ways of action—as,
for example, in using proclamation rather than statute for a
certain action—they took pains to explain at great length the
reason for their procedure and its essential correctness and
legality. Elizabeth aimed to keep, and in general succeeded in
keeping, the discussion of matters of state in the privy council
and out of the common law courts and parliament. At times
James and Charles tried to prevent parliament from discussing
foreign affairs and matters of state, but at other times they
themselves initiated and encouraged the discussion of those
questions.[31] They also encouraged the common law courts to
debate such matters. The graciousness of the king in letting
Bate's case be judged in the law courts was called to parliament's attention in 1606.[32] Heath said that although Darnel's
case "be a case which concerns himself in a high degree, yet
he [i.e., the king] hath been so gracious and so just as not to
refuse to leave the examination and determination thereof to
the laws of this kingdom." [33] Coventry, the lord keeper, told
the judges in star chamber concerning the equally famous and
important case of ship money that "you have cause to declare

[31] As, for example, in the 1623–24 parliament.
[32] C. J., I, 317.
[33] S. T., III, 32. Miss Relf points out, however, that the king did not
want this case tried in the courts. F. H. Relf, *The Petition of Right*,
(University of Minnesota Press, Minneapolis, 1917), p. 2.

it with joy that in so high a point of soveraignity he would consult with you." [34] In each of the famous constitutional issues of the period, royalist judges tried to prove that the particular prerogative of the king under discussion was his legally. Although the royalists did not have all the law on their side, they took such great pride in the fact that they were acting legally that they wanted others to realize the correctness of their actions.

This striving of the Stuarts for legal absolutism was a very important way in which they departed from Tudor practice. It was also the most threatening and dangerous policy they followed, certainly the one most feared by their parliamentary opponents. It is therefore necessary to try to discover why they so persistently wanted legal recognition of the king's absolute power to act for the general welfare.

The answer is essentially a simple one. They needed the support which only the law could give to their position and claims. They needed this support, for one reason, because legal precedents were numerous and strong in support of the subjects' property and rights. There were few cases in the common law courts, as the royalist judges themselves pointed out,[35] where the law had taken direct cognizance of the king's absolute power of government, whereas the main function of the common law courts had long been to protect the subjects' rights. The need of the royalists for securing such legal support was especially acute in the first half of James's reign, for during those years they had to meet the challenge of the common lawyers, led by Coke, to extend the common law jurisdiction. The attempt to limit and whittle down the personal jurisdiction of the king, the jurisdiction of chancery and of the ecclesiastical courts, to the point where such jurisdictions would be definitely dependent upon the all-controlling de-

[34] St. P. Domestic, 16/346:20. See also the statement of Crawley in the ship-money case on the same point. S. T., III, 1078.

[35] Bacon said in the proceedings in star chamber against Mr. James Whitelocke "that there is in all our law not three cases of it." S. T., II, 768.

termination of the common law courts,[36] must inevitably have been a contributing factor in the royalist effort to write the absolute prerogative into law.

Legal decisions in the king's favor would also enable them better to meet the fact of parliament's great legal competence. Judges and lawyers had long recognized that the king in parliament could legally perform many actions which the king could not do out of parliament. Would not the king's absolute power out of parliament be strengthened if judges and lawyers put the stamp of legal approval upon it? Legal decisions would also win them support within parliament, where they must face the skill of leaders of the opposition, many of whom were trained lawyers, generally better prepared than the privy councillors to marshal in their favor all the law on a particular issue. It is clear, for example, that James and his councillors took the initiative in bringing Bate's case to trial in the exchequer court partly in order that a legal decision based on weighty reasons might stop all questioning and criticism in and out of parliament.[37] In 1628 the royalists had to face the great attempt of some of the parliamentary opposition to reduce legally the king's power. If the royalists by that time had not established legal precedents in favor of the king, they might not have been able successfully to prevent the opposition from drawing up a statute sharply curtailing the king's absolute power.

It is also true that the more legal the argument the royalists could put forth in any parliament, the greater general approval and support they could secure from the great group of moderates. When in the 1610 parliament Yelverton departed from law, exalting the king too exuberantly, his speech was

---

[36] James said that the absolute prerogative of the crown ought not to be disputed, "but that of late the courts of common law were grown so vast and transcendent, as they did both meddle with the King's prerogative, and had incroached upon all other courts of justice; as the High Commission the Councils established in Wales and at York the Court of Requests." Spedding, V, 363.

[37] Gardiner, II, pp. 5–6.

not received with favor.[38] Nor was Ashley's when in 1628 he ventured to suggest the truth—that the issue between king and parliament was beyond the law's competence to solve.[39] Most of the royalists, like most of their parliamentary opponents, preferred to rest their case upon the sure ground of the law rather than to ascend to lofty heights of political philosophy. The king and his councillors needed the law to win the necessary support from legally minded Englishmen, particularly those who were endeavoring to strengthen common and statute law on behalf of the subjects' rights and against the king's prerogative.

They also needed the law desperately in order to carry on the work of government effectively. Towards the end of Elizabeth's reign Hawarde noted the "intent" of members of the "Queens Council and Judges" that the decrees and proclamations of the council "shall be a firm and forcible law, and of the like force as the common law or an Act of Parliament." [40] Although such an "intent" was somewhat restrained by the decision in the case of proclamations, James and Charles needed more urgently than the Tudors to rely upon the prerogative institutions for governing the country. Unlike the Tudors who had carried out their greatest changes in parliament, the Stuarts were unable to achieve constructive measures, like the union with Scotland, by statute law. With parliament persistently blocking the crown, and with the common law courts for a time under James rendering several decisions not to his liking, the government quite naturally turned more and more to the council and those prerogative courts where the king's absolute authority was undisputed.

[38] D. Carleton wrote to Sir Thomas Edmondes, ". . . this Henry the hardy did absolutely the worst, and for tyrannical positions, that he was bold to bluster out, was so well canvased by all that followed him, that he hath scarce shewed his head ever since." *The Court and Times of James I,* ed. R. F. Williams, 2 vols., (London, 1848), I, 121, as quoted by Gardiner, *Parl. Debates in 1610,* p. 85, n. b.
[39] L. J., III, 759.
[40] Hawarde, p. 78.

Quite naturally also, the government wished to establish the unquestioned legality of any actions of these bodies. For example, when in 1614 Oliver St. John expressed his opinion in a letter to the mayor of Marlborough that the king's attempt to collect a benevolence was illegal, he was imprisoned and fined by star chamber, and provision was also made for "recognition of his offence in all the courts at Westminster." [41] The fact, however, that he was quickly released and his fine remitted seems to indicate, according to Spedding, that the court desired "not to punish the man but to make an impression upon opinion by a judicial sentence accompanied with authoritative declaration." [42]

Earlier, in the case of James Whitelocke, coming before the council in 1613, that body tried to secure an authoritative declaration on the legality of its own jurisdiction. Whitelocke's questioning of the legality of the proceedings of the naval commissioners appointed by the king was treated by the council as contempt of its authority and of the absolute prerogative of the king, particularly his military and naval power. ". . . the opinion broached by the said Whitelocke did manifestly (by consequence) overthrow the King's martial power and the authority of the Council Table, and the force of his Maty's proclamations, and other actions and directions of State and Policy applied to the necessity of times [and] occasions which fall not many times within the remedies of ordinary justice, nor cannot be tied to the formalities of a legal proceeding . . ." [43] Any claim by Whitelocke that *lex terrae,* mentioned in Magna Carta or in other statutes, protected the subject legally from action taken by the council or the naval commissioners acting under it was invalid, for "his Maty's Prerogative and his absolute power incident to his sovereignty is also *lex terrae* and is invested and exercised by the law of the

[41] Spedding, V, 135.
[42] *Ibid.,* 146. The case of Oliver St. John was cited by R. Berkeley in his argument in the ship-money case. S. T., III, pp. 1110–11.
[43] Spedding, IV, 350.

land, and is part thereof." [44] It is clear that in the cases of James Whitelocke and of Oliver St. John, the council and star chamber were primarily concerned to proclaim the complete legality of their proceedings against the subject.

Even more essential for the adequate functioning of the government than the assertion of the legality of the absolute prerogative in council and star chamber was the need to secure legal sanction in the common law courts for the financial policies upon which the Stuarts were forced to embark. These rulers had inherited from the Tudors a national state with some up-to-date governmental machinery to administer it, but their heritage also included medieval machinery and ideas which the Tudors had left intact. The widest and most shocking gap between the nature of the Tudor state and its governmental machinery existed in the realm of finance. Except for their capital levies upon church and crown lands, the Tudors financed a government rapidly becoming modern in the sphere of its activities with sources of revenue inherited from the medieval period. Although many men were rapidly growing richer in the sixteenth century, and therefore were well able to pay higher taxes to finance the state activities benefiting them, public finance had not been brought up-to-date. There was truly one state in England in 1603, but men still insisted that the king must live of his own "estate." Parliamentary grants were not regarded as routine taxes for the normal and regular expenses of the nation, but as free gifts to supplement the king's own revenue for extraordinary expenses; and parliament was not generous with its gifts in the seventeenth century. Despite recent attempts to present the Stuart kings more objectively than they were treated by historians in the nineteenth century, neither James I nor Charles I naturally arouses the student's sympathy; but no scholar of English history in the first half of the seventeenth century, who reads of the efforts of those monarchs and their treasurers to solve an impossible

[44] *Ibid.*

financial problem, can fail to be touched by this predicament bequeathed them by the Tudors.

One way to meet that situation was to secure legal decisions in the regular courts in favor of special taxes. By such decisions legal precedents would thereby be established in the common law for a new imposition, custom, or ship, which the king in the exercise of his absolute power might judge necessary. With a foothold secured in the common law—that great inheritance and bulwark of the subjects' rights—the consolidation of the royalist position would be infinitely easier to achieve in this age when most Englishmen looked to the law to settle all disputed questions.

Even when the common law courts had rendered decisions in favor of the king's absolute prerogative, legal difficulties still remained. According to the evidence presented by their notes and papers, financial devices and legal perplexities occupied the minds of harassed treasurers. Caesar, Cranfield, and Weston managed to evolve financial schemes and plans, but these had to be translated into money actually collected from men who were well known to be stubborn about parting with money, particularly if there might be a loophole in the legal correctness of the form and procedure employed. One of the difficult problems the council often faced under the Stuarts was how to act—what form and procedure to employ in connection with a particular issue. Of what use were their decrees if they were not obeyed, and if the government could not legally coerce those who disobeyed? The fact that agencies of absolute government like the council lacked ways of acting and of securing obedience was recognized by some of the royalists. Weston insisted that the king's prerogative be written into the Petition of Right, for "One reason why the power cannot bee tacite for that power which is not knowen and confest cannot bee obeyed." [45] "The King," Dorset said in 1628, "hathe as much right to *Legem terrae* for matters of State

[45] *Lords Debates in 1628*, p. 173.

as the Subjecte for their rights." [46] Ashley made another telling remark in the same parliament when he said that "if they have jurisdiction of matters of state they ought to have power to coercion." [47] There was the deadlock. Parliament could not coerce the king, but the "absolute king" also lacked adequate ways and means of coercing the subject. The Tudor privy council could sometimes persuade a stubborn subject to contribute money for a ship, but the Stuart council needed to have adequate legal means for coercing his more recalcitrant descendant. This dilemma played a very significant part in the disputes over ship money. The government needed a legal decision in support of the new "tax," but they also hoped by such a decision to be able to resort, if a man refused to pay, to the traditional legal way of forcing payment. They wanted to be able to distrain his property. [48]

This imperative need to secure for absolute government the use of established legal forms, procedures, and officials became necessary because the Tudors had failed to bring the governmental machinery of absolutism up-to-date. There had been much practical high-handed absolutism under the Tudors, particularly in council and star chamber, but the general day-by-day government of the country had been carried on in traditional ways. [49] The medieval common law courts survived and towards the end of the sixteenth century experienced a revival. Local officials continued to function in their accustomed ways as in earlier centuries, and parliamentary sanction was generally secured for important new policies and departures. This studied concern for legality and tradition on the part of the Tudor rulers has often been commented upon

[46] *Ibid.*, 130.

[47] Mass., 4/17/28. Berkeley said, in his argument in the ship-money case, that the king "hath as incident to his regal office, power of coercion." S. T., III, 1095.

[48] D. L. Keir, "The Case of Ship-Money," *Law Quarterly Review*, L II, (1936), 556 and 572.

[49] On this subject, see particularly F. W. Maitland, *English Law and the Renaissance*, (Cambridge University Press, Cambridge, 1901), and C. H. McIlwain, "The English Common Law, Barrier against Absolutism."

as the greatest proof of their skill and tact in ruling, for such ways of acting were familiar, winning as much popular support for them as spectacular pageants and processions. The survival throughout the sixteenth century of these medieval forms of action, institutions, and officials has very great constitutional significance in the seventeenth century. That significance lies in the fact that the Stuarts and their officials had either to carry on the routine of government using old forms and traditional officials, or to create new administrative machinery and officials possessing adequate sanctions for enforcing the absolute prerogative. The Tudors had not made such changes, nor, as far as we know, did they desire to do so. The existing machinery was reasonably adequate and also cheap. Parliament granted money and justices of the peace worked for nominal pay. The common law, practiced and expounded in the common law courts, protected the property rights of the king as well as of the subject, bringing in lucrative fees to the government. Nor could the Tudors, even if they had so desired, afford to create new machinery for enforcing absolutism.

Whether or not the Stuarts consciously desired to erect a new machinery of absolutism, to include not only the council and common law courts but also the local courts and officials, is a question I am not qualified to answer; but certainly had they desired to create this machinery, the difficulty of securing the money necessary for the job would have constituted an almost insurmountable obstacle in their path. The mere task of running a government rapidly becoming quite modern in the extent of its activities, but remaining medieval in the sources of its regular revenue, was difficult at all times and almost impossible when the country became involved in foreign wars. The acute problem of public finance which the Stuarts faced has long been recognized as a fundamental cause of the constitutional controversy in the seventeenth century; but there has been much less realization of the connection between the amount of money necessary to run the government and the attempt of royalist lawyers and councillors to secure legal decisions which would enable them to use existing machinery and forms of actions to carry on absolute government under the sanctions of law.

In view of the different compelling reasons for securing the law as their ally, the persistent effort of royalist councillors and lawyers to establish absolute government on a legal basis becomes understandable. To summarize, it was imperative in the first place that the absolute power of the crown be stated and accepted in a law court in order that a legal precedent could be cited in its support. This need was particularly great because of the financial and administrative problems the government faced. In the second place, such power must in any decision be recognized legally as a legitimate and true exercise or manifestation of government's authority, even though the opposition should claim that the action under discussion trampled upon the rights of the subject. In the third place, any attempt by the opposition, either in court or parliament, to reduce or deny any part of the absolute power of the king must be stopped before the opposition could win a legal victory in a court decision or parliamentary statute.

In attempting to secure these legal objectives, royalist judges were handicapped by the fact that they must base their case, not primarily on law, but on the nature and necessities of absolute government. In the discussion over impositions in the exchequer court in 1606 and in parliament in 1610 and 1614, the royalist judges realized clearly that they could find little help in common law cases bearing directly upon the point. Fleming contended that the matter in question was "material matter of state, and ought to be ruled by the rules of pollicy." [50] Clarke held that the judgment should not be according to the rules of common law but according to the precedents of this court (i.e., the exchequer), which he insisted was of a different nature from the common law courts.[51] For these judges to

[50] S. T., II, 390.
[51] *Ibid.*, pp. 382–83.

pronounce so positively in a court of law that the matter did not come within the competence of the law, and at the same time for them to push for a legal decision upon it, brings out in sharp relief a basic inconsistency of the royalist cause which was never entirely resolved.

Because of this basic inconsistency, the nature of the arguments they employed in the courts of law is complex and often confusing. Determined to secure the support of law for the cause of legal absolutism, and yet unable to base their arguments squarely upon clearly defined and accepted legal precedents bearing exactly upon the point at issue, judges and lawyers tackled this problem of winning the law to their side, not by a frontal and direct assault, but by employing oblique and circuitous tactics. They so defined the issue as to bring it within the accepted powers of the crown; they argued very skillfully from analogy; and they discovered general legal principles favorable to their contention. At times they deserted the law for more philosophical and political arguments, but seldom rested their case solely on these grounds, generally preferring to shift from general concepts to law or from law back to general concepts, with the shift cleverly conceived and well timed to win the law, at least by implication, to their side.

In each of the three major cases of the period, that is, in Bate's case, Darnel's and the ship-money case, royalist counsel and judges defined the issue in such terms as to bring it within the king's prerogative. In Bate's case, they contended that the imposition on currants was not a tax upon an Englishman's goods or a "commoditie of this land" [52] but an impost on foreign imports and therefore not subject to the ordinary law of the land, since, in ports leading to the open sea, the king "hath absolute power . . . to include and exclude whom he shall please." [53] Such impositions, so the argument ran, are the effects of commerce, and are therefore related to the treaty

[52] S. T., II, 390.
[53] *Ibid.*, 389.

power of the king, which everyone knows falls within the realm of his absolute power.

In Darnel's case Heath made it clear that the government was not claiming that a man "shall be imprisoned without due process, and never brought to answer," for "that is unjust," [54] but was only asking "whether the ordinary courts of justice have power to bail him or no." [55] If the courts had such power at all times, it would sometimes be impossible for the king, responsible for the welfare and safety of all, to protect his people from dangers the ordinary judges "who walk below stairs," not always "privy" to all the circumstances in the case, might be ignorant of. [56] Since men agreed that the king was responsible for the general welfare of all, they must therefore accept his right to commit a person without immediately showing the reason for it. Since the king was trusted with so much, why should there be any question about trusting him with this necessary emergency power to commit?

In the ship-money case, the king's judges insisted that the subject was not asked for money which might be regarded as a tax or tribute, but for a contribution towards a ship which the king, charged with defending the realm, needed immediately in order to carry out his kingly responsibility. Since the king knew that ships were necessary to defend the coasts and English merchants from pirates, might he not "command such aid by the Writ for saving and preserving the kingdom and people?" [57]

Such were the arguments used by the royalists to bring matters in controversy within the limits of the king's absolute power. They were not allowed to ignore common and statute law precedents altogether; this, the opposition would not allow. But they did find it difficult to cite appropriate legal precedents and, consequently, had to rely primarily upon the fact that legal precedents could not easily be cited against them,

[54] *Ibid.*, III, 39.
[55] *Ibid.*, 41.
[56] *Ibid.*, 39.
[57] *Ibid.*, 924.

or, secondarily, that general principles of law or of statutory interpretation favored their contention. For example, in the debate over impositions, Clarke insisted that no common or statute law could be shown against these particular impositions. Darcy's case did not apply, "for that is of a commodity within the land, and betwixt the patentee and the king, and not between the king and the subject." [58] Bacon said that since the question of impositions at the ports "were never brought into the king's courts of justice, but still brought to parliament, I may most certainly conclude, that they were *conceived* not to be against law." [59] In fact "they were *thought* to *stand with law.*" [60]

On the question of statutes, the royalists relied upon the general rule that statutes do not bind the king's prerogative by general words but only by specific ones. There are "many authorities," Bacon said, "that kings shall not be bound by generall words." [61] Montagu reminded the commons in 1610 that there is "A saving in every act of the King's prerogative." [62] In regard to the statute of 45 E. 3 cap 4, enacting that no new imposition should be levied on woolfels, wool, or leather, Clarke explained that "this extends only to the king himselfe, and shall not binde his successors; for it is a principal part of the crown of England, which the king cannot diminish." [63] To the parliamentary argument that because poundage and tonnage were granted in parliament, it therefore was a basic principle that any further impositions should be levied only in parliament, Bacon replied: ". . . it is not strange with kings, for their own better strength, and the better contentment of their people, to do those things by parliament, which nevertheless have perfection enough without Parliament." [64]

---

[58] *Ibid.*, II, 387.
[59] *Ibid.*, 396. Italics are mine for emphasis.
[60] *Ibid.*, 398. Italics are mine.
[61] *Parl. Debates in 1610*, p. 70.
[62] *Ibid.*, p. 63.
[63] S. T., II, 385.
[64] *Ibid.*, 399.

Fleming admitted that statutes had been passed against im-
posts within the land, but maintained that "All these Statutes
prove expresly, that the king had power to increase the impost,
. . . and that he continually used this power notwithstanding
all acts of parliament against it." [65]

In general, the royalists in their treatment of statute followed basic principles of statutory interpretation, always emphasizing the fact that in all statutes the essential prerogatives
of the king were saved by implication. Yelverton went so far
as to say in parliament in 1610, "No Act of Parliament yet
made nor any can be made, but the King may impose." [66] Such
extreme statements, however, were exceptional in 1610.

The king's judges in the ship-money case made a determined
effort to prove the legality of the king's power of defense by
common and statute law. Banks in particular insisted that he
rested his case on the "law of the land," and would not take
this "occasion to discourse either of the law of nature, . . .
nor of the law of God, . . . nor of the law of nations, . . . nor
of the imperial law." [67] He tried to demonstrate that according
to English common and statute law the king had the legal
right to demand a ship, yet the common and statute laws he
cited did not bear directly on the issue. They were only illustrative of the general powers of the king for defense. For
example, he cited the Statute 24 Hen. 8 "that this realm of
England is an empire, and hath been so accepted in the world"
as one proof of the fact that the king of England was an absolute monarch. Then he argued that since he was an absolute
monarch he possessed all the *Jura summae majestatis*. Next
he attempted to show that these *Jura summae majestatis* "are
given unto his person by the common law." [68] To prove this
point he cited common law cases and legal authorities supporting particular rights of absolute monarchy—the right,
for example, of "supreme dominion," of "sovereign jurisdic-

[65] *Ibid.*, 393–94.
[66] *Parl. Debates in 1610*, p. 85.
[67] S. T., III, 1019.
[68] *Ibid.*, pp. 1022–23.

tion," of pardoning, and of "concluding war and peace." [69]
Because he could cite legal cases and authorities recognizing
those rights of the king, he implied that the common law recognized his right also to take ships for the defense of the
land.[70]

Banks employed the same devious technique in another argument, citing "those supreme titles, which the common law
of England giveth unto the king." [71] Because he could quote
common law references concerning the king's title as *Vicarius
Dei*," as the "fountain of common right," as *"Capitalis Justi-
ciarius totius Angliae,"* [72] he concluded that the king's power
of defense to command a ship "is implied out of the sovereign's
titles given unto him by the common law of England." [73]
Arguments like these reveal that even when Banks tried hard-
est to rely on common law, he had essentially to argue from
analogy and general principles rather than from concrete and
exact legal precedents.

When the royalist judges considered statutes in the ship-
money case, they again insisted that the statute either did not
apply to the particular point at issue, or must be so interpreted that the king's power remained intact. At times they
treated precedents dear to the parliamentary opposition in a
very high-handed and cavalier fashion. Banks, for example,
would not accept the evidence of the particular text of Magna
Carta drawn up in John's reign, because it was "an inforced
act from a distressed king," and had never been restated in
exactly that form.[74] Finch discarded altogether the evidence
of Fortescue because he had written in extraordinary times
when civil wars were taking place.[75] Banks insisted that no
royal power was taken away by the Petition of Right, for "there

[69] *Ibid.*, pp. 1023–24.
[70] *Ibid.*, pp. 1064–65.
[71] *Ibid.*, p. 1032.
[72] *Ibid.*
[73] *Ibid.*, p. 1017.
[74] *Ibid.*, p. 1052.
[75] *Ibid.*, p. 1230.

was never a word spoken in that debate of taking away any power of the king for the shipping business." [76] Berkeley argued in the same way, pointing out that the statutes cited in the Petition of Right, and even the petition itself, "must have a reasonable intendment and that by a common and just equity, for exposition of those three statutes, aids, and charges, for so necessary a purpose as the defence of the kingdom; and '*salus reipublicae*' will be clean out of the law, as fully as if they had been precisely excepted; and if other exposition be made according to the letter only, it might truly be said of such a literal exposition . . . that laws made for the good of the commonwealth, will prove the bane and ruin of it." [77]

In short, the royalists denied that the king's absolute prerogative could ever be taken away or reduced by general words of statutes or general principles of the common law cited by their opponents; whereas they themselves justified by general words, principles, and implications any exercise or extension of the king's absolute power affecting the realm of the subjects' property. On the basis of the strict letter of the law narrowly defined, the royalist judges failed to produce arguments which could not at least be legally challenged.

Their reasoning became more straightforward and convincing when they ignored common and statute law and turned to other more exalted branches of law. During these years of controversy they often seemed to have recognized consciously or unconsciously that the known and generally accepted law could be their ally only up to a certain point, for they certainly did not try to rest all their case on law and precedent. At times they deserted the known law and constitution and became

[76] *Ibid.*, p. 1056.

[77] *Ibid.*, pp. 1109–10. Concerning the statute of *De Tallagio non Concedendo*, which was passed "without the exception or the saving of the antient aids which was in *Confirmatio Chartarum*," Berkeley said: "But it is plain, that these general words were never meant, either on the king's, or the great lords and other subjects sides, to be absolutely general for all cases." *Ibid.*, p. 1108.

more aggressive, looking to natural law and the law of nations for support, and relying upon the nature of monarchy and natural allegiance to the person of the monarch. Their thinking along these less legal and traditional and more political and theoretical lines must now be considered.

Even before a concrete issue had arisen, Doderidge, in the skeleton outline of his treatise on the prerogative, proposed to base his discussion not only on English law but on "divine philosophy and Law of Nations." [78] In so doing, he claimed he would be imitating a learned judge in the time of Edward I who said "that when newe matter was considered whereof no former Law is extant we do as the Sorbonists and Civilians resorte to the Lawe of Nature which is the Grounde of all Lawes." [79]

Arguments which were based on natural law and the law of nations were very common in James's reign, particularly in connection with the discussion of the *post nati*. In arguing the case Bacon philosophised on different kinds of law, pointing out that as "the common law is more worthy than the statute law, so the law of nature is more worthy than them both." [80] In this particular case, he argued, the general principles of natural law should prevail:

> Is it not a common principle that the law favoureth three things, life, liberty, and dower! And what is the reason of this favor? This, [he answered] because our law is grounded upon the law of nature . . . by the law of nature all men in the world are naturalized one towards another, they were all made of one lump of earth, of one breath of God; . . . It was civil and national laws that brought in these words and differences of . . . alien and native . . . the law favoureth not them, but takes them strictly; . . . all national laws whatsoever are to be taken strictly and hardly in any point wherein they abridge and derogate from the law of nature.[81]

[78] Sir J. Doderidge, *op. cit.,* p. 4.
[79] *Ibid.,* p. 4 v.
[80] S. T., II, 581.
[81] *Ibid.,* pp. 594–95.

Calling upon the principles of natural law, as Bacon did in the statements just quoted, was a common practice of many lawyers in the early seventeenth century. Coke himself seems to have employed such philosophical arguments in the case of the post nati.[82] A full discussion of the law of nations in relation to English law occurs in the treatise on impositions by Sir John Davies. The question Davies raised was this: "Whether the Impositions which the King of *England* hath laid and levied upon Merchandize, by vertue of his Prerogative onely, without Act of Parliament, be lawful or warranted by the Law of *England*." [83] To answer this question, he first defined his terms as follows:

> By the Law of *England,* we understand not only our customary Common Law, and our Statutes of *England,* which are Native and peculiar to our Nation only, but such other Laws also as be common to other Nations as well as to us; have been received and used time out of mind by the kings and people of *England* in divers cases, and by such ancient usage, are become the Lawes of *England* in such cases; namely, the generall Law of Nations, and the Law-Merchant which is a branch of the Law, the Imperiall or Civil Law, the Common or Ecclesiastical Law, every of which Laws so far forth as the same have been received and used in *England,* time out of mind, may properly be said to be the Laws of *England*.[84]

In proving this point Davies marshaled impressive authorities, citing Justinian, St. Germain, Baldus, Strabo, and Bodin in support of the fact that in affairs of commerce, the law of nations prevailed. Bracton and Staunford were called upon as witnesses of the fact that the king of England had by the law of nations other prerogatives than the old customary ones.[85]

[82] *Ibid.,* p. 629. It is not clear from Coke's report of the case who is speaking.

[83] Sir John Davies, *op. cit.,* pp. 1–2.

[84] *Ibid.,* pp. 2–3.

[85] *Ibid.,* pp. 5–8.

Davies's treatise in which this definition of the law of England was given was not published until 1656, but since it was
written towards the end of James's reign, it might well have
circulated in manuscript in the years before 1628. Though it
is impossible to judge whether or not his comprehensive
definition of the law of England was known in 1628, the
royalists in parliament in that year defined *lex terrae* in the
same way as he had. When the parliamentary opposition
raised the issue by insisting that *lex terrae* was only common
law, and that common law protected the subject against such
commitments as in Darnel's case, the royalists replied that *lex
terrae* included not only common law but other laws as well,
and that according to one of these other laws, that is, martial
law, such commitment was legal. As Sir Henry Marten said,
"Martiall Lawe is not against the Common Lawe: Martiall
lawe cannot bee set downe but it must bee according to occasions in time of warr." [86] Secretary Coke took part in this
discussion, saying, "The marshall lawe is parte of an essentiall
lawe of the Kingdome; we all sweare that the King is supreme
governor of all lawes, and the Comon Lawe is not the only
lawe of the Kingdome." [87] We must, according to Secretary
Coke, "consider as well the government of a state, as the legall part Kings as well commanders of people, as leaders." [88]
Sergeant Ashley made even more sweeping statements concerning the *lex terrae*. In addition to the common law, he
argued, "there are divers other Jurisdictions exercised in this
Kingdom, which are also to be reckoned the Law of the
Land." [89] These include the ecclesiastical law, the law of the
admiralty, martial law, the law merchant, and also the law
of state. When monarchs act by this law of state, "their Acts
are bounded by the lawe of nature,[90] the Common lawe doth

[86] Mass., 4/18/28.
[87] Nich., 4/22/28.
[88] Harl., 4/22/28.
[89] L. J., III, 758.
[90] Mass., 4/17/28.

not provide for matters of state . . . when the Necessity of State requires it, they do and may proceed according to Natural Equity." [91]

The royalists also talked of the law of nature and the law of state in the ship-money case. Crawley stated that the king was entrusted by the law of nature with the defense of the realm, and that his responsibility for defense implied the right to raise the taxes necessary for carrying it out.[92] Littleton, the solicitor-general, carefully explained that he was basing his arguments on reason, and that his reasons rested "First, upon the law of nature: Secondly, of state, and Thirdly, of public safety, necessity and convenience." [93] By following this method, he promised that the result should not "be against the statute law, common law, or any of the hereditary rights and liberties of the subjects of England, but consonant to, and warranted by all." [94] Concerning the third kind of law he said "Salus populi suprema lex. All other laws positive are subordinate to this law and are to be regulated by it." [95] "Positive laws are abrogated by reason, when the safety of the king and people are in danger." [96] Crawley also stated that the letter of the law could not always be followed. In some cases, he wrote, it has been shown by the author of the *Doctor and Student* that "it is necessary to leave the words of the law, and to follow that which reason and justice requireth: and to that intent equity is ordained, which is no other but an exception of the law of God, or law of reason, from the general rules of the law of man. Which exception is tacitly

[91] L. J., III, 758.

[92] S. T., III, 1084.

[93] *Ibid.*, 925.

[94] *Ibid.* Concerning the phrase *salus populi* Banks made the following comment: "Surely the grammarians tell us that *salus* is taken '*pro incolumitate*,' as well for safety as for health," *Ibid.*, p. 1061. Weston said the same, *Ibid.*, 1066. See also, Spedding, III, 379 for this remark, probably by Bacon: "And if *salus populi* be *suprema lex*, then though law and usage and prerogative were all against us, yet *bonum publicum* should always be preferred."

[95] S. T., III, 926.

[96] *Ibid.*

understood in every general law." [97] Statements like these
just given reveal, from one point of view, how far the royalists
were departing from known and traditional laws, and, from
another, how zealously they worked to justify their position
by law of any sort.

Berkeley at one point in his argument resolved all difficulties very simply by completely identifying king and law:

> I never read nor heard, that Lex was Rex; but it is common
> and most true, that Rex is Lex, for he is a 'lex loquens';
> a living, a speaking, an acting law: and because the king
> is 'lex loquens,' therefore it is said, that '*rex consetur habere
> omnia iura in scrinio pectoris sui.*' [98]

In this statement Berkeley of course abandoned the distinction
between the absolute and ordinary prerogative of the king;
but it is significant that even this judge, holding more extreme
views than most royalist judges, did not think of claiming
that the king's absolute prerogative was sheer power which
could override the law. Berkeley maintained only that since
king and law were identical, all the king's actions were legal.
This belief in a legal rather than a power theory of government was still a basic assumption with Berkeley, and, I believe,
with all of the royalist judges and councillors prior to the civil
war.

The royalists could also look to divine law and to God to
strengthen their position. All of them would undoubtedly
agree that the great power they desired for the king was
warranted both by natural and divine law. As Ellesmere said,
"the kinge's Ma[jes]tie, as it were inheritable & descended
from god, hath absoluteye monarchichall power annexed

[97] *Ibid.*, p. 1085. The lord keeper declared in 1624 that the king "never
spared the Execution of any Law but for a great Law, *Salus Reipublicae.*"
L. J. III, 213.

[98] *Ibid.*, p. 1098. The Earl of Clare used the same phrase. In writing
to Thomas Wentworth, his son-in-law, he said that "we live under a
Prerogative Government, where Book-Law submits into *Lex Loquens.*"
W. Knowler, *The Earl of Straffordes Letters and Dispatches . . .* , 2 vols.,
(London, 1739), I, 31.

inseperablye to his Crowne & diademe, not by Common lawe nor statute lawe, but more auncyente than eyther of them." [99] Bacon also pointed out that "the King holdeth not his prerogatives of this kind [i.e., his absolute prerogative] mediately from the law, but immediately from God, as he holdeth his Crown." [100] When Strafford was defending himself before the lords, he reminded his accusers and judges that although the fundamental laws of the land included the property rights of the subject, yet "the Prerogative of the Crown is the first Table of that Fundamental Law, and hath something more imprinted upon it: For it hath a divinity imprinted upon it, it is God's Annointed: It is he that gives the Powers." [101] Royalist judges and councillors could well have made the divinity of the prerogative, so clearly stated by Ellesmere, Bacon, and Strafford, a cornerstone of their whole position, but few of them chose to present and build up their case on the basis of this concept. Perhaps, as Jones half implied in his argument in ship money, they, being judges, preferred to leave such arguments to the divines. [102]

A more common argument employed by the judges and councillors, when they deserted the letter of the law and became more theoretical, was a consideration of the nature of monarchy in general and the English monarchy in particular. The basis of their position here was the traditional and generally accepted concept that England was governed by a monarch responsible to no one, not even to the emperor or pope. The royalists saw the value of such a concept for their own position since they knew that Englishmen in the seventeenth century were proud of the independence of their ruler. His freedom from any foreign jurisdiction was theirs also, so completely did they identify themselves with their head and king when they considered England's place in the world. The

[99] Hawarde, p. 188.
[100] Spedding, III, 371. Spedding attributes this statement to Bacon, p. 368.
[101] Rushworth, VIII, 182.
[102] S. T., III, 1184.

royalists pointed out that such a great and independent monarch as the English king must possess great authority. In the debate on impositions in 1610 Crompton declared that even the German emperor could prevent his subjects' goods from going out of the kingdom; and drew the conclusion that "if the Emperor may do this there is no question, but a free king who is more absolute in his dominions than the Emperore may do like to his subiects." [103] In his book on impositions, Davies claimed that the king of England "having all Imperiall Rights within his own Kingdoms, hath and ever had as absolute a Prerogative *Imponere victigalia,* or to lay Impositions as the Emperor of *Rome* or *Germany,* or any other King, Prince, or State in the world, now have, or ever had." [104] Here was a challenging argument which must surely have been heard and approved by some men during these years when Englishmen were lustily proclaiming the greatness of their nation.

Nevertheless, most royalist judges and councillors responsible for carrying on the government did not make this argument a cornerstone of their position. In 1637 in the ship-money case, several royalist judges talked of the nature of true monarchy, and yet no one of them developed and used that argument as fully as one might expect. Banks, for example, introduced his argument by announcing that the king had the right to command a ship for purposes of defense "not only by his kingly prerogative, but also *jure majestatis.*" [105] "This power," he continued, "is not only *'inter prerogativa regis, sed inter jura summae majestatis.'* " [106] It is also "innate in the person of an absolute king." [107] Here was a good starting point for a general discussion of the nature of true monarchy,

---

[103] Tho. Crompton on Impositions, Cotton MSS. Titus F IV, Brit. Mus., p. 242v.
[104] Sir John Davies, *op. cit.,* pp. 147–48. Davies pointed out, however, that the king of England used his great power with moderation, pp. 148 ff.
[105] S. T., III, 1016.
[106] *Ibid.*
[107] *Ibid.,* p. 1017.

but Banks never really entered into that discussion. Instead, he turned his attention to the prerogatives of the king of England, to English precedents, and to English law. Another judge, Sir Robert Berkeley, also said that "the King of England hath a monarchical power, and hath *'jura summae majestatis.'* "[108] ". . . the rights of free monarchy appertain unto him."[109] Berkeley, however, like Banks, did not theorize further upon these statements but confined his case largely to English law and precedent.

Sir Francis Crawley discussed the nature of monarchy at greater length than any other royalist judge in the ship-money case. In particular he listed eight regal prerogatives which existed not only "by our laws" but "by all laws."[110] His list included those generally accepted as belonging to the English king, such as the appointing and pardoning power, the power to make peace and war, to coin money, and "to have allegiance, fealty, and hommage." His list also included the two most controversial of the king's prerogatives. According to Crawley, the first of the king's eight prerogatives "that containeth all the rest, is That the king may give laws to his subjects: and this doth not detract from him, when he doth it in parliament."[111] The eighth is "to impose taxes, without common consent in parliament."[112] It would be natural to expect Crawley to develop further his significant statement concerning the king's prerogative to give laws to his subjects. Since he explicitly said that this prerogative "containeth all the rest," it looks as if he had learned from Bodin, who had built the monarch's sovereignty around his lawmaking power. Crawley did know Bodin, as two references to him testify,[113] but in neither of these citations is he concerned with Bodin's views on the lawmaking power. Crawley cited Bodin both times only to fortify his own

[108] *Ibid.*, p. 1090.
[109] *Ibid.*, p. 1098.
[110] *Ibid.*, p. 1083.
[111] *Ibid.*
[112] *Ibid.*
[113] *Ibid.*, p. 1081 and p. 1083.

contentions that in emergencies the king of England might lay a charge upon parliament without waiting to ask his subjects for it. At no point in his argument did Crawley build up his case around the far-reaching prerogatives he listed for the English king and for all true monarchs. Like Banks and Berkeley, he confined most of his arguments to a much narrower sphere: the right of the king to secure money from his subjects in an emergency without waiting for parliament.

Essentially then, royalist judges preferred legal arguments based on English precedents to those based on the general nature of monarchy and to those involving divine and natural law or the law of reason. When they did resort to those more theoretical ideas, they failed to develop them to their full potentialities. If, on the one hand, they started out, as Banks did, with a discussion of the general nature of absolute monarchy, they developed their position by turning to specific English laws and precedents. If, on the other hand, they started with the specific English situation, as most of them did, they introduced these more theoretical arguments to strengthen a particular point of English law. Thus the royalists did their best to build up a legal absolutism upon the basis of law, even though they generally had to argue from definition, from analogy, and from general legal principles rather than from concrete cases bearing directly upon the issue under dispute.

Whatever arguments they might employ, each case they won in a court of law was a great legal victory for their position; and it must never be forgotten that the royalists were the victors in the great law cases of the period. A few more legal decisions in their favor, like those rendered in Bate's case, in Darnel's or in ship money, and the cause of the subject and his legal rights would have been black indeed.

The seriousness of the attempt of the judges to rest their case on law and thereby to build up a legal absolutism, and the magnitude of the legal victories they actually did win, were clearly realized by their parliamentary opponents, who

gave more time and energy to blocking and opposing the legal
and quasi-legal views of royalist judges and councillors than
to refuting the high-flown divine-right talk of James or of
some of his clerical favorites. In the 1614 parliament Sandys
said, concerning the decision in Bate's case, "other princes have
imposed but never claymed right to doe it." [114] In 1628
Wentworth voiced the same sentiment when he remarked,
"That which passes from White Hall is but a gust which
russeth the wether calms: but that which is legally done
stinges us." [115] So strong was the feeling of the parliamentary
opposition in 1628 that they must stand firm against all
royalist effort to secure legal, i.e., judicial or statutory, recognition of the absolute prerogative, that, although they tried to
write into law their own rights, they successfully blocked every attempt of the royalists to write the king's prerogative
into law. Intrinsical prerogative, Coke said, is "a word that
we find not but once in the law"; [116] while Pym said, "And for
reason of state, I desire itt may never come amongst Lawes." [117]
Seldon stated that if the absolute prerogative were admitted
in a statute, "wee shall have a law to that sence and soe wee
shall destroy our fundamentall liberties wee have allready resolved." [118] "I would knowe," he said, ". . . what person liv-
inge is excluded from arbitrary appointments, for in effect this
is to lett out the liberty of the Kingdome upon trust." [119] These
speakers and the group supporting them were determined that
the law which had been their "trusty servant" "should not fail
them" now. Their instinct was sound, for any admission in
law, particularly in statute law, if coupled with the victories already won in the law courts, would establish the absolute pre-

[114] Hastings Parliamentary Papers, Report of Sandys 5/12/14. On June
4th, 1614, the commons told the king that "if they shoulde graunt the king
releife it might in after ages be accompted a reall Confirmation of the
kinge [s] absolute power of ymposinge." *Commons Debates 1621*, VII, 652.
[115] Gros., 5/1/28.
[116] Gros., 4/26/28.
[117] Bor., 4/26/28.
[118] Mass., 4/26/28.
[119] Bor., 4/26/28.

rogative so firmly that the king would then be in the position to use the law and all its forms to win one practical victory after another. In 1628 the parliamentary opposition prevented the absolute or intrinsic prerogative from being written into a statute or into the Petition of Right,[120] but again in 1637 the royalists strengthened the position of legal absolutism by the decision in the ship-money case.

In all their legal victories the royalists had relied on English law and precedent and upon their skill in defining a disputed issue so as to bring it within the accepted powers of the king. They had also used to some extent arguments based on the law of nature, of nations, and the law of *salus populi*. The parliamentary opposition had also employed some of those more theoretical arguments, but they feared and attacked them when they found the royalists using them to strengthen their case for the legal absolutism of the crown. They feared them for good reason. If the royalists established their claim that natural law not only reinforced common law, but could, upon occasions determined by the royalists, override it, then the safeguards to property and other rights of the subject provided by the common law would be of no avail. The first bulwark of defense would be gone because the royalists would have won this important beachhead within the common law. Securely entrenched upon such a beachhead, the royalists could, with the help of natural law, advance further with only a weakened line of defense to resist their penetration. That last line would crumble quickly if the royalists used to the full their telling argument that only the law of preservation prevailed in times of danger. Since the royalists were admittedly the judges of such times, the parliamentary opposition was afraid that all law would be absorbed into the law of preservation.

With such thoughts and fears, the leaders of the opposition seized the opportunity given them in the Long Parliament in 1640 and 1641 to reply to the royalist judges and to the dangerous arguments by which they had won their legal victories.

[120] See chapter VI.

They were equal to the occasion and directed the full fury of their anger and fear against those judges who had decided for the king in the ship-money case. The instinct of the leaders of the parliamentary opposition was sound. The royalists had used the law as their ally, and they had done it openly—by decisions in the law courts. By such decisions they had done much towards erecting legal absolutism in England.

Exactly how far did judges and councillors working for this legal absolutism go in their own thinking? Did they believe that the monarch's authority was so exalted that no place was left for the subjects' rights, for parliament, or for the law of the land, except for those laws they chose to retain as sustaining and advancing their own concept of monarchy? Which qualities and public powers of their absolute monarch did they emphasize most? The answers to these and similar questions can best be given by again turning to the ideas expressed by some of the royalists who helped to govern England in the first forty years of the seventeenth century. Although no one of them ever put together for our benefit his complete constitutional and political views, some of them did reveal their basic conceptions concerning the monarch's authority.

First they agreed that in the English government the monarch was trusted with much. In fact trust was implicit in their concept of monarchy. Within the realm of the absolute prerogative, the king was free—free to choose such counsels and such forms of action as he would. Absolute power "useth all meanes to know the verity." [121] Since, as Fleming said, "his absolute power hath no lawe to dyrecte him," [122] he must be trusted in its exercise. When in 1628 the parliamentary opposition tried to pass a law to restrict his freedom of action and direct his absolute power, the royalists reminded their opponents that their king was one who had been trusted with much. No one presented this point of view more clearly than

[121] Ellesmere, *Certaine Observations concerning the Office of the Lord Chancellor*, (London, 1651), p. 44.
[122] Hawarde, p. 363.

Heath, who bore the brunt of the royalist defense against the attempt of the opposition in 1628 to limit the prerogative more narrowly than it had ever been before. Heath said:

> God hath trusted the King with governing the whole. He hath therefore trusted Him with ordering of the Parts; and there are many Cases of infinite Importance to the Subject, and of undoubted Trust, reposed in the King, wherein notwithstanding it was never questioned by a Subject of the King why He did thus or thus. As the King is trusted with the Coins and Monies of the Kingdom, of His Absolute power, He may abase, He may inhance them; He may turn our Gold and Silver money into Brass or base Money, and in one instant, undo his People thereby. The Answer is, He will not do it: He is trusted. He may make Wars, He may conclude Peace, or Leagues. These are fatal to the whole Kingdom, to the Liberties, and to the Lives of His Subjects. The Answer is, He will not do these unfitly, for the Hurt of his People: . . . The King will not break the Trust committed unto Him by God. But, my Lords, do I by this say, or maintain, that a King hath Liberty to do what He list? No, God forbid: He is set over His People for their Good; and, if He do transgress, and do unjustly, there is a greater power than He, the King of Kings: *Respondet Superiori*. And as *Bracton,* an Old Writer of the Law said, *Satis ei sufficit ad Poenam quod Dominum expectet Ultorem*: . . . these Gentlemen of the Commons House . . . have overdone; they have made their Proposition so unlimited, and so large, that it cannot possibly stand, but is incompatible with that Form of Government, which is Monarchy, under which we happily live.[123]

The English monarch had always been trusted with much, and royalists rightly feared that should the parliamentary opposition win a complete victory in 1628, true monarchy, a form of government implying much trust, would be seriously threatened. Bishop Laud revealed his fears in comments he scribbled in the margin of a manuscript copy of Rudyard's speech supporting the attempt of the commons to clarify and restrict the king's power to imprison for reasons of state. "For suppose

[123] L. J., III, 757–58.

such a Lawe could be made," Laud wrote, "yett it could not take of all Trust from the King." Laud was shocked that Rudyard had spoken of Magna Carta as reducing the regal power and wrote, "To reduce is a hard phrase." [124]

The royalists insisted that the monarch must be trusted and also maintained that this trust included a wide discretionary power to be used in emergencies. The power they claimed in both Darnel's case and in ship money was essentially an emergency power—in the first case, the power to imprison for reasons of state in an emergency, and in the second, the power to demand contributions for ships to meet an emergency. They maintained that their monarch possessed this extensive discretionary power, that he alone was the judge of when such power should be used, and that when this power was invoked, no other law or right could prevail against it. Here was perhaps the greatest trust resting in their monarch. Few of the royalists claimed that this great power could be used except in an emergency, but all of them believed it was an essential part of the monarch's prerogative.

The views of Strafford on this power reveal very clearly how an efficient and practical administrator regarded it. Strafford wrote to Hutton:

> *Salus populi suprema lex,* nay in cases of extremity, even above acts of Parliament . . . the Mischief which threatens States and People are not always those which becomes the Object of every vulgar Eye; . . . therefore it is a safe Rule for us all in the Fear of God to remit these supreme Watches to that Regal Power whose Peculiar indeed it is . . . than feed ourselves with the curious Questions, with the Flatteries of imaginary Liberty, which, had we even our silly Wishes and Conceits, were we to frame a new Commonwealth even to our own Fancy, might yet in Conclusion leave ourselves less free, less happy than now, . . .[125]

[124] St. P. Domestic 16/102:43. Rudyard had said that "the very point, scope and drift of Magna Charta was, to reduce the regal to a legal power, in matter of Imprisonment . . ." S. T., III, 173.

[125] Knowler, *op. cit.,* II, 388–89.

Again in 1641, when Strafford was defending himself before
the lords, he consistently maintained that the king's prerogative must include an emergency power: "The Prerogative must
be used, as God doth His omnipotency, at extraordinary occasions . . . there must be a prerogative if there must be extraordinary occasions." [126] To Strafford, as to other royalists, a
monarch with such great prerogatives was thought to occupy
the key position in government. "The authority of a King," he
said, "is the keystone which closeth up the arch of order and
government, which contains each part in due relation to the
whole, and which once shaken, infirm'd, all the frame falls together in a confused heap of foundation and battlement, of
strength and beauty." [127]

The royalists attributed great power to the king, but most
of them did not claim that his absolute power normally included the right to take his subjects' property. Such power was
no part of royal monarchy, but as Bodin had pointed out,
existed only when the form of monarchy was seigniorial—not
the highest and truest form of monarchy.

The attitude of the judges towards property in the Bate's
case and in ship money has already been discussed. In both
cases they took pains to point out that neither the impositions
upon currants nor the contribution towards a ship was a direct
tax upon the subjects' property. They also maintained that the
ships the king asked his subjects to furnish were justified only
under the king's emergency power to provide for the defense
of the land.

Most royalists also never denied that in their form of monarchy parliament occupied a proper place, even though, in
the reigns of both James and Charles, reports were circulated
that perhaps the king would dispense with parliament. As
early as 1607 the Venetian ambassador reported to the doge

---

[126] *Cal. St. P. Domestic, 1640–1*, p. 542.
[127] Tanner MSS. LXII. f. 300, printed in *The Academy*, 5 June 1875,
pp. 352–53, as quoted in C. V. Wedgwood, *Strafford*, (J. Jonathan Cape,
London, 1935), p. 75.

and senate that the king had said "in private" that if the commons continued to oppose the union with Scotland, "he will be forced to carry it through by his own absolute authority." [128] Again in 1620 Chamberlain commented to Carleton upon Bacon's speech "exalting the King's prerogative as the perfection of law,—a doctrine [Chamberlain said] meant to prepare the way for subsidies without Parliament." [129] Early in the reign of Charles, the king's vice chamberlain, Dudley Carleton, told the commons publicly that, glorious as their monarchy now was, perhaps the king would be forced by their actions to become a different kind of ruler. In other kingdoms, he warned them, when men "changed there parliamentary liberty into tulmultuary indevors: it was changed by the Soverange to an other forme of government: We are the happiest of nacions. In this kingdome I see men looke like men: they have flesh on their backs and clothes to cover that flesh. In other places the men looke like ghosts ther bodyes clothed with canvas suits and wodden shooes." [130]

This threat of new counsels and of a new kind of monarchy aroused a storm of opposition. In 1628 the royalists, for the most part, did not threaten to change their monarchy, but liked to point out how glorious it was. England had, according to Doderidge, "A Monarchie of the best composocion, ever renowned in all the world, the Crowne Imperiall holdes of none but God." [131] Heath said, "the Parliament is a great Court, a great Counsell, the great Counsell of the King," and added "but they are but his Counsell, not his governours." [132]

[128] *Cal. St. P., Venetian*, X, 488.

[129] *Cal. St. P., Domestic, 1619–1623*, p. 184.

[130] Gros. 5/12/26. See also, Whit. 6/12/26, where the following remark of the chancellor of the exchequer is recorded: "If wee make a happy consultation this day, wee make the king safe att home and feared abroad. If we doe it not I cannot tell that we shall have another day of Consultation."

[131] *Lords Debates in 1628*, p. 106. The lord keeper did say in this parliament that if parliament should refuse to grant money, "Necessity and the Sword of the Enemy will make way to others." L. J., III, 688.

[132] *Speech of Sir Robert Heath, . . . in the case of Alexander Leighton*, ed. S. R. Gardiner, (Camden Society, 1875), p. 9.

In these frank words Heath denounced the bold attempts of the parliamentary opposition to achieve some control of the king. Most royalists would share Heath's views on this point, for they assigned to parliament a subordinate place in the government of the country. Many of them would also agree with Berkeley who looked upon parliament as "a most ancient and supreme court," but pointed out that its proper function was for the peers and commons there to "shew the estate of every part of the kingdom; . . . make known their grievances (if there be any) to their sovereign, and humbly petition him for redress." [133] To the royalists, parliament was the king's council, meeting when the king called it, dispersing when he dissolved it, and, when it was in session, granting the taxes and passing the laws which the monarch in his great wisdom deemed necessary. They admitted that parliament was the king's council but did not accept its position as the council and representative body of the kingdom.

It is true that most of the royalist councillors and judges believed that the king could not normally collect taxes which had not been freely granted him, but they seemed to assume in their public utterances that subjects would always respond freely and generously to the declared needs of the king. The Earl of Northhampton said that for subjects to supply the king was as "proper and fit" as for "rivers to give tribute to the sea." [134] Ellesmere expressed his attitude in these words: "Benevolence is the parte of a dutifull and lovinge Subject to shewe unto their prince . . ." [135]

[133] S. T., III, 1098.

[134] *Parl. Debates in 1610*, p. 18.

[135] Hastings Parliamentary Papers, 1614, A booke of remembrances of those thinge that doe happen . . . in the higher house of Parliament . . . See also the remark of Clarke in Bate's case: "As it is not a kingdom without subjects and government, so he is not a king without revenues." S. T., II, 383. In the parliamentary debate on impositions in 1610 Montague said, quoting Bracton: "All kingdoms supported by 2 things, Government, Revenue. Take either of theise away, the kingdome falls to ruyn." *Parl. Debates in 1610*, p. 63. In the 1614 parliament someone remarked, "The King *pater patriae; communis parens*, therefore all good Children to relieve him." C. J., I, 462.

It is not easy to determine exactly how the royalists felt about the lawmaking power, for, like their parliamentary opponents, they seldom discussed it. Perhaps the reluctance of both groups to state their position clearly is due to the fact that both knew that, according to English law and the constitution, lawmaking was the joint action of king, lords, and commons. The average royalist would assert, I believe, that the king made the laws in parliament. He would not claim that the king made the laws alone, and yet he would maintain that laws made in parliament were truly the king's laws. There appears to be no evidence that many royalists believed that the lawmaking power was the highest and most supreme act of government. Judge Crawley stated that it was, and he also said "That the king may give laws to his subjects: and this doth not detract from him, when he doth it in parliament." [136] Nevertheless, Crawley did not rest his case for the king on his lawmaking power nor discuss its relation to other parts of the government. The first royalist I have discovered who stated his views clearly on the relation of the lawmaking power to the supremacy of the king was Henry Ferne, who did not write before the civil war. According to Ferne, the two houses were "in a sort Coordinate with his Majesty, *ad aliquid,* to some act or exercising of the supream power, that is to the making of Lawes by yeelding their consent," [137] yet they did not share supremacy with the king in many other ways, as, for example, in making war and peace, in appointing, etc. Ferne certainly did not regard the legislative power as more important than many other powers of government. It happened to be a power which the king shared with parliament, but that fact did not detract from his supremacy since he was completely supreme in so many other important ways. Ferne's reasoning on this question would, I believe, have been accepted by most royalist judges and councillors prior to the civil war. They, like Ferne,

[136] S. T., III, 1083.
[137] Henry Ferne, *Conscience Satisfied* . . . (Oxford, 1643), p. 6. See chapter X for a fuller discussion of Ferne.

belived that the king was truly absolute, but that normally he made laws as well as secured taxes in parliament.

A revealing indication of Charles's views on the subject during the years between 1630 and 1640, when no parliament was called and money was actually secured by non-parliamentary means, occurs in his remarks concerning certain passages in a play, *The King and the Subject,* by Phillip Messinger. The play, as originally written, included the following lines spoken by Don Pedro, king of Spain, to his subjects:

> Monys? Wee'le rayse supplies what ways we please,
> And force you to subscribe to blanks, in which
> We'le mulct you as wee shall thinke fitt. The Caesars
> In Rome were wise, acknowledginge no lawes
> But what their swords did ratifye, the wives
> And daughters of the senators bowinge to
> Their wills, as deities, etc.

When Charles read these lines he "set his marke upon the place with his owne hande, and in thes words: 'This is too insolent, and to bee changed.' " [138] True kings, so Charles must have wished his subjects to believe, did not raise supplies any way they pleased and did not claim that their wills alone made laws.

Royalist judges and councillors had some respect for parliament's place in granting taxes and making laws, and they also regarded the king as part of the state and not above or outside it. It is true that the divine-right ideas of James and some of the clergy served to set the monarch outside and above the state, but there is no evidence that judges and councillors subscribed to that view, which certainly could not be reconciled with the legal arguments they employed in their attempt to erect a legal absolutism. They did not argue for a king outside the state who ruled people far below him by his mere will, but for a king whose authority over his people rested on the law of

---

[138] *The Dramatic Records of Sir Henry Herbert, Master of the Revels, 1623–1673,* ed. J. Q. Adams, (New Haven, 1917), p. 23. See also p. 38. I am indebted to Professor Gerald Bentley of Princeton for this reference.

the land and his kingly responsibility to provide for the welfare of all. It was consistent with the general royalist position for them not to separate the king from the state, for here they stood on firm legal ground. Ellesmere had said in the case of the post nati: "This is a daungerous distinction betweene the king and the crowne, and betweene the king and the king-dome: it reacheth too farre; . . . It was never taught, but either by traitours, as in Spencers bill in Edward the second time . . . or by treasonable papists, . . . or by seditious Sec-taries and Puritans . . ." [139] In the years after Ellesmere made these remarks, members of the parliamentary opposition who were not "seditious Sectaries" advanced subtle arguments con-cerning parliament's position in the state. Those arguments, when carried to their logical conclusion, thrust the king clear out of the state. The royalists bitterly resented parliament's growing claims, but I have not discovered that any of them before the civil war actually stated that the parliamentary argu-ments denied the king a place within the state. When, however, in 1642 the arguments of that opposition became less subtle and more open and bold, Ferne and Digges, the two keenest thinkers supporting the king's cause at that time,[140] pointed out that the parliament had thrust the king out of the state—a completely illegal act, since he most assuredly was a part of it.

If, therefore, the royalist position is viewed from the point of view of the claims its supporters did not make for the king, it seems essentially moderate and legal, for they did not believe that normally the king could secure taxes or make laws without parliament, nor did they put the king outside the state. On the other hand, if the position of the king advocated by royalist judges and councillors is viewed from the point of view of the nature and extent of their positive claims, it appears less mod-erate and more extreme. They actually did put forward a concept of monarchy attributing to the king such extensive and

[139] S. T., II, 690. In his speech to parliament, Nov. 18, 1606, James said, "But for himself, he would never make a Separation of the Peoples Will and the Will of the King." C. J., I, 314.

[140] See chapter X.

comprehensive prerogatives that his position, as they viewed it, was legally and constitutionally more absolute than most Englishmen had believed it to be in the early seventeenth century.

The way in which royalists departed from the traditional and existing constitution and law was not primarily in the particular precedents they cited, but in the cumulative effect of their reasoning. By extending the emergency and discretionary power of the king and by enlarging his trust, they so exalted the absolute power that little room was left for the subjects' rights and property, and they so tipped the scales in favor of the prerogative that the old balanced constitution no longer prevailed. They actually extended the monarch's absolute power so far into realms which the law had generally recognized before as belonging to the subject that the law no longer did afford adequate legal protection for his rights and liberty. For these reasons the conception of monarchy which the royalist judges and councillors evolved during these years of controversy was a real departure from the views most men had earlier held.

Whether or not it could be justified on the basis of legal precedents is a question I am not prepared to answer. A study of all the precedents cited by both the royalists and parliamentarians would undoubtedly throw some light on the question, but I doubt that such a study would yield substantial results. Were such a study made, it probably would be found that in general the precedents and laws cited by both sides were substantially correct. According to the interpretation presented in the opening chapters of this book, men believed that the law favored both the king and his prerogative and the subject and his rights, and aimed to preserve a balance between the two. If such views were held as late as the seventeenth century, after a century of strong Tudor rule, it is probable that they survived as a heritage from the medieval period. If, therefore, a study were made of the medieval precedents so freely cited by both sides, it might well be discovered that both sides could unearth legitimate medieval precedents supporting their respective contentions.

Whatever the legal validity may be concerning the precedents cited, the reader of the debates and arguments in the seventeenth century is constantly impressed by the failure of either the royalists or their parliamentary opponents to meet squarely the arguments and precedents on the other side. In their arguments "they slid past each other," [141] each side citing its own precedents and each side presenting an interpretation of opposing precedents which made them of little avail. Raleigh pointed out the nature of the impasse when he said, "If the House press the King to grant unto them all that is theirs by the Law, they cannot, in Justice, refuse the King all that is his by the Law. And where will be the Issue of such a Contention. I dare not divine, but sure I am, that it will tend to the Prejudice both of the King and Subject." [142]

Despite Raleigh's warning, that is exactly what happened. Each discovered the precedents enabling it to push deep into the realm of the other. In their claims the royalists reduced the realm of the subjects' rights and liberty to such a narrow margin that the parliamentary opposition rightly feared that the net result would be a new kind of monarchy more absolute than English law had known before; and yet that same opposition did its best to curtail the powers of government so sharply that the king and his councillors rightly feared that monarchy, as England had long known it, would be changed into another form of government. Because both sides pushed so deep into the middle realm where the law had never established a fixed line clearly separating the realm of the king's government from the realm of the subjects' property, but where mutual respect and love between king and people were supposed to maintain a proper balance between the two, both sides were guilty of de-

[141] C. H. McIlwain, *Constitutionalism Ancient and Modern*, p. 130.

[142] *The Prerogative of Parliaments*, 1644, Harleian Miscellany (ed. of 1745), V, 208 as quoted by C. H. McIlwain, *Constitutionalism Ancient and Modern*, p. 114.

parting from established legal and constitutional traditions concerning the nature of government in England.

If the royalists could rightly point to established law and tradition favoring the king and recognizing his government as absolute in many important realms, the parliamentarians could rightly point to established law and tradition protecting the subjects' rights and to parliament itself where subjects granted taxes and co-operated as partners with the king in passing laws. If, as Hunton contended in 1643,[143] the king was supreme only in parliament, then the position of the royalist judges and councillors can be called unjustified since they denied this truth. If, on the other hand, as Ferne contended, the king's supremacy did not depend upon the few powers whose exercise he shared with parliament, then the royalist position was essentially correct. Between these points of view, which unfortunately were not presented clearly before the civil war, there is, in my judgment, no certain legal choice. Both were half truths. It was possible for the views of each to be half true, legally speaking, because the doctrine of parliamentary supremacy was not fully developed, not completely accepted, and its implications not clearly understood in those decades before the civil war when the constitutional arguments were being drawn up and presented. Hunton realized more clearly than Ferne and other royalists that lawmaking had become the supreme act of government; but it is true that lawmaking had not always occupied such an important place in government—in particular, not in the medieval period from which so many legal precedents were drawn. Ferne stood on the firm ground of law and established tradition when he insisted that the king alone was absolute in many important realms of government other than lawmaking; but he consciously or unconsciously refused to recognize the growing part which legislation had played in the government of England in the century and a half before the civil war.

[143] See chapter X.

The fact that there were precedents and traditions recognizing the subjects' rights helped to prevent royalist judges and councillors from establishing the complete legal absolutism of the monarch. The king never received blind support from his judges. Not only the leaders of the parliamentary opposition, but men believing that the king possessed great prerogatives to be used for the general welfare, were perplexed by such precedents. They were not at all sure that the king could override established form and procedure to secure a necessary tax. In the debates in parliament over impositions in 1610 Hobart saw the problem clearly, explaining it as follows:

> If he [that is, the king] myht sett an imposition by his absolute power, then he might gett an imposition by his absolute power by seising his goods and imprisoning his body. But, if you cannot gett it but by the legall power, therefore he cannot sett it by his absolute power.[144]

This problem of "getting" perplexed several judges in the ship-money case, where the government had insisted that a service (the service of a ship) and not a tax was being asked of the subject. But, argued an unknown person interested in the decision, if this is a service, then the appropriate form to receive such a service must be employed, and English law did not possess such a form for securing the service of a mythical ship not yet built from "inland areas." "Money for new ships cannot be levied by writ," but must be by "Acte of Parliament. . . . Judges must not deliver what hath beene done *de facto*, but what may be done *de jura*."[145]

Though opinions such as these were minority opinions, they highlight the problem the royalists faced in running the government. They also indicate how much easier a complete victory would have been for them if these medieval forms of

---

[144] *Parl. Debates in 1610*, p. 119.

[145] Stowe MSS. Legal opinion regarding assessments of ship money, Hunt. Lib. There is no indication in the manuscripts concerning the author of these opinions. See also the Hastings MSS. on Ship Money in the Huntington Library where many questions concerning procedure were raised.

action had not checked and partially blocked the establishment of a complete legal absolutism. Moreover, if perchance the Stuarts had by some miracle found the money and used it to set up an administrative absolutism with paid intendants and an efficient standing army, the amount of support they would have had is problematical. Certainly not much in parliament, and perhaps not too much in the council and law courts. Although many lawyers argued in favor of legal absolutism, men like Ellesmere, Heath, Strafford, and possibly Bacon, who were steeped in English law with its emphasis on form and procedure, might have withdrawn their support from the king if the royalist cause meant that old traditional forms and procedures would be permanently trampled down. When, for example, in 1628 the king wished to secure an opinion from the judges, they cautiously refused to commit themselves until the actual facts and circumstances were before them.[146] It is quite probable that some of the judges whose legal arguments played an important part in building up a theory of legal absolutism might have refused to give their support to it if the net result meant new officials, new forms, and new ways of acting. Thus the law upon which the royalists built so much of the edifice of legal absolutism did not give them complete support. It proved to be something of a stumbling block when they tried to "set" taxes by the absolute power which they could not "get" by existing forms and procedures. The survival of older forms and procedures during the century of Tudor rule served to keep alive the idea that subjects as well as kings possessed rights during those years between 1630 and 1640 when parliament could not act as the guardian of those rights.

There is a second way in which the earlier precedents and traditions proved to be something of a legal stumbling block to the royalists. Since most of the judges and councillors admitted that the king could not normally take taxes nor make laws without the consent of parliament, they were really faced with the fact that the king's government could not function

[146] St. P. Domestic, 16/141:44.

effectively without the co-operation of his subjects. Neither James, nor Charles, nor their royalist councillors could ever secure the sustained co-operation of parliament, and the only effective control they had was to dissolve it or to refuse to call it. As long, however, as most of the king's judges and councillors still held to the belief that parliament was necessary for taxes and laws, the royalists were always under a legal handicap in their attempt to establish legal absolutism. In the administration of government also, they had to depend essentially upon the willing co-operation of amateur officials. They could not rely primarily upon paid bureaucrats who could be controlled and coerced.[147] The Stuart attempt to rule by the "law of state" could never completely succeed as long as the "law of state" lacked coercion. Thus the failure of the medieval law and constitution to provide adequate legal sanctions against the monarch's encroachment upon the subjects' rights was paralleled in a sense by its failure also to establish legal means by which the monarch could correctly and easily carry on kingly government without securing the co-operation and consent of his subjects. The lack of adequate coercion in medieval law was a major problem which both the royalists and parliamentarians had to face in the constitutional crisis of the seventeenth century, and neither side was able to solve it entirely successfully within the established framework of the existing law and constitution.

There is yet another legal flaw in the arguments of the royalists. On the one hand, they wanted to link absolutism with existing forms and procedures in order to be able to use the established law and machinery of government for their own purpose. On the other hand, they claimed that an essential characteristic of the absolute prerogative was its freedom of action. When the government acted under the absolute prerogative, it was free from the limitations of form and procedure, even when its actions penetrated deep into the realm of the

[147] On this point see D. L. Keir and F. H. Lawson, *Cases in Constitutional Law*, (Clarendon Press, Oxford, 1928), p. 33.

subjects' rights, where the law normally limited the king's authority. In short, the royalists wanted both greater freedom of action for the monarch's absolute prerogative, and also the legal right to use traditional forms and procedures which had normally sharply curtailed the king's freedom of action. Although to my knowledge no royalist thinker ever spoke of this basic inconsistency, and no parliamentary opponent ever seized upon it as a weapon to turn against his adversaries, the fact that such a fundamental flaw existed in royalist thinking sheds light upon our understanding of the nature and validity of the arguments used in the attempt to construct legal absolutism in England.

The royalists were also faced with the fact that the arguments which they used in advancing their cause contained political weaknesses and fallacies. By the very arguments they employed in exalting the monarch, they exposed the glaring contrast between their conception of monarchy and the actual kings, James and Charles, who sat upon the English throne.

The parliamentary opposition was quick to recognize and capitalize upon this political weakness in the royalist edifice. They resented, in the first place, the royalist claim that the king's absolute power was something beyond the ken of ordinary mortals. The royalists spoke of such power as a "mystery," a "secret" which only a king and councillors close to him could understand. Fleming said in his argument in Bate's case, "It is not reasonable, that the king should express the cause and consideration of his action, for they are *arcana regis*." [148] Coventry remarked in star chamber in 1637, "Noe man will expect that *Arcana Regni* should be published," [149] while Crawley said in the ship-money case, "*Arcana Regni* not fit for public debate." [150] Such sentiments were also proclaimed by royalists in parliament whenever the opposition ventured to discuss matters of foreign policy which it believed were of general concern

[148] S. T., II, 394.
[149] St. P. Domestic, 16/346:20.
[150] S. T., III, 1078.

to all Englishmen. The royalists even maintained that though parliament granted money, the spending of such money was a private prerogative of the king. When in 1614 St. John protested against the illegality of a benevolence asked by the king, Ellesmere was shocked at such boldness on the part of a mere subject and wrote: "Herein he showeth his ignorance, his pryde, and presumption, viz That he would be of the K[in]gs pryvie Counsell and would have all the Comons to be also. Which is to turne a monarchie into Democracie." [151]

The inconsistency and uncertainty of the royalist position is revealed in statements like this. On the one hand, they claimed that the absolute power existed for the general public welfare and, on the other, that the king must not be questioned or criticised in the exercise of it, because such power was mysterious, fit only for the king or a select chosen few to understand. The need for a well-defined public-welfare power existed because of the integrated state England had become, but many of the important subjects in that state would accept such a power only if they shared in its exercise—certainly not if they were told that, although such power was necessary for the general welfare, all questions concerning its use must be left to the king, and that its secrets were not to be revealed to the public.

In the second place, it was a political blunder for the royalists to make so much of the emergency power of the king. In their studied concern to rest their case on law they found that his emergency power served their purpose well, for by it, so they contended, the king could justifiably in any emergency take money from his subjects and imprison them without due process of law. If the royalists had used this great power only for emergencies, there could have been little sound opposition to such use; but since they employed what was essentially an emergency power for the ordinary routine of government, they aroused great fears in their parliamentary opponents that legal absolutism would be permanently established in England.

[151] Ellsmere MSS., El., 454, "A matter conserning Seynt John." Hunt Lib. For the case of Oliver St. John in star chamber in 1615, see S. T., II, 899 ff.

When, therefore, those opponents gained the upper hand in the Long Parliament, they were not satisfied to stop this abuse of kingly power, but went on to deprive the king of most of his prerogative powers and institutions of government which had been built up since the accession of Henry VII. In their fear that the emergency power might again be used as it had been between 1630 and 1640 on behalf of kingly absolutism, they reduced the king's power to extremely limited proportions.

It was also, in the third place, politically unwise for the royalists to talk so much about the great powers with which the king was trusted. Although this argument was strong legally, it was weak politically. The actions of James, and particularly of Charles, even in those realms like foreign affairs still accepted as within the king's absolute power, did not inspire confidence. On the contrary, they aroused profound distrust on the part of the parliamentary opposition of the monarch's qualifications for trusteeship in such realms. Leaders in the commons never lost completely their trust in James, but during the first four years of Charles's reign their distrust of Buckingham, his favorite minister, developed so rapidly that the reader of the parliamentary debates in 1628 feels that although leaders of the opposition still professed their faith in Charles, profound distrust was already present, coloring and influencing their thinking and policies. By 1640 that distrust had increased greatly and had become the single most important factor influencing their actions during the first year of the Long Parliament. In the last six months before the civil war broke out, the leaders of the opposition moved on to claim revolutionary powers for the two houses because they had lost all trust in their king. During these years of growing tension between them and him, the emphasis put by royalist councillors and judges on the great powers with which their monarch was trusted only served to remind the leaders of the opposition that the throne was occupied by Charles, whom they did not trust, and that their liberties and rights could never be safe as long as English law and the constitution allowed such great trust to the king. When Charles lost his head on the scaffold in 1649, he was, from one point of view, paying the supreme penalty for that great trust committed to the monarch and for the attempt made by his royalist councillors and judges to erect a legal absolutism upon the basis of that trust.

Again, a fourth argument used by the royalists to erect legal absolutism proved to be a political boomerang. Most Englishmen in the early seventeenth century attributed great and not too carefully defined powers to their king; but when Strafford spoke of the king's position as the keystone by which government was held together, the parliamentary leaders were not at all certain that such a king as Charles was a very stable keystone. They preferred to make the law and parliament the keystone of their government.

A fifth and last way in which the legal arguments used by the royalists exposed their political failures can be seen in connection with their claim that the king was part of the state. There was truly, as Doderidge had said, a political union between the king and his subjects; but James and Charles and their advisers were never able to achieve this union in reality. Instead, they used parliament for their own "party" purpose, not, as the Tudors had used it, to achieve by common action a community of interest between king and subject. Any talk, therefore, by the royalists that the king was part of the state could hardly fail to remind the parliamentary leaders that he actually was ignoring them who were also a part of the state, for he was refusing to work with them co-operatively in passing laws and in raising money to support the state.

In all of these ways, then, the success achieved by the royalists in their legal arguments was somewhat offset by the fact that the actual monarch whom they exalted, whom they trusted with so much, and whose authority formed the keystone of government, fell so far short of the ideal monarch they pictured England's king to be. The success they achieved legally also served to reveal, to those concerned with the subjects' rights, the legal flaws and inadequacies of the traditional law and constitution, and thereby encouraged (perhaps unconsciously) the parliamentary opponents of the royalists to grasp for greater political power for themselves as the only effective way to limit the king and maintain the rights and liberties of Englishmen.

Up to this point this chapter has been concerned with the general ideas of royalist judges and councillors who did so much to erect legal absolutism in England. Their ideas are important, not because they reflect a profound or original philosophy, but because the men advocating them were in high places, charged with the responsibility of government. Their views are important because the men holding them were important, and because for several decades they were able to achieve some success in administering government on the basis of their ideas of legal absolutism.

There were, however, some statements made which were more extreme and more significant in the history of political thought than any already presented, and these ideas must now be considered. Some few royalists tried to show that the English monarch might correctly take the property of his subjects. Although most royalist judges and councillors never denied that the subject possessed property and other rights, some of them who discussed the nature of monarchy argued in ways which really broke down the rights and property of the subject. Three illustrations of this more extreme point of view will be considered. The first occurs in Davies's treatise on impositions in which he wrote as follows:

> That the King doth not take the Land or Goods of any without his consent; but . . . there is a particular and expresse consent, and there is an implicit and general consent . . .[152]

> . . . when subjects who live under a Royall Monarchy, do submit themselves to the obedience of that Law of that Mon-

[152] Sir John Davies, p. 96.

archy, whatsoever the Law doth give to that Monarch, the subjects who take the benefit of the Law in other things, and doe live under the protection of the Law, doe agree to that which the Law gives by an implicit and general consent, and therefore there are many cases where the king doth lawfully take the goods of a Subject without his particular and expresse consent, though the same be not forfeited for any crime or contempt of the Owner.[153]

In time of war, for example, if the king take my house in order to build a fort, I implicitly consent "for that I being a member of the Common-weal cannot but consent to all Acts of necessity tending to the preservation of the Commonwealth." [154]

Archbishop Harsnett is a second royalist who so defined and treated the relation between the monarch's absolute power and the subjects' property that the monarch was really given all power and the subjects left little or no assurance of their property. Harsnett's interpretation occurs in his comments on the propositions drawn up by the lords in 1628: [155]

Fundamental propriety and fundamentall Libertye is conceived to bee that property and Libertye wch upon the first submission to a Monarchicall Government was allowed to the Subjects of this Kingdome. For this Kingdome beinge a Monarchie Royall and not Seigneuriall, and the relation beeinge between King and Subject; and not Lord and Slave: The Subjects are free Subjects, haveinge propertye and Libertye; and not Slaves or Villaines wch have neither. Yet the Subject hath his Propertye and Libertye, not Absolute but Subject-Like: that is soe longe as Hee liveth subject-like: Under and according to the Lawes. For Servire Legibus Libertas. But by transgressing the Lawe, the Subject, in Divers Cases, looseth and forfeiteth his Property to the Kinge, as by Outlawrie, Attainder, etc. And soe Hee forfeiteth both liberty and life, by like Capitall offences. For then Hee is out of the Lawe wch made Him a Proprietor. And therefore it may bee truly sayd of this Kingdome. Ad Regem Potestas omnium pertinet, ad Singulos Proprietas. And Omnia Rex Im-

153 *Ibid.*, pp. 96–7.
154 *Ibid.*, pp. 97–8.
155 St. P. Domestic, 16/102:14.

perio posidet, Singuli Domino, wch is the ground of all for-
feitures, & Eschetes to the Crowne.[156]

The third illustration of royalist theorizing about monarchy
in a way which extended the monarch's power into the realm
of the subjects' property comes from a speech of Judge Berkeley
in the ship-money case. He spoke as follows:

A fundamental policy of our laws . . . is this, That the
King of mere right ought to have, and the people of mere
duty are bound to yield unto the king, supply for the defence of the kingdom. And when the parliament itself doth
grant supply in that case, it is not merely a benevolence of
the people, but therein they do an act of justice and duty to
the king.[157]

Statements like the foregoing by Berkeley, Harsnett, and
Davies make clear the dangers inherent in the royalist interpretation of monarchy, for if these statements should ever
become the established royalist position, it would mean that
any government run on that model would not be limited by
the property rights of the subject. With that bulwark of his
liberty gone, absolutism completely sanctioned by law and not
limited in any way could easily come into existence.

There was also great danger inherent in the royalist view
that allegiance was owed to the person of the king by natural
law. The nature of the issue and of the arguments employed
in the case of the post nati focussed attention upon the person
of the king and natural allegiance to him as a person. Several
of the judges taking part in that case, including Ellesmere and
Coke, talked of the natural allegiance due the king, but it was
Bacon who presented the most complete and theoretical argument on that basis. He pointed out that the king possessed
both legal and natural authority, but insisted that the natural
came first and was never obliterated by later laws.[158] Relying
on political thought to strengthen his argument, he philoso-

[156] *Ibid.*
[157] S. T., III, 1099.
[158] S. T., II, pp. 578 ff.

phized as follows: "It is evident that all other commonwealths, monarchies only excepted, do subsist by a law of precedent." [159] In monarchies "especially hereditary . . . the submission is more natural and simple, which afterwards by subsequent laws is perfected and made more formal; but that is grounded upon nature." [160] In discussing the particular nature of the English government, he admitted that laws and parliaments were important, "yet nevertheless there is but one and the self-same fountain of sovereign power depending upon the ancient submission." [161]

This concept of allegiance due the person of the king was used by Nethersole, one of the most extreme royalists, in his defense of the king in the parliament of 1628. What shall a king do, Nethersole asked, if the people refuse to support him? [162] His answer was: "A kinge must use sutch wayes as hee can. Every man hath a naturall obligation towards his owne life and goods, and the same hath a kinge to his kingdome which cannot bee abrogated no more by law then the other by nature." [163] Again in the arguments in ship money, Banks, the attorney general, talked of natural allegiance due the person of the king, calling this absolute power *ius summae majestatis* and saying that it was "innate in the person of an absolute king, and in the persons of the kings of England. That this power is so inherent in the king's person, it is not any ways derived from the people but reserved unto the king, when positive laws first began." [164] "All magistracy it is of nature, and

[159] S. T., II, 578.
[160] *Ibid.*
[161] *Ibid.*, p. 600. In 1614, the Bishop of Lincoln said that the lords should not confer with the commons concerning impositions "ffor it is a *Noli me tangere;* and none that have ether taken the othe of Supremacye or Allegeance may doe it wth a good conscience for in the othe of Alegiance we are sworne to maintayne the priviledges of the crowne." Hastings Parliamentary Papers, A booke of remembrance . . . May 21, 1614.
[162] Bor., 3/26/28.
[163] *Ibid.*
[164] S. T., III, 1017.

obedience, and subjection. It is of nature. And before any municipal law was, the people were governed by the law of nature, and practice did rule according to natural equity: this appeareth in the Reports of Sir Ed. Coke . . ." [165]

Such emphasis upon power innate in the king and upon natural allegiance due his person was obviously a threat to all law and custom which the subject believed the constitution provided for his security. A king possessing this innate power and claiming this natural allegiance could always, if he so desired, call upon it to override all else. It would have been perfectly consistent for Bacon or Banks to have made this concept the foundation and starting point of a theory of sovereignty in which all power in all realms rested ultimately in the person of the monarch. Neither of them, however, did work out such a complete and absolute theory.

One more extreme statement by a royalist lawyer must be considered. At one place in his treatise on impositions Davies wrote as follows:

> By the Law of Nature all things were comon and all persons equal, there was neither *Meum* nor *Tuum*, there was neither King nor Subject; then came in the Law of Nations, which did limit the Law of Nature, and brought in property, which brought in community of things, which brought in Kings and Rulers, . . . and all these things, namely Property, and Contract, and Kings, and Customes, were before any positive Law was made; then came the Positive Law, and limited the Law of Nations; whereas by the Law of Nations the King had an absolute and unlimited power in all matters whatsoever. By the positive Law the King himself was pleased to limit and stint his absolute power, and to tye himself to the ordinary rules of the Law, in common and ordinary cases, worthily and princely, according to the Roman Emperour, *Dignissimum Principe Rex se allegatum legibus confiteri*, retaining and reserving notwithstanding in many points that absolute and unlimited power which was given unto him by the Law of Nations . . .[166]

[165] *Ibid.*, 1019.
[166] Sir John Davies, pp. 29–30.

Davies's statement that "by the positive Law the King himself was pleased to limit and stint his absolute power" really means that all limitations upon the king were voluntary. Had Davies followed up this statement with a theoretical discussion of sovereign power, he might have been the first important royalist in this period to have developed a theory of absolute sovereignty for the king in all realms, but Davies failed to use and work out the implications of this important statement. Like other leading royalist lawyers and councillors, who talked of absolute power and sometimes exalted it more than the law had ever exalted it before, he too stopped short of the concept of sovereignty.

So did Bacon, the most theoretically minded of all royalist judges and councillors. Since Bacon was more of a political philosopher than any other man considered in this chapter, his ideas should be viewed as a whole before the chapter is concluded. Bacon's constitutional and political thinking is perplexing to the modern reader, for his ideas do not on the surface always seem consistent. At one time he eulogized the law and parliament; at another, the king and his divine authority. He spoke of the king's prerogatives as legal, and again as transcending the law. These different emphases do not, in my opinion, mean that Bacon moved from one concept to another as fancy suited him or the situation of the moment required. Essentially he believed in the constitutional ideas presented in the first part of this book—in a king having great authority, in subjects possessing rights, and in law moulding the body politic together and adjusting and balancing its separate component parts. To him parliament was a necessary institution to be used to bring the king and subject together in love and harmony in order that together they might work constructively to perfect their body politic. Had the actual body politic functioned as smoothly and harmoniously as Bacon philosophically believed it should, he might never have expressed other views than these on constitutional and political questions. Bacon, however, possessed a flexible mind. If harmony could not be achieved at the normal level of the law and constitution, he would move upward to a higher level. To ascend higher, it was both legal and natural to follow the way of prerogative, for the law ascribed great and extensive prerogatives to the king and did not define or limit them too closely in the sphere of government. In fact, the prerogative was but "the perfection of the law." Moreover, the king's great prerogatives came not only from the law but from God. Since they were reflections of divine law, they might be a mystery beyond most human comprehension; and since they might lie outside the range of ordinary law, they might transcend its human limitations and frailties; but, by their very nature, they could not, if properly understood, really overthrow or truly contradict the law of the land. These exalted prerogatives, resting on law and yet transcending it, enabled the king to provide for the general welfare of all, and to achieve at the higher level of the prerogative the unity and harmony of the body politic in which Bacon believed almost passionately.

His facile ability to see all operating together in harmony might be interpreted in the twentieth century as the mental gymnastics of an opportunist shifting his ground with every new situation. Bacon, however, lived in the early seventeenth century when the medieval ideal of the ultimate harmony of all laws, from divine to human, remained as a heritage from the past, and when the new discoveries in science opening up before men's minds seemed to many, understanding and accepting them, only a further revelation of new and wider harmonies in God's universe. If again we marvel that Bacon could find an exalted place for James I in this hierarchy of law and order, we might with proper humility note the contrast between the noblest expressions of our own democratic faith today and the actions at times of our chosen representatives in Congress.

Bacon's ideas were essentially those of his own age and must be interpreted in that frame of reference. If some few of his many statements on the king's prerogative sound like sovereignty, we can not correctly isolate them and draw conclusions from them alone. On the contrary, such statements must be interpreted in relation to all his constitutional and political thinking. From that point of view, the evidence indicates that Bacon never really grasped the concept of sovereignty and certainly did not make it a basis of his thought. His contribution to constitutional and political thought in these years of controversy lay in furnishing and developing ideas concerning the prerogative which the royalists used to justify the legal absolutism they tried so hard to establish in England.

Some of the royalist clergy were bolder, more extreme, and also more profound in their political thinking than any councillor or judge prior to the civil war. At least two of them definitely grasped the concept of sovereignty. Their ideas, in relation to the great constitutional and political controversies going on in England in the first forty years of the seventeenth century, will be the subject of the next chapter.

CHAPTER V

ROYALIST CLERGY EXALT
THE DIVINE RIGHT OF
THE KING

During the reigns of the first two Stuarts an important group of the clergy supported the royalist cause, and a considerable number of them played an active and vital part in setting forth doctrines of monarchical power more significant in the general history of political thought than the ideas of royalist councillors and lawyers.

In view of the history of the previous century, it was perfectly natural for the English clergy to support the king. For almost seventy years before James ascended the English throne, the clergy had known and accepted the king as supreme head (or governor) on earth of the church in England. Under the leadership of the monarch all ties with Rome had twice been broken, and an Anglican form of worship set up. Before Elizabeth died a truly national church existed in England. For a bishop or clergyman to accept the monarch's supremacy in both church and state had become the conventional traditional pattern to follow.

It was also the path which many clergy, sincerely and actively interested in reconstructing and perfecting the Anglican church, quite naturally followed. Leaders in the church in the early seventeenth century, who wished not only to retain bishops but to emphasize their divine authority, and who desired not only to preserve the form of service in the Prayer Book but to emphasize and strengthen the Catholic tradition within it, looked to James and Charles, rather than to parliament, to find support for their ideas. As parliaments slowly but steadily became more Puritan in their policies and personnel, the Anglican clergy who were not Puritans looked more and more to the king to support their views; while reciprocally the king, angered by parliament's persistent refusal to grant him money and its encroachment upon his kingly government, defended and favored the non-Puritan clergy within the church. From a theological point of view also, clergy who were beginning to find some Calvinist doctrines too strict and dogmatic, and were attracted by Arminian views of free will, could turn only to the king for support for this more liberal theology. On good and valid grounds, therefore, great numbers of Anglican clergy sided with the king, and not with parliament, as the issue between the two sharpened.

Their support of the king and his claims did not mean that the monopoly of holiness had passed to the Puritans. Puritan preachers were zealous for God and goodness and aroused against the devil and sin, but so were many Anglican divines. Like the zealous Puritan, many an Anglican preacher attacked vigorously the evils of individuals and of society, often displaying in his treatment of human beings a sympathetic and keen understanding of profound psychological and spiritual problems and values.

To state these grounds and reasons naturally leading many clergy to side with the king does not deny that preferment in the church lay in the king's hands, nor that clergy who spoke or wrote well in support of the king received lucrative positions. There was much bitter truth in the contemporary remark that the Arminians "held all the best bishoprics and deaneries in the kingdom." [1] James's and particularly Charles's appointment to high places of clergy who held and expressed royalist views of kingship did much to intensify and sharpen the Puritan opposition to bishops, and eventually to kings.

These Stuart monarchs not only favored the Anglican clergy

[1] J. Hunt, *Religious Thought in England,* 3 vols., (Strahan, London, 1870–73), I, 148 as cited by J. R. Tanner, *English Constitutional Conflicts of the Seventeenth Century,* (Cambridge University Press, Cambridge, 1928), p. 13.

who exalted kings, but expected them to assist their rulers and benefactors when they needed help.[2] From the point of view of ideas, James needed no help, for he had already as King of Scotland set forth a complete theory of the divine right of kings [3]—a theory more comprehensive and more extreme than most of his clerical supporters ever enunciated. Shortly after James became King of England, he entered actively into the great battle of books going on at that time in western Europe between the champions of the claims of the church and the exponents of the state's supremacy. James entered the lists on behalf of the state against Bellarmine and other Jesuit writers who were setting forth with clarity and vigor the pope's right, as head of the church, to use all means, including the temporal weapons of deposition and regicide, in order to attain the ultimate spiritual purpose of the church. James as a writer achieved a European reputation by his defense of the complete independence of kings from papal control or interference, and by his justification for the oath of allegiance imposed upon all Catholics in England in 1606.[4] In this task his "literary assistants" were the bishops and other clergy, who, as Professor D. H. Willson has recently shown,[5] helped him with his own writings, making corrections and translations of them, and also contributed, often at James's suggestion, substantial works of their own on behalf of the independence of temporal rulers from papal jurisdiction. One of the books written in this way, *God and the King,* ascribed to Richard Mocket, "was a textbook for the instruction of youth, and James commanded its

[2] D. H. Willson, "James I and His Literary Assistants," *Huntington Library Quarterly* VIII, (1944), pp. 35–57.

[3] "James's whole political theory appears full-blown in *The Trew Law of Free Monarchies,* written in 1598, five years before he succeeded to the throne of England . . ." C. H. McIlwain, *The Political Works of James I,* (Harvard University Press, Cambridge, Mass., 1918), Introduction, p. XXXVII.

[4] On this whole subject, see C. H. McIlwain, *The Political Works of James I,* Introduction; and J. N. Figgis, *The Divine Right of Kings,* (Cambridge University Press, Cambridge, 1922).

[5] D. H. Willson, "James I and His Literary Assistants."

use in all schools and universities and by all ministers of the church." [6]

The clergy were useful assistants to the king and the cause of monarchy in other ways also. As early as 1615, Bishop Andrews of Winchester said in a council discussion concerning the summoning of parliament "that he thought it a very good preparation that the people might be instructed and taught that relief to their Sovereign in necessity was *jure divino,* and no less due than their allegiance and service." [7] Godfrey Davies [8] has shown us how the government came to use the church for official purposes. Particularly, "sermons in London were of special importance, and were often made the occasion for an announcement, or a pronouncement, of policy." [9] The sermon of James Usher at the opening of the 1621 parliament, of Isaac Bargrave before the 1624 parliament, and of Bishop Laud in 1628 [10] might well have been inspired by the government, so strongly did each preach the value and need of unity in church and state.

From the beginning of his reign Charles, like his father, looked to the clergy to support and strengthen the throne. Above all he wanted financial assistance, for by 1625 the financial needs of the government were exceedingly acute. Due to rising prices, foreign wars, and meager parliamentary grants, the money in the treasury was hardly adequate to meet the day-by-day running expenses of the government. Forced loans were now resorted to on a larger scale than before. To secure the necessary response from people for these loans, and also to arouse in parliament a sense of the pressing financial needs of the government, the privy council turned for help to the clergy. In royal instructions to all the bishops, which the two archbishops were asked to deliver, the council frankly admitted that

[6] *Ibid.,* p. 54.

[7] Spedding. V, 202.

[8] "English Political Sermons, 1603–1640," *Huntington Library Quarterly* III (1939), pp. 1–23.

[9] *Ibid.,* p. 8.

[10] See pages 196 and 198.

the state, being "pressed beyond her strength," was calling for assistance upon the church, so closely "united and knit" to the state.[11] It was, the government claimed, the duty of the church, which in the past had so often been helped by the state, to come now to its assistance. The clergy were instructed to plead for unity and to point out that Charles's needs must be relieved. They were asked to preach that when people refused him financial support for foreign affairs and war desired by parliament, such action was "Sinne, because ayde and supply for the defence of the Kingdome, and the like affaires of State, especially such as are advised and assumed by Parliamentary Counsell, are due to the King from his People, by all Law both of God and men." [12] Some of the leading clergy did respond to this appeal, and in the next few years spoke out more openly and more boldly on behalf of the king's great power within England than they had done before. In the years between 1630 and 1640 many clergy continued to support the king in their sermons and writings, and until 1636, when Henry Burton denounced the bishops, the government seems to have succeeded quite well in maintaining its censorship against books and sermons coming from the parliamentary or Puritan opposition.[13]

In the realm of ideas, the Anglican clergy made significant contributions to the royalist cause. As royalist councillors and lawyers gave the crown its strongest support in the realm of legal and constitutional ideas, so royalist clergy provided the strongest support in the realm of theological and political ideas. Because they attempted to base the claims of monarchy on law, the king's councillors and judges proved to be the most dangerous enemies the parliamentary opposition faced; but in the realm of ideas, their arguments were not particularly

[11] *Instructions directed from the Kings Most Excellent Majestie, unto all the Bishops of this Kingdom* . . . , (London, 1626), p. A2r-v. These instructions are discussed by G. Davies, "English Political Sermons," pp. 14–17.

[12] *Instructions, op. cit.,* p. A3.

[13] This remark is based upon my own research and the opinion of G. Davies, "English Political Sermons," p. 19.

original, or penetrating in their theoretical implications. On the other hand, the more extreme and profound ideas of the royalist clergy never came so close to practical success as the ideas of judges and councillors; and consequently, although they were attacked and denounced by the parliamentary opposition, they were never feared in the same degree. From the point of view of political thought, however, the contribution made by the clergy was more original and profound than that made by councillors and judges.

Royalist lawyers and councillors had linked the cause of absolutism to law, bolstering and sanctifying it by all the support which the law afforded. The royalist clergy went higher than law for support for the king's power, position, and claims. They linked his cause with God's—with His purpose and plan for the world, with His commands as revealed in Scripture, and with His omnipotence and will. God was the foundation upon which many aspects of clerical thought rested. It was God who ordained kings and who decreed that they should not be resisted but obeyed—two of the most common notes sounded by the clergy.

There was good reason why these ideas should be proclaimed in England. The belief that the king's power came immediately from God had a goodly medieval heritage which had served the Tudors well. Most Englishmen, including members of the parliamentary opposition and leading Puritan clergy, agreed in the early decades of the seventeenth century that kings were ordained by God. Most of them also agreed that the king should not be resisted. Here the medieval precedents were less certain, but the belief in non-resistance had become common in England in the sixteenth century, for the Tudors in strengthening the state had exalted the king above all subjects, and in breaking from Rome had made the monarch head of the church immediately under God. The "new monarchy" of Henry VIII had been fashioned by secular hands, but justified and explained to the people, not by secular Machiavellis, but by clerical pamphleteers. They, drawing upon the medieval concept that ruling power came directly from God to the king without any mediation of pope or priest, had demonstrated that the king's actions were in accord with God's will and plan, and that the monarch, being God's agent on earth, acting in His place, must not be resisted.[14] The international situation during the reign of Elizabeth had given added support to such views. Each crisis brought out more clearly that resistance to her meant civil dissension, foreign war, and possible conquest, whereas obedience afforded the best guarantee of that order and security which was desired and regarded as an ideal. By the time that the Stuarts came to the throne, these beliefs had become firmly established without the help of James and his divine-right theory. At this time Englishmen were divided on many issues, but not on the supremacy of God in human affairs. They believed that man was ruled by God who had decreed, as the Scriptures demonstrated in so many places, that kings should rule on earth. Belief in a divine right of kings meant belief in God.

It was also associated with national pride in their country, for divine right meant that the king of England received his authority immediately from God, and not from any temporal or spiritual power on earth. He as their king was exalted, but so were they as Englishmen. With the independence of the government from any foreign authority which had been achieved in the sixteenth century had come more unity and greater international importance for their country. Englishmen were naturally proud of the divine right of their ruler, for in his greatness they and their country shared.

Moreover, there were many events and circumstances in the first quarter of the seventeenth century working to keep these beliefs alive and strong. A reformed and militant Catholic church had turned the tide against the first Protestant successes

[14] See F. V. Baumer, *The Early Tudor Theory of Kingship*, (Yale University Press, New Haven, 1940).

and was bringing back into the fold some of the territories and lands earlier lost. Austria and Spain were still aggressive and still winning victories for Catholicism. An impartial observer, taking stock of the situation at any time in the first three decades of the century, might well look to England, as the Puritans did, as the last strong defense of Protestantism. Nor were men too sure that England was really secure. Gun Powder plot aroused great fears of Catholic plotting and internal dissension. God had intervened, so men said, to prevent Guy Fawkes from destroying king and parliament in 1605, but God might not always choose to save England. After all, a Jesuit had succeeded in murdering Henry IV of France in 1610.

English kings and subjects might well look to God for help against Catholics within and without the country, for these men were claiming that the spiritual power must exercise an indirect jurisdiction over all temporal power in order that it might obtain its spiritual end. James and many of his clerical supporters in England answered this argument, as imperialists had done since the time of Dante, by asserting and demonstrating that the power of earthly kings came directly and immediately from God. According to the canons agreed upon by the clergy in 1606, God had ordained that man should be ruled first by Adam and then by succeeding fathers, which kind of patriarchal power "was in a sort *potestas regia.*" [15] After due time true kings were set up by God to rule His people, and such kings and all later monarchs received their authority directly from God. Moreover, such kingly power was supreme over the priestly. Aaron was subordinate to Moses, Christ to the Roman government, the early Christians to pagan emperors. Any temporal power ever exercised by popes was a usurpation in oppo-

[15]*Convocation Book of 1606, commonly called Bishop Overall's Convocation Book,* (Oxford, 1844), p. 3. These canons were not put into effect. Concerning the patriarchal origin of kingly power, Roger Manwaring wrote that "Adam had *Dominion* settled in him, before there was either *pope,* or People." *Religion and Alegiance: In Two Sermons Preached before the Kings Majestie . . . 1627,* (London, 1627), p. 13. Manwaring's political ideas are discussed in some detail at the end of this chapter.

sition to God's plainly revealed truth that kings held their power immediately and completely from God.[16]

A king whose power was so close to God, and so sanctioned by Him, possessed an immense advantage over any other kind of authority, and the proponents of such beliefs made telling and effective use of the advantage which was theirs. The cause of the king was God's cause, for kings were, John Buckeridge announced from the pulpit, "God's ministers serving for that purpose." [17] "Your Highness," John White wrote to James, "is more than an ordinarie man: God hath set his owne image, as it were upon his gold, in an eminent manner upon you, which he hath not done upon other men: your cause is Gods cause, your zeale and constancie is for Gods truth; they are Gods inheritance and peculiar people you defend, it is your right you stand for; and a blessed government you maintane." [18] "Of all the creatures of the Universe," Robert Sherwood wrote, "none draweth neerer to the Creator then man; neither any degree of men, so much as doth the King, whether wee consider his person or his Office. As the face of *Moses* descending the Mount from God, shone bright and glorious: so the Majesticke looke of a King (reflecting divine beames, received from the King of Kings) daunteth the most proud and savadge hearts of Inferiors. Therefore Kings are in holy Writ called *Lights,* for their glory; *Gods* for their power; and the *Lords annointed,* to testifie their graces, and the dignity of their Office." [19]

John Rawlinson talked of kings, using some of the same comparisons as Sherwood:

[16] *Convocation Book of 1606, Passim.*

[17] *A Sermon Preached at Hampton Court before the Kings Majestie . . . 1603,* (London, 1606), p. 3. Buckeridge became bishop of Rochester and Ely.

[18] John White, *A Defence of the Way to the True Church . . . ,* (London, 1624), Epistle Dedicatorie [to King James], sig. B1r. White, who had been at Caius College Cambridge, became chaplain in ordinary to James.

[19] John Bede, *The Right, and prerogative of Kings Against Cardinall Bellarmine and other Jesuites . . .* Translated by Robert Sherwood, (London, 1612), Introductory letter to James, A2v. Sherwood was a lexicographer. According to the D. N. B., it is doubtful that it was he who translated Bede.

The excellency of Princely dignity shines in the *very face* and countenance of a King. For there is a *Character tremendus in vultibus Regum*: An impression or character of dreadfull Majestie stampt in the very visage of a King . . . it is said of *Moses*, Exod. 34: that after *his conference with God, the skin of his face shone so bright, that the people were afraid to come neare him.*[20]

Of all creatures on earth, the king was closest to God. "All Governours . . . are Gods Pictures." Subordinate magistrates are "half pictures," but "Kings are the Pictures of God at length, and represent him in such due proportions, that as *God is our invisible King,* so the *King* is our *visible God.*" These words were uttered by Henry Valentine in St. Paul's Church the 27th of March, 1639.[21]

Men proclaiming such a close identity between king and God believed that the king must partake of God's supernatural power and receive His grace in order to maintain government upon earth. To them, only God could rule the turbulent spirits of men, and God had chosen to have kings rule in His stead on earth. To enable them to rule in His place He bestowed a full measure of grace upon them.[22] God gave kings "wisdome, fortitude, knowledge, vivacity of Spirit, goodness of nature," etc. above and beyond the common people.[23] God made the king

[20] John Rawlinson, *Vivat Rex. A Sermon Preached at Pauls Crosse on the day of his Majesties happie inauguration,* March 24, 1614 . . . , (Oxford, 1619), p. 9. Rawlinson was chaplain to Ellesmere, and chaplain in ordinary to James.

[21] Henry Valentine, *God Save the King* . . . , (London, 1639), pp. 5–6. Valentine was vicar of Deptford and at one time a lecturer at St. Dunstan's in the West.

[22] L. Andrews, *Works, Library of Anglo Catholic Theology,* (Oxford, 1841–1854), II, 20. Andrews said that the care of kings in looking after their people was "supernatural," for the ordinary man did not wish "to afflict and vex his soul with the care of others." Andrews was bishop of Winchester.

[23] Henry Peacham, *The Duty of all True Subjects to Their King: As also to their Native Country in time of extremity and danger,* (London, 1639), p. 6. Peacham was not a clergyman, but a writer, best known for his *Compleat Gentleman.*

the "guardian of Gods Law." [24] The King must obey this law, and, "as the child of God" and also as a "King annoynted of God, he must commaund it." [25] Kings were set up to do God's work on earth. They were ordained "Not to take their owne ease and pleasure, but to governe others; Waking when others sleepe, and taking care, that all men else may live without care." [26] A king's "owne pillow must be stuffe with *thistles* that he may stuffe the pillowes of his people with downe." [27] Had all kings proved worthy of the high calling and divine responsibility assigned them by some royalist clergy, they would truly have been Gods on earth.

In exalting a king, these clergy did not proclaim that a king wielded irresponsible power. On the contrary, they asserted his responsibility to God, who had ordained him and in whose stead he was ruling, and his duty to the subjects whom God had put in his charge. Anglican as well as Puritan preachers reminded a king that God would hold him responsible for the manner in which he discharged his task. God was more exalted and more searching in His judgment than any human tribunal, and He was more demanding of a king than of other mortals, for He had bestowed special blessings and favors upon him to enable him to rule as God should rule upon this earth. The royalist clergy in England did not advocate a theory of government devoid of responsibility.

The difficulty lay in the fact that kings were men who fell short of their divine mission. In that contingency only God could deal with them, for no monarch was to be resisted by man.

> Let him rage, kill, Massacre, hee is but a storme, sent of God to chastise his children, . . . we may not *conspire* against them; our *hands bound,* we may not so much as *lift up* our little finger against them.[28]

[24] John Buckeridge, *op. cit.,* p. 20.
[25] Arthur Lake, *Ten Sermons,* (London, 1641), p. 131. Lake was bishop of Bath and Wells.
[26] John Buckeridge, *op. cit.,* p. 4.   [27] John Rawlinson, *op. cit.,* p. 16.
[28] William Goodwin, *A Sermon Preached before the Kings Most Excel-*

If we break into tumult and disorder, we resemble those Giants of whom the Poets write; who making offer to scale the skies, and to put Jupiter out of his throne, were overwhelmed in a moment with the mountaines which they had heaped together.[29]

Royalist preachers spared no pains to condemn resistance to kings. During the reign of James they denounced Roman Catholics and the doctrine proclaimed by some of them that resistance to temporal rulers was sometimes necessary in order to glorify God and attain His purpose in the world. One of these preachers, Robert Tynley, asked his congregation:

But who seeth not, . . . that this Religion falsely termed *Catholike,* utterly perventeth the lawful subjection of people to their Sovereignes, and that Hell is not more opposite to Heaven, then the bearing of armes by the subject against his Prince, . . . to depose Kings, to dispose of their dominions, to take the Crowne from one, and give it to another, as men tosse a tenice ball in the Court, from *Henrie* to *Rodulph,* and so along; to assoile subjects of their fidelitie; these and such like, which are after the decrees of later Popes, overthrow the very foundations of Kingdomes and Commonweales.[30]

The Roman Catholics and their doctrine of rebellion were favorite targets at which royalist preachers aimed during most of James's reign, but Brownist and other extreme groups with like beliefs were condemned also. John White said that Ana-

lent Majestie at Woodstocke, Aug. 28, 1614, (Oxford, 1614), pp. 23–24. Goodwin was vice-chancellor of the University of Oxford and a chaplain to James.

[29] John Hayward, *An Answer to the First Part of a certaine conference, concerning succession, published not long since under the name of R. Dolman,* (London, 1603), N3v. Hayward was a laymen, not a clergyman. His ideas are discussed by W. K. Jordan, *The Development of Religious Toleration in England,* 4 vols., (Harvard University Press, Cambridge, Mass., 1932–1940) II, 473–75.

[30] *Two Learned Sermons, . . . Preached, the one . . . the 5 of Nov, 1608. The other . . . the 17 of Aprill, 1609 . . . ,* (London, 1609), pp. 19–20. Tynley was Archdeacon of Ely in 1609.

baptists, and "such as are enemies to Monarchie, and all con-
spirators, Assasines, rebelles, and turbulent persons, are beasts,
and enemies to God's ordinance and to nature." [31] Joseph Hall,
more moderate in his language but more searching in his
thought, went straight to the heart of the Brownist contention
that resistance to earthly kings might sometimes be necessary
in order to obey God and conscience and that men advocating
non-resistance were disloyal to God. To this argument Hall
replied, "While you accuse our loyaltie to an earthly King, as
treasonable to the King of the Church, Christ Jesus: If our
loyaltie bee a sinne, where is yours? If we be traytors in our
obedience; what doe you make of him that commands it?
Whether you would have us each man to play the *Rex,* and
erect a new governement, or whether you accuse us as rebels
to Christ in obeying the old: God blesse King *James* from such
subjects." [32]

During the reign of Charles, Isaac Bargrave, chaplain to the
king and dean of Canterbury, spoke out vigorously against
rebellion. Rebellion, Bargrave said, preaching before Charles,
March 27, 1627, "causeth all sinne in generall, and is as great
as the foulest sinnes in *particular,* even as witchcraft and Idolatry." [33] "No men hath learn'd to disobey his *King,* but he had
learn'd before to disobey his God." [34] Henry Valentine believed
that too many people had come to advocate rebellion. Preaching before the king in 1639, he denounced the Jesuits who had
advocated rebellion and added significantly: "And I would
to God this was the doctrine of the *Jesuites* only, for we know
the men, and we know their communication, but this leaven

[31] *Two Sermons; The Former Delivered at Pauls Crosse . . . March 24,
1615, . . . The Latter at the Spittle . . . in Easter weeke, 1613 . . . ,*
(London, 1615), p. 19.
[32] J. H. [i.e. Joseph Hall], *A Common Apologie of the church of England: Against the unjust Challenges of the over-just Sect, commonly called
Brownists . . . ,* (London, 1610), p. 85. Hall was bishop of Norwich.
[33] *Sermon preached before King Charles March 27, 1627,* (London, 1627),
p. 6. Text 1 Sam. 15. 23—"Rebellion is as the sinne of Witchcraft, and
stubborness as the wickedness of Idolatry."   [34] *Ibid.,* p. 20.

hath spread further, and even soured them that take upon them to be reformers of the reformed Churches." [35]

To disobey and rebel was to sin, whereas to obey and submit was to be pleasing in God's sight. Submission, John Dunster said in a sermon at St. Marie's Oxford, "is *proper to man,* not *instituted by man;* for it hath its beginning from God." [36] We must obey for the Lord's sake. Christ himself lost his life "that he might not loose his obedience," [37] and in the early church the Christians submitted even to pagan rulers.

In enjoining obedience, in condemning rebellion, in comparing kings to God, and in asserting that kings received their authority directly from God, royalist preachers relied primarily upon the Scriptures and Christian tradition and theology, and thereby linked the cause of kings with God's plan and command for mankind. To many Englishmen such arguments were the most weighty of all, compelling enough to lead them to cast their lot with the king in the fateful summer of 1642. The romantic picture of gay cavaliers fighting for king and country and the pleasures of this earth against sober Puritans fighting for God and the establishing of His heavenly kingdom on earth contains a little truth, but perverts more. Many Puritans fought for property and political power, as well as for God, and many royalists supporting the king truly believed they were defending God's cause and his word against men who had committed the awful sin of rebellion against their king and their God.

Some preachers and writers more philosophically minded also believed that in supporting and defending the king they were acting in harmony with the order so necessary in the affairs of man and in the universe at large. To Englishmen in the early seventeenth century "The universe was a unity, in which everything had its place, and it was the perfect work of

[35] H. Valentine, *op. cit.,* p. 26. Valentine mentions Mariana and Buchanan by name (p. 26), but does not name any contemporary Puritan.
[36] John Dunster, *Caesar's Penny or A Sermon of Obedience . . . ,* (Oxford, 1610), p. 3. Dunster became chaplain to archbishop Abbot.
[37] *Ibid.,* p. 8.

God. Any imperfection was the work not of God but of man," [38] and man's part lay in working with and not against the divine harmony in earth and in heaven. "Take away Kynges, Princes, Rulers, Magistrates, Judges, and suche states of God's ordre, no man shall ride or go by the high way un-robbed, . . . and there must nedes folowe all mischief and utter destruccion, bothe of soules, bodies, goodes, and common wealthes." [39] So ran the *Exhortation concerning good Ordre and Obedience to Rulers and Magistrates* in the book of Homi-lies published in 1547, and so ran the advice and warning sounded from pulpit and press by royalist divines in the first half of the seventeenth century. "Order is the good of every creature: with whome it is better not to be, then to be out of order. . . ." [40] Wicked kings "may be the cause of many dis-orders," but for man to depose them "must needes bee the Mother of perpetuall confusion." [41] Princes occupy a key place in human society and also in God's vast universe. They are "the precedents of God in respect of universall power and generall obedience." [42] "Every Prince in his kingdome, being the helme by which the whole body is moved and inforced to move as hee is moved." [43] "Monarckie is like the pole of the world, where all the meridians meet, and cannot be dislocated in the person vested therewith, but universall perturbations must follow." [44] "God hath set apart your Majestie," Joseph

[38] E. M. W. Tillyard, *Shakespeares History Plays*, p. 11, published by The Macmillan Company New York (copyright 1946) and used with their permission.

[39] As quoted by E. M. W. Tillyard, *op. cit.*, p. 19. Used with the permission of The Macmillan Company. The homilies were reprinted in 1635.

[40] John Buckeridge, *op. cit.*, p. 2.   [41] William Goodwin, *op. cit.*, p. 25.

[42] [Christopher Lever], *Heaven and Earth, Religion and Policy*. Written by C. L. . . . , (London, 1608), p. 57. Lever took orders, but did not secure a living in the church. He wrote both prose and poetry.

[43] *Ibid.*, pp. 56–57.

[44] *Nero Caesar or Monarchie depraved an Historical work dedicated to the D. of Buckingham* . . . By the Translatour of L. Florus (London, 1627), p. 287. This tract is attributed to Edmund Bolton or Boulton by the Huntington Library. Bolton was an antiquarian, an historian, a poet, and a Roman Catholic.

Hall wrote to James, "as a glorious instrument of such an universall good to the whole Christian world: . . . the burden of the whole world lies on the shoulders of soveraigne authority." [45]

Not only kings but all magistrates had their appointed place and ordained task in the universal scheme. In a sermon preached before Sir Henry Hobart and Sir R. Haughton, William Pemberton said:

> Sith the God of heaven and earth is the first mover, in his supreme orbe of government, all you his secondarie movers, in this your orbe of government, . . . ought to move after the will and ordination of God, and not . . . from your private affection, . . . You must in your motion run the same course, or use the same end with God himselfe; namely, the glory of God. . . . And such subordination will surely cause an heavenly harmony, and heart-pleasing consent, in a circular revolution thus. [46]

It was Francis Gray, a minister living at New Castle upon Tyne, who presented the most comprehensive discussion of the whole order in heaven and earth. Because the comparisons Gray made in a sermon preached in July, 1635, throw so much light on seventeenth century assumptions and attitudes, his remarks will be given at some length:

> Wee see God in the very first Creation of the World, observing order, and establishing a Superiority amongst his Creatures, willing *The greater Light to rule the Day, and the lesser to governe the Night.* And when hee comes to the Creation of Man, whom you may be pleased, as it were, to call the Master-piece of that his Divine Work-manship, [he gives] *him command over the Birds of the ayre, the Beasts of the field, and Fishes of the Sea.* . . . If we compare the body Politick to the body Celestiall, there wee find an Hyerarchy; the Apostle therefore speaks of *Principalities* and *Powers,*

[45] *A Recollection of such Treatises as have been heretofore severally published* . . . , (London, 1615), Dedication to James.

[46] *The Charge of God and the King To Judges and Magistrates for execution of Justice,* (London, 1619), Epistle Dedicatory to Bacon. Pemberton was rector at High Ongar in Essex.

Dominions and *Thrones;* mention wee find made of Cheru-
bins and Seraphins, Arch-angels and Angels: If to the body
Astronomicall, the same Apostle sheweth us, that *One Star
differeth from another in glory*: If to the body Ecclesiasticall,
you have the same Apostle affirming, *How that God hath
given to some to be Prophets, some Apostles, some Evangel-
ists, and some Pastours and Teachers*: If to the body Naturall, there wee see all the members of the body to be guided
by the governance of the head: If to a body Oeconomicall,
the Apostle sheweth us, and observation may teach us, that
as there be vessels of gold, and vessels of silver, so also, vessels of inferiour mettall: If to the body Military or Martiall,
if there were not Generalls, Captaines, and the like Officers
to command, as well as the common Souldier to obey, there
were but small hope of victory: If to an hive of Bees, there
this superiority is, *Ipsius naturae thesis,* the very instinct of
Nature hath taught them to acknowledge a King, *Et Rege
incolumi mens omnibus una.* If likewise we shall resemble
the Commonwealth to a Ship, the Orator could tell us, that
. . . some are ready to pumpe, some to sound the depth by
casting in of the plummet, and some also to sit at the stern.
If lastly, to an Instrument of Musicke, there we see the
sweetest harmony to arise from differing notes. Thus in the
Commonwealth, God will have an higher and a lower; some
to governe, and some to be governed; some to command,
and some to be commanded.[47]

The ideas set forth by Francis Gray in this passage dramatize
the way in which the royalist cause rested in part on basic ideas
Englishmen had long cherished. Few Englishmen could accept
the ideas of James in their entirety, but many would naturally
agree with those views of the royalist clergy which have been
presented up to this point. Moreover, many men who might
not follow or comprehend the involved legal arguments of
royalist judges and councillors in the Bate's case or in ship
money could listen to clergymen admonishing them from the
pulpit that God in His infinite wisdom had ordained kings to

[47] *The Judges Scripture . . . A Sermon Preached in St. Nicholas Church
of Newcastle upon Tyne, before the Judges, Justices, and Gentlemen of
the Towne and Countrey, at the Assizes holden there the three and
twentieth day of July, 1635 . . .* , (London, 1636), pp. 3–6.

rule them, and that for man to resist them was to defy God and
disturb the order of the whole universe. Men could easily understand and be swayed by sermons sounding such familiar
notes. By using these arguments the royalist clergy played a
significant role in strengthening the conservative basis of the
royalist position. If a man must ultimately choose between
king and parliament, the claims of a king who was part of
God's plan for the world, and who fitted into the divine order
and degree of the universe, must not be lightly dismissed.
"Take but degree away, untune that string, and hark what discord follows." The royalists would hardly have been able to
win, as they did, many men of moderate views to their side,
if their supporters had not presented such compelling arguments on behalf of kings.

The clergy, however, like the councillors and judges, did not
confine their appeal just to familiar conservative ideas. Some of
them turned to nature and natural law to justify kingly rule,
while others talked as if the king were the whole state—the
only binding cohesive force in human society. Here their
thinking was more original and more significant in the general
history of political thought, and here their views aroused more
opposition because they ran counter to the basic beliefs held
by so many Englishmen.

In turning to nature and natural law for support of kings,
royalist clergy showed that they were more than theologians—
that they were intellectual leaders in their own age. The seventeenth century was an era when thinkers desiring to achieve
intellectual stature could not talk only of God and theology,
but must discuss nature and natural law. On the basis of natural law many different and often conflicting political theories
were set forth in this century. By one interpretation of it, absolute monarchy was justified; by another, democracy; by one,
a contract theory of government in which the people transferred all their power; by another, one in which they maintained their fundamental rights. On the basis of natural law,
the foundations of international law were also laid. In line

with the all-pervading influence of natural law, royalist clergy in England turned to it to strengthen their arguments for kingly rule.

The clergy also argued from natural law in order to meet their adversaries on their own grounds. Catholic and Puritan opponents of the divine right of kings had discovered in the sixteenth century that, according to natural law, the consent of man played an important part in government. Consequently, the divine-right theorists found it particularly necessary to demonstrate that nature and natural law, if properly understood and interpreted, spoke unequivocally on behalf of kingly rule. As Professor Wormuth reminds us, "The naturalism of King James has been too much slighted. As prominent as references to divine authority in his writings are expressions like 'natural king,' 'natural allegiance,' 'natural obligation,' 'natural duty.' " [48]

Among James's clerical supporters also, such references and concepts were set forth. Overall's *Convocation Book,* agreed to by the clergy in 1606, referred to the Son of God "ordaining by the law of nature" that children should obey their parents, and mankind their rulers.[49] George Carleton, one of James's most staunch episcopal supporters and assistants, gave his interpretation of the law of nature in answer to "some of the Pope's flatterers" and "others also," who had "written that the power of government by the law of nature is in the multitude." [50] Such an interpretation, Carleton contended, is completely wrong. "Every man of reason carrieth this much light and understanding about him, as to judge this thing without errour. Because no man can conceive in the first beginning any other government of a family, then by one whom God and nature made *Patrem familiae,* the father of the familie. . . . And what is a King by nature, but the father of a great family? and what is

[48] F. D. Wormuth, *The Royal Prerogative 1603–1649,* (Cornell University Press, Ithaca, 1939), p. 88.
[49] *Op. cit.,* ch. 2, p. 2.
[50] *Jurisdiction Regall, Episcopall, Papall . . . ,* (London, 1610), p. 12. Carleton became bishop of Chichester.

the father of a familie by nature, but a little King? and therefore the first governement of states by the lawe of nature, was by Kings." [51]

John Rawlinson looked to nature and also to Aristotle as authorities for the excellence of princes. "And *Nature* herselfe (saith that *Chiefe Secretary* of Nature) hath made the *Physiognomy* of Princes to bee such, as strike's an awfull feare and reverence into as many as behold them." [52] The prince is naturally called the head of the body politic "because as the *Head* is the Prince of the Naturall body; so the *Prince* is the Head of the Politike body; being to it as the head to the rest of the members, the fountaine both of sense and motion." [53]

Kings, so royalist clergy asserted, existed by natural law, and obedience to them rested on natural law also. The "Duties of *fearing* God and King," Matthew Wren announced from the pulpit in 1627, "are charged upon us, not so much by any written Law, as by a Law within us also, by the Rule of Reason, and the Divine Law of Conscience . . ." [54] William Goodwin pointed out that the tie binding king and subject "exceeds al other Bonds, and cancels al other obligations." All obligations, as of a "Son unto his Father, a Wife unto her husband" are binding, "*Nature, Sense, Reason, Humanitie, Christianitie, Divinitie* binds them to Obedience, with a Bond which cannot bee broken: but the Bond of Allegiance to our KING containes them all, exceeds them al." [55] Calybute Downing, who championed the right of the civil state to supremacy over the ecclesiastical, wrote that "orderly subjection and superioritie proceed from the instinct of pure nature: for in Heaven there is order amongst the blessed Angels, and in the state of in-

[51] *Ibid.*, p. 12.
[52] John Rawlinson, *op. cit.*, p. 9. Rawlinson cites Aristotle in the margin.
[53] *Ibid.*
[54] *A Sermon preached before the Kings Majestie on Sunday Feb. 17,* (Cambridge, 1627), p. 34. Wren was master of St. Peter's Cambridge and chaplain to Charles.
[55] *Op. cit.*, pp. 22–23.

nocency there was superiority, not onely betwixt man and all other creatures, but also betwixt man and woman; and had they lived in Paradise till there had beene father and sonne, there should have been *Patria potestas* . . ." [56] Natural law was made the foundation of monarchical authority by Peter Heylyn, who gave a royalist answer to Burton's bold attack upon prelates in 1636. In answering Burton, Heylyn wrote that "the law of *Monarchie* is founded on the law of *nature,* not on *positive lawes*: and *positive lawes* I trowe are of no such efficacie, as to annihilate any thing which hath its being and originall, in the *law of nature.*" [57]

Arthur Lake also set forth an elaborate and involved argument on the importance for human welfare of the naturalness of a prince. Puritan preachers liked to point out that God had allowed the people of Israel to choose their king, but Lake gave his own interpretation of that point of view in this fashion:

In the Law God commanded the Israelites, *If they chuse a King, they shall chuse one of their owne brethren.* The reason why the Israelites resolved jointly to take David for their king, is because they were his bones and flesh: there must bee a naturall conjunction, where wee looke for a naturall affection. Grafts doe alter their stockes in nature; for sweet fruite graft into a sowre stocke doth not yeeld fruit answerable to the sowre juice which is naturall to the stocke. But it is not so in Policy: the Prince which is the stocke, will communicate the nature of his owne juyce unto his people, which are to him as grafts. Our Chronicles (to seeke no further) record wofull experience hereof in the sundry alterations in this state by Picts, and the Danes, the Saxons, and the French: yea although by counterfeit pedigrees they

---

[56] *A Discourse of the State Ecclesiasticall of this Kingdome, in relation to the Civill* . . . , (Oxford, 1632), p. 64. Downing later supported the cause of parliament, probably because he failed to win the preferment in the church which he deliberately sought. (See pages 347–48.)

[57] *A Brief and moderate Answer to the seditious and scandalous Challenges of Henry Burton,* (London, 1637), pp. 32–33. Heylyn, a disciple and supporter of Laud, wrote on both theological and historical subjects.

doe pretend themselves to be naturall, yet when occasion serves, they will betray themselves to bee unaturall.[58]

In this discourse on the importance of a natural tie between king and people, Lake may possibly have been arguing for divine hereditary right.[59] In the sermons I have read from this period, the majority of royalist clergy exalting the king's position do not stress the necessity of the strict hereditary right of a king,[60] but many of them would agree with Lake's emphasis on the value of a natural tie binding king and subject.

They liked to compare the king to a shepherd of his flock. Such a comparison implied that as sheep only constituted a flock when they had a shepherd, so a people only became a society when they possessed a king. Another meaningful comparison likened the king to a fountain. John White wrote to James: "Your Highnesse most happy government is the fountaine of our well-doing: when Princes maintain religion, and execute justice, punishing wicked men, and rewarding the godly, then they *come downe like raine upon the mowen grasse, and as showers that water the earth.*" [61] Henry Valentine said from the pulpit, "Kings were of old Crowned neare some Fountaine, because they are Fountaines and common blessings . . ." [62] William Dickinson compared the king in relation to the commonwealth to the foundation in relation to the whole house. All others than the king "are but parts of the frame raysed upon this foundation. Some are main crossebeames, some polished pilasters, others smaller Rafters: some are for use, some for ornament, some set up in places of honour, some of dishonour; all have their dependance more or

---

[58] *Op. cit.,* p. 110.

[59] Not clear from context.

[60] On this point, see C. H. McIlwain, *The Political Works of James I,* Introduction, pp. XXXIII and XXXVI.

[61] *A Defence of the Way to the True church . . . ,* (London, 1634), Epistle Dedicatory to James, B1r-v.

[62] *Op. cit.,* p. 18. To Henry Peacham "Every good Prince is another Orpheus, who by the well-tuned harmony of wholesome Lawes, Mercy, and his owne example, laboureth to draw unto him the whole body of his people." *op. cit.,* p. 1.

lesse: onely the *King* is the *Foundation;* and as it were the *Selfe-praexistence* and *axis* of the common-wealth, upon whose wel-being and good Lawes the whole state of things, and the good and ill of his Subjects and Cittizens relie." [63]

So important was the king for the commonwealth that in praying for him "wee pray for ourselves, our prayers returne unto our owne bosomes." [64] The people should pray for the king because of the *"Necessity* of it in reguard of themselves. *Vivat Rex, ut Vivat Regnum.* Let the King live, that his king- dome may live; for the Kings life is the life of the whole King- dome." [65] "A King then being *Totum populi,* the total summe (as I may say) of all the peoples welfare, good reason that *Totus populus,* not some, but *all* the people should jointly pray for His welfare." [66]

The king was said to be not only the foundation of the people's welfare, but the very "soule of the Commonwealth." There, as in the natural body, the soul gives life—"inanimates" the whole.[67] Without the soul there could be no real life in either the natural or the politic body. In the language of Dick- inson:

> . . . as in the body of man the soule is said to be at once in the whole and every part, the hand, the eye, the foot, every member receiveth its enablement and measure of working from the soule, . . . Even so it is in the *Republike,* the *King* is not limited, his power is diffused through the whole and every particular, and according to the instruments hee works by, so is his power denominated. In the *Chauncery* hee is called *Lord Chauncelor,* in other courts *Judge, Justice,* and so of the rest. . . . from him that rideth on the *Kings* horse unto the petty *Constable* the worker & moover is the

[63] William Dickinson, *The Kings Right, Briefly set downe in a Sermon preached before the Reverend Judges at the Assizes held in Reading, for the County of Berks, June 28, 1619,* (London, 1619), p. C.4v. Dickinson was a fellow of Merton at Oxford. His ideas are discussed more fully at the end of this chapter.

[64] Henry Valentine, *op. cit.,* p. 24.

[65] John Rawlinson, *op. cit.,* p. 28.

[66] *Ibid.,* p. 29.

[67] Henry Valentine, *op. cit.,* p. 17.

same, all are as it were animated & enabled in their places
and offices by one and the same Soule, *the King*.[68]

In making these fanciful comparisons, royalist preachers and
writers generally assumed that a king would rightly animate
his people as the soul permeated the whole body, that he
would rightly lead his people like a true shepherd, that justice
would flow from him as water from a fountain, and that he
would actually be a firm foundation upon which the whole
superstructure of the commonwealth might safely be built. The
possibility that a king might not always act as he should towards his people—that he might become a tyrant—was generally ignored.

A few writers, however, ventured to discuss tyranny. The
great value and virtue of monarchy, even when it was corrupt, was the theme of an interesting tract entitled *Nero
Caesar*, first published in 1624. In it the author admitted that
Nero was wicked. Nevertheless, the fact "That sacred monarchie could preserve the people of Rome from finall ruine,
not-withstanding all the prophanations, blasphemies, and scan-
dals of tyranous excesses, wherewith Nero defiled and defamed
it, is the wonder which no other forme of government could
performe." [69] Henry Valentine dared to say from the pulpit
in the year before the Long Parliament met that "a bad *King*
is a Thing which the oldest man here cannot remember, yet
let me tell you that *Tyranny* is rather to be chosen than *An-
archie* . . . Better it is to feare *one,* then *many,* better one
Lion, then all the *Beares,* and *Bores,* and wilde beasts of the
Forrest." [70] Without a king, Valentine was really anticipating
Hobbes in saying, life is "nasty, brutish, and short"; there can
be no organized society, only the strife of each individual
against every other. Consequently even under a tyrant, there
is some order and a possibility of organized society—a condi-

---

[68] William Dickinson, *op. cit.,* pp. C4v-Dr. It is interesting to note that
this advocate of strong kingly power uses naturally the word republic, with
no anti-monarchical bias implied.

[69] *Op. cit.,* p. 69.   [70] *Op. cit.,* p. 14.

tion infinitely preferable to the anarchy of individuals, who, when there is no rule over them, act like the "beasts" and "bores" of the forest.

Valentine was really saying that without a king there was no state—no people in any organized sense. No preacher in England actually proclaimed that *l'etat, c'est le roi*, but those preachers and writers who pointed out the blessings of tyranny were implying that the king was the state. So also were those preachers who made the king the shepherd, the fountain, the foundation, or the soul of the state. Comparisons of this sort could be made, as they earlier had been, without any implication that the king was truly the state; but most royalist clergy, whose comparisons have been presented here, took pains to point out the all-pervading and all-controlling part which the king in these roles occupied in the commonwealth. To them the king was the all-pervading binding force in the state without which there could be no commonwealth. Royalist clergy went much further than royalist councillors and judges in emphasizing the king's value to the body politic. A royalist councillor and judge believed that the king must possess the general-welfare power to use in emergencies. It is true that he tended to regard too many matters of government as emergencies, but he never even implied that the king was the state. Berkeley said, "Rex is Lex"; [71] he did not claim more. Some royalist clergy, however, made the very existence and being of the commonwealth depend upon the king. In this respect, their thinking went much further than the thinking of their fellow advocates of strong monarchical rule. By their emphasis upon the indispensable role of a king for the very existence of a commonwealth, they made a significant contribution to the political thought of the seventeenth century, although such a concept did not win Englishmen to the royalist cause.

Many of the royalist clergy who discussed the king's power in relation to his position in the commonwealth, and in relation to divine and natural law, did not discuss specifically his

[71] S. T., III, 1098.

power in respect to the laws of the land. Their talk of non-resistance, of obedience, and of kingly authority resting on divine and natural law is no guarantee that the speakers or writers believed the king was absolute in relation to the laws of the land.[72] Many of them, and some of the ablest, seemed surprisingly unconcerned with the great constitutional and political controversy of their own age.

A goodly number, however, preached and wrote on subjects in ways which indicate directly or indirectly their awareness of the issues of the time. Some of them not only discussed the power of a king in general, but entered into some of the particular controversies of their age concerning the nature and extent of the English monarch's power. Puritan preachers and parliamentary pamphleteers played an important part in strengthening the opposition to James and Charles, but these preachers and writers had no monopoly of pulpit and press. Their royalist opponents spoke out boldly also. As basic disagreements in church and state sharpened and widened the differences between the two groups, royalist preachers took special pains to preach on the value of peace and unity in church and state.

James Usher, preaching before the commons at Westminster on February 18, 1621, made unity the keynote of his sermon, saying:

> If in some other things wee bee otherwise minded, than others of our brethren are; let us beare one with another, untill God shall reveale the same thing unto us: and howsoever we may see cause why we should dissent from others in matter of opinion; yet let us remember, that there is no cause why wee should breake the Kings peace, and make a rent in the Church of God.[73]

[72] See J. W. Allen, *English Political Thought 1603–1660*, (Methuen & Co., London, 1938), pp. 97–101.

[73] *The Substance of That Which was Delivered in a Sermon before the Commons House of Parliament,* . . . *the 18 of February, 1620*, (London, 1621), pp. 6–7. Usher was professor of divinity in the University of Dublin. His text for this sermon was 1 Corinthians 10, Verse 17, "Wee being many, are one bread, and one body: for we are all partakers of that one bread."

The sermon preached by Walter Curll at Whitehall, April 28, 1622, and published by special command, spoke of the blessings of peace, internal as well as external, and openly attacked those leaders who were trying to make changes which could only lead to discontent and disorder. The significant parts of Curll's sermon are as follows:

> For *peace* is one of those good things, whereof wee know not the worth, till we feele the want. Therefore though we have peace, yet let us *follow peace,* follow it with our prayers, and with our thankes: . . . For the better keeping and continuing whereof, *Solomon* gives us this rule, *not to meddle with them that are seditious,* or, *that are given unto change,* Prov. 24. 21. For desire of change and alteration, it is the mother, and mover, and maker of much sedition; and they that are troubled with this itch of Innovation, they cannot but be rubbing upon Majestie it selfe, and could be content to turne Monarchy into Anarchy, or into any thing, so they might be doing. And some such turbulent Tribunes there are in every State, who out of their glorious, vaineglorious humur of popularity, would be counted Angels, though it bee but for stirring and troubling of the waters. Yea not onely the desire, but the very feare of alteration, and toleration, may some time proove seditious, when busie men will be busying themselves, and buzzing into others, a feare of that, whereof there is no feare. Which privie murmurings, and mutterings what are they, but the spirit of sedition, speaking low out of the ground, and whispering out of the dust? as the Prophet speaketh, Esa. 29. 4, and would speake out, if it durst: But *into their Councels let not our soules come,* if wee will be the true *followers of Peace.*[74]

Here indeed was plain speaking from the pulpit.

Humphrey Sydenham must have believed that members of parliament needed to be reminded of the value of obedience, for in the sermon he prepared to preach before the parliament held at Oxford in 1625 he said:

> *Command* and *obedience* are the *body* and *soule* of *humane societie,* the *head* and *foot* of an *establisht Empire.* Com-

[74] Published in London, 1622, pp. 21–23. Curll was civil dean of Litchfield.

mand sits as *Soveraigne*, . . . *Obedience,* as 'twere the *subject.* . . . where they kisse mutually, there is both strength and safety; but where they scold and jarre, all growes to ruine, and combustion.[75]

At the opening of the 1628 parliament, Laud preached before the commons, choosing as his text Ephesians IV. 3: "Endeavoring to keep the unity of the spirit in the bond of peace."[76] He pleaded eloquently for the need and value of unity in church and state, pointing out the positive good wrought by the spirit of unity, and the dire disasters brought about when it did not prevail. In 1628 when the highest statesmanship and greatest compromise was necessary to maintain any real unity between the royalists and their parliamentary opponents, the shallowness and poverty of Laud's political insight is woefully revealed in his concrete suggestion that a way to maintain unity "is for the governors to carry a watchful eye over all such as are discovered, or feared, to have private ends."[77]

Patrick Scot denounced the "late Insolencies of some Pseudo-Puritans, Separatists from the Church of Great Britaine."[78] Such men, he wrote, are "factious spirits, violently *agitated* with outragious passion of *signularitie,* envy, anger, desire of rule, and popular applause."[79]

> The motto of *Jacke Straw, Wyat* & *Kett* was *vivat Evangelium,* & how the pretext of conscience is a cullour of disobedience to every casheerd *Levite* or ignorant *consistorian,* whose studies are by wresting Scripture to destroy unitie,

[75] *Moses and Aaron or the Affinitie of Civill and Ecclesiastick power* . . . , (London, 1635), p. 135. Because the parliament at Oxford was suddenly dissolved in 1625, this sermon was not preached before it, but was delivered at St. Mary's Oxford on Feb. 26th, 1625/6. Sydenham was chaplain to Lord Howard of Escrick.

[76] William Laud, *Works,* 6 vols., (Oxford, 1847–60), I, sermon 6.

[77] *Ibid.,* p. 167.

[78] *Vox Vera; or Observations from Amsterdam* . . . , (London, 1625), Title page. Scot was not a clergyman, but a Scottish writer who came to England after the accession of James. In 1618, according to the D. N. B., he helped to raise voluntary gifts for the king.

[79] *Ibid.,* p. 24.

beget a scisme in the hearts of subjects, and make it their common place in writings, discourse, or in the Pulpit to leape from the lives of their flockes, to enveigh against government, and presumptuously incroach without all reverence upon the affaires of Princes, as they were able to demolish the walles of the Church, shake the foundations of the State, and live Libertines without controlement.[80]

Scot seems to talk directly against some of the parliamentary leaders in England:

They are bad *States-men* that unjustly take from the subject to add to the *prerogatives* or *revenues* of *Kings,* thereby they weaken *soveraigntie,* deprive it of the love of the people, make the life of it troublesome and subject to diseases: but you like worse *Statesmen,* touch the string of *soveraignty* with too rough a hand, or rather breake it in pulling the natural feathers from it, to enlarge *popular* libertie. In advancing this *Anarchy,* you open a dore to all manner of evils, which with licentiousnesse and disobedience rush into the commonwealth and make the great *frame* of *soveraigne Empire* unproportionable, uncomely, and altogether unserviceable, either for restraint of vice, advancement of vertue, or for uniting of inward power against forraine force, which are the main ends of royall institution.[81]

Scot believed in frank speech, as the selections just given reveal.

So did Robert Skinner, who in 1634 took the opportunity in a sermon on the beauty of worship to stress the value of public worship and to point out the dangers of private worship:

. . . Conventicles, and private meetings, under colour of Religion, too often serve unto dangerous practices; Seditious opinions, and turbulent positions have beene ever first *invented* and *vented* in private. There it is, that peremptory pens, and sawcie tongues are thought *consciencious,* because *audacious,* and hee commonly reputed the *bestman,* that is the *worst subject.*[82]

[80] *Ibid.,* p. 25.   [81] *Ibid.,* p. 53.
[82] *A sermon preached before the King at White Hall Dec. 3,* (London, 1634), p. 40. Skinner was bishop of Oxford.

Five years later Henry Valentine spoke out directly on the evils of his day as he saw them, exclaiming:

> But oh the strife of tongues! Oh the great thoughts and divisions of heart that are amongst us. Contempt of Authority is become the character of a Christian . . . libelling and speaking evill of dignities the language and dialect of Gods people; preaching Obedience to the Magistrate civill, and Ecclesiasticall, is interpreted downe right flattery, and gaping after preferment.[83]

Some of the clergy ventured in their sermons and writings to discuss the highly significant and controversial question of the king's relation to law. As the parliamentarians stressed the rule of law, so some royalist writers and clergy talked of the king's complete freedom from the binding sanction of law. Important as laws are in human society, R. Willan said in his sermon before the judges on November 5, 1622: "I speak not of Princes; Lawes were not written for them. . . . of good Princes their high calling makes them above Law . . ."[84] William Goodwin discoursed at some length upon the fact that the English king could not be coerced, invoking Roman law and scripture to strengthen the accepted English legal doctrine. The king, he wrote: is "ipse solutus Legibus, himselfe exempted from his lawes, not from the *Direction,* and Observance of them, but from the Punishment and penalty of them, . . . There is no Tribunall, to which he may be cited; no law by which he may be punished. . . . *God hath planted him above all men, and hath given no man authority to punish him.*"[85]

[83] Henry Valentine, *op. cit.,* p. 19.

[84] *Conspiracie Against Kings, Heavens Scorne. A Sermon preached at Westminister-Abbey befor the Judges, upon the fifth of Novemb. 1622* . . . , (London, 1622), p. 25. Willan was a chaplain to Charles I.

[85] William Goodwin, *op. cit.,* pp. 20–21. Goodwin continued his remarks as follows: "[kings] shall not escape the hands of God neither alive nor dead, But the *Lawes* of *God,* of *Nature,* of *Nations,* of the *Church,* of *free Monarchies,* the *Lawes Imperiall* all *Priviledge* and *Exempt* them; they cannot be deposed by the sentence, they may not be *deprived* by the force of any *Mortall Man.*" (p. 22).

Some writers and clergy joined hands with some royalist councillors and lawyers in stating definitely that law was derived from the prince. As early as 1603, Robert Pricket in a poem to James wrote:

> The lawes of England will themselves derive,
> From great king *James* his high perogative.[86]

Christopher White, in a sermon delivered at Oxford preached not only of submission in general to the king, but also to the laws made by kings, "For in that *generall power* of governing, is included that of *giving Lawes,* as being but a branch of the generall." [87]

A more extreme and complete statement on the question of the king's dependence upon the law came from the pen of Calybute Downing:

> Our King then being a most absolute Monarch, hath this prerogative, and from that wee have and hold our priviledges, not from that written prerogative, abstracted out of *Fitzherberts* Abridgement, by Sr *William Stanford,* . . . But from an unwritten unrestrained right of dominion, whereby he hath plenarie power, not onely to make legall propositions of validitie, or voyde in their first institution, or to interpret them either by declaring them to bee corrected in some poyntes and cases, especially if hee correct them by a more particular expresse pressing law, as hee may correct the law of nature by the law of nations; the law of nations, by the law of armes; the law of armes, by the law of particular Leagues; and all by the power of dominion.[88]

Such statements as this one by Downing, or even the less extreme ones by White or Willan, lead the modern reader to ask whether the men making them did not have a real concept of sovereignty upon which their thought primarily rested.

[86] *A Souldiers Wish Unto His Soveraigne Lord King James,* (London, 1603), B4. This poem is ascribed to Pricket by the Huntington Library catalogue. Pricket was a poet who eventually took holy orders.

[87] Christopher White, *The Oathes, . . . 3 Sermons in Oxenford . . . ,* (London, 1627), Second Sermon, p. 26. White, a bachelor of divinity, was a student at Christ Church.

[88] Calybute Downing, *op. cit.,* pp. 90–91.

As I interpret their writings, the answer must be no, for none of them, not even Downing, of whom it is impossible to be quite certain, developed and pointed out all the implications of the remarks they made, or used their more sovereign-like statements as the core of their thinking. There were, to my knowledge, only two royalist supporters of the king, prior to 1640, who viewed kingly power as sovereign.[89]

Before their contribution to the development of the concept of sovereignty is discussed, another common argument employed by royalist clergy in relation to the immediate issues of their own time should be examined. The clergy loved to point out to their congregations and to their readers that the consent of man played no part at all in the institution of government. It was perfectly natural and strictly consistent with their own premises for them to hold such a view, for they had long proclaimed unequivocally that government arose and functioned only by the command of God. To them the concept that man had any part or authority in government was a damnable doctrine, advocated only by traitorous Jesuits or Protestant sectaries, who also preached the right of resistance. Such views and the writers proclaiming them were squarely condemned by many of James's clerical supporters in the battle of books they waged against Bellarmine and all others holding his dangerous views. To them all books against the complete authority of princes were dangerous and damnable, and they spared no pains to denounce them.

Among the many clerical writers taking part in the campaign against such poisonous views, David Owen [90] was outstanding, not primarily because of the originality of his thought, but because of his thoroughness in piling up all possible authorities to support his own views, and because of his penetration in discovering the enemy under any guise and in condemning all who were responsible for advocating damnable

[89] See the end of this chapter.
[90] Owen was a controversial writer who became chaplain to John Ramsay, Viscount Hadington.

views. Owen, like most of the royalist clergy and many of the Puritans and members of the parliamentary opposition, believed that the king's power came directly from God—"the Author and Ordainer of it." [91] Consequently, the people had no part in setting up kings and must not resist them. In support of these views, Owen turned to scripture, church fathers, nature, the law of nations, civil and canon law, and even cited English statesmen—Burleigh, Ellesmere, Stafford, and Coke—as agreeing with his own views.[92] Starting with the usual scriptural authorities, he proceeded systematically through Christian history in three-hundred-year intervals, piling up examples and authorities to support his views. He looked to English and continental history for examples of the authority of temporal kings, and also cited the civilians, Baldus, Hostiensis, William Barclay, Adam Blackwood, etc., in defense of his views.[93]

More interesting and significant than Owen's defense of his own position was his attack upon his opponents. Here he set out to demonstrate the "concord of Papist and Puritan for the deposition of Kings." [94] "*The Puritan-Church Policie,*" he wrote, "and the *Jesuitical society* began to-gether: the one in *Geneva,* 1536, and the other in *Rome, 1537.*" [95] They by their doctrines and practices endanger church and state, the Puritans perhaps more subtly and less openly, but no less dangerously.[96] "The Puritan-Papists tell us the Fundamentall Laws, are (I know not what) contracts, or conditionall Covenants, betwixt the King and the People, entred, and establisht by Oath at the Kings first Inauguration; which being broken,

[91] David Owen, *Anti-Paraeus or a treatise in the Defence of the Royall Right of Kings,* (York, 1642), p. 77. This tract was first published in Latin in 1622.

[92] David Owen, *Herod and Pilate reconciled, or, the concord of Papist and Puritan for the Deposition, and Killing of Kings,* (London, 1610), Epistle to the dutifull Subject.

[93] David Owen, *Anti-Paraeus,* pp. 74–75.

[94] David Owen, *Herod and Pilate reconciled,* Title page.

[95] *Ibid.,* Epistle to the dutifull Subject.

[96] *Ibid.,* See particularly chs. 7 and 8.

they will have the People free, and loose from all **Bonds of Allegiance** and **Religion** to their Soveraignes." [97] Such a doctrine, Owen declared, is absolutely wrong and dangerously malicious. So also is their view that people play a part in instituting government. On the contrary, "the authority of the People is nothing," and "the absolute power [of the king] is (under God) Supreame, in every part perfect." [98] Owen looked back into history to discover the origin of the Puritan position on rebellion and sedition, and found "no ground of this leud learning, beyond 220 yeares in the Christian world. The first authors of it beeing Johannos de Parissiis, Jocabus Almain, and Marsilius Pativinus." [99] In the sixteenth century Goodman, Knox, Beza (the authors of *Franco-Gallia* and of the *Vindiciae contra Tyrannos*), Cartwright, Buchanan, and Danaeus were condemned by Owen as the most dangerous exponents of Puritan political beliefs.[100] David Owen was a vigorous writer who spared no pains to denounce both Jesuits and Puritans holding "seditious" views. He must have done much to popularize the belief which increasingly, and particularly in the civil war, came to be held by royalists—namely the idea that the political views of Papists and Puritans were woven from the same cloth and equally dangerous to the authority of kings.

During the latter part of James's reign, there was considerable activity against individuals and groups holding the dangerous ideas which Owen and others had condemned. An attempt was made to rout out the views of dangerous writers from Oxford and Cambridge. In May, 1622, the council received a declaration from the Archbishop of Canterbury and twelve bishops stating "that they consider the positions of Pareus and others, . . . contrary to Scripture and the Church of England, and therefore caution the heads of colleges, etc., to beware of allowing students in divinity to read them." [101]

---

[97] David Owen, *Anti-Paraeus*, pp. 2–3.   [98] *Ibid.*, p. 76.
[99] David Owen, *Herod and Pilate reconciled*, p. 45.
[100] *Ibid.*, pp. 47–53.   [101] *Cal. St. P. Domestic, 1619–1623*, p. 396.

On July seventeenth, 1622, the university reported to the council: "Have publicly condemned the doctrine of Pareus as seditious, and burned a copy of his book, not doubting [they optimistically add] that all contagion of his doctrine is purged from the University." [102] The authorities at Cambridge were also concerned, and at a meeting of the senate of the university "Sundry propositions, relative to the kingly power being subject to none save God, and the impiousness of resistance thereto, were carried unanimously, and the books of Dr. Pareus Bucanus, condemned to eternal infamy and forbidden to be read." [103]

Neither the council, the universities, nor the clergy in their dioceses and parishes were successful in suppressing the ideas the government regarded as dangerous. Although during the twenties talk of non-resistance was very unusual, the conviction that the king's authority was limited by law, and that government rested on man's consent as well as the king's authority, was developing rapidly.[104] Again the clergy played some part in denouncing and trying to suppress such views. Robert Sibthorpe, for example, preaching during the stormy sessions of the 1626 parliament at the Northhampton Assizes, said, "let not the People stand so much upon pretence of Libertie, as to lose Saftie." [105] Two doctrines have been set forth which he emphatically denounced, one "which makes the *Church above the King, and the Pope above the Church.*" [106] The other "makes the Law above the King, and the people above the Law, and so deposes Princes, by their *Tumults and Insurections.*" [107]

In 1636 Henry Burton came forth with one of the most outspoken and ringing challenges the Puritans in England had yet made. It was in answer to Burton's two tracts that Peter

[102] *Ibid.*, pp. 426–27.
[103] *Ibid.*, p. 427.
[104] See chapter VIII.
[105] *Apostolike Obedience Shewing the Duty of Subjects to pay Tribute and Taxes to their Princes, according to the Word of God* . . . , (London, 1627), p. 23. Sibthorpe was vicar of Brackley in Northhamptonshire.
[106] *Ibid.*   [107] *Ibid.*

Heylyn stated so emphatically that the "law of *Monarchie* is founded on the Law of *nature,* not on *positive lawes.*" [108] He also accused Burton of subtly, if not openly, advocating the *"Puritan tenet,* that Kings are but the Ministers of the Commonwealth, and that they have no more authority then what is given them by the people." [109] Burton, Heylyn implied, may have learned such a dangerous and erroneous idea from Buchanan. Heylyn concluded from his analysis of Burton "that out of doubt the *Puritan religion is rebellion,* and *their faith faction.*" [110]

Less than three years after Heylyn wrote these words, Thomas Morton, Bishop of Durham, condemned the Puritan idea that princes are made by the consent of the people. On the contrary, "The powers that be are . . . *ordained of God,* that is, orderly constituted: but if, when the *People* have constituted a Ruler over them, there remaineth in them a power dormant, upon *Occasion,* to over-rule, and un-king, and un-make him, to whom they are *Subjects*; this were an unorderly and ougly a confusednes, in the Bodie politique, as it would be in the body naturall to stand on its head with the heels upwards." [111] Once powers are established "they *are* of God, *God* owneth them, they may not be disturbed. For as silver, whilest it is mere Plate, if it be tendred for exchange, may be either taken, or not, by the partie to whom it is offered: but if it once receive the Kings stampe, and be coyned, it is currant money, and may not be refused." [112]

In the same year, 1639, Henry Valentine also condemned the idea that people played any part in government. The doctrine of the "Consistory," he proclaimed from the pulpit, "cannot be good, for it advances the *Thistle* above the *Cedar,* the people above the Prince, witnesse these, and the like

[108] *Op. cit.,* p. 32.
[109] *Ibid.,* p. 26.
[110] *Ibid.,* p. 156.
[111] *Sermon preached Before the Kings most Excellent Majestie, in the Cathedrall Church of Durham, May 5, 1639,* (Newcastle, 1639), p. 10.
[112] *Ibid.,* p. 11.

dangerous and seditious positions." [113] Like other royalists, Valentine condemned Buchanan by name and added: "And another of the same stamp affirmes that the power of the people over the King, is the same that the power of a generall Councell is over the Pope." [114]

Royalist clergy did their best to keep the people submissive. They also did their best to induce the people to pay money to the king. One of the most positive constructive contributions made by them to the royalist cause was in relation to the all-important question of securing adequate revenue. The belief that a man's property was his own—that a parliamentary grant was a gift to the king—was the cornerstone upon which the parliamentary opposition rested its case. Royalist lawyers and councillors tried to justify and prove the legality of the extra-parliamentary means used by James and Charles to raise revenue, but they were cautious and conservative on the subject of direct taxation without parliamentary consent. Few of them ever directly denied that property fundamentally belonged to the subject and not to the king. The royalist clergy, however, were less cautious and constitutional in their approach to the question. It was they, rather than lawyers and ministers, who went farthest in advancing the doctrine that taxes, even direct ones, were tribute due the king, which the king had the right to demand and take without asking for them. The earliest sermon I have discovered where this point of view is stated was preached in 1606 by John Buckeridge, later Bishop of Rochester and Ely. He told his congregation: "You pay tribute & customs, and Subsidies of duetie and Justice; You give them not of courtesie; and they are *stipendium Regis,* not *praemium,* they are the Kings stipend or pay, not his reward." [115] In the next few years other royalist clergy also spoke of the tribute due kings.[116] Chamberlain

---

[113] Henry Valentine, *op. cit.,* p. 10.

[114] *Ibid.,* p. 11. Valentine does not name this other "of the same stamp."

[115] John Buckeridge, *op. cit.,* p. 3.

[116] See [R. Mocket], *God and the King: Or, A Dialogue shewing that our Soveraigne Lord King James, being immediate under God within*

wrote Carleton, "The Bp. of London, preaching at St. Paul's cross on the benevolence, argued that what we have is not our own, and that giving to the King is only restoration." [117] When in 1626 Charles wrote to the clergy, requesting them to assist the state by preaching certain doctrines, some of them rallied to his support by enunciating more complete views on the subject of tribute due the king than they had ever before expressed. Robert Sibthorpe, in his sermon on *Apostolike Obedience,* proclaimed that a prince should be maintained not only by crown lands and private revenues, but by taxes imposed on trade and on landed property. Tribute, he wrote, is due the Prince by divine law and as "a sign of our subjection," by natural law as a "reward of their paines and protection," and by the law of nations "as the sinewes of the States preservation." [118] In support of these bold assertions Sibthorpe cited Polycorp, Tertullian, Gregory, Ambrose, Anselm, and even Luther, Melancthan, Calvin, Beza and Cranmer.[119]

Roger Manwaring was even bolder than Sibthorpe in his statement of the case for tribute. He talked not only in general terms of divine and natural law but dared to mention parliament in specific terms. It is true, he wrote, that although "such *Assemblies,* are the *Highest,* and *greatest Representations* of a *Kingdome,* the most *Sacred* and *honourable,* and *necessary* also for those ends to which they were at first instituted: yet know we must, that, ordained they were not to this end; to contribute any *Right* to Kings, whereby to challenge *Tributary* aydes and *Subsidiary* helpes; but for the more equall *Imposing* and more easie *Exacting* of that, which unto *Kings* doth appertaine, by *Naturall* and *Originall Law*

his *Dominions, Doth rightfully claime whatsoever is required by the Oath of Allegeance,* (London, 1615), p. 34. Mocket became chaplain to archbishop Abbot, warden of All Souls Oxford, and "one of the king's commissioners concerning ecclesiastical affairs."

[117] *Cal. St. P. Domestic, 1619–1623,* p. 418.
[118] Robert Sibthorpe, *op. cit.,* p. 14.
[119] *Ibid.,* p. 15.

and Justice; as their proper *Inheritance* annexed to their *Imperiall Crownes* from their births." [120] Upon urgent necessity, therefore, taxes may be imposed without parliament. There are times when the "Deliberation and Motion" of great bodies takes too much time for "Necessities of State." [121] In another sermon Manwaring argued in the same way, pointing out that "by natural *Justice;* hath *Caesar* a *Right* unto, and a *Portion* in that, which beares his *Image,* and *Superscription.*" Christ willingly admitted that tribute was due Caesar. "And this, our *Blessed Lord* did with that *Readinesse,* not expecting any *Parliament,* at *Rome,* or in *Judea,* to bee first assembled; Nor had *Caesar,* at this time, any Warres in hand, the whole world being then at Peace." [122]

During the decade between 1630 and 1640, the government managed its finances somewhat more successfully than it had during the stormy decade of the twenties, for now foreign wars with their pressing financial needs were over, and the treasury was under the able administration of Weston. The state was not so sorely pressed that it needed at this time the help of the church in raising money. At least there do not seem to be in the sermons and clerical writings of the period from 1630 to 1640 any such complete, such theoretical, or such outspoken statements on the subject of tribute as those earlier made by Sibthorpe and Manwaring.

The many political views sounded by the royalist clergy from pulpit and press brought them into disrepute by 1640. The remedies they had advocated for the profound and complex problems of their age were too simple. They had talked of peace and unity without seeming to realize that such a desirable state could not be achieved if fundamental differences and problems remained unsolved. In the face of growing discontent they had preached more loudly and extravagantly than ever before on the virtues of obedience and the

[120] Roger Manwaring, *op. cit.,* p. 26.
[121] *Ibid.,* p. 27.
[122] *Ibid.,* Second Sermon, p. 37.

sin of rebellion. Although such talk appealed to many conservatively minded Englishmen, it also added to the mounting wave of criticism of the church. In an age when a man's religion and his politics were closer together than they are today, it was not easy or necessary always to separate one's religious and political views. Some men who probably had never questioned the forms or doctrines of the English church began to have questions and doubts about a church whose clergy preached like Bargrave and Morton. We know that between 1620 and 1640 the movement called Puritan grew, and that, by the time the Long Parliament met, there had developed a strong group determined to take the control of the church from the king's hands and place it in parliament's. Many factors contributed to the growth of that movement, but among them must be included the part which the royalist clergy played in talking politics—and politics of a royalist brand—from the pulpit.

As the Puritan movement grew strong in church and state in the twenty years prior to the Long Parliament, so also did the constitutional and political opposition to the crown increase. By 1640, parliamentary leaders attacking the king's ministers, his policies, and his instruments of government had joined forces with Puritan clergy who were attacking the prelates, policies, and doctrines of the established church. The strength of the forces arrayed against the crown and church in the first months of the Long Parliament might never have been so great, if the royalist clergy had not tried to assist the crown by advocating and developing political doctrines on behalf of kingly power. By 1640, the leaders of the parliamentary opposition were thoroughly aroused against royalist councillors and lawyers who had used the courts to establish legal absolutism, and also against royalist clergy who had used the pulpit and press to proclaim the divine right of kings to rule their people without their consent, to tax them against their wills, and to be supreme over the law of the land.

These ideas, proclaimed by the royalist clergy for almost

forty years, ran directly counter to the basic beliefs of the parliamentary opposition. As the clergy preached and wrote that tribute was due kings, parliamentary leaders stood staunchly on their property rights. As the clergy preached that the king was above and free from the laws of man, parliamentary leaders looked more and more to the law as the foundation of all government. As the clergy rested the king's power and position on the law of nature, so eventually parliamentary leaders and pamphleteers discovered that the law of nature allowed self defense and, in the last analysis, justified resistance to kings. As the clergy preached that the king's power came only from God, that the consent of man played no part in government, and that the very commonwealth itself depended upon the king, parliamentary leaders and Puritan preachers must have been alarmed. They had earlier accepted the belief in the divine origin of kingly power and in non-resistance, but had never believed that the people had no share in government or were not part of the state. They had always maintained that, although the king's power came from God, he must in his government take account of the consent of man. Slowly however, they began to push God aside and stress more the part played by man in government. Eventually they came to advocate resistance to kings, and finally some of them thrust the king out of the state, proclaiming that the people in parliament constituted the state. It is probable that some of the extreme views of the opposition would have developed even if the royalist clergy had not asserted the opposite beliefs. The impact and thrust of idea upon idea can never be categorically determined, but in the ferment of political thought prevailing and developing in England in the first half of the seventeenth century, the views set forth by royalist clergy must have contributed in no small degree to the crystallization and development of the views of the parliamentary and Puritan opposition.[123]

Henry Parker, the keenest pamphleteer supporting parlia-

[123] See chapters VI to X.

ment's cause between 1640 and 1645,[124] attacked the clergy and
their divine-right ideas in his first important pamphlet:

> [These clergy] wed the King to their quarrell, perswading
> him that Parliaments out of Puritanisme, doe not so much
> aime at the fall of Episcopacie, as Monarchy: and that Episco-
> pacie is the support of Monarchy, so that both must stand
> and fall together. Howbeit because they cannot upbraid Par-
> liaments of attempting any thing against Monarchy further
> then to maintaine due liberty, therefore they preach an un-
> limited prerogative, and condemne all law and liberty as
> injurious to Kings, and incompatible with Monarchy. . . .
> And the common Court doctrine is that Kings are bound-
> lesse in authority, and that they onely are *Caesars* friends
> which justifie that doctrine; and from this doctrine hath
> grown all the jealousies of late between the King and his best
> Subjects; and this is that venemous matter which hath laien
> burning, and ulcerating inwardly in the bowels of the com-
> mon-wealth so long.[125]

The political ideas of the royalist clergy have been discussed
in this chapter without reference to a doctrine of sovereignty,
although sovereignty was implicit in their concept that the
king had the power of God, that he was above the law, that he
was responsible to no man, and that he was the state. Sovereignty, however, may be implicit in a concept without the pro-
ponent of the idea being aware of it, or fashioning consistently
all his views around it; and it appears that, with two exceptions, the royalist clergy prior to the civil war did not fully
grasp the concept of sovereignty. The parliamentary opposition did not attack them because of their views of sovereignty.
Manwaring, one of the two men who proclaimed a theory of
sovereignty, was bitterly condemned in the commons because
he had proclaimed that tribute was due princes, whereas his remarks attributing sovereign power to kings were ignored.

[124] See chapters IX and X for a fuller discussion of Parker.
[125] Henry Parker, *The Case of Shipmoney briefly discoursed* . . . 1640,
pp. 33–34. On Nov. 7th, 1640, Pym complained of the clergy "Preaching
for absolute monarchy that the King may doe what he list." *D'Ewes
(Long Parl.)* ed. W. Notestein, p. 9.

Both Roger Manwaring and William Dickinson actually arrived at a concept of sovereignty, and both were members of the clergy. Manwaring's contribution to the development of the concept has recently been pointed out and discussed by Professor Wormuth.[126] Dickinson, who stated his views in 1619, eight years before Manwaring, seems to have been unnoticed by students of political thought.

Dickinson set forth his ideas in only one sermon, *The Kings Right,* but in it he revealed himself as one of the most constructive and most extreme thinkers on the royalist side prior to the civil war. In this one sermon he stated clearly most of the leading ideas of the royalist clergy. He asserted that the king was the "Foundation" and *"axis of the Com-mon wealth, upon whose wel-being & good Lawes the whole state of things, and the good and ill of his Subiects and Cittizens relie."* [127] The king's authority in the realm, like the soul's in the body, was "diffused" through the whole body politic.[128] His power was in accord with "that reason engrafted into every mans understanding." [129]

It was in connection with his discussion of the meaning of the words "to judge" that Dickinson revealed clearly that he regarded the king's power as truly sovereign. There are, he explained, different degrees of judging. In one sense to judge is to "interpret Law, and settle differences betweene particulars according to that scantling and measure which is prescribed them and others to be ruled by. But to be *The Judge,* is to be that Majesty and Architectonicall power, which out of its owne absolutenes setteth downe a Law, and appointeth a publike measure, *Quatenus, Quomodo, & quousq;* whereby all mens actions are to be squared and adjudged whether they be good, or whether they be evill. The Latines have divers Phrases to express this power by, as *Ius Majestatis, Ius summi imperii,*

---

[126] *Op. cit.,* pp. 93–98.
[127] *Op. cit.,* C4v.
[128] *Ibid.*
[129] *Ibid.,* C.

Principatus, Arbitrium: And the person endued with this greatnes is called *Arbiter rerum, Princeps, Dominus rerum temporumq; vitae, necisq; Dominus,* and (as the *Hebrewes* will have it) *Judex super nos,* a Judge over us." [130] Moses and later rulers in Israel also possessed this full power of judging. In that country, according to the testimony of Samuel, the king was "not onely to have *Jurisdiction,* but *Dominium* over their persons and estates. . . . Let it therefore be understood that to be *The Judge,* (the word so taken in my text) is to have the right of supremacy over all persons and causes, and to governe and moderate them and their actions according to that proportion of Law and reason which hee pleaseth to set down to be observed." [131]

In this discussion of the meaning of judging, Dickinson clearly ascribed sovereign power to a king. To him the king's power was supreme and unlimited except by God, it extended over men's property, and most significant of all, the king "out of his owne absolutenes setteth downe a Law." Dickinson's identification of the king's supremacy with his absoluteness in making law stamps him as perhaps the first thinker on either the royalist or parliamentary side to grasp fully the idea of sovereignty. It was not until the civil war broke out that some few theorists in both camps began to discuss the nature of supremacy with the same penetration Dickinson brought to the question. Even Manwaring, whose contribution to the development of a doctrine of sovereignty in the years before the civil war was significant, never made a clear and close identification between the king's supremacy and his lawmaking power.

Roger Manwaring, however, is probably the best known of the royalist clergy advocating extreme views of the king's power in the period before the civil war. His two sermons, *Religion and Alegiance,* preached before the king in July, 1627, brought down upon him the wrath of the parliamentary opposition, for in those sermons he asserted, as has been already shown,

[130] *Ibid.,* B3r.
[131] B3v.

that tribute was due princes by natural law, and that parliament had no right to deny money to them. In those sermons also Manwaring set forth many of the leading ideas of the clergy: that the king's power came from God, that man had no part in it, and that the obedience of subjects to a king was enjoined not only by God but by nature.

Manwaring's contribution to the development of the concept of sovereignty lay, as Professor Wormuth has pointed out, first in his identification of the king's power with the omnipotency of God, and second in his viewing the king's decrees as commands. "That sublime *Power* therefore," he asserts, "which resides in earthly *Potentates* is . . . a *participation* of God's owne *Omnipotency*, which hee never did communicate to any *multitudes* of men in the world, but *onely*, and *immediately*, to his owne Viceregents." [132] "All the *significations* of a *Royall pleasure*, are, and ought to be, to all *Loyall* Subjects, in the nature, and force of a *Command*." [133]

In connection with this second general statement that the king's pleasure is in the form of a command, Manwaring made three significant remarks. "The *Lawes*," he wrote, "which make provision for their [i.e. the subjects] reliefe take their binding force from the *Supreame* will of their *Liege-Lord*." [134] His second pertinent statement is as follows:

And for his Soveraigne *will* (which gives a binding force, to all his *Royall Edicts*, concluded out of the Reasons of *State*, and depth of *Counsell*) who may dare *resist* it, without incurable waste and breach of Conscience? [135]

His third important statement occurs in connection with his treatment of rebellion:

[132] Roger Manwaring, *op. cit.*, p. 11. Manwaring's ideas were attacked in parliament in 1628 and his book suppressed, but he himself won preferment in the church, receiving a good living at Stanford, and in 1635 the bishopric of St. Davids.
[133] *Ibid.*, p. 17.
[134] *Ibid.*, p. 9.
[135] *Ibid.*, pp. 17–18.

. . . if any *King* shall *command* that, which stands not in any opposition to the originall Lawes of *God, Nature, Nations,* and the *Gospell*; (though it be not correspondent in every circumstance, to Lawes Nationall, and Municipall) no Subject may, without hazard of his own Damnation, in rebelling against God, *question,* or *disobey* the will and pleasure of his *Soveraigne.* For, as a *Father* of the Countrey, hee commands what his pleasure is, out of *counsell* and *judgement.* As a *King* of Subjects, he injoynes it. As a *Lord* over Gods inheritance, hee exacts it. As a *Supreme head* of the body, he adviseth it. As a *Defendour* of the *Faith,* hee requires it as their homage. As a *Protectour* of their persons, lives, and states, he deserves it. And as the *Soveraigne procurer* of all the happinesse, peace, and welfare, which they enjoy, who are under him, hee doth most *justly* claime it at their hands.[136]

These three different specific statements, taken in connection with his more general ideas of the king's power as a participation in God's omnipotency and of the king's decrees as commands, indicate that Manwaring grasped the concept of sovereignty. Nevertheless, it should be noted that nowhere does he explicitly ascribe all lawmaking power to the king or state that his will is law. Laws making provision for the king's relief (not all laws) receive their "binding force" from the king. His sovereign will gives "binding" force, not to all laws, but to "Royall Edicts, concluded out of the Reasons of State, and depth of Counsell." It is at least possible that Manwaring was thinking here of that portion of the king's lawmaking power which was included within the realm of his absolute power exercised for reasons of state through the council. He did not explicitly say that all laws, including those passed in parliament, came only from the monarch's royal will. Finally, in Manwaring's third statement, he discussed nonresistance and the king's power to compel obedience only in connection with laws not "in any opposition to the originall Lawes of God, Nature, Nations, and the Gospell." In his general discussion of the king's power and the king's commands,

[136] *Ibid.,* pp. 19–20.

Manwaring talks in terms of sovereignty; in his more concrete illustrations of his general statements, he appears to be more cautious, causing some doubt to arise in the reader's mind whether or not he understood the full implications of the king's position as power and of his will as law.

With both Manwaring and Dickinson, however, a different and more sovereign note was sounded than most royalist clergy or their parliamentary opponents voiced prior to the civil war. Despite the inadequacy of older theological and legal ideas to solve the constitutional and political problems men faced in England between 1603 and 1642, both royalists and parliamentarians clung as closely as possible to the tried and true— to the law and to God's plan and decrees. The law was stretched to serve both royalist and parliamentary lawyer and politician, and God was claimed by both royalist and Puritan clergy as sanctioning their views and claims. By 1630 leaders on both sides had departed in some measure from the ideas which were their common heritage, and which most men had earlier agreed upon. The ideas each side developed in the years prior to 1642 came to full bloom only during the years of civil war. Then a few men saw clearly for the first time that the issue was one of sovereign power, and not of law or of God's will. During that struggle a few theorists frankly deserted the older ideas and set forth theories of sovereign power.[137] These theorists recognized that the law, no matter how much it was exalted or stretched on behalf of king or parliament, was inadequate. They ceased to make God a vital force in the political affairs of men and came to talk of power and supremacy in modern political language. In the period before the war, neither Manwaring nor Dickinson arrived at the point in their discussion of sovereignty which Parker, Herle, Digges, and Filmer reached during the war, but both of these royalist clergy deserve to be remembered as preachers who seem to have grasped the concept of sovereignty at an early date.

[137] See chapter X.

CHAPTER VI

PARLIAMENT DEFENDS RIGHTS, THE LAW, AND THE CONSTITUTION

THE MEN who made up the parliamentary opposition were in many respects like the royalists, particularly the royalist councillors and lawyers. Both groups belonged to the upper classes. Members of the house of commons were largely country gentlemen with possibly some business interests and connections. A minority were leaders in the expanding industry and trade, but such leaders were also building up their landed holdings and strengthening their country connections. The economic and social complexion of the royalists was not very different. Although there were more great lords and fewer businessmen among them, many great noblemen at this time were not averse to supplementing their landed wealth with business ventures, particularly if a monopoly for a profitable enterprise could be secured from the king. Many members of the parliamentary opposition were lawyers and judges, trained in the same way and tradition, following the same laws, and serving in some of the same courts with their royalist opponents. In their constitutional and political thinking, some of their views were similar to those of the royalists, for most leaders of the opposition, as well as most royalist judges and councillors, entered into the constitutional controversies of this period holding the moderate views of the king's authority, the subjects' rights, the law and balanced constitution, and the place of parliament in their polity which have been presented in the first part of this book. The parliamentarians, like the royalists, departed from those views only slowly and reluctantly. In religion many of them were moderate Anglicans, proud of their national church and loving its services. When in 1641 and 1642 the Puritan minority threatened to make the Anglican church Puritan, many members of parliament who had earlier opposed the king left the parliamentary ranks and joined with him to preserve the Anglican religion. From the economic and social point of view, from the professional and intellectual, and in some respects from the religious, there was no great cleavage between the men supporting parliament's cause and those supporting the king's.

So similar were these parliament men to the best councillors and advisers carrying on the king's government that many of them could have served the crown well had the Stuarts been wise enough to give them, rather than some of their court favorites, responsible positions in the privy council. If the Stuarts had been sufficiently far-sighted, particularly in the earlier years of the struggle, to take men like Sandys, Alford, or Phelips into the government, it is at least possible that there would have been few constitutional crises and no civil war. Whenever the crown did secure the support of men who had been in the opposition, as happened between 1628 and 1631, when Wentworth and Noy deserted the parliament and went over to the crown, or again in 1641 and 1642 when many more, led by Falkland and Hyde, went over to his side, the king's cause grew strong. Whether monarchs with more insight and more political wisdom than either James or Charles displayed could have won over the parliamentary opposition is at best problematical; but there is no doubt that both rulers by their stupid blunders, stubborn actions, and high-handed policies showed so little perception of the tide of events or pulse of public opinion that they drove men, few of whom were natural rebels, into an opposition which eventually brought on an unnatural civil war.

The leaders of the parliamentary opposition had become too important by the time James became king for them to be treated lightly. Moreover, the king could ill afford not to take them into his confidence, for he needed their financial support to run the government. It is true that the financial problem the Stuarts faced was inherited from the Tudors. Those rulers had taught the country gentry and the merchants in the House of Commons the business of government, but had not been able to persuade those same men to bear a fair proportion of the expense of government. As always, the expense of government was mounting in the seventeenth century, and at the same time the regular revenues of the crown brought in less money, for prices were going up, and land values, from which much of the regular revenue was derived, advanced more slowly than prices. The financial problem could no longer be solved by a confiscation of monastic lands. Faced with this financial dilemma, the Stuart kings needed help from their subjects and needed it desperately. James and Charles recognized that need and asked for help, but they still thought they had only to ask as the Tudors had done, and they would receive. Neither James nor Charles seems to have understood the full import of the financial problem which vexed and tried the souls of their ministers. The kings tried to bargain—to offer a few crumbs of the prerogative—in order to secure parliamentary grants, but they did not understand that the stakes were higher now than they had been under the Tudors, and that their opponents were more skillful players and better bargainers than they themselves were.

The price these men demanded now for substantial parliamentary grants was not just redress of grievances, but a greater share in the government of the state. In parliament there was some opportunity for them to take part in governmental policies, but not enough. Important decisions on foreign policy, peace and war, religion, and economic questions were still made, policies formulated, and administrative machinery set in action without reference to parliament. The upper classes represented there were too prosperous and their business interests reached out too far for them not to be affected by foreign policy. It now concerned them as well as the king. To merchants who traded with India or who invested capital to trade in the new world, the relations between England and Spain were vital. It is certainly no accident that the most aggressive spirits, Pym and Warwick, were members of trading companies.[1] More research concerning the business interests of the members of parliament would undoubtedly reveal the wide-flung interests of many of them, for they were not apart from the world of economic affairs. If they were expected to contribute greater sums of money to the state, they naturally asked questions about state policies and wished greater participation in fashioning them. They desired to help direct those policies into channels which took account of their own interests and activities.

Desiring more participation in government, the influential leaders at the same time became fearful that parliament might lose that position and power which it had long possessed, for kings, with the help of royalist judges and councillors, had raised some money without parliament, and the legality of such action had been sustained by the king's judges in Bate's case and later in ship money. The law had been used against them, and their rights were no longer secure. If the king's councillors and judges made the king's prerogative any more absolute, what need was there for calling parliament? And if kings no longer needed to ask parliament for money, how long would they need parliament for any purpose? Without parliament the liberties of Englishmen would be lost, and their land no longer the commonwealth their ancestors had known and cherished. When that happened, the last country in Europe where subjects had rights would disappear. Absolutism would then prevail in all Europe. "Wee are," Phelips said, "the last monarchy in Christendome that retayne our originall rightes and constitutions." [2] Phelips and other members of the parliamentary opposition were sincerely alarmed by the growing

[1] See J. H. Hexter, *The Reign of King Pym*, (Harvard University Press, Cambridge, Mass., 1941), pp. 77 ff.
[2] *Commons Debates in 1625*, p. 110.

success of the royalists in erecting a legal absolutism which could only mean ultimately the end of their rights and their parliaments.

Such a combination of fear and desire makes men stubborn and inflexible in insisting on maintaining all which is theirs and drives them to seize every opportunity to criticize or checkmate the adversary, whether such criticism or acts are justified or unjustified. The leaders in the commons became so zealous and vigilant to take advantage of any small opportunity to increase their power that, although most of them clung to fairly moderate constitutional and political views, it became increasingly difficult for them to work out practical solutions to difficult questions on moderate grounds. To remain moderate and to accept compromise was particularly difficult when they came to distrust the honesty of Charles's intentions. Bitter as many of the conflicts were between James and his parliaments, there was never revealed in the parliamentary debates during his reign the same suspicion of him and his intentions as poisoned the relations between Charles and his parliaments from the beginning of his reign.

The difficulty of achieving a moderate compromise and of continuing to hold moderate constitutional views was also increased because some members of the house of commons were Puritans. Many times the spark which ignited criticism and kept it burning bright, when interest might have lagged or fears been calmed, came from a Puritan leader. Most members of the lower house feared and distrusted Spain, but hatred of Spain, "the Catholic harlot," seared the soul and inflamed the tongue of a Puritan merchant or country squire. It takes an inner unquenchable conviction of righteousness to stand firm or to move ahead in the face of odds, and the Puritan possessed just that kind of conviction. Elect of God, he feared no man, not even a king. If one parliament was dismissed, he laid plans for the next. If the royalists controlled the press and pulpit, he found hidden subtle ways to air his views in pamphlet and sermon. Called by God to lead himself and others

in righteous ways, he scented out possible danger before anyone else realized trouble was brewing. Believing that he was
right because his ways and beliefs were God-given, he had the
zeal to work for reform and truth as he saw it with greater
determination than men who were swayed more by economic
than by religious motives. Wishing to make the Anglican
church Puritan, because that was the will of God, he was not
turned from this purpose even during those years between 1630
and 1640 when no parliament met, and Laud, guiding the
Anglican church in ways of holiness, persecuted Puritans ruth-
lessly. Dogmatic in his theology and unused to adjusting the
scriptures to tradition and the habits of man, the Puritan
hated compromise and stood firmly and stubbornly for the
right, as he saw it, when others believed compromise possible.

No amount of research can prove that the Puritans were always the aggressive leaders in this struggle between king and
parliament, but no serious reader of the parliamentary debates
during these years can deny, I believe, that the Puritans gave
to the parliamentary cause that dynamic leadership which enabled parliament to stand firm in the face of royalist claims
and actions, to checkmate the king, and eventually to become
supreme in the state.[3]

Any analysis of the reasons for the differences between English and French constitutional development must take account
of this part played by the Puritans in parliament. In France

[3] For a popular poem illustrating a contemporary attitude towards the
Puritans, see C. H. Firth, *Stuart Tracts 1603–1693*, (London, 1903), pp.
237–38.
For contemporary statements of the importance of the Puritans in
parliament, see also *Cal. St. P. Venetian*, 1603–1607, pp. 202 and 285.
On December 16, 1628, Salvetti wrote concerning preparations for the
1629 parliament: "With regard to lay Catholics, they are to be confined
to certain places and must pay punctually the usual exactions. All this
is to please the Puritans and conciliate the new Parliament; but, as with
these people it is a maxim to oppose everything, never to be satisfied
with the present, nor to agree with what is proposed for the future," he
doubts that such preparation will be effective. Skrine MSS., H. M. C.,
XI, 173.

for some time after the Edict of Nantes the Huguenots had their own church, their own institutions, almost their own state. In those respects their position was better than the position of English Puritans, who failed under Elizabeth and James to make the Anglican church more Puritan or to win the legal right within the church to worship according to Puritan beliefs. Under Charles, with his approval of Arminian beliefs and practices, and particularly under Laud, the position of the Puritans within the Anglican church became even more difficult. The English Puritan, however, was an integral member of the English nation, forced to conform to its ecclesiastical laws of which he disapproved, but privileged to play his part as a member of the realm in parliament. Denied the legal right to worship as he believed God willed men should worship, and denied the legal right to create and enforce a Godly regime on English soil, he turned his Calvinistic fervor and conviction into other channels. In the pulpit he became the reformer lashing out against the ecclesiastical and moral, the social and economic abuses of his age.[4] In parliament he played the part of a reformer also. In that role the disciple of Calvin made an important contribution to modern democracy and liberty.

The arguments upon which the parliamentary opposition based their case fall into two main categories, the legal and the political. Whenever possible the leaders looked to the law to preserve their rights. This approach was often used because the concept that to the subject belonged rights, notably property rights, was an old one generally recognized in law and in the machinery of administration. To harass and irritate monarchs who encroached too much upon the subjects' rights and to remind their kings of the legal limitations to their rule was relatively easy for men as informed and as convinced as Sandys, Coke, Phelips, and Wentworth. To coerce the king was another matter. Here the parliamentary opposition ran into

[4] For an outstanding treatment of this subject see W. Haller, *The Rise of Puritanism*, (Columbia University Press, New York, 1938). See also chapter VIII of this book for a discussion of the political ideas of the Puritan clergy.

real difficulty, for the problem was one for which the law afforded no solution. Nevertheless, law and constitutional precedent could furnish at least the starting point for arguments involving certain rights of the subject.

The parliamentary opposition, however, was not content to limit the king's prerogatives when they encroached upon the rights of the subject. They wished also to control the policies of the king in realms belonging to him and generally accepted by law and practice as within his jurisdiction. This desire could only be realized by political, not legal means — by the effective control of parliament over government; and as early as the first decades of the seventeenth century, parliamentary leaders were struggling with ways and means of achieving such control. To do so effectively demanded new tactics and new ideas, and they produced both. In the realm of ideas they proclaimed that parliament, and particularly the house of commons, was responsible for the welfare of the nation at large. Because of this great responsibility, certain parliamentary actions and claims were just and necessary, even though not backed by law nor supported by definite precedents. In short, parliament based part of its case not on legal but on political arguments.

The kind of argument employed by the parliamentary opposition depended upon the nature of the issues under discussion. Since in 1610 and 1614 the question of impositions was essentially legal, the attack upon them in the parliaments of those years was made on the basis of the law and constitution. In 1621, 1624, 1625, and 1626, however, when the debates concerned foreign policy and monopolies admittedly falling within the sphere of the king's prerogative, the opposition attacked the king's policies in these realms on the basis of parliament's responsibility to the nation. By 1628 when the main argument (the extent of the king's discretionary power) had again become legal, the arguments on the Petition of Right fell largely within the realm of law and right. When the Long Parliament met, the leaders still looked to the law to preserve their rights, and tried on the basis of law to impeach the ministers of the crown, whom they accused of ruling illegally; but when they failed to impeach Charles's ministers by means of the law, they quickly resorted to political actions and arguments and succeeded in passing bills of attainder against their most dangerous opponents. More and more in the Long Parliament the arguments became political, as the aggressive demands and desires of the leaders increased. Their growing claims, beginning with the Grand Remonstrance, and continuing right up to the Nineteen Propositions, could not be presented on the basis of the law and constitution, but only on the basis of their responsibility to the nation. After the civil war began, this was the argument upon which they justified their actions. A convincing legal case could not easily be made, for by their aggressive policies they had given the royalists an opportunity to be the guardians of the law and constitution. The royalists were wise enough to take advantage of this situation and to make their appeal to the nation a legal, constitutional one. Nevertheless, even after the civil war broke out, some of the champions of the parliamentary cause presented their case in the following semi-legal and constitutional way. Parliament, they claimed, was acting as the guardian of law and right, as the interpreter of the constitution, as the last remaining constituted authority in the realm able to save the country from the misuse of the king's power and from the dissolution of all government and authority.

In the rest of this chapter [5] the arguments put forth by the parliamentary opposition and their supporters on the basis of law and right and the "legal authority" of parliament will be discussed. From the accession of James right up to the outbreak of the civil war, those leaders turned to legal and constitutional arguments as the soundest and surest ground upon which they could stand in many of the issues of the period. Although some of those men were grasping and aggressive, the

[5] See chapters VII, IX, and X for further discussion of the parliamentary arguments.

great majority were basically conservative and moderate in their thinking. They checked the king and encroached upon his authority, but at heart most of them remained good monarchists, incapable of thinking ill of James in 1621, and sorely distressed in June, 1628, when they feared Charles had broken faith with them. Since these leaders tended to be conservative in their thinking, they naturally turned to conservative arguments based on law and precedent whenever the issues were of such a nature that legal or semi-legal arguments could be found. In the second place, these leaders, like their royalist opponents, were clever interpreters of public opinion and knew well that a legal argument, or one based on precedent, would be the most appealing one to the great group of moderate men whom they hoped to convince of the justice of their cause. A third and most significant reason for the parliamentary attempt to rest its case upon law was the nature of the arguments used by the royalist judges and councillors. The success of those men in securing decisions in the law courts in favor of the king's absolute power, and in winning those decisions by legal arguments, made it imperative that the opposition not lose the law as its ally. Although the judges in the courts never gave full support to the cause of complete legal absolutism, the royalists did win great victories in the law courts. By those victories, however, they only intensified the determination of the parliamentary opposition to prevent them from registering any legal victories in parliament.

If the royalists won in the law courts, their opponents won in parliament. In 1610 and 1614, even though they failed to secure a complete victory by passing a statute against impositions, they succeeded in discussing the question in parliament, and in presenting powerful legal arguments against the king's right to take impositions by his absolute prerogative. The arguments which Clarke and Fleming had advanced in Bate's case were reasserted and developed by royalist judges and councillors in parliament in 1610; but now they were opposed and matched by such telling and effective arguments on the other side that the royalists might well have wished that they had left the question of absolute prerogative as a matter of "policy and government," [6] and had never argued it at all in a court of law. Yelverton, an ardent royalist, tried to stop the parliamentary discussion in 1610 by asserting, as Fleming had done in the exchequer, that the question was beyond the competence of the common law; [7] but Martin quickly replied, "Mr. Yelverton hathe concluded that this matter is not determinable by law; but Bate's case was adjudged by the judges of the lawe; and so he hath brought the judges into a *premunire* already." [8] By turning to the law courts for legal decisions in favor of the absolute prerogative, the royalists were able to secure some money for the depleted treasury; but they paid too high a price for such sums in terms of the opportunity they afforded the opposition, whenever parliament met, to argue against the legality of the absolute prerogative, and against the legal arguments by which royalist judges and councillors had supported it.

Since the royalists had made it a matter of law, their opponents had to be concerned with the question of right. Sandys drove home this point very effectively in parliament in 1614, when he remarked that "other princes have imposed but never claymed right to doe it." [9] He also said "that it is not vallewe that accreweth to the kinge yearlye by ymposicions that is so much stood uppon as that the kinge doth take to his sole authority to ympose." [10] The leaders in the 1614 parliament were determined that the some three hundred new members of the commons should see the matter of impositions in its true light, and therefore decided the question "should be considered in

[6] S. T., II, 16.

[7] *Parl. Debates in 1610*, p. 87.

[8] *Ibid.*, p. 88.

[9] Hastings Parliamentary Papers. Report of Sandys, May 12, 1614, on the committee for a conference with the Lords upon impositions, Hunt. Lib. MSS. See also, C. J., I, 481.

[10] *Commons Debates 1621*, VII, 653. Appendix C in vol. VII is a parliamentary diary for 1614.

the Committee of the whole House," where the new members "might hear the arguments." [11] They seemed to realize that parliament was fast becoming the last guardian of the subjects' rights, and that they must pass on to younger members the solemn responsibility which was theirs. We must not, Brooke said, "leave our Posterity in worse case, than our Ancesters have left us." [12] The determination of the leaders to make a major constitutional issue of the question of impositions was again revealed when, in the last days of this short parliament, the king and his councillors tried desperately to secure some supply. The commons replied that "before these ympositions were Layed downe if they shoulde graunt the kinge releife it might in after ages be accompted a reall Confirmation of the kinge[s] absolute power of imposinge." [13] The king dissolved parliament and stopped for a time their arguments; but he failed to secure a parliamentary grant, and even more important, he and his councillors also failed to prevent the parliamentary opposition from presenting a strong case in favor of the subjects' rights against the absolute prerogative.

In their arguments in those early years the leaders of the parliamentary opposition set forth their interpretation of the law and constitution which remained the cornerstone of their position until 1640. For them the issue in the question of impositions was simple. To take impositions was to take property, and to take property was against the subjects' rights and the law and constitution of the land. From this statement of the case the parliamentarians never wavered. As the royalists defined the issue as one concerning the absolute power of the king in the realm of foreign affairs and trade, so with equal firmness the parliamentarians defined the question at stake as one of property, for in that realm the subjects' rights were believed to be beyond the king's authority. Because property

[11] Gardiner, II, 237.
[12] C. J., I, 467.
[13] *Commons Debates 1621*, VII, 651–52.

was at stake, the issue was fundamental. "It is," Whitelocke said, "a question of our very essence; . . . whether we shall have any thing or nothing . . ." If the king's claims are true, "we are but tenants at his will of that which we have." [14]

Because the issue was so fundamental, "long travel" was taken in 1610 "in searching Ancient Records in the Tower of London and in other places" [15] to secure support for their case. Such "long travel" did not reveal any common law cases or statutes bearing so directly on the exact point that the royalists would accept them. Whitelocke, the most forceful and profound of all the parliamentary debaters and thinkers in these years, admitted that "there is nothing in our law-book directly, and in point of this matter; neither is the Word (imposition) found in them,. until the case in my lord Dier, 1 Eliz 165." [16] Important as common and statute law precedents were to the parliamentarians in defending their position on the question of impositions, speakers used those laws in their arguments more often to present a general principle illustrated by the law rather than to rest their arguments on one or many specific cases or laws. For example, in their petition in 1610, the commons spoke of this "law of propriety" as "carefully preserved by the common laws of this realm, which are as ancient as the kingdom itself." [17] Whitelocke said concerning the fundamental principle "That the king of England cannot take his subjects goods, without their consent, it need not to be proved more than a principle. It is *jus indigenae,* an old homeborne right, declared to be law by divers statutes of the realme." [18]

Hakewill found another old right and general principle to support his argument that the king could not legally take impositions. He discovered that the common law loves "certainty," and that certainty is particularly "requisite in cases

[14] S. T., II, 479.
[15] *A Record of Some Worthy Proceedings: In the Honourable, Wise, and Faithfull Howse of Commons in the Late Parliament,* (1611), p. 12.
[16] S. T., II, 487.
[17] *Ibid.,* p. 521.
[18] *Ibid.,* pp. 483–84.

where the common law giveth the king a perpetuall profit or revenue to be raised out of the interest and property of his poor subjects estate." [19] If, therefore, in this case of impositions, where the subjects' goods are the issue, the law "hath omitted and neglected it [i.e., certainty] we must conclude the law to be most unreasonable, improvident, and contrary to itself." [20] To back up his general statement that the common law is certain when the subjects' goods are involved, Hakewill gave several illustrations of where such certainty prevailed. For one thing, "the common-law giveth the king a fine for the purchase of an original writ," [21] and in each case the fine is a certain definite known amount which the king cannot change. From several such illustrations he concluded that any duty allowed the king by the common law on customs was "limited and bounded by the common-law to a certainty, which the king hath not power to increase." [22] An argument of this sort reveals that Hakewill, like his royalist opponents, tried to establish the illegality of the king's actions by arguing from general principles and from analogy rather than from direct cases.

In his treatment of statute law, Hakewill made a clever interpretation of statutes to suit the parliamentary claim that impositions laid by the absolute power were illegal. He interpreted specific words in some statutes broadly and others strictly, in order always to favor the parliamentary position. For example, in a statute like Magna Carta in which freedom of trade was granted to merchants, the word merchants must be interpreted liberally and generously to include native as well as alien merchants, for Magna Carta is a "beneficial" statute (i.e., for the subject) and therefore "particular and Speciall words doe always admit a general extent." [23] Hakewill also claimed that since the statute of 25 E. 1. c. 7 was beneficial, the king's promise in it to take "no such things" must be inter-

[19] *Ibid.*, p. 414.
[20] *Ibid.*
[21] *Ibid.*, p. 416.
[22] *Ibid.*
[23] *Ibid.*, p. 457.

preted liberally in such a beneficial statute to mean "no charges upon all kinds of merchandise." [24] In insisting on a liberal interpretation of special phrases in these statutes, Hakewill was claiming that, according to the spirit and intent of the English law and the constitution, the subjects' property must remain secure against the king's absolute prerogative. On the basis of this principle he insisted that words in other statutes which might justify the king's absolute prerogative be interpreted very strictly. For example, in the statute of 11 R.12.cap.2 where it was decreed that non-parliamentary impositions should not be put upon wools, leather, or woolfells, "saving always to the king his ancient right," this saving could not refer to "the pretended right of impositing," for then it would "be contrary to the body of the act." [25] In the case of the increase of customs secured by Edward I in the Carta Mercatorum, Hakewill seemed to admit that this was an imposition levied by the king's absolute power, but insisted that such a precedent had no bearing upon the issue under discussion because it concerned foreign merchants.[26] Thus, even in his treatment of statutory as well as of common law precedents, Hakewill discovered an interpretation for the different statutes which favored the parliamentary contention that the law guarded and protected the subjects' property.

The royalists did not in general deny that the subjects' property was their own. They had presented their case for the absolute prerogative on other grounds, but the parliamentary opposition was ready in 1610 and 1614 with their answers to the royalist claims. To Fleming's argument that the matter was one of policy and not of law, Martin replied, as has already been pointed out, that in taking the case into the law courts the royalists had made it a matter of law. To the royalist claim that the king's absolute prerogative included his right to take impositions, Crew answered that the proof is on "our side," for

[24] *Ibid.*, p. 466.
[25] *Ibid.*, p. 444.
[26] *Ibid.*, pp. 429–30.

such a prerogative is not mentioned in the Statute *Prerogativa Regis,* in Fortescue, or in Frowick's *Reading upon the prerogative.*[27] To the royalist argument that the king must have an emergency discretionary power to handle difficulties, Whitelocke said, "Our rule is in this plain commonwealth of ours, *'oportet neminem esse sapientorem legibus.'* If there be an inconvenience, it is fitter to have it removed by a lawful means, then by an unlawful."[28] Thomas Hedley went even farther in insisting that "This question determinable onely by the common lawe of England, for lawe of State he knowes not."[29] In actual war, Hedley explained, law is silent, "But in peace the comon law is to lymitt the prerogative of the King, because the King cannot dispence with it."[30] Blocking out the prerogative by extending so far the sphere of the common law came to be a commonplace among parliamentary leaders in 1628, but in 1610 Hedley appears to be the only man who made such a sweeping claim for the absoluteness of the common law. A more prevalent point of view concerning the emergency power would be the attitude of Carleton, who said: "And in our lawes, though prerogative be not so hembed in, but that it may break out upon extraordinary occasions, as *tempore guerrae,* . . . yet is it so entangled as it can not goe at pleasure . . ."[31]

The royalists had made much in their arguments of the king's responsibility for the general welfare, and of the important powers entrusted to him in order that he might carry out

[27] *Parl. Debates in 1610,* p. 94.
[28] S. T., II, 518. See also, A. Wilson, *The History of Great Britain, being the Life and Reign of James the First,* (London, 1653), p. 52. Wilson says in connection with the parliament of 1610 that the king talked of *Arcana imperii,* "But the *Parliament* were apprehensive enough, that those hidden *mysteries* made many dark steps into the Peoples Liberties, and they were willing by the light of *Law* and *Reason,* to discover what was the Kings, what theirs."
[29] *Parl. Debates in 1610,* p. 72.
[30] *Ibid.* Martin also said, "The comon lawe extends as farre [as] the power of the Kinge extends." *Ibid.,* p. 89.
[31] *Ibid.,* p. 111.

his great responsibility. This argument was effectively answered by Hedley, Jones, and Whitelocke. Hedley put the case this way, "if it be not for the good of the Comon wealth, without paying money, then it is not good, paying money." [32] According to Jones, "he may restrayne for the good of the Commonwealth, and dispence: but to take a some of money for a dispensation he cannot." [33] Whitelocke also admitted that the king possessed power for the public good, but insisted he could not "make gain and benefit by it. The one is protection, the other is expilation." [34] In short, the parliamentarians insisted that the general-welfare power of the king could not override property, for without the subjects' right to property there could be no well-being in their commonwealth.

When their answers to the royalists and their own arguments are combined, the outlines of the parliamentary interpretation of the constitution become fairly clear. In their view of that constitution, the right of property was basic. Property rights were extended to take in merchant's goods upon the sea, for, as Martin said, the merchant "hathe as good right to plowe the sea as the plowman hathe to plowe the land." [35] "The merchant is not the man alone that is subject to taxes, and all other men free." [36] In their view of the constitution, the king was limited by law, particularly in reference to the taking of the subjects' property. If there was no certainty on that point, Hakewill said, "it were to the utter dissolution and destruction of that politike frame and constitution of this commonwealth." [37] The king was also limited in the making of law. In the Petition of Grievances to the king in 1610, the commons explicitly said:

> The policy and constitution of this your kingdom appropriates unto the kings of this realm, with the assent of the parliament, as well the sovereign Power of making laws, as that

[32] *Ibid.*, p. 73.	[33] *Ibid.*, p. 64.	[34] S. T., II, 514.
[35] *Parl. Debates in 1610*, p. 88.
[36] S. T., II, 472. Hakewill made this remark.
[37] S. T., II, 420.

of taxing, or imposing upon the subjects goods or merchandizes, wherein they have justly such a propriety, as may not without their consent be altered or changed.[38]

Many parliamentary speakers waxed eloquent on the importance of parliament's part in lawmaking and taxing. Some of them even stated that the king was most absolute in parliament and called attention to the many different ways in which the king in parliament could legally do certain things which he could not correctly do outside of parliament.

From that position James Whitelocke advanced to a real concept of complete parliamentary supremacy. He argued that because the king's power was greater in parliament than out of it, his power in parliament was *"suprema potestas* The soveraigne power, and the other is *subordinata."* [39] Moreover, he recognized that supreme power is "a power that can controule all other powers, and cannot be controuled but by itself." [40] He pointed out that since the power of imposing "hath ever been ranked among those rights of sovereign power," it must rest where sovereign power was, that is, in the king in parliament.[41] Whitelocke's argument is important because he recognized that the supremacy lay not in the king alone, nor in the law, but in parliament. The legal illustrations he cited for that supremacy were sound and could not be denied. The implications he drew from them showed a grasp of reality more penetrating than that of any other parliamentary leader between 1603 and 1640.

Whitelocke gave the parliamentary opposition an argument by which they could have presented their most convincing legal case against the king's absolute prerogative. Some men, notably Martin, Fuller, and Sandys, talked during these early years of the ways in which the king was supreme only in parliament; but no one except Whitelocke used the fact of his

[38] *Ibid.*, p. 522.
[39] *Ibid.*, p. 482.
[40] *Ibid.*
[41] *Ibid.* See also, *Commons Debates 1621*, VII, 631 and 642 for additional opinions on this question in 1614.

supremacy in parliament as the one supreme proof of the subordination of all of his prerogatives to that supremacy. Instead, the leaders of the opposition still thought in terms of law and right and precedent. In 1614, when they worked out a careful plan of procedure to present their arguments before the lords, they chose Whitelocke to present the precedents from Edward I to Edward III, and Sandys to discuss the frame and policy of the kingdom.[42] Whitelocke's brilliant analysis of the frame and policy of their kingdom had apparently not been understood or accepted by them. They did not realize the extent of parliament's sovereignty. Their failure to grasp, as Whitelocke did, the necessary subordination of all powers to the sovereign power may surprise us today, but it is more easily understood if we remind ourselves that the concept of sovereignty, as a supreme final authority controlling all others, had not yet become an accepted basis of men's thinking in England. Moreover, during those many years when parliament did not meet, they saw the king alone carrying on the government as a supreme ruler. Like most of us, they naturally looked to old rather than new concepts to defend their position. Their law and their rights had a goodly heritage which all men knew and most men accepted. Their parliament was old too, but its complete and final sovereignty in the state was too recent a development, and too uncertain a doctrine, for legally minded Englishmen to use as the cornerstone of their legal case against the absolute prerogative.

The leaders of the parliamentary opposition stopped short in these years of claiming complete sovereignty for parliament. Instead they talked of the sanctity and inviolability of the subjects' rights from any encroachment by the king's prerogative, insisting that in times of peace no property could be taken from the subject except in parliament. They also rested their case upon the legal limitation of the king, extending the boundaries of such limitation into the area claimed by the royalists as the realm of the absolute prerogative, where the king was

[42] Hastings Parliamentary Papers, Reports of Sandys.

free to act as he pleased. Most of them did not deny that in real emergencies the king could act by his prerogative, but they felt that most difficulties in their commonwealth should be settled by law. Although most of them did not grasp the meaning and significance of Whitelocke's statement of complete parliamentary supremacy, they did make the taxing and lawmaking power of parliament a most fundamental part of their policy and constitution. They talked of the importance of the lawmaking power, but, like some of their royalist opponents, did not yet regard the legislative power as supreme above all others. They still accepted certain matters, such as foreign affairs, appointments, coinage, and defense, as belonging within the realm of the king's absolute prerogative, and apparently still accepted those powers as co-ordinate with, and not subordinate to, his power in parliament.[43]

The parliamentary conception of the constitution was strong in its emphasis on property, law, and the place of parliament. It can not be called a complete theory of government, for, with the exception of Whitelocke, its exponents did not clearly work out the relation of all parts of the government to each other. In 1610 and 1614 they were not prepared to claim for parliament all the powers in different realms exercised by the king. They were still willing to allow him some discretionary power, and they were not ready to deny that he was responsible for the general welfare; but they opposed any use of such powers which touched the sanctity of their property rights. This parliamentary interpretation of the constitution tipped the scales of the old balanced polity in favor of the subjects' right and the law, and against the realm of the king's absolute prerogative.

Already in 1610 and 1614 the parliamentarians were backing up their interpretation of the law and constitution by appeals to the law of nations, the law of God, the practice of other nations, and the nature of true monarchy. Mr. Went-

---

[43] These last two paragraphs are a summary of some of the material discussed more fully in chapters I and III.

worth, a Puritan, reminded the commons that "The King is subject to another King, and wee all pray *veniat regnum tuum.*" [44] He also pointed out that "the lawe of God is the Decalogue, which is that subjects as well as kings should enjoy theyre owne." [45] Fuller quoted "Deut. 24 Not to take the milstone to pawne, for that is his living," as an argument against the king's right to take his subjects' goods. [46]

Roger Owen was the parliamentary speaker in 1610 and in 1614 who discussed most fully the law of nations and the practices of other nations. He asserted that "Theise impositions are not agreeable to the lawe of nations, nor to the practise of modern nations, nor the law of the land." [47] Concerning the law of nations he said, "Properties of goods, by lawe of nations, according to Austyn Therefore it is contrary to the lawe of nations to take away the property of man's goods." [48] Owen examined systematically the practice of other monarchies, pointing out here that, although the Roman emperors took customs from those whom they conquered, they did not from their subjects. [49] He admitted that the French monarchs took customs, but explained that such power had been given them in 1355 by act of parliament. [50] A special and definite act of parliament had granted impositions to Alfonso II of Spain. [51] The emperor of Germany could not impose, whereas in the Low Countries "They pay to theymselves." [52] Owen admitted that the Medici had imposed, but "the Dukes of Medicis did usurpe." [53] In England "The King hathe not the customes by the comon lawe and constitution of this kingdome." [54] Such a

[44] *Parl. Debates in 1610,* p. 61.
[45] *Ibid.*
[46] *Ibid.,* p. 59.
[47] *Ibid.,* p. 112.
[48] *Ibid.* Austyn refers to St. Augustine.
[49] *Ibid.,* p. 113.
[50] *Ibid.,* p. 114.
[51] *Ibid.*
[52] *Ibid.*
[53] *Ibid.*
[54] *Ibid.*

limitation upon his power, however, did not detract at all from his stature as a great king, for "the King of *England* hath as much Power, as any other King of the World." [55] In not taking his subjects' property, he was ruling as a true king. If the king might impose, leaving the subject no property, Whitelocke said, "you make him no king; for, as Bracton saith, . . . *'ex est, ubi dominatur lex, non voluntas.' "* [56]

From the point of view of the nature and scope of the arguments, little was left unsaid by the parliamentary leaders in 1610 and 1614. In 1628, there were, according to the surviving records, more speakers, longer speeches, a little more theory, and some different emphases, but comparatively few new ideas advanced. It is also true that in these earlier years the parliamentary opposition could not counter the royalist claims with arguments based exclusively on English law. Desirous as those parliamentary leaders were to cite common and statute law on behalf of their claims, they argued, even when these laws were being discussed, more from general principles illustrated by such laws than from exact and definite precedents. They also appealed to the law of nations and of God frequently and apparently effectively.

The thoroughness and effectiveness of the parliamentary arguments were not unnoticed by their royalist opponents. In 1614, Ellesmere, then an old man, warned the lords what to expect from the parliamentary leaders if the lords went into a joint conference with the commons on the subject of impositions. He insisted that the lords had not sufficiently considered the case and the records; whereas the commons "goe both high and lowe and looke of all things that concern their purpose, and we can say nothinge, having not seen records. They perhaps will tell us of the lawe of nature and Nations, beinge learned and able gentlemen, who have studied this case longe, if any man in this house thinke himselfe able to dispute with them, lett him doe it, for myselfe I must desire to be ex-

[55] C. J., I, 467. Owen made this remark in 1614.
[56] S. T., II, 486.

cused . . ." [57] Ellesmere was too old to cope with these ardent leaders who were so well fortified with arguments of all kinds to support their interpretation of the constitution.

The second great attempt of the parliamentary opposition to check the royalists on the basis of law, precedent, and the constitution took place in parliament in 1628. In the years before that parliament met, the fears and apprehensions of the men leading the opposition had grown. They had seen how the royalists had used and extended the doctrine of public welfare to shield and justify all actions of government, no matter how much such actions encroached upon the rights of the subject or how grievous they were to him. In 1621 and 1624, parliament-men had attacked monopolies as grievances for which remedy should be given, but the royalists had tried to prevent parliamentary discussion and action upon them on the ground that monopolies were "matters of state." In 1625 and 1626, the opposition had attacked Buckingham, whose policies they regarded as most grievous, but the royalists had insisted that he was a minister appointed by the king and responsible only to him. The parliamentary opposition in 1626 was in no mood to accept this royalist interpretation. "I have observed," said Eliot at that time, "a new wisdome in this house in this, that the faults of private men shall be shaddowed under secretts of state." [58] So fearful had the opposition become of royalist actions and claims that they even wondered if parliaments themselves might not be doomed, and as Alford had said in 1621, "farewell parliaments and farewell England." [59]

Men of moderate views, as well as the more aggressive parliamentary leaders, were fearful of the future. A good index of the state of mind of a moderate conservative in the year before the parliament of 1628 is furnished by examining Archbishop Abbott's protest against the views proclaimed by Sibthorpe in

[57] Hastings Parliamentary Papers, A booke of remembrances . . . May 25, 1614.

[58] Whit., 4/21/26.

[59] *Commons Debates 1621*, VI, 155.

his sermon on Apostolic Obedience. Abbott denounced Sibthorpe's assertion that subjects are bound to support their
prince, even when he demanded taxes from them without parliament. Such a doctrine, according to Abbott, might lead to
sedition, for "There is a *Meum* and a *Tuum* in Christian-
Common-wealths, and according to Laws and Customes
Princes may dispose it, that same being true, *Ad Reges potestas
omnium pertinet, ad singulos proprietas.*" [60] Abbott denounced
the loan which the king had demanded and the means he had
used to secure it. "And when afterwards I saw, that men were
to be put to their Oath . . . And yet further beheld, that
divers were to be imprisoned: I thought this was somewhat a
New World." [61] Abbott dared also to criticize Buckingham to
whom Charles had delegated such great power. Elizabeth, he
pointed out, was wise enough not to let any one man be so all-
important. It is necessary to distinguish between the king and
the duke, ". . . the one is our Sovereign by the Laws of God
and Men, the other a Subject as we are." [62] Abbott even voiced
the fear "that the Duke had a purpose to turn up side down
the Laws, and the whole Fundamental Courses, and Liberties
of the Subject." [63]

Men were truly alarmed before the parliament of 1628 met,
for soldiers had been billeted, martial law proclaimed, forced
loans taken, and men committed to prison for refusing to pay
—and all these actions had been carried out on the plea of
necessity in government. Even more alarming, the judges in
the five knights' case had rendered a decision in a court of law,
putting the stamp of legal approval upon arbitrary imprisonment at the command of the king.[64] Here was the greatest blow

[60] Rushworth, I, 443.
[61] *Ibid.*, 455.
[62] *Ibid.*, 451.
[63] *Ibid.*, 455.
[64] For a full discussion of the nature of the judgment and the parliamentary discussion of it, see F. H. Relf, *The Petition of Right*, (University
of Minnesota Press, Minneapolis, 1917), ch. I. The two best recent treatments of the Petition of Right are by Miss Relf and by E. R. Adair, "The
Petition of Right," *History*, V, 99–103.

of all for the parliamentary opposition. In 1610 and 1614, the decision in Bate's case had set the stage and determined the temper of the arguments in parliament, and now in 1628 the legal problem, arguments, and decision in the five knights' case colored and affected the arguments and actions in parliament. To the leaders of the opposition and to many men of more moderate views, such legal decisions constituted the greatest danger of all to their cause—the cause of the subjects' rights, the law, and the future existence of parliament. Therefore their great aim in 1628 was to do their utmost to keep as much of the law as possible on their side, and to prevent the royalists from winning it over completely to theirs.

This fear that the law which had been their "trusty servant" for so long might fail them now was expressed time and time again in the debates in 1628. Eliot wondered "whether there be a power in the Law to preserve our goods." [65] Selden called the royalist doctrine of general welfare "a new lawe, the lawe of state," [66] while Sir Edward Coke hoped that God would not "send" him "to live under the lawe of convenience and discretion." [67] Phelips was concerned that there were "acts of power against acts of Law." [68] These men did not object to some emergency powers of government and occasional discretionary actions, but feared that such powers might become established and accepted as legal. Shervile objected to the "distinction discovered of late *inter legalum et regalem potestatem regis.*" [69] He wished "it had slept." [70] Only in a pulpit, which "is of no waight" according to Selden,[71] had any "ever denied or doubted that we had a fundamentall propriety of our goods." [72] Although Selden asserted that the pulpit's de-

[65] Mass., 3/22/28.
[66] Mass., 4/19/28.
[67] Mass., 4/18/28.
[68] Bor., 3/22/28.
[69] Bor., 3/29/28. According to Professor Hartley Simpson, the name Sherfield in the Borlase diary is actually Shervile.
[70] *Ibid.*
[71] Mass., 4/26/28.
[72] Nich., 4/26/28.

nunciation of property was of no consequence, other men revealed by their remarks that this doctrine, which had been preached in the twenties from the pulpit, did trouble them. Seymour, for example, said, "It hath binne preached or rather prated in the pulpitts, that all is the kings . . ." [73] If such royalist doctrines became established and accepted in law and eventually in the administrative machinery of government, the cause of parliament would be black indeed. The precedents and laws would truly have been turned against them. When that happened, nothing would be left of their rights as subjects. Even kingship in its highest form, which they believed England possessed, would disappear, for, as Digges once said, "That King that is not tyed to the Lawes of the Kingdome is a Kinge of slaves." [74] To prevent such a calamity became the aim of the parliamentary opposition in 1628.

To achieve this objective they must first of all re-establish the subjects' rights upon a firm legal basis. In the parliamentary debates and discussions they therefore presented the case for the subject as carefully as if the issue were being debated and decided in a court of law. Throughout the debates in this parliament, the lawyers rather than the politicians held the floor. [75]

The starting point of their argument was the inherent right which the subject had in his property. They insisted that it is "an undoubted and fundamentall Point of this so ancient a Law of *England,* that the Subjects have a true Property in their Goods, Lands and Possessions." [76] This right was recognized and guaranteed, they asserted now, as they had in 1610, by old and established principles and precedents of the common law. "The Common Law hath so admeasured the King's Prerogative as He cannot prejudice any Man in his inheritance." [77]

[73] Bor., 3/22/28. [74] Mass., 3/22/28.
[75] See F. H. Relf, *The Petition of Right,* p. 1.
[76] S. T., III, 84–85. Sir Dudley Digges was the speaker.
[77] L. J., III, 762. E. Coke was the speaker. He was citing Plowden, 4 Eliz. Pl. 236.

Together with the property rights of the subject belonged, in the parliamentary view of the case, his personal rights—his liberty as a free Englishman. "If the King have no absolute power over our Land or Goods, then *a fortiori* not over our Persons, to imprison them, without declaring the Cause . . ." [78] This linking together of property and personal rights was the cornerstone of the parliamentary case. Though logically and historically they could be linked together, the actual precedents for liberty were less definite and clear-cut than those for property.[79] This fact was not openly admitted by the leaders in the commons but must have been tacitly recognized, because, when they talked of liberty, their arguments became more indirect and based more on analogy than when they discussed property rights. One of their favorite statements was that if the subject had no freedom against the king's right to imprison him, he would be worse off than a villein.[80] The king would also be less glorious, for he would be ruling over bondmen and not free subjects.[81]

Another argument advanced by Selden and Coke ran in this fashion:

> In all cases, my lords, where any Right or Liberty belongs to the subjects by any positive law written or unwritten, if there were not also a remedie by law, for the enjoying or regaining this Right or Libertie, when it is violated or taken from him, the positive law were most vain and to no purpose . . .[82]

Habeus corpus being "the highest remedy in law" [83] for the person of the subject must prevail at all times if the liberty of the subject is to have meaning. Coke showed that since the law had provided many remedies for the person of the subject,

[78] Rushworth, I, 507. Creswell was the speaker. According to Professor Hartley Simpson, Creswell is Richard Cresheld.
[79] See Gardiner, VI, 241.
[80] S.T., III, 128.
[81] Mass., 3/22/28.
[82] S. T., III, 95.
[83] *Ibid.*

the principle was thereby established that the king could not imprison at his pleasure.[84] He also pointed out that it was not unusual, but according to practice and precedent, for the courts regularly to pass upon the king's actions and to see that such actions were in accord with the correct form. The "way and mannerr" in which the king should act "is debated every day in every Court in Westminster." [85] Because form and procedure did to a certain extent protect the subjects' rights, that fact was made another cornerstone of the parliamentary case. The commission for martial law, as interpreted by the royalists, could mean that a man might "suffer death without a Jurie and tryall." [86] That is impossible, Banks argued, for "it is noe dash of a pen that dashes and takes away many a man's life." [87] The proper form must be followed. In 1628, as in 1610 and 1614, parliamentary leaders tried to prove the correctness of their position by citing general principles, and then arguing that such fundamental principles must apply to the question at issue.

They also tried to demonstrate that specific laws and statutes were on their side. The commons took their stand on Clause 14 of Magna Carta, Littleton pointing out that the words *per Legale judicium* gave the protection of the common law to subjects for trials "at the king's suit." [88] In fact, in the words of Rudyard, "the very scope and drift of *Magna Charta* was, to reduce the Regal to a Legal Power, in matter of Imprisonment." [89] To hold, as the royalists did, that Magna Carta and other statutes exempted the king from the law was, in the opinion of the opposition, unhistorical and illegal. At one point in the debate on statutes and precedents, the parliamentarians turned the tables very cleverly against the royalists. Sir Francis Nethersole "Moved to read the Preamble of the

[84] S. T., III, 129–30.
[85] Mass., 4/15/28.
[86] Mass., 4/16/28.
[87] *Ibid.*
[88] S. T., III, 86.
[89] Rushworth, I, 551.

statue made in the 31 yeare of H. the 8: for Proclamacions, because," he explained, "there may be some exposicion of the
King's prerogative. For possibly that which was done by the
state at that tyme may be of use to us now. The preamble was
read." [90] And then Sir Edward Coke said: "the gentleman did
well to bring forward authority for what he sayd that the Act
was repealed: and in that Act was proviso, that a proclamacion
made out of the prerogative shal neyther bynd lands bodies
or goods." [91] The implication was clear. Here was a statute
recognized as one giving great power to the king, and yet even
it exempted from his prerogative important specific rights of
the subject.

It was impossible, however, for the parliamentary opposition in the debates in 1628, as it had been impossible in 1610,
to present a completely convincing case on the basis of statutes
or precedents. The precedents did not exactly fit the issue
under discussion,[92] and Magna Carta and the other statutes
cited could be interpreted by the royalists as not applying to
the particular kind of law or imprisonment under discussion.

The royalists did not deny that, in general, common and
statute law afforded protection to the subject; but insisted that
the phrase "law of the land" included other than common laws,
as for example, martial law, the law of the admiralty, merchant law, and the law of state.[93] They also held that although
the king might not imprison without just cause, the cause need
not always be expressed, nor the procedure always follow the
ordinary common law forms.

To meet this royalist argument, the parliamentarians had
to do more than to cite common and statute law principles and
precedents. They had to try to demonstrate that the common
law or statutes confirming common law principles protected
completely the property and individual rights of the subject.

[90] Gros., 4/26/28.
[91] *Ibid.*
[92] See F. H. Relf, *The Petition of Right*, p. 20.
[93] See chapter IV.

Accordingly, for a few weeks leaders in parliament talked as if their whole case rested only on the common law and its principles. They insisted that, according to the correct legal exposition, the phrase *per legem terrae* meant "the Common Law, which is the generall and universall law by which men hold their inheritances." [94] To them the common law "is the principall and generall Law, and is always understood by the way of excellencie, when mention is of the law of the land generally: and that though each of the other laws (i.e., ecclesiastical law, admiralty, merchants, etc.) which are admitted into this kingdome by custome or act of Parliament, may justly be called *a* law of the land, yet none of them can have the preheminence to be styled *the* law of the land." [95] In the words of Selden, "The Cannon and Civill lawe or Admiralty are lawes that are in force by the lawes of the land, but they are not the lawes of the land." [96] Digges maintained that although the king was God's image and as absolute as any king, "yet the Common law provide for all." [97]

Perhaps the most extreme lengths to which this particular argument went occurred in connection with the proposition suggested by the lords that the king should declare that the subject had a fundamental property and a fundamental liberty. Coke, who himself had often spoken in such terms, now said concerning the word "fundamental": "a word I understand not." [98] He wanted the property and personal rights of the subject to rest upon definite common and statute law principles and precedents. Coke was so desirous of defining and blocking off the king's prerogative in order that the subjects' liberty, protected by common law, might be absolutely inviolate, that he admittedly in this parliament changed his mind on the question of imprisonment for reasons of state *per mandatum regis*. In his own words: "When I had read Stanford, I enclinde, I

[94] S. T., III, 153.
[95] *Ibid.*
[96] Nich., 4/15/28.
[97] Harl., 4/22/28.
[98] Gros., 4/26/28.

confess, to his opinion but afterwards lookinge on records and acts of Parliament, for tenants at will, and for liberty, I was converted . . ." [99]

Parliamentary leaders were so eager to secure the law as their ally that they tried to surround their rights with a strong stockade built of common law, within which no legal action of government could penetrate. Because of their well-grounded fears that the royalists would secure all law on their side, the leaders of the parliamentary opposition tried to secure for their position the monopoly of the common law. From the point of view of law and precedent, they went too far in this eulogy of common law, for they too were denying, as the royalists often denied also, the necessary balance and adjustment between government and rights. They were trying to establish, as Heath said, "a new Mathematical Line that admits of no Latitude at all," [100] which would make it impossible for government to function.

Historians have sometimes talked as if the whole parliamentary case between 1603 and 1640 rested on common law. Such an interpretation is, in my opinion, quite incorrect. During those forty years of constitutional debate and conflict, the parliamentary case rested not on one but on many arguments, some of them legal and constitutional, others more political. In finding the telling argument in connection with the particular issue at stake at different times, the parliamentarians showed themselves to be as clever and as historically and philosophically minded as the royalists. They, like their opponents, claimed time and time again that natural and divine law, as well as English law, were on their side, and that their interpretation of the case was supported by the true nature of their monarchy. "The Kings of England," Shervile said, "have a Monarchecall state not a Segnioraill. The first makes freedome,

[99] Bor., 3/29/28. It was in connection with Coke's confession that Phelips said "that Sir E. C. is *Monarcha Juris* and thoughe it were the pleasure of the State to remove him from the King's bench here, yet he hopes he shall have a place in the King's Bench in Heaven" (Nich., 3/31/28).

[100] L. J., III, 763.

the second slavery" [101]; while the speaker implied that subjects who were free, as well as rich, were "most able to do your Majesty service, either in Peace or War." [102] According to Nathaniel Rich, "if the Subject hath noe propriety then there is noe Mercy (?) and honour and then noe Justice, for to Justice is the distribucion of Mercy (?) and honour, if noe Justice, noe throwne; for Solomon saith that Justice establisheth the King's throwne." [103] Phelips referred to English and foreign writers who had stood for the property and liberty of the subject, saying, "foraine and home writers agree that the propriety of the Subject is that his goods ought not to be taken from him [but] by his voluntary Consent, without consent in Parliament." [104] "Even our neighbours the french, whereof du Haillian the historian is one that can tell us mutch. Wee have 2 Authers at home for us Fo[rte]scue, Hen[ry] VI, and Sir Thom[as] Smyth Secretary to Queen Elizabeth. They say, that the kings of England can not make lawes, nor rayse monny, but in Parliament." [105]

The customary appeal to the Bible was frequently made. Coriton said that "the Kings of Israell must read in the law of God that his hart might not be lifted up above his brethren: he is the minister of God for our good." [106] Seymour insisted that property and liberty belong to us by "the Law of God, and of the land," [107] and Cresheld, pleading for the liberty of one's person, reminded them that Christ had said, *"Is not the Body* of more worth than the Raiment?" [108]

At times, in their eulogy of property and liberty, these men even called upon natural law and spoke of *salus populi,* despite the fact that they had condemned the royalist use of

[101] Bor., 3/29/28.
[102] Rushworth, I, 541.
[103] Nich., 3/26/28.
[104] *Ibid.*
[105] Bor., 3/26/28.
[106] Gros., 5/6/28.
[107] Rushworth, I, 500.
[108] *Ibid.*, p. 508.

these terms and doctrines. Eliot remarked, "It is proved, (this liberty of oures), By way of Law of nature and nations to bee sutch as does beelonge to us." [109] Cresheld went further, saying "that by the very Law of Nature, service of the Person of the Subject is due to his Soveraign; but this must be in such things which are not against the Law of Nature . . ." [110] Selden ventured to say, "The *Salus populi* is *libertas populi*. Festus sayd so to Agrippa." [111] Since the parliamentarians had tried so often in March to strengthen their case by resorting to natural and divine law, it is remarkable that the royalists did not turn the tables against them in April, when the commons rested everything upon common law.

It was relatively easy for the parliamentary opposition to agree upon general principles and impressive arguments in favor of their case. It was much more difficult to find a proper legal remedy for the recent encroachments of the king against their liberties. The major difficulty confronting them when they sought a remedy lay in the fact that they were determined to find a legal remedy, i.e., one in harmony with past laws and the traditional constitution. To find such a solution in the law presented almost insurmountable obstacles. Both the supporters of the king and of parliament insisted, with considerable justification for their stand, that the law favored their interpretation of the issue. The law itself was not clear-cut. As has been shown in earlier chapters, precedents in the past had been quite clear and definite in favor of both the king's prerogative and the subjects' rights, but had not been clear when the question was one involving the general welfare, where a necessary adjustment between the king's prerogative and the subjects' rights had never been worked out legally.

[109] Bor., 3/31/28. Eliot continues as follows: "There is for it reason, example and auctority, Reason and *conservationem generalem,* for as Pliny sayes though auctority beelonge to the greatest, punishment does not, and therefore instances in Bees, where though all of them have stings, the king only is excepted and allowed none . . ."

[110] Rushworth, I, 508. Cresheld maintained that it was against the law of nature "to have the body imprisoned without any cause declared . . ."

[111] Bor., 3/28/28.

On this vital problem there was no law and there were no precedents which both groups would accept, and yet any suggestion that the issue could not be solved legally was regarded as almost treasonable by leaders on both sides. Sergeant Ashley was bold enough to suggest that the dilemma could not be solved by legal means. It was, he explained:

> . . . a Question too high to be determined by any legal Decision; for it must needs be a hard Case of Contention when the Conqueror must sit down with irreparable Loss; as in this Case, if the Subject prevail, Liberty but loses the Benefit of that State Government, without which a Monarchy may too soon become an Anarchy; or, if the State prevail, it gains absolute Sovereignty, but loses the Subjects not their Subjection, for Obedience we must yield, though nothing be left but Prayers and Tears; but it loses the best Part of them, which is their Affections, whereby Sovereignty is established, and the Crown firmly fixt on His Royal Head. Between Two such Extremes, there is no Way to moderate, but to find a medium for Accommodation of the Difference . . .[112]

In reading the debates now, it is refreshing to come upon these words of Ashley, for they make sense to us. Here was a man not bogged down in law and precedent, but one who recognized that the time had come to face the facts: to desert the law if it would not help them, and to work out a new compromise, not on the basis of law, but of politics. Ashley really was saying in 1628 what Hobbes said later in the *Behemoth*, but he was distinctly out of order in the first part of the seventeenth century. The lords reprimanded and imprisoned him for his speech, and the commons regarded it as almost treasonable. Both sides wanted to rest their case on law, and would not admit at this time that the law had failed them.

In condemning Ashley and in insisting that a legal remedy

[112] L. J., III, 759. *Author's note:* Ashley's earlier views on this subject have been discussed in a valuable and comprehensive study by Miss Faith Thompson which was published as this book was going to press (F. Thompson, *Magna Carta, Its Role in the Making of the English Constitution, 1629,* pp. 284–93. University of Minnesota Press, Minneapolis, 1948).

be found, the leaders in the parliament faced a difficult task. Statute was the normal way in which king, lords, and commons came together to handle matters common to all, and statute was the first method which the leaders in the commons hoped could be found to remedy the difficulties. The Petition of Right was decidedly a second choice.[113] On April first, the grand committee of the commons passed certain resolutions condemning arbitrary imprisonment by the king or privy council and declaring "That the ancient and undoubted Right of every free Man is, that he hath a full and absolute Property in his Goods and Estate and that no Tax, . . . Loan . . . or other like Charge, ought to be commanded or levied by the King, or any of his Ministers, without common assent by Act of Parliament." [114]

The lords gave their answer to the commons by drawing up their own resolutions, the first four of which reiterated in general terms the property and individual rights of Englishmen. Their fifth proposition reads as follows:

> And as touching his Majesty's royal prerogative intrinsical to his sovereignty, and entrusted him from God *ad communem totius populi salutem, et non ad destructionem*, that his Majesty would resolve not to use or divert the same to the prejudice of any of his loyal people in the property of their goods or liberty of their persons; and in case, for the security of his Majesty's Royal person, the common safety of his people, or the peaceable government of his kingdom, his Majesty shall find just cause, for reason of State, to imprison or restrain any man's person, his Majesty would graciously declare that, within a convenient time, he shall and will express the cause of the commitment or restraint, either general or special; and, upon a cause so expressed, will leave him immediately to be tried according to the common justice of the kingdom.[115]

[113] F. H. Relf, *The Petition of Right,* p. 27 and p. 35.

[114] C. J., I, 878–79. For the resolutions "with notes showing the alterations made in the house," see F. H. Relf, *The Petition of Right,* (University of Minnesota Press, Minneapolis, 1917), pp. 61–62.

[115] Harl. MSS. 4771, fol. 110, as quoted in S. R. Gardiner, *History of England from the Accession of James I to the Outbreak of the Civil War,* 10 vols., (Longmans, Green, and Co., London, 1883–84), VI, 260.

In the latter part of this fifth resolution, the lords had made an honest attempt to safeguard the king's power of commitment from being abused, but their reference in the first part of the proposition to "his Majesty's royal prerogative intrinsical to his Sovereignty" could not be accepted by the parliamentary opposition. On the other hand, it quickly became apparent that the lords and many moderate members in the commons would never agree to any bill based upon resolutions which omitted all reference to the king's prerogative. Any law—and statute would be law—asserting the absoluteness of the subjects' rights, as the parliamentary opposition insisted they should be set forth, and failing to include also a statement of the king's right to act in an emergency for the general welfare of all, would be, as the royalists and many moderates correctly pointed out, a legal denial of the powers long exercised by the crown. To be true to law and precedent, the king's prerogative as well as the subjects' rights must be written into law. If, however, the prerogative were written into a statute, it could all too easily be cited in the future as justification for any further encroachment upon the subjects' rights, no matter how strongly those rights might be proclaimed in the statute. The leaders in the commons, keenly aware of earlier royalist interpretations of the prerogative set forth and accepted in the courts, realized that any mention of the prerogative in a statute, in relation to the general-welfare or emergency power, would be another great legal victory for absolutism. This they were determined to prevent, even though they admitted in the heat of parliamentary debate that the king could act extra-legally in a real emergency.[116] These leaders feared most, not sovereignty in action when an emergency occurred, but that such sovereign power might be accepted as legal and written into the law of the land. In the face of recent royalist policies

---

[116] Coke, for example, said in the debates on the Petition of Right, "I had rather for my part have the Prerogative acted and I myself to lie under it, than to have it disputed." Pym said, "And we cannot leave to him a Soveraign Power: Also we never were possessed of it" (Rushworth, I, 562).

they were determined that any bill coming out of this parliament should be a legal victory for their side, and not another one for the royalists who had won the earlier rounds of the legal struggle. The more extreme and the more moderate leaders in the commons agreed that "intrinsical" prerogative, included in the lords' resolutions, "is no worde of the Law." [117] If they should now write it into statute law, that would be "in effect to lett out the liberty of the Kingdome upon trust." [118] There was sufficient agreement in the commons to enable them successfully to prevent the royalists from including in a statute any mention of the prerogative.

On the other hand, the leaders in the commons could not draw up a statute satisfactory to themselves which asserted the subjects' rights and liberties. When, on April 28, the commons, led by Wentworth and Coke, ignored the lords for the time being and moved ahead to translate their own resolutions into a bill,[119] legal difficulties and clear-cut differences of opinion immediately arose in the committee of the commons. Men who had stood together in April against the lords' attempts to write the prerogative into law, and who acted together in May when the lords tried to include a saving for the prerogative in the Petition of Right, divided sharply in the debates taking place in committee between April 29 and May 6 on the proposed bill for the liberties of the subject.[120] Their major problem was this: the law clearly recognized the subjects' rights, and few men, even in the lords, disputed or denied that constitutional principle; the king, however, had violated their rights, and a stronger remedy than the restatement of a principle was necessary. To find such a remedy within the law proved to be impossible. The medieval English law and government had been

[117] Mass., 4/26/28.
[118] Bor., 4/26/28. Noy, Digges, and Rudyard all agreed that the lords' fifth resolution should be omitted. Bor., 4/26/28; Gros., 4/26/28; Rushworth, I, 551–52.
[119] For the text of the bill, see F. H. Relf, *The Petition of Right*, p. 63.
[120] For a detailed discussion of the differences, see *ibid*, pp. 27–35.

strong in the assertion of general principles; it likewise had
been woefully weak in recognizing and establishing legal sanctions which should operate when general principles were violated.[121] According to both medieval and Tudor precedents, a
king could not be coerced, he could pardon penalties if penalties should be attached to a bill, and he must not be completely
tied to legal forms but be left some freedom of action.

The recognized and accepted law on these points convinced
Digges, Noy, Seymour, and Rudyard that they could not support a bill in which the king's prerogative was limited more
completely than precedents warranted. Their remarks reveal
clearly their legal perplexities. Digges said: "The Bill is too
strict in some parts, it recites that neyther the King, Councell
nor other shall committ, restrayne or detayne etc. it tyes the
Kinge too mutch, and makes him say that that never King saied
beefore." [122] "Was ever act of Parliament spoke in this language
that the King shal not, etc." [123] Noy said: "it was wel resolved
that men imprisoned shold have cause expressed. Q[uestion]:
whether it be convenient to express this in an act: quere: what
good: by it: what inconvenience to leave it: we can not make it
with any coertion. nor payne: for the King may pardon . . ." [124] Seymour believed that "to make ourselves greater
then subjects is to make the King less than his predecessours." [125] Rudyard looked at the dilemma in a typically conservative manner, remarking, "If we can save ourselves by the
old laws, wisheth we should be sparing to make a New . . .
Let not us lock upp the King, for thereby we shall make that
which is vertue in him to be a constreint. We take it ill that he
imprisons our bodies, let not us then seeke to imprison his
goodnes." [126]

[121] See C. H. McIlwain, *Constitutionalism Ancient and Modern*, pp. 69–
126.
[122] Bor., 4/29/28.
[123] Gros., 4/29/28.
[124] Gros., 4/30/28.
[125] Mass., 5/1/28.
[126] Nich., 4/30/28.

In striking contrast to the attitude revealed by the remarks just given, was the point of view expressed by Coke, Eliot, and Phelips. These men were not such sticklers for the law. Beginning in 1621 they had led the way in the parliamentary encroachment upon the king's rights. In the debates in April, 1628, they did not answer Digges and Noy by quoting the law, for there was no law for them to quote; but, as in other emergencies of the past and future, they reminded the members of the commons that they, as representatives of the nation, were responsible to the nation and to posterity for acting constructively upon this great problem. Phelips insisted that "we are to deall for the good of posterity." [127] Eliot also looked ahead, reminding them that "wee seeke not to diminish the kings honour or power but to inlarge it and render it for his honour to posteritie." [128] Coke expressed his convictions in these words: ". . . wee are accomptable to a publique trust to our Countrey . . . after a publique violacion hath beene made by his ministers, less will not sattisfye his subjects then a bill . . ." [129]

These men, who talked of their responsibility to the nation and to posterity, were willing, when the strict law failed them, to move ahead and write a bill which would coerce the king. This bill, however, was never written, because the parliamentary leaders themselves could not agree upon the kind of bill it should be. Wentworth, for example, agreed with Coke that they were "accountable for a publique trust," [130] but would settle for a bill that provided quick legal remedy for the subject against commitment by the king or council, but did not prevent or condemn such arbitrary imprisonment in the first place. To him a trust must be left in the crown, "but for that that concerns Westminster hall that that concerns the habeus Corpus, lett us soe secure it that the Judges in Westminster Hall dare not denie us." [131] Wentworth would reassert the sub-

---

[127] *Ibid.* For a fuller discussion of these views, see chapter VII.
[128] Mass., 4/30/28.
[129] Mass., 5/2/28. According to Borlase, 5/2/28, the speaker may be Wentworth, not Coke.
[130] Nich., 5/2/28.   [131] Mass., 5/1/28.

jects' rights and improve the means by which they could be secured, but he would not encroach directly upon the sphere of government belonging to the king.

It proved impossible for the commons to agree upon "An Act for the better securinge of every free man touching the proprietie of his goods and libertie of his person." [132] Although extremists, moderates, and even conservatives were agreed that the subject possessed rights, as their acceptance later of the Petition of Right so clearly demonstrated, any attempt "for the better securinge" of them in a statute would encroach upon the sphere of the king's government, and on this point men differed sharply. Much as they believed in the subjects' rights, very few were willing to try to apply effective sanctions against the king. The problem of sanctions is in its nature ultimately political, not legal, and even the leaders of the parliamentary opposition were not agreed nor prepared at this time to challenge the king politically. From this point of view, it is understandable why they failed in 1628 to settle legally by statute the long-standing problem of the relation of the subjects' rights and the king's prerogative.

Despite their inability to agree upon a statute, no member of parliament wished in 1628 to draw up a party manifesto for one part of the nation which would further divide men and might ultimately lead to war. In 1628 they desired almost passionately to find a common ground upon which all Englishmen and their king could unite in order that the unity which they believed was the foundation of their commonwealth might be restored. In the Petition of Right, the form which they finally agreed upon and which the lords and eventually the king accepted, specific royalist actions were condemned and declared to be against the rights of the subject. Common and statute law, and in particular Magna Carta and six statutes, were cited as the authority for the absoluteness of the subjects' rights against such actions of the king.

[132] F. H. Relf, *The Petition of Right*, (University of Minnesota Press, Minneapolis, 1917), p. 63.

In two ways this statement of their rights was far from satisfactory. In the first place, it was only a restatement of the rights they believed they already possessed by the law and constitution. It carried no guarantee (beyond the king's formal acceptance of it) that he would not in the future, as he had in the past, use his prerogative in such a way that their rights would again be menaced. In the second place, the petition was in its form not a public statute,[133] the highest kind of man-made law in England. The leaders knew well that in failing to secure a statute which wrote into law their case, i.e., the absoluteness of certain rights of the subject, they had suffered a legal defeat. Since the petition was not a statute, it did not represent either an adjustment between the king's prerogative and the subjects' liberties, nor even an acceptance by all of their rights in the form of a statute.

Despite the failure of the parliamentary opposition to win a victory surely guaranteeing their rights in the future, the Petition of Right represents a significant achievement. Although they had "falen from a statute and a new lawe to a petition of right," [134] they were able to secure one in which the subjects' rights, recognized in Magna Carta and in certain statutes, were set forth as absolute, without any reference to the king's prerogative or intrinsic sovereign power. Nothing less would have been accepted in 1628 by the parliamentary leaders, who had become so fearful of the way the royalists had turned the law to their own advantage. Now, if ever, the law must be stated and principles proclaimed unequivocally in favor of the subjects' rights. In their judgment it was preferable to state those rights absolutely in a petition rather than conditionally in a statute. Moreover, this petition was not one of grace, where the subjects asked the king of his grace to bestow something of his own upon them, but a petition of right where the subjects recorded what was legally their own, not the king's. It is true that they had to ask—to petition for their own rights—because, ac-

[133] *Ibid.*, p. 54.
[134] Mass., 5/22/28, Wentworth speaking.

cording to English law and the constitution, the king could not be coerced, but must be humbly petitioned, even concerning rights not his own but belonging to others. In declaring the absoluteness of their rights and in doing it in the form of a petition, parliamentary leaders were making their case as strong as it could possibly be made on the basis of the medieval law and constitution. Medieval law had been strong in its recognition of the principle of the absoluteness of the subjects' rights, and their petition asserted those rights unequivocally. Petition was the strongest medieval form the subject possessed when approaching the king, but it was only petition. It lacked sanction. The parliamentary opposition, well versed in medieval law, were perfectly well aware of this weakness, but in 1628 the majority in the commons were not yet ready to apply sanctions. They still thought they might save themselves by the law and constitution. They still hoped that basic principles formally stated would be strong enough to be accepted and followed by all.

And the remarkable fact is that in June, 1628, the "whole realm" in parliament, including the king, did accept the principle of the absoluteness of the subjects' rights. That was the greatest victory won in these critical years by the parliamentary opposition on the basis of the law and constitution, and it would not have been possible had they not used the form of a Petition of Right. The fact that they used that form, in which the subjects' rights could be unequivocally stated, partially explains why practically everyone in the commons, a majority in the lords, and eventually the king himself, finally accepted it in the manner drawn up by the opposition, with no mention in it of the king's prerogative and no saving clause concerning his sovereign power, which the lords had tried so hard to write into the petition.

Nothing is more striking in reading the debates in both the commons and the lords than the agreement upon the Petition of Right which was reached by men who had disagreed for years, who had continued those differences in many sessions of this parliament, and who would in the future fight on opposite sides in a civil war. In accepting the Petition of Right, they agreed to the legal absoluteness of the subjects' rights. They might and did hold different views on the king's prerogative; but their willingness to agree to the petition was tremendously significant, and can best be shown by presenting the key ideas put forward by speakers on May 20 and the following days in connection with the amendments submitted by the lords, who asked that the petition, as drawn up by the commons, include a clause saving of the king's sovereign power. One by one, men in the commons spoke to the point, and each insisted that the petition contain no saving clause which would weaken the rights of the subject. On this point Digges, Noy, and Rudyard were at one with Coke, Wentworth, and Pym; and eventually enough conservatives in the lords agreed also.

This agreement was reached because certain fundamentals were stressed and finally accepted. In the first place, men agreed that their petition was a petition, and one concerned solely with the rights of the subject. Though many moderates had earlier claimed that a saving of sovereign power should be included in a resolution or a statute, now they unanimously agreed that it had no place in a petition concerned with the rights of the subject. Hakewill, one of those moderates said, "I have seen divers Petitions, & where the Subject claimed a Right, there I never saw a Saving of this nature." [135] Sir Henry Marten, who had not always gone with the leaders in the commons, spoke against the addition proposed by the lords being included in a petition of right. Such an addition he said, "is not competible with the frame and fabrick of our petition, our petition is a petition of right, wee lay downe in it that by the lawes of this Realme noe man may bee enforced to lend money and wee shew that hee hath such a proprietie in his goods that hee may not bee charged but by common assent in parliament." [136] Selden was another member of the commons, who earlier in the

[135] Rushworth, I, 562.
[136] Mass., 5/23/28.

debates had insisted on the king's rights, but he now agreed
that this petition should contain no saving of them, for sovereign power "is altogether impertinent to the matter in the
Petition." [137]

Men agreed also that their petition concerned law and nothing else. Policy was ignored. "All our Petition," Pym declared,[138] "is for the Laws of *England*," while Alford said, "Let
us give that to the King that the Law gives him, and no
more." [139] They also stressed the fact that in the past certain
laws, in particular those protecting the subjects' rights, had always been stated as absolute without any saving or exception
being written into the law. To include a saving now, Coke
pointed out, "weakens Magna Carta, and the other statutes for
thei are absolute, no saving in them, thei are the foundation
of our petition, and wee shall shake them" [140]—"this fellow
Magna Carta is such a fellow as will have noe savinge." [141]
Wentworth agreed to this interpretation, since, if we admit any
addition, it will mean "that where the Law is absolute, we
shold make it with a Savinge" [142]—"these Laws [meaning
Magna Carta and the six statutes] are not acquainted with
Soveraign Power." [143] Even Noy, who had not agreed in April
to a statute on the subjects' rights, said, concerning any reservation of the prerogative in the petition, "To add a Savinge is not
safe, doubtful words may beget ill construction; and the words
are not onely doubtful words, but words unknown to us, and
never used in any Act or Petition before." [144]

In support of this point—that Magna Carta and the supporting statutes were absolute—Glanville presented lengthy
arguments based upon principles applied by lawyers and
judges in the interpretation of statutes. "I consider," he said,

[137] Rushworth, I, 566.
[138] *Ibid.*, 562.
[139] *Ibid.*
[140] Harl., 5/20/28.
[141] Gros., 5/20/28.
[142] *Ibid.*
[143] Rushworth, I, 562.
[144] *Ibid.*, p. 563.

"our petition is uppon the Common lawe and statutes, there is in the King concerning some statutes and lawes, a trust, but in some there is not, there is noe trust whatsoever to bee above the Common lawe, for the statutes in them that are paenall that prohibit *mala prohibita* and are paenall, for those lawes the Kings of England have dispensed with the breach of them, *non obstante,* but those statutes that are not under anie penaltie, but absolute commaunds according to the Common lawe and of the nature of Common lawe, I never heard any trust to dispince with them, . . ." [145]

Undoubtedly there were many in this parliament who would not accept in its entirety this interpretation of Glanville's, for in it he gave, as all the members of the parliamentary opposition did at this time, a wider and more general latitude to the subjects' rights than to the king's. Yet it proved to be a telling argument against the incorporation of the king's prerogative in a petition concerned with the rights of the subject, because the fundamental principle upon which he based his argument —the principle that the king might dispense in statute with his own rights but not with the subjects' rights—had long been applied by lawyers in the interpretation of statutes.

Another important point made by Glanville, to which many subscribed, was his assertion that "the end of the petition is not to inlarge the bounds of Law but their Liberties, being infringed to reduce them to their auncient bounds." [146] The fact that the parliamentarians claimed they were asking not for something new, but for something old, provided a firm foundation for their argument that in the past all formal legal or parliamentary statements of the rights of the subject did not contain any reference to sovereign power. In previous records, they argued, the subjects' rights had been stated as absolute. There had been no reference to sovereign power. Consequently, their petition should not include one now. "Looke into all the acts

[145] Mass., 5/22/28.

[146] *The Copies of two Speeches in Parliament. The one by John Glanville Esquire. The other by Sir Henry Martin Knight* . . . , the 22 of May, 1628, p. 3.

of parliament and you shall never see peticion of right mingled with the Kinges power nor the subject use the words of soveraigne power . . ." [147] If such a term were included now, their record would be different from all previous ones—it would be a departure from precedent. More important: it would mean "that the Rights and Liberties of the Subject, declared and demanded by this Petition, are not theirs absolutely, but *sub modo*." [148] The result would be that they as subjects would be worse off now and in the future than their ancestors had been in the past.

In the lords, too, where the supporters of the king were more numerous, many men argued in favor of accepting the petition without a saving clause. Their reasoning, as revealed by the debates on the issue, is very interesting. Lord Pagett said: "the kg. cannot divest himselfe of his prerogative no more than he can of his Crowne. Yt, secured wth out addicion . . . if nothing that wee can add to this petition can adde or weaken the prerogative no neede of addicion." [149] The Earl of Hertford remarked that he was "not satisfied if need a saving no saving for it is but the right of the Subject." [150] Viscount Say expressed the same point of view, saying, "the right of the subject toucheth not upon the Prerogative." [151] "If there bee nothing in the peticion more then the libertie of the Subject, there neede no saveing of the Prerogative of the King." [152] Bristol maintained that "This addicion is not an essentiall parte of the business. . . . The right of the Sub[jects] before us. Why questioned, because infringed. The King's prerogative not before us, but came to be named accidently." [153] To these men the right of the subject could always be overridden in an emer-

[147] Bor., 5/20/28. Sir E. Coke is the speaker.
[148] L. J., III, 815. Glanville is the speaker.
[149] Ellesmere MSS., nos. 7785, 7786, 7787, 7788. Notes in the handwriting of the first Earl of Bridgewater . . . relating to . . . discussions on the Petition of Right . . . , Hunt. Lib. MSS., 5/20/28.
[150] *Ibid.*, 5/21/28.
[151] *Ibid.*
[152] *Lords' Debates in 1628*, p. 189, n. 5.
[153] *Ibid.*, p. 185.

gency by the prerogative, but at least they agreed in 1628 to this petition in which the subjects' rights were stated as absolute.

To secure the formal assent of the king in a manner satisfactory to the commons was no easy task. On June 2 the king delivered the following answer to the petition:

> The King willeth that right be done according to the laws and customs of the realm; and that the statutes be put in due execution, that his subjects may have no cause to complain of any wrong or oppressions, contrary to their just rights and liberties, to the preservation whereof he holds himself as well obliged as of his prerogative.[154]

Such an answer, the leaders of the commons maintained, was too general, too evasive, and too open to ambiguous interpretation. The commons had drawn up their rights and stated them absolutely in a petition of right, defeating all efforts of the lords to include a reference to or a saving of sovereign power. Their leaders were determined that the king's answer also should omit any reference to the prerogative, for as Coke said, "In a doubtfull thinge, Interpretation goes alwayes for the Kinge." [155] The king's answer was "defective," [156] Pym declared, because it "hath noe relation to the peticion, nor hath any proporcion to the peticion, the answere being left att large to the lawes, whereas we have in our peticion alledged certeyne lawes." [157]

On June 7 the king again came to parliament and gave his answer, "Whereupon the Commons returned to their own House with unspeakable joy." [158] According to the Statutes of the Realm, the words of assent were: "Soit Droit fait come est

[154] S. R. Gardiner, *The Constitutional Documents of the Puritan Revolution,* (Clarendon Press, Oxford, 1906), p. 70.

[155] Bor., 6/7/28.

[156] Gros., 6/6/28.

[157] Nich., 6/6/28. See also, S. T., III, 999–1000. Holborne, in defending Hampden in the ship-money case, refers to the king's first answer and says, "yet in the close there is put in a saving of the prerogative; but this Answer did not satisfy."

[158] Rushworth, I, 613.

desire." [159] In these words the king decreed that right be done as is desired. He thus related his answer to the petition, mentioning only right, omitting any reference to his prerogative, and stating that he was agreeing to what had been desired. Such an answer registered his acceptance of the statement of rights which the lords and commons had presented to him.[160] Because he agreed to the rights which they desired, this second answer was completely satisfactory. "Wee could never have had a better answer," [161] the king "granteth all we desire," [162] Coke hastened to declare.

This interpretation of the king's answer is strengthened, I believe, if the exact wording given in the Borlase and Massachusetts diaries is examined. According to Borlase the words were these: "Soit droict faict come ils desirent" [163] (let right be done as they [i.e., the lords and commons] desire). The idea is the same as in the usual form, but the importance of the king agreeing to that which the lords and commons desired is made active, instead of passive, and therefore emphasized. When Coke spoke on the second answer, contrasting it with the earlier one, he used the same words, as *they* desire. According to the Massachusetts diary, Coke said: ". . . now it is Soit droit fait comes ills desire, if this had beene a private bill, it is Soit fait come il desire, if a publique Le roy vult, but the King now saith Soit droit fait come ils desire." [164]

The joy which the leaders in the commons expressed was well founded.[165] For once, in the long struggle between the

[159] 3 Car. I, special enrolment of Petition of Right.
[160] The legal and technical questions involved in the form of the king's assent are discussed at considerable length by F. H. Relf, *The Petition of Right,* pp. 44–58, and by E. R. Adair, *op. cit.*
[161] Mass., 6/7/28.   [162] Gros., 6/7/28.
[163] Bor., 6/7/28. In the Mass. diary (Mass., 6/7/28) the words are, "Soit droit fait come il est desire par le Petition." In the *Lords Journals* (III, 844), the words are, "Soit Droit fait com est desiré;" in Rushworth (I, 613), "Soit droit fait come il est desire." The answer is not recorded in any other diary.
[164] Mass., 6/7/28. Coke's speech is also given in Grosvenor as follows: ". . . the King now sayth: Soit droit fait com il desire!"
[165] See Gros. and Mass., 6/7/28, for expressions of joy in the commons.

king's prerogative and the subjects' rights, the king had agreed to their rights and to their desires in the form in which they had drawn them up. Previous controversies in which both sides had claimed the law as theirs had ended with the royalists writing into law their own point of view, the absolute right of the king's prerogative. In this crisis the supporters of the king and the king himself had tried and failed to include a saving clause for the prerogative in the Petition of Right. Had they succeeded they would have won another legal victory—and this one in parliament. Their failure, therefore, to write in a saving clause was a legal defeat for the absolute prerogative, and a victory for the rights of the subject.

The leaders of the parliamentary opposition hoped that the Petition of Right, containing no saving of the king's prerogative, would not be legally disregarded in the future as Magna Carta, and certain statutes had been bypassed since the accession of the Stuarts. Phelips "would faine know what Judge durst go against a resolution of the King the Lords and us. This is no skrowle to bee lost at Whitehall or else where, but a record fitt for the Tower." [166] Pym believed "that noe Juge will recede from it." [167] According to Coke, the way of petition was sound "for whatever the lords house and this house have at anie time agreed upon noe Judge ever went against it, and when the Judges in former times, doubted of the law they went to the parliament, and there resolucions were given, to which they were bound." [168]

In the twelve years after this solemn petition was drawn up, a majority of the king's judges did disregard it, and again in the ship-money case win another victory for the cause of legal absolutism. That victory, however, was of short duration. The Petition of Right was not permanently "lost at Whitehall," but remained as a living record, influencing the decisions of judges in later ages when the judgment in the ship-money case

[166] Bor., 5/27/28.
[167] Mass., 5/27/28.
[168] *Ibid.*

had become a mere historical document of interest only to those caring to know English history in this period.

The significance of the Petition of Right can best be evaluated from the point of view of the ideas and principles stated in it. The parliamentary opposition won a truly great victory in the realm of ideas and principles when the Petition of Right was agreed to by the whole parliament of commons, lords, and king, for they succeeded in putting on record and in securing an interpretation of the law and constitution which was in accord with the spirit, if not always the letter, of the medieval constitution. The significance of that record and victory is very great, despite the fact that for the next ten years royalist concepts and policies of government prevailed, and despite the fact that parliament was only really successful when it abandoned the law and constitution and carried through a political revolution in the civil war period. In the Petition of Right, however, the concept of the absoluteness of the subjects' rights was stated as unequivocally guaranteed by the law and constitution. In that point of view practically everyone in the commons, and eventually a majority in the lords, and the king himself, concurred. Men who differed in many ways, and who later fought on opposite sides in the civil war, agreed to the Petition of Right. For one brief moment the realm was united—and united on the basis of men's rights.

The parliamentary party was now much stronger because this legal victory was theirs, if only temporarily. Without the support of the law and constitution upon which the principles announced in the Petition of Right were based, it is, in my opinion, very doubtful whether the parliamentary politicians could have secured enough support from moderates to have destroyed the king's ministers and his instruments of prerogative government in 1641 and to have waged a civil war. In that civil war the moderates are found on both sides. One important reason for the peculiarities of the division is that, when men's opinions were being formed, the law and constitution could be cited, not only as supporting the cause of the king, but also the cause of parliament. The principle of the absoluteness of certain of the subjects' rights in law, stated so unequivocally and accepted so formally by the whole parliament in the Petition of Right, was a great source of strength to the parliamentary opposition.

The petition is also significant because no such direct, complete, comprehensive, and formal a statement on behalf of the subjects' rights had been put forward and agreed upon by the whole realm since Magna Carta. After the interval of strong rule under the Tudors, and in the midst of the successes of absolute government won by the Stuarts, such a restatement of a basic principle of the medieval law and constitution did much to keep those principles before men's eyes. From the point of view of the enforcement of those principles, the Revolution of 1688 marked a greater victory than the Petition of Right. From the point of view of the principles themselves, the Petition of Right was the great victory won in the seventeenth century. It must never be forgotten that the petition came first, and came during those years when the royalists had their greatest chance during the entire century of establishing legal absolutism. Without the Petition of Right, agreed to by the whole realm, the medieval concept of the absoluteness of the subjects' rights might easily have died. Had that happened, any victory for the parliamentary opposition (assuming that there could have been a victory) would not have included a Bill of Rights as part of the revolutionary settlement.

With the Petition of Right, the parliamentary cause was immensely strengthened, and its ultimate victory was one in which both medieval law and modern politics triumphed. In the Bloodless Revolution, parliament became the dominant and controlling partner in the government; in the Bill of Rights, the concept of the absoluteness of the subjects' rights, woven into the medieval English constitution, was transmitted to modern times to play its great part in shaping ideas and institutions in the modern world. In the period after 1688 the rights recorded in the Bill have been increased in number and extended to other lands, until today the existence of rights guaranteed by law is accepted as an indispensable basis of modern democracy. To extend those rights to include economic and social rights for all, and to achieve a bill of rights which will prevail throughout the world, is one of the most challenging and important tasks upon which men interested in building a better society and world are today engaged. If at the present time we are concerned with rights, it is in large measure because we in the western world have been born in lands where the belief in rights is part of our heritage and has been woven into our thinking and our institutions of government. The history of the rights of man is a long one, and one which is still being written. Its roots and beginnings reach back into the Middle Ages and beyond to Roman law, Stoic philosophy, and Christian belief. In that long history, a high place of honor should be given the Petition of Right, which was agreed to by the whole realm in parliament at a time when it seemed as if everywhere absolute government was winning out over the rights of man.

For the next eleven years, however, the victory lay with the royalists. During that long interval when no parliament met, they made their greatest bid for absolute power resting on the law and constitution. Ship money was not the first but the last of many ways they discovered of raising money without parliament. In winning the decision in the exchequer chamber in favor of ship money, the royalists presented all of their strongest arguments in favor of the legality of the absolute prerogative. It is their ideas, and not the ideas of the lawyers and judges disagreeing with them, which are of greatest interest to the student of constitutional and political thought in this period.

In contrast to the sweeping statements made by the royalist judges, the arguments advanced by St. John and Holborne defending Hampden, and by Croke, Hutton, Davenport, and Denham, rendering a minority decision against the king, make far less significant reading. The first point which strikes the modern reader is the fact that the lawyers and judges on Hampden's side seemed to concede so much to their opponents. St. John, for example, admitted that the king possessed as part of his general-welfare power the power of defense, that he alone could judge when the kingdom was in danger, and that "means of Defense" were in his hands. In short, he did not deny the king's discretionary powers, but stated that "in this business of Defence, the *suprema potestas,* is inherent in his majesty, as part of his crown and kingly dignity." [169] The question at issue was by what means he could legally exercise this power of defense.

A second point which strikes the modern reader is the skill with which the lawyers and judges supporting Hampden chose the ground on which they stood, and the firmness, even stubbornness, with which they clung to their position. Their refusal to give way, when they admitted so much, must have been irritating to those royalist lawyers pressing home their contention by so many different arguments.

St. John and Holborne took their stand primarily upon the absolute right of the subject to his property, and upon its corollary that the king must legally secure money, even for the defense of the land, in parliament. Their arguments on these points are largely a repetition of what the parliamentary opponents of the king had long been saying. Their contribution to the parliamentary thinking on the subject lies in the clarity, effectiveness, and thoroughness with which they closed the loopholes through which the king's prerogative could ever operate against them. Although they agreed that in actual war or invasion all laws became silent, and that all men, including the king, might act in extraordinary ways to save themselves, they did not agree that the king by his prerogative could take property without the consent of the subject. Holborne refused to admit that the law ever allowed the king to take property upon extraordinary occasions, but maintained that the law must pro-

[169] S. T., III, 860–61.

tect the subject absolutely from infringement by the king's
prerogative, implying that if there were any loopholes at all,
bad kings might take advantage of them.[170] Against the royalist
extension of prerogative into the realm of the subjects' property and their claim that the law of the land sanctioned such
an invasion, Holborne set up the law as an absolute barrier to
the prerogative and an absolute protector of the subject in all
cases. Upon his view of the constitution, it would have been
practically impossible for the king to carry on his government
at all, except upon the sufferance of parliament.

In most of his argument St. John stopped short of insisting,
as firmly as Holborne did, upon the complete protection the
law always afforded the subject. There is one statement, however, made by St. John which calls for comment. It is a very
direct and complete answer to the royalist claim that the king
must act for the general welfare. "In his majesty," St. John said,
"there is a double capacity, natural and politic. All his Prerogatives are *jure coronae*, . . . such things are *patrimonia et bona
publica*, to be employed for the common good . . ." [171] St.
John used this statement to demonstrate that many accepted
revenues of the crown, such as treasure trove, existed in order
to enable the crown to provide for the general defense. He
never explicitly drew the conclusion that all rights of the king,
belonging not to him personally but to the crown, were really
the rights of the nation; but, four years later in 1641, that argument was used by the parliamentary opposition to justify their
encroachment upon the remaining prerogatives of the king.
St. John may well have paved the way for such a sweeping
argument when, in 1637, he asserted that all the king's prerogatives were "to be employed for the common good."

The judges who gave verdict against the king did it on narrower and more technical grounds than had been presented by
either Holborne or St. John. They agreed, as members of the
parliamentary opposition had in 1628, that, in an immediate

[170] *Ibid.*, p. 972.
[171] *Ibid.*, p. 873.

and overwhelming emergency, the king might act extra-legally, but they denied that in the present issue such an emergency existed. "Royal power," Crooke said, "is to be used in cases *of* necessity, and imminent danger, when ordinary courses will not avail; . . . But in a time of peace, and no extreme necessity, legal courses must be used, and not royal power." [172] The fact that the king had employed a legal procedure (for a writ was a normal form of procedure for many actions) played squarely into the hands of the judges supporting Hampden. Since the royalists claimed that the writ was legal, it was the judges' task to pass upon its legality. "We that are judges are bound," Crooke said, "according to the law, not according to our own imaginations, both to judge according to the law, and the law of this land, either of the common law or of the statute law: and I see no book, nor know of any authority that doth maintain this writ; but contrariwise, there are books and authorities in law that say, this writ ought not to be maintained." [173] Not only Crooke, but Hutton, Davenport, and Denham, as well as St. John and Holborne, found that in several respects the writ was technically defective for doing what the royalists asked it to do. Therefore it could not be legally used, and therefore judgment could not be given for the king.[174]

It is true that these men were resting their decision on technicalties in this case involving great issues; but it is also true that they were resting it on the constitution, which consisted in part of basic principles easily grasped by all, and in part on forms and procedures. Some of the latter, such as the necessary consent of all in parliament to taxation, were not mere technicalities. Moreover, in the seventeenth century most forms and procedures protecting private rights were inextricably mixed with those assuring public rights. Therefore, in insisting that any writ by which the subjects' property was taken must be technically correct, these judges opposing the king were not basing

[172] *Ibid.*, p. 1162.
[173] *Ibid.*, p. 1129.
[174] On this point, see D. L. Keir, "The Case of Ship Money," *Law Quarterly Review* LII, (1936), pp. 546–74.

their decision on a procedure which a seventeenth-century English-man would label a technicality.

At the time when questions concerning the correctness of the writ were being raised, men were searching their souls and making up their minds whom they should support if ever parliament should be called. In the decision they ultimately took, law counted for much. The Petition of Right, asserting the principle of the absoluteness of the subjects' rights and agreed to in a form which the whole parliament accepted as correct, had strengthened the parliamentary cause. So also the decision in the ship-money case of four minority judges, who found that the king had not used the correct legal form in his procedure in this case, weighed heavily in the minds of men in the seventeenth century, when correct form and procedure were extremely important. In that minority decision, the royalists suffered a real defeat. For at least thirty-four years they had worked to establish legal absolutism, and now, as late as 1637, four out of twelve judges appointed by the crown would not agree that the law allowed the king to use the ordinary machinery of government to administer his absolutism. Here was a victory for medieval forms of action, as the Petition of Right had been a victory for medieval principles and beliefs.

By 1640, when the Long Parliament met, the leaders of the opposition challenged the legality of the decision in ship money and attacked the whole royalist case for legal absolutism on broader grounds than any judge or lawyer had earlier advocated. The discussion of the nature of their arguments during the first year of the Long Parliament must be postponed, however, until other developments in parliamentary thought before 1640 are examined.

CHAPTER VII

PARLIAMENT SPEAKS FOR THE NATION

RIGHT up to the outbreak of the civil war, parliamentary leaders looked to the law and constitution to vindicate and justify their stand against royalist claims and actions. Resting their case on law and right, they prevented the opposition from winning a complete victory for legal absolutism, and by their defensive stand they strengthened the belief in the seventeenth century (when the current of absolutism was running strong) that government rested on law and could not encroach upon or overthrow certain basic rights of Englishmen.

During all these years of tension and struggle, the parliamentary leaders never waged just a defensive battle. Recent studies have shown conclusively that parliaments in the first decades of the seventeenth century were aggressive, taking and "winning the initiative" [1] in the struggle against the crown. Self-appointed leaders of parliamentary committees, rather than privy councillors, directed the sessions of parliament, planning programs of action, working together in and out of parliament to achieve them, and often checking with considerable success the government in its domestic and foreign policies. Yet all their success was not enough. They wished to check and limit the king more completely, and also to share authority with him. Their ambition did not stop with leadership of the commons, but went on to thoughts of leading the nation.

It was not easy to justify these aggressive desires by appeals to law, rights, and medieval precedents, and parliamentary

[1] W. Notestein, *The Winning of the Initiative by the House of Commons*, (London, [British Academy], 1924). See also D. H. Willson, *The Privy Councillors in the House of Commons*, (University of Minnesota Press, Minneapolis, 1940).

leaders never rested all their case upon such grounds. As their tactics and ambitions became aggressive, so did their ideas. If a legal argument could be used, it was employed. When, however, the law supported the claims of the royalists, as it often did, the more ardent parliamentary leaders refused to accept a legal defeat, but pushed forward as representatives of the nation at large, claiming that parliament, and particularly the house of commons, was entrusted with the responsibility for the general welfare of the commonwealth.

This concept was grounded more on political realities than legal precedents, and it certainly was more revolutionary than the ideas discussed in the preceding chapter. It was not, however, invented in the seventeenth century. Its history is part of that larger story, still awaiting its historian, of the development of the idea of the peoples' consent to government and of the emergence of institutions of government where such consent became a functioning reality. The full story of this important subject must take account of Greek philosophy and Roman law, in both of which the importance of the peoples' consent to law was stressed. It must deal with the contribution made in the early Middle Ages by the Germanic tribes: that law belonged to the folk and could only be changed by the folk. In the later Middle Ages, this story could show how consent by people to law, and co-operation between king and people in declaring and making law, became commonplaces of medieval political thought; and also how this idea of consent came to life in obscure ways, about which we know too little, as first local and then more central institutions of government grew up in western Europe, affording to some people the opportunity to participate in declaring and making law.[2]

---

[2] For this whole subject, see especially B. Wilkinson, *Studies in Constitutional History of the thirteenth and fourteenth Centuries*, (Manchester University Press, Manchester, 1937), ch. 2; C. H. McIlwain, *Constitutionalism Ancient and Modern*, pp. 117–18; G. Barraclough, "Law and Legislation in Medieval England," *Law Quarterly Review*, LVI (1940), 75–92; and F. W. Maitland, *Collected Papers*, 3 vols., (Cambridge University Press, Cambridge, 1911), III, 247.

When the sixteenth century is reached, this unwritten history could well call attention to the growing divergence between England and the continent. Theorists in Spain and France in the sixteenth century wrote more fluently and forcefully than any English writer on the idea of consent in government; but as they wrote, the actual consent of people to government became a hollow mockery, as more absolute kings ruled without using or even calling together their representative Estates or Cortez. In England, on the other hand, parliament came to play a more important part in governing the country than ever before. The Tudors wisely chose to govern with the co-operation and consent of their people in parliament. Consequently, the idea of consent to government lived on in England during the sixteenth century, not primarily in the writings of political thinkers, but in the minds of men who in parliament consented to laws.

If parliament in England had a long and continuous history as the concrete embodiment of the idea of consent to government, the historian of ideas and institutions would like to know the nature of parliament's relation to the country at large. How early was it viewed as the embodiment of the realm, possessing the full power of the realm? Under what circumstances did such a concept develop? Did it come to be a normal and generally accepted one? These questions are fundamental, and in recent years medieval historians have substantially increased our knowledge of significant parts of the story.[3] The story, however, is not complete, and for the Tudor period particularly, much needs to be done. The conflicting nature

[3] Outstanding treatments of the subject are: J. G. Edwards, "The *Plena Potestas* of the English Parliamentary Representatives," in *Oxford Essays Presented to H. E. Salter,* (Clarendon Press, Oxford, 1934); S. B. Chrimes, *English Constitutional Ideas in the Fifteenth Century,* (Cambridge University Press, Cambridge, 1936), ch. 2; H. M. Cam, *The Legislators of Medieval England,* (London [British Academy], 1946); G. L. Haskins, "Parliament in the Later Middle Ages," *American Historical Review,* LII, (1947), 676–83; and F. M. Powicke, *King Henry III and the Lord Edward: The Community of the Realm in the Thirteenth Century,* 2 vols., (Clarendon Press, Oxford, 1947).

of the evidence in that period can be illustrated by the fact that Sir Thomas Smith said, "For everie Englishman is entended to bee there present. . . . And the consent of the Parliament is taken to be everie mans consent"; [4] whereas a study of legal material reveals the fact that in the sixteenth century some areas were still regarded as exempt from the binding effect of statutes.[5]

Obscure as the history of the concept of parliament's relation to the nation is, by Elizabeth's reign there is sufficient evidence to enable historians to see the situation somewhat more clearly.[6] From D'Ewes *Diary* the following conclusions may be drawn. In the first place, some members of the commons were talking both of their responsibility to their own country (county) and also of their responsibility to the nation. In the second place, talk of this sort often occurred when the issue under discussion concerned a matter which the queen and council viewed as within the realm of the royal prerogative, and which some leaders of the commons believed was the concern of the nation. The more ardent Puritan members of the commons refused to be silent when Elizabeth tried to prevent the House from discussing religion. In his famous speech of February 8, 1575, Peter Wentworth insisted that there must be freedom to discuss religion, if the commons were to do their duty to God, the queen, and the commonwealth. "Liberty of free Speech . . . is the only Salve to heal all the Sores of this Common-wealth . . ." [7] "Yes truly, we are Chosen of the whole Realm, of a special Trust and Confidence by them reposed in us to forsee all such Inconveniences." [8] "It is a great and special part of our duty and office, Mr. Speaker,

[4] Sir T. Smith, *De Republica Anglorum*, p. 49.

[5] S. E. Thorn, *A Discourse upon the Exposicion & Understandinge of Statutes*, p. 31.

[6] For the most significant treatment of this problem in Elizabeth's reign and in the period of the early Stuarts, see L. F. Brown, "Ideas of Representation from Elizabeth to Charles II," *Journal of Modern History*, XI (1936), 23–40.

[7] D'Ewes (Elizabeth), p. 236.

[8] *Ibid.*, p. 238.

to maintain the freedom of Consultation and Speech, for by this, good Laws that do set forth Gods Glory and for the preservation of the Prince and State are made." [9] ". . . I am now no private Person, I am a publick, and a Councillor to the whole State in that place where it is lawful for me to speak my mind freely . . ." [10]

Monopolies were a second subject upon which many members in the commons spoke out on behalf of their responsibility to their towns, counties, and the whole commonwealth. In the words of Mr. Francis Moore, "there is no Act of hers that hath been or is more derogatory to her own Majesty, more odious to the Subject, more dangerous to the Common-wealth than the granting of these Monopolies." [11] Mr. Spicer defined a monopoly as a restraint of any thing publick in a City or Common-Wealth to a private use," [12] while Martin labelled monopolists the "bloodsuckers of the Common-Wealth." [13]

Already then, before the accession of James, leaders in the commons who would not accept the monarch's direction of questions which she claimed were her concern and her prerogative, had justified their interest in such questions by appeals to the nation at large whose representatives they were. Men advancing such views, however, were not numerous, and with the exception of those who entered into the discussion on monopolies, not successful in convincing the commons at large that the time had come for parliament to claim on behalf of the nation the right to discuss all questions. On the contrary, the statements of Peter Wentworth were too extreme for his fellow members in the commons, who took the proper measures in 1575 to have him imprisoned in the Tower.

The idea, however, that parliament was responsible to the nation, suggested by comparatively few men in Elizabeth's reign, quickly developed and matured in the first three decades

[9] *Ibid.*, p. 240.
[10] *Ibid.*, p. 241.
[11] *Ibid.*, p. 645.
[12] *Ibid.*, p. 644.
[13] *Ibid.*, p. 646.

of the seventeenth century. The parliamentary opposition employed it as their most potent weapon in the clash of ideas during these years of crisis. They used it in the first place to strengthen an argument based on law and right, in the second place to justify an encroachment upon the realms of the king's absolute power, and in the third place to justify a new and aggressive procedure on the part of the commons. The second way was the most frequent and important and will be discussed at greatest length.

The concept of parliament's responsibility to the nation was frequently employed when law and right proved to be inadequate for meeting the particular constitutional issue under debate. For speakers to turn from talk of law and right to talk of parliament and the nation was a natural sequence, for the law and right to which they appealed were the law of the land and the right of the subjects of the land. Speakers could effectively drive home an argument whose starting point was law and right by appealing to the country at large or the subjects in general. In 1628, for example, law and right furnished the basis of the attack made by the parliamentary leaders against the right of the king to imprison without cause being shown, to levy forced loans, to quarter soldiers, etc.; and yet in those debates speakers frequently strengthened their legal arguments by pointing out that in standing for law and in checking the king, parliament was acting for the nation's welfare. As *"Trustees* for the Countreys good," [14] as well as the defenders of law and right, the parliament of 1628 opposed the king. Especially in times of greatest crisis the parliamentary leaders turned to the nation for support. When the Petition of Right was drawn up, the commons would not accept proposed amendments to it which admitted the legality of an undefined discretionary power in the king. In standing firm against the proposed amendments, leaders in parliament claimed to be acting for the sake of the nation. Glanville spoke as follows: "I thinke the happines of the people consists

[14] *Ephemeris Parliamentaria*, (London, 1654), Preface.

in the preserving of the lawes, it is not safe to acknowledge a power that is above the lawes for the safetie of the Realme." [15] Hoskins declared that "we come not in this assembly but to preserve the Liberties of the kingdome." [16] On June 5 the king threatened to dissolve parliament, and the situation at the moment seemed hopeless to the leaders of the opposition. Their work for the nation was not yet complete. Was all lost? Must they end their efforts? Did their responsibility as parliament-men stop there? Should they now remain silent? No! Sir Nathaniel Rich said, "Wee have a charge to save the Kinge and Kingdome." [17]

Unable to find in strict law an effective way of coercing the king, they literally turned to the nation at large to remedy a long-standing weakness of the law, which, however strongly it had asserted the principle of the legal limitation of the king, had remained woefully inadequate in effective means of enforcing such limitation against kings who refused to act legally. In looking to the nation at large to remedy the defects of the law and constitution, the men advocating this idea were starting on its long history the significant political concept which only became fully translated into the actual government of England when the political control of parliament over the king slowly became a reality in the years after the Revolution of 1688.

In the preceding chapter it was shown that in this same parliament of 1628 the more aggressive leaders of the commons tried unsuccessfully to draw up a statute which would furnish more adequate sanction for the subjects' rights and liberty against the king's prerogative than established law and precedent provided. Although a committee of the commons could not agree upon the bill, the men willing to go beyond law and precedent to coerce the king rested their arguments upon their responsibility to the nation, upon the "publique trust" owed

[15] Mass., 5/22/28.
[16] Gros., 5/20/28.
[17] Bor., 6/5/28.

their country. In 1628 there was only a handful of men beginning to think, much less to act in such terms, but it is profoundly significant that the idea was set forth by even a few at
this early date.

The controversies between king and parliament covered a
wide range of issues. With some of them, as with the question
of impositions debated in 1610, or the extent of the king's
discretionary power debated in 1628, law and right furnished
the bulwark for the parliamentary stand. With others, where
the question concerned foreign affairs, religion, monopolies,
or ministers appointed by the king, parliamentary leaders defended their position by presenting many lines of reasoning.
Law and precedent were appealed to, the subjects' right was
talked of, but the parliamentary case could not be built up
effectively around such arguments. And with good reason, for
these matters came within the realm of the king's absolute
prerogative. When the first Stuart ascended the English throne,
foreign affairs were still admitted to be within the sphere of
the king's absolute power. Before 1621 few members of the
commons ventured to discuss foreign affairs without first securing the permission of the king, and until 1642 parliament did
not ask outright that authority in this realm be transferred
from the king to the two houses. In the case of monopolies, the
serious attempt of parliament to interfere with the exercise of
the king's absolute power in that realm had been going on only
since the latter part of Elizabeth's reign. Whether religion
should ultimately be controlled by the king in or out of parliament was an older dispute reaching back at least as far as the
time of Henry VIII. Yet the question in its active form started
only with the Puritans in Elizabeth's reign, and despite growing demands and desires of parliamentary leaders, complete
parliamentary control over religion was not demanded of the
king until late in 1641. In the case of ministers of the crown,
there existed numerous medieval precedents for impeaching
those ministers who broke the law, but impeachments had
slumbered during most of the Tudor period. The leaders in

the commons revived them in the twenties, but waited until late in 1641 before demanding actual parliamentary control of the appointing power.

At those times, therefore, when religion, foreign affairs, monopolies, or unpopular ministers of the crown were being discussed, as they were particularly in the parliaments of 1621, 1624, 1625, 1626, and 1629, the arguments used by leaders of the commons in their stand against the crown were more complex and less conservative than the arguments employed when law and precedent could form the basis of their stand, as in 1610 and 1628. The kind of reasoning used by parliamentary leaders in many of the sessions of the 1621, 1624, 1626, or 1629 parliament indicates that they were more conscious than some modern historians have been of the uncertain or confused support which law and precedent afforded them. It was comparatively easy to harass and partially limit a king in realms touching the right of the subject; but to oppose or restrain him in the realms mentioned above was more difficult, for here law and precedent were inadequate or confused, and the extent of the king's absolute power within those realms still admittedly great. We who read the commons debates of the twenties can watch the more daring parliamentary leaders like Pym and Phelips and Eliot struggling with this difficult constitutional problem. To obtain some authority with the king in the realm of foreign affairs, religion, monopolies, etc., they encroached upon his power in those spheres, and to justify their encroachment they appealed to the people at large, whom the members of the house of commons represented and for whose general welfare they now claimed responsibility. Unable to base their arguments too completely on law and precedent, and yet determined to push on, parliamentary leaders came more and more to look for political rather than legal or constitutional sanction for their claims and actions. In the name of the people of England, whose representatives they were, they challenged the absolute power of the king in those realms where law and precedent failed to provide convincing or sound arguments. The idea of parliamentary responsibility to the nation developed so rapidly in the twenties because the issues debated in those years involved realms of government where the king's power was admittedly so great that the parliament's claim to enter into those realms could only be advanced by the almost revolutionary appeal that parliament, as the guardian of the nation's welfare, must examine all questions affecting that welfare.

The exponents of this idea were setting up a concept directly counter to a cornerstone of royalist thought, namely, that the king was responsible for the general welfare of the nation. They were refusing to accept the monarch's tutelage, for they had come to believe that he was not a true guardian of the happiness of the commonwealth of which they were a part and in the government of which they now desired a greater participation than in earlier ages.

In claiming for themselves responsibility for the nation's welfare, these men were also laying the foundations for one pillar of democratic thought: that the ultimate responsibility of representative government is to the people governed. It is quite unlikely that the parliamentary advocates of this concept were truly conscious of the democratic implications of the idea they did so much to develop. In the twenties they still based the great majority of their actions and claims on the law and constitution, and they never explicitly denied that the king as head of the state had a general responsibility for the nation's welfare. Although they were advancing ideas important in the history of democratic thought, they themselves were wealthy country squires or merchants with a classical contempt for the political understanding or ability of "the mob" for whose welfare they pleaded so eloquently.

There is ample evidence, however, that parliamentary leaders knew they were encroaching on the king's prerogative in areas generally recognized in the past as within his absolute power. They knew well that a constitutional dilemma existed which they must face. In one of the debates in 1621 Sir James

Perrot raised the question confronting them all. "The Kinge had by Proclamacion forbidden to speake of affaires of state, of matters of Prerogative. Howe can we," Perrot asked, "deale in grievances without examineing Pattents, which are effects of prerogative? Howe shall we treate of provision for the Pallatinate and not meddle with matters of state?" [18] Phelips also recognized the impasse. On December 12, 1621, after the king had ordered the commons to stop their discussion of foreign affairs, Phelips said, "Wee are in a terrible Dilemma either to forfeit our liberties by dealinge onelie in such busines as the kinge shall appoint, or to disobey the king's command." [19]

In 1625 Charles tried to prevent the commons from discussing the case of Montagu by reminding them that, since Montagu was the king's servant, the matter should be handled by the king and not by the commons. Alford, who so often saw straight to the heart of a question, opposed the king's request with the following argument: "All Justices of Peace, all Deputy Leiutenants are the King's servants, and indeed no man can committ a publicke offence but by color and oportunity of publick imployment and service to the Kinge: so that, if wee admit this, wee shall take the way to destroye Parliaments. . . ." [20] Here in a nutshell was the constitutional dilemma confronting the house. In the parliament of 1628 the same problem again arose. The leaders in the house insisted that religion could properly be discussed by the commons, for "how cann wee make lawes and not debate Religion, never was there more need for this house to bee carefull in Religion for Religion cannot bee devided from the State." [21]

The constitutional dilemma which these leaders clearly recognized was resolved in the name of the nation. When questions involving foreign affairs, religion, monopolies, or min-

[18] *Commons Debates 1621,* IV, 15.
[19] *Ibid.,* V, 235.
[20] *Commons Debates in 1625,* p. 70.
[21] Mass., 3/24/28. Mr. Shervile asked earlier in the same speech, ". . . were there not Acts of Parliament for the Articles in H:8 was not our Religion established in E: 6 time?" Mass., 3/24/28.

isters of the crown were discussed, the speakers asserted the right of parliament to consider the matter, because parliament was responsible for the welfare of the nation. In the eight years between 1621 and 1629, as we now can discover by reading the parliamentary diaries of those years, the idea of parliament's responsibility to the nation became one of the most common arguments used by leaders in the commons. During this decade, it was primarily within the walls of parliament, and not in the press or pulpit, that this very significant development in the history of democratic thought took place, as leaders in the commons freely and boldly entered into the discussion of matters which the royalists insisted, on good grounds of law, came within the realm of the king's prerogative.

The realm in which the absolute power of the king was least controversial was that of foreign affairs; yet, beginning in 1621, leaders in the commons discussed those questions freely, criticized policies advocated by the king, suggested counter policies, and claimed in the name of the nation that parliamentary privilege gave them the right to debate such questions. They admitted that the king could make a treaty, but insisted that if the effect of any such treaty constituted a grievance to the people, parliament must do its duty and consider the question. When in April a treaty with Spain concerning tobacco was under discussion, Phelips said that this treaty "is resolved to be inconvenient for the state." [22] In November and December, when foreign affairs were again debated, the parliamentary leaders opposed the land war on the continent favored by James. Such a war would be disadvantageous to the commonwealth, Pym explained.[23]

It was in connection with the right of the commons to discuss foreign affairs that the question of free speech was debated so hotly in many sessions of the 1621 parliament. Although the house did not yet ask to control foreign policy, it did

[22] *Commons Debates 1621*, III, 9.
[23] *Ibid.*, IV, 442.

claim the right to discuss it and tried to advise the king concerning it. In Elizabeth's reign only a handful had pleaded for freedom of speech. Now, in 1621, many leaders in the commons rose to speak on the question. Hakewill insisted that the privileges of the commons were "the principall parte of the Lawe of the Land, . . . the Custom of England," not only theirs, but the kingdom's. In fact "The privileges of the kingdom are the preservation of the kingdom." [24] Crewe was willing to grant that the king might call and dissolve parliament, "yet, when we are called, we are, without Limitation, to deal in what Business ourselves think best; for otherwise shall we not be able to do their Business, for whom we come hither, which is that of the Country." [25] "I have read nothinge in the negative," Mr. Wentworth said, "what busines for the common wealth wee may not treat of or meddle with." [26]

On December 15, in the midst of the discussion leading up to the Protestation, Coke made the following famous and frequently quoted statement:

> I never spake here but for the honour of the kinge and the good of the kingdome. If I should not now speake, my silence would strike mine own conscience. The libertie of everie Court is the Lawe of the Court. Magna Charta is called *Charta libertatis quia liberos facit.* I will not dispute with my Maister for his words, but when the kinge sayes he can not allowe our liberties of right, this strikes at the roote. Wee serve here for thousands of tenn thowsands.[27]

These remarks of Coke are assuredly worth the attention they have been given. It is significant to note that they open on a legal note and close on a political one, and are thus symbolic of the past and of the future—of the past when legal checks

[24] *Ibid.,* VI, 243.
[25] Nicholas, *P. and D.,* II, 357–58.
[26] *Commons Debates 1621,* V, 243. Mr. Wentworth was Thomas Wentworth, M. P. for Oxford and son of Peter Wentworth. In this speech he told his audience to "see Sir Thomas Smith of parliaments, and Crompton, 34 H.8."
[27] *Ibid.,* V, 239–40.

like Magna Carta had been generally regarded as sufficient to limit the king and protect the subject, and of the future when political control by the "thousands of tenn thowsands" in the nation, acting through their representatives in the commons, would be achieved as a more effectual guarantee of freedom.

Religion was another realm in which the king's policies proved grievous to the commonwealth, as leaders in parliament, acting on behalf of the nation, pointed out time and time again. An especially objectionable policy, particularly to the Puritans in the House of Commons, was James's moderation towards Catholic recusants. This policy was cleverly attacked in 1621, not directly on religious grounds, but on the grounds of its danger to the state,[28] Pym pointing out that the errors of papists extended "to the Distemper of the State." [29] Speaking to the king, he admitted that "as the Image of God's Power is expressed in your royal Dignity, so is the Image of his Goodness by your Lenity and Clemency," yet he wondered "if this Goodness do not shine upon the Popish Priests and Jesuits without some Hazard to your State." [30]

The parliament of 1624 was agitated because of recent books and pamphlets written by those divines who had raised the king's power to greater heights than most Englishmen would accept. In May, a book by Montagu was denounced because it was "so offensive to the state." [31] At that time, however, since the commons were "not willing to become judges in so deep points of religion, it was ordered to send the book and petition to my Lord's Grace of Canterbury." [32] In the 1626 parliament the commons again took up the question of Montagu. The committee in charge of the matter cautioned "Not to meddle with the doctrinall parte of his workes, but as they disturbe the peace of the Church and Commonwealth." [33] The parliament of 1628 found time to consider again the case of Mon-

---

[28] *Ibid.,* II, 463–64.   [29] Nicholas, *P. and D.,* II, 233.
[30] *Ibid.,* 234.   '   [31] D'Ewes, 5/13/24.   [32] *Ibid.*
[33] St. P. Domestic, 25/10, as quoted in *Commons Debates 1625,* p. 179.

tagu, and now they moved ahead less cautiously. According to Pym, the committee of religion discussing Montagu said, "Wee sitt here to consult of matters concerning the Commonwealth and the Church. This is within our jurisdiction . . . for truth that is clear, it is in this house to defend and protect it. . . . Religion in a Kingdome is as the Soule of the Kingdome . . ." [34]

Religion was one of the most important issues debated in the 1629 parliament, and by this time the leaders of the opposition had become so fearful of Charles's Arminian tendencies and appointments that they boldly entered into the discussion of all aspects of religion, including doctrinal questions. By 1629 some leaders in the commons had become aggressive Erastians, claiming full parliamentary control of religion in order to halt those religious policies of Charles which Puritans and many moderate Anglicans believed menaced their souls and their nation. The temper of these men was expressed most dramatically by Mr. Rous. To him the Petition of Right was important, "but there is a right of an higher nature that preserves for us far greater things, eternal life, our souls, yea our God himself; a right of Religion derived to us from the King of Kings, conferred upon us by the King of this Kingdom, enacted by laws in this place, streaming down to us in the blood of the martyrs, and witnessed from Heaven by miracles, even by miraculous deliverances. And this right, in the name of this Nation, I this day claim, and desire there may be a deep and serious consideration of the violations of it." [35]

In their consideration of the question in 1629, speakers boldly claimed that parliament should be supreme in matters of religion. Parliament, Pym asserted, should "know the established and fundamental truths, . . . for Parliaments have confirmed acts of General Councils, . . . and Parliaments

[34] Mass., 6/11/28.
[35] *Commons Debates for 1629*, p. 12. In the same speech, Rous said: ". . . when the soul of a Commonwealth is dead, the body cannot long overlive it" (p. 13).

have enacted laws for trial of heretics by jury." [36] Pym also claimed that only parliament, and not convocation or high commission, could deal with the question of heretics. Since the convocation was "but a provincial synod," its power was "not adequate to the whole Kingdom"; and since the authority of high commission was set up by parliament, "the derivative cannot prejudice the original, the judgment of Parliament being the judgment of the King and of the three estates of the whole Kingdom." [37] Littleton also asserted parliament's final control over religion, saying "The Convocacion house hath noe power to make any Cannon of the Church or to put it uppon the State but by the assent of the State" [38] in parliament. Thus in the name of the nation, the parliamentary opposition claimed control over religion as early as 1629.

The welfare of the commonwealth was also stressed during these years in connection with the important and controversial question of monopolies. Monopolies granted by the king had been attacked vigorously in parliament in the latter years of Elizabeth's reign, and by 1621 the public prejudice aroused by them became very acute. The whole question was debated and discussed at great length in this year and again in 1624. Parliamentary leaders still admitted that the king possessed the power to grant them, but they insisted with mounting fervor that his grants must be for the welfare and not the harm of his people. Moreover, the fact that the privy council certified that a particular grant was beneficial to the realm no longer satisfied the aggressive parliamentary opposition. Because they, not the council, best represented the nation, theirs was the

[36] *Ibid.*, p. 21.
[37] *Ibid.*
[38] *Ibid.*, p. 120. D'Ewes made the following comment on the zeal of men in parliament for religion: "I cannot deny but the greater part of the House were either truly religious, or morally honest men; but these were the least guilty of the same fatal breach, being only misled by some other machiavelian politics; who seemed zealous for the liberty of the Commonwealth, and by that means drew the vote of those good men to their side . . ." *The Autobiography and Correspondence of Sir Simonds D'Ewes . . .*, 2 vols., (London, 1845), I, 404.

responsibility to examine the grant—to see if it were truly beneficial and not grievous to the people. They denied that monopolies granted by the king were matters of state outside their jurisdiction.

All the bitterness of their pent-up antagonism concerning monopolies came out in the attack on Mompesson in 1621. Among the arguments used against him was one that his monopolies were "mischeevous to the Comon-wealth," [39] and also oppressive to it.[40] He was accused in the interest of the "justice of the kingdom." [41] Even the king's grants for monopolies overseas were attacked as against the welfare of the nation. Gorges, who had been granted a monopoly in Maine, told the following story before the committee of grievances in February 1624:

> . . . this (as it seems) was a grievance of the *Common-wealth*, and so complained of in respect of many particulars therein contained contrary to the Lawes and priviledges of the subjects, as also that it was a Monopoly, and the colour of planting a Colony put upon it for particular ends, and private gaine, which the House was to look unto, and to Minister justice to all parties, assuring me further that I should receive nothing but justice, and that the House would do no wrong to any, that I was a Gentleman of Honour and worth, and the Publique was to be respected before all particulars . . .[42]

Parliamentary leaders in 1621 and 1624 criticized and challenged mercantile companies and trade policies which benefited a few men or a small number of companies. The arguments on these questions stressed the point that the public good of all, not the private gain of a few, must be considered. Alford said, "We must not see a private gaine to particular men be the decay of the shipping of the Land . . . when we are heear for the Kingdom in generall." [43] Sandys was active in

---

[39] *Commons Debates 1621*, IV, 85.

[40] *Ibid.*, VI, 43.   [41] *Ibid.*, II, 191.

[42] J. P. Baxter, *Sir Ferdinando Gorges and his province of Maine*, 3 vols., (Prince Society, Boston, 1890), II, 36–37. I am indebted to Professor Hartley Simpson for this reference.

[43] *Commons Debates 1621*, III, 106.

denouncing the privileges of the Merchant Adventurers, pointing out in 1624 that it might be "dangerous for the commonwealth to give so much liberty to the Merchant Advanturers." [44] "Sir Dudley Digges saith that upon all the interruptions of the liberty of the trade of the Merchant Adventurers they have ever gotten more privileges and liberty and wrought advantages of profit to themselves to the prejudice of the state . . ." [45] The privileges of the clothiers were also attacked on the ground that they were a menace to the public welfare. Sir William Spencer showed "That it was proved at the Council Board, that all the Clothiers of this kingdom are scarce able to buy the Tenth Part of the Wool of this Kingdom; and therefore it would be a great Prejudice to the State, that the Clothiers should have the sole buying of it." [46] Coke dramatized this grievance in the following language: "If the stealinge of a sheepe be felonie, much more the robbinge of a whole state by carryinge out wooll or fulling earth, a blessing appropriated to this kingdome." [47]

A similar point of view was expressed in the debates over the act for the free trade of cottons made in Wales. To the argument that this act would take away the charters of Shrewsburye, the answer was given that "Common Good is to be preferred before any perticuler Towne." [48] In the discussion of the act for "Free Fishing on the Coast of Newfoundland, New England, etc." the secretary pointed out that in the regions under discussion monopolistic privileges had already been granted, and "That if Regall Prerogative have power in any thinge it is in this." [49] The following reply was made to this explanation:

(1) The King's Prerogative never soe magnificent as in Parliament. And yf theis partes may be Ordered by his private Graunte, much more by the Publique Graunt of the King and Kingdome. (2) Ireland, Gersy, and Garnsey are under the jurisdiction of this Howse. The Seignory is the Kings,

[44] Nich., 5/5/24.
[46] Nicholas, *P. and D.,* I, 53.
[48] *Ibid.,* IV, 252.
[45] Nich., 4/8/24.
[47] *Commons Debates 1621,* V, 115.
[49] *Ibid.,* IV, 256.

but the Land is the Planters and the Trade is the Kingdoms.[50]

A nice distinction here—one which attributed governmental authority to the king, maintained that the property belonged to the subject, and claimed that the privilege of trading with the area belonged neither to king nor subject individually, but to the nation at large. By distinctions like this, parliamentary leaders were in reality encroaching upon the recognized medieval rights of both king and subject, and in the name of the nation were laying the foundations for future parliamentary sovereignty.

In the name of the nation, too, ministers of the crown were criticized, attacked, and sometimes impeached during these years. Neither the importance nor the closeness of a minister to the crown restrained the aggressive leaders. George Moore remarked concerning Bacon, "Were the Lord Chancellor never so great, never so dear unto him, yet the Commonwealth (the Mother of us all) is to be preferred before all." [51] As the opposition to Buckingham intensified, the same argument was used against him. Phelips said in 1625, "It is not fit to repose the safety of the kingdome upon those that have not parts answerable to their places." [52] In 1626 it was declared that his actions "assume the Nature of the highest Offences. . . . The Welfare and Safety of the People and State, is the supreme Law. Thus they are fit for so great a Council as the Commons of *England* to declare . . ." [53] Among the charges hurled at Buckingham, none was pleaded with more passion than the charge that he was a menace to the state. Some of his offences, Mr. Ball said, were "agaynst the Kings dignity: some agaynst the Crowne: some agaynst the Libertyes of the Subjects, and kingdom." [54] Mr. Kirton showed "That the Duke hath hindered the good proceedings of the Commonwealth and desire him to put no

[50] *Ibid.*
[51] Nicholas, *P. and D.*, I, 186.
[52] *Commons Debates in 1625*, p. 118.
[53] L. J., III, 597.
[54] Gros., 5/9/26.

man in ballance with the commonwealth." [55] Another speaker
said, "The Dukes growing greater and greater in power is
nothing butt setting himselfe agaynst the Commonwealth." [56]
The same sentiments against Buckingham were expressed in
1628. Coke attacked him at this time, saying, "whoever violat-
eth lawes doth not hurt certen Citizens but goeth about to over-
thro the whole Commonwealth. . . . The Duke of Buckingham is the man . . . lett us present this as our grevance of
grevances . . . " [57] So great was the hatred and fear of Buckingham that parliamentary leaders often went to ridiculous
lengths in criticizing him. In the name of the nation, his election as chancellor of the University of Cambridge was denounced in 1626 by Pym, who considered it "to be a publique
grievance that the government of the university should be committed to a man accused of great crimes in parliament." [58] To
Pym and to other aggressive leaders in the commons in 1628,
the nation was not safe as long as the appointing power remained in Charles's hands. "And since the House was the
greatest Council of the Kingdom," Eliot asked, "where, or
when should his Majesty have better Counsel than from
thence." [59] No leader, not even Eliot, was prepared at this date
to demand full parliamentary control of the appointing power;
but many men in the commons, fearful of Charles and desirous
of playing a greater part in governing the country than the law
and constitution afforded to them, did during the critical years
of the twenties encroach upon and attack the king's appointing
power, justifying their actions on the basis of their responsibility as parliament-men to the nation at large.

   The argument that some person, some policy, or some action
constituted a public grievance, and therefore was a matter of
parliamentary concern and responsibility, was used in different
ways during the turbulent parliaments of this period. It was

[55] Rich., 5/12/26.
[56] Whit., 6/12/26.
[57] Gros., 6/5/28.
[58] Whit., 6/7/26.
[59] Rushworth, I, 609.

an important weapon employed by parliamentary leaders in their encroachment on the king's power at this time. As they encroached on that power, it was often necessary that bolder tactics or new forms of procedure be developed to enable the house to play its new role in the affairs of the country. The general lines on which the procedure in the commons developed during these years have been brilliantly set forth by Professor Notestein.[60] It is not my intention in this chapter to treat procedure as such; but it is relevant to its main theme to indicate that lines of action and forms of procedure—either new or long-used—were often explained or justified in the name of the nation. In 1610–11, for example, parliament debated the question of impositions, despite the fact that a decision in favor of their legality had already been rendered in a great law court. Parliament, however, was determined to discuss the matter because it concerned "the whole kingdome" and was "a question of our very essence" [61]—because parliament, being "the representative body of the commonwealth," expressed "the public judgment of the whole state." [62] According to Hitcham "If any imposition be not for the good of the commonwealth, it is not lawfull." [63] In 1614, when impositions were again under discussion, Sandys explained to the lords that the judges' decision in Bate's case might be correct in law, but "some cases are above a Comon Courte and fitt only for this highe Courte, for noe king will sett his Crowne nor Subject his Liberty upon the judgment of any Comon Courte." [64]

When, in 1621, the house of commons attacked Mompesson and other holders of monopolies granted by the crown, the question arose of the extent of the jurisdiction possessed by the commons. To determine this question Noy and Hakewill were asked to examine the precedents—"to show how far and for what offences, the power of this House doth extend to punish

[60] *The Winning of the Initiative by the House of Commons.*
[61] S. T., II, 479.
[62] *Ibid.*, pp. 480–81.
[63] *Parl. Debates in 1610*, p. 77.
[64] Hastings Parliamentary Papers, Report of Sandys, May 12th, 1614.

delinquents against the State as well as those who offend against this House." [65] Sandys claimed that it was correct to accuse a man when thereby "the honor of the king, the justice of the kingdom and the livelihood and liberty of the subject shall be defended." [66]

By 1624, the committee procedure which had welded the house of commons into an organized body able to oppose the king successfully, had become very effective. Committees of the house were often charged by speakers to remember their responsibility to the nation. Digges moved, for example, that the "committee of the grievances may select all such things wherein we may do our country service by commanding them up to the King." [67] When the parliament of 1624 attacked Cranfield and accused him of levying certain impositions, the leaders in the commons realized that law and precedent were in favor of the impositions. Nevertheless, they did not drop the matter but pushed on in the interest of the commonwealth. Phelips advised them "To let the Right of imposing sleep a while. Necessary to represent this, as a Fault in the Lord Treasurer, and an Injury to the Commonwealth." [68] "The Lord Treasurer," Coke explained, "is sworn to serve the King and his people, to do right to all both poor and rich . . ." [69] The commons should press their charges against this high official. "The assembly of knights, citizens and burgesses of the House of Commons do represent the whole body of the commons, great multitudes. We are the best inquisitors." [70]

Several questions of doubtful procedure arose in 1626 when the commons wanted to discuss the king's action in making Coke a sheriff. Eliot urged that this matter making Coke ineligible for election to parliament should be considered be-

[65] Nicholas, *P. and D.*, I, 103, as quoted by F. H. Relf, *Lords Debates in 1628*, p. XIII.

[66] *Commons Debates 1621*, II, 191.

[67] Diary of Sir Thomas Holland for the parliament of 1624, Tanner MSS. 392 and Rawl. D, 1100, (Bodleian Library, Oxford), 4/26/24.

[68] C. J., I, 764.

[69] Erle, 4/12/24.

[70] Erle, 4/15/24. Coke speaking.

cause "the case is the case of the kingdom." [71] In the midst of the accusation of Buckingham in 1625–26, the question arose of whether or not the duke should be accused on the basis of common rumor. Littleton believed that they should proceed with the accusation, pointing out that there was "A great Difference between common Fame, and Rumour. The general Voice is common Fame." [72] Sherland expressed the same belief: "If in cases that concerne the life of a particular person common fame is allowed, shall it not be likewise in a case that concerns the life and soule of the commonwealth, which though wee cannot call legall treason, yett wee may call it reall treason." [73] Eliot also urged that the house should continue to consider all questions relating to Buckingham. "If we desert our fredome: we wrong ourselves. Have not we power to enquire of such things as are for the honor of the King for the safety of the Commonwealth." [74]

Eliot was prepared to push forward along almost any line in the interest of the commonwealth. During the opening days of the 1626 parliament, he urged the commons to give first consideration to the misgovernment in the country and to those men who would divide king and subject. He would not delay discussing this matter until later in the session, no matter what the traditional order of procedure might be, for "We have formerly broken presidents on the Countreys behalf." [75] Eliot moved ahead boldly along procedural lines again in 1628. In the parliament of that year he wanted to probe into the king's pardoning power, a realm belonging most intimately to the monarch, through which he bestowed grace. Eliot, however, moved "that wee may have a sight of the heads of the pardon before it bee engrossed, lett it appeare playnly that the pardon stretches not soe farr as to take of those from censure whome

---

[71] Rich., 2/14/26.
[72] C. J., I, 847. Littleton did not believe common fame was adequate reason for a definitive judgment.
[73] Whit., 4/22/26.
[74] Gros., 5/3/26.
[75] Rich., 2/10/26

our Duety to the Kinge and conscience to our selves and our Countrey would cause us to question." [76] There is little doubt that Eliot's conscience for himself and country outweighed his sense of duty owed the king.

The question of the king's pardoning power came up again in 1629, when the commons discussed the pardons which had been granted to Montagu, Cosin, Manwaring, and Sibthorpe. Rous declared that these four men "made the Commonwealth sick;" [77] and the commons, trying to find out how the pardons had been issued, set up a sub-committee to send for records.[78] Charles quickly dissolved this parliament which had become so aggressive, but eleven years later the Long Parliament immediately demonstrated that it had not forgotten the great advances which leaders in the commons had made in the twenties in the name of the nation.

The ideas which have been discussed up to this point reveal a group of aggressive parliamentary leaders who talked much of the commonwealth as they encroached upon realms claimed by the king as his. When the matter under discussion did not lend itself to an appeal to law or precedent, they appealed to the nation and, through such an appeal, developed a powerful weapon in the realm of ideas. Although the idea of responsibility to the nation was not invented by them, this concept was used more often and more effectively during the sixteen twenties than ever before.[79] Along with aggressive leadership,

[76] Bor., 6/16/28. Pym was another leader like Eliot who employed frequently the argument that new or doubtful actions of the commons were justified because of the commons' responsibility for the nation. In 1628 he advocated that the commons might suspend J. Baber, recorder of Wells, because he had issued a warrant for billeting soldiers in his town. The commons, Pym said, "may expell out of the house such as offended against the commonwealth, as Sir G. Mompesson. And we may expell any man that hath bene too busy, or offended against the Commonwealthe. As unworthy to be member of this house . . ." Nich., 4/8/28.

[77] *Commons Debates for 1629*, p. 37.

[78] *Ibid.*, pp. 37–38.

[79] As early as 1610 or 1611 Ellesmere noted that leaders in parliament "kepte secrette and privye Conventicles and Conferences. . . . And besydes they stuyded and Labored much to contrive and sett forth many supposed

improved procedure, and the weakening influence of the privy councillors, it played a significant part in the growing importance of parliament in this period.

Most of the leaders in the group opposing the king contributed to the development of the concept—Coke, the lawyer, Wentworth, Digges, and Noy, who later went over to the king, as well as the more fiery Phelips, Pym, and Eliot.[80] The reason for their agreement appears to be this. Despite the fact that some of their basic constitutional ideas differed, so that eventually the more conservative group and the more radical group parted company, in the twenties they could unite in opposing those policies of the crown which they found both illegal and oppressive. They agreed that the king had encroached too

grievances in the State and government." Ellesmere MSS. vol. 39, 2599, Hunt Lib. MSS.

The author of *A Record of Some Worthy Proceedings* wrote in 1611: "Well, I pray God; that whensoever we shall have an other parliament, Counties, cities and burroughes may not be moved by letters from such common-wealth-men, as the penman of the said publication is feared to be, to chuse such Knightes and burgisses, as will have less zeale for the ease and freedom of the subjects, than had the Knightes and burgisses of the late Parliament" (p. 5).

In 1616, Sherburne, in a letter to Carleton, quoted a friend writing to Coke as follows: "Hopes his standing so stoutly for the commonwealth proceeded from a love of justice, not from a disposition to oppose greatness; . . ." *Cal. St. P. Domestic*, (1611–1618), p. 415.

Arthur Wilson referred to the more aggressive leaders in the commons in 1621 as "the *Pilots* of the Commonwealth." A. Wilson, *History of Great Britain*, p. 161, as quoted by D. H. Willson, *The Privy Councillors in the House of Commons*, p. 155. For a full discussion of aggressive leadership in the commons, see D. H. Willson, particularly pp. 120 ff. and 155 ff.

[80] In Sir John Eliot's, *The Monarchie of Man*, A. B. Grosart, 2 vols., 1879, written when Eliot was in prison, it is clear that Eliot, in his ideal government discussed in this book, wanted a parliament to share, perhaps to direct, the king in the realm of government. Eliot wrote: "A Prince cannot have that universalitie of science to comprehend all things in his braine; and therefore a Senate was thought necessarie to be auxiliar and assistant" (pp. 69–70). In large parts of this treatise Eliot seems to ignore the problems and issues of his own day and to philosophize in literary clouds where true harmony prevailed. When, however, he discussed the position of the prince or pilot, he did not ascribe any real independent power to him, but limited him by the law and insisted that a senate be associated with him in the realm of government.

much on the subjects' right and liberty, and they also must have agreed that some encroachment on the king's power must be made, especially in view of the fact that he was asking parliament for money for foreign wars.

The concept developed to meet a practical situation, and it developed in a practical way. Little theorizing went along with it. Natural or divine law was not often appealed to by speakers in the commons, the Bible was seldom cited, and English or foreign writers were not commonly mentioned at this time in connection with this particular concept, whereas such authorities were frequently cited to back up common law or to prove the sanctity of property. The fact that the concept of parliament's responsibility to the nation was not bolstered up in this decade by such appeals and such authorities strengthens the belief that it was being used to meet a practical dilemma, and that its exponents were perhaps aware of the fact that the idea injected a political and radical argument into the controversies of the age.

During this same decade of the twenties, a few of the leaders, whose remarks have already been given, went further than others in the lengths to which they carried this idea of parliamentary responsibility for the nation. The more extreme developments of it came from the more aggressive and fiery of the leaders—from the politicians Pym, Eliot, and Phelips, not from Wentworth, Digges, or even Coke. These radical leaders began to talk of the unity necessary between king and people and to put forward the idea that anyone menacing or threatening that unity was dangerous to the state. Unable to control the king's ministers and favorites legally, they turned from accepted legal arguments to an interpretation of the law essentially political. They extolled the safety of the state as a supreme good—back of law and underneath the authority of kings. They denounced the actions of ministers of the king as threatening the safety of the state, and claimed that such danger to the state justified parliamentary consideration of those actions. Here in essence was the important political argument used against Strafford and other ministers of the crown in the impeachments and attainders of 1640–41, and here was the idea which became a cornerstone of the parliamentary case in the immediate controversies leading up to the civil war.

It was first put forward in parliament, it appears, as early as 1621. In the parliament meeting in that year, Pym delivered a long oration attacking a speech which Shepherd had made against the Puritans, Pym claiming that Shepherd's speech was an offence to the state. And why? Because he sought to menace the great unity between king and people by bringing the Puritans "into the ill opinion of the king." [81] The danger threatening this necessary unity was again stressed in the charges and speeches made against the lord treasurer in 1624. Sir Miles Fleetwood said concerning Cranfield's iniquity, "There are 2 kinds of perturbers of the good (of) this kingdom: 1, the priests and Jesuits . . . 2, those that are offenders in this kingdom and seek to keep a difference and distance between the King and his subjects." [82] Phelips insisted "That he that gives the King bad counsel or denies good may justly be proceeded with for stirring the King against the people and for breeding a coldness of fear between the people and the King." [83]

When Montagu was attacked in 1625, he also was charged with menacing the necessary unity between king and people — with laboring "to put a jelosy betwixt the Kinge and his well affected subjects." [84] In the attempted impeachment of Buckingham, the same argument was used. According to Rushworth, Pym was the speaker who elaborated the ideas contained in the eleventh article drawn up by the commons. In part of his speech, Pym said:

> There be some Laws made that are particular, according to the temper and occasions of the States: there are other Laws that be coessential and collateral with Government; and if those Laws be broken, all things run to disorder and con-

[81] *Commons Debates 1621*, IV, 63.
[82] Nich., 4/5/24.
[83] Gurney, 4/9/24.
[84] *Commons Debates in 1625*, p. 49.

fusion. Such is that Rule observed in all States, of suppressing Vice to encourage Virtue, by apt Punishments and
Rewards: And this is the fittest Law to insist upon in a Court
of Parliament, when the proceedings are not limited either
by the Civil or Common Laws, but matters are adjudged
according as they stand in opposition or conformity with
that which is *Suprema lex, salus populi.*[85]

Again, in the parliament of 1628, when Manwaring was attacked, Pym worked out and presented the case against him,
using the same basic arguments. Manwaring's offence was said
to lie in the fact that he had written and preached in favor of
beliefs subversive to the state. He had advocated the doctrine
that the king's power was so absolute that if the people refused
to grant taxes to the king he might take them from them without their consent. Manwaring, so Pym maintained, "strikes at
the roote of all government." [86] It is "the antient and fundamental Law, issuing from the first frame and constitution of
the Kingdom" [87] that taxes and loans must be granted by common consent in parliament. Change that law and you alter the
form of government. A truly unified government exists when
the people have the opportunity to show their love by giving
of their own to the king. To take away that opportunity is to
break the necessary unity between king and people and so to
change the form of government. Forms of government can not
be changed "without apparent danger of ruine to that State." [88]
In the 1629 parliament, Pym again attached Manwaring, saying this time: "Verily they, that shall thus go about to seduce
or corrupt a Prince, deserve to be hated of all men; as much as
those that attempt to poison a public spring or fountain
whereof all drink." [89] Arguments of this sort were common
enough in the forties, but not in the twenties. In that earlier
decade, however, Pym was already setting forth the arguments

[85] Rushworth, I, 335.
[86] Bor., 5/14/28.
[87] Rushworth, I, 596.
[88] *Ibid.* Pym's argument has been greatly condensed.
[89] *Commons Debates for 1629*, p. 69.

which he and others later employed with telling effect against Strafford, Laud, and other supporters of the king. He was already claiming such great parliamentary responsibility for all the realm that he was actually bypassing the king who for so long had been the head of the commonwealth.

This doctrine of the welfare of the state was presented in still another extreme way in this period. During the sessions of parliament in 1626, Eliot was committed to prison at the command of the king, and a violent debate over his commitment took place in parliament. In the course of the debate Mr. Mason insisted that no member of the house of commons should be questioned except for offenses against the commonwealth:

> We sitt not heere as private men but as publique vested for the commonwealths service, and therefore ought not to be questioned for anything butt wherein the Commonwealth hath an interest and for offences done agaynst the Commonwealth. There may be offences agaynst the king and high crimes which may not tend to the destruction of the Commonwealth, as contempts, encroaching upon the libertyes of the Crowne, etc.[90]

The idea put forward by Mason in this statement is far-reaching in its implications. Mason was claiming that although the king might call parliament, its members should not be questioned for their actions against their ruler, unless such actions were judged by parliament to be "offences done agaynst the Commonwealth." Their duty and responsibility to the commonwealth came first, before their duty and responsibility to the king. The doctrine of parliamentary responsibility to the nation was never stated during the decade of the twenties in more startling or more revolutionary form than by Mason in this speech in 1626.

Since the idea of parliament's responsibility to the nation could be carried in the early part of the century to such lengths as have been suggested, several questions related to the whole

90 Whit., 5/17/26.

development of the concept should be considered. As parliament-men were using this commonwealth argument, were they at the same time working out ways and means of bringing parliament, and especially the commons, into closer contact with the nation? Were they recognizing that parliament's authority was delegated—was derived from the nation? In answer to these questions, the first thing to note is that members of parliament often referred during the twenties to their own constituents and to the country at large. In a discussion of whether or not to grant subsidies to the king in 1621, Alford said, "I take it *pro concessu* wee must give, but lett us remember that England sent us. That must be satisfied. Wee must not leave England miserable and looke onelie to the palatinate." [91] Phelips also urged restraint in granting subsidies, "For we must take care that we give not such advantages for the future, that our country may find fault with us." [92] When again, in 1626, the question of giving a subsidy arose, Brown reminded the commons that if they should "give away the peoples money with [out] having redresse of our grievances, the countrey will blame us." [93] By 1628 references to their constituents by members of the house of commons were very frequent. Sir Henry Marten said, ". . . every day our members come to the house, with their pockets full of letters from their wives and Families of the disolute doings of the Soldiers." [94] Sir Henry Wallop complained that the soldiers in the Isle of Wight "leave bastards in every parish to bee a perpetual charge" [95]; and Digges told how farmers and landlords in East Kent complained of the billeting of soldiers.[96] Wentworth advocated "that his Majestie bee informed that if wee doe not goe home with our hands full of confidence and securitie in our liberties, wee shall bee the wonder of our Countree." [97]

These numerous references to the country by parliament-men were undoubtedly sincere, but were not accompanied by

---

[91] *Commons Debates 1621*, V, 219.
[92] *Ibid.*, II, 448.   [93] Whit., 6/12/26.   [94] Mass., 5/23/28.
[95] Mass., 4/8/28.   [96] Bor., 4/2/28.   [97] Mass., 4/7/28.

any suggestion that leaders in parliament believed the nation at large possessed active political power. For all political purposes, they in parliament were not only the representatives of the nation but the nation itself. The members of the house of commons, Coke said, "appear for Multitudes, and bind Multitudes; and therefore they have no Proxies. They are the Representative Body of the Realm." [98] Pym expressed the same sentiment when he called parliament the "great eye of the kingdom." [99] To Alford parliament was "the Counsell of the Land." [100] It was the only council which the kingdom possessed,[101] and "where Counsell fayles, the people perish." [102]

In 1621, the commons proclaimed in the Protestation that the priviliges of parliament were the "ancient and undoubted birthright and inheritance of the subjects of England." [103] In 1628, the privileges of the commons became "the harte strings of the Commonwealth." [104] In 1629, Phelips said, "If we suffer the liberties of this House, out of fear or complement to be abused, we shall give a wound to the happiness of this Kingdom." [105] In all their talk of parliament's responsibility for the welfare of the nation, leaders in the commons made a close organic (almost mystical) identification between parliament and nation. In the Middle Ages parliament had been viewed, at least at times, as possessing the full power, the *plena potestas,* of the realm. In the first decades of the seventeenth century this identification of parliament and nation was a very real belief, and one which increasingly played an important part in the thinking of many leaders of the commons in the period just before and during the civil war. In the years before

[98] L. J., III, 307.
[99] *Commons Debates 1621,* II, 303.
[100] *Ibid.,* III, 354.
[101] *Ibid.,* V, 185.
[102] *Ibid.,* II, 354.
[103] C. Stephenson and F. G. Marcham, *Sources of English Constitutional History,* (Harper & Brothers, New York, 1937), p. 429.
[104] Bor., 4/10/28. Coke speaking.
[105] *Commons Debates for 1629,* p. 7. Complement may be complaint. *Ibid.,* n. 7.

1640 no one in or out of parliament seems to have reminded parliament-men, as later Lilburne and other radicals did, that the great power of parliament, if wielded for the nation, must be truly responsible to the nation and must work out ways and means to enable it to be controlled ultimately by the nation. On the contrary, as parliament during these years encroached upon the king, claiming more and more of his power in the name of the nation, parliament seemed to assume without question that its voice was truly the voice of the nation.

Another series of questions arising in the historians mind, as he follows the development of the concept of parliamentary responsibility to the nation, concerns the place which men advancing this concept assigned to the king. Did they view him, so long the head of their commonwealth, as a part of the nation or outside it? Did they regard the nation as an entity bound together to bargain with the king or, if bargains failed, duty bound in the last analysis to resist him? There exists insufficient evidence to enable the historian to answer these questions with any finality, but a careful reading of the commons' debates throws some light upon them.

As direct evidence bearing on the problem, the more extreme statements made by parliamentary leaders must first be considered. As early as the 1610 parliament, Hoskyns, perhaps the most radical member of that parliament, reminded the house that "The regal power [is] from God, but the actuating thearof is from the people." [106] Sandys also talked of the people's place in government, claiming that both elective and hereditary monarchs "come in by Consent of People, and with reciprocal Conditions between King and People." [107] During the debates in 1628, Phelips, Pym, and Mason spoke of the contract between king and people. Phelips put it this way: "It is well known, the people of this State are under no other Subjection, than what they did voluntarily consent unto by the original

[106] *Parl. Debates in 1610*, p. 76.
[107] C. J., I, 493. According to Sir John Holles, "Sir Edwin Sands was questioned for his speech of elective and successive kings." Portland MSS., H. M. C., IX, 138.

contract between King and people . . ." [108] Pym injected the same idea into his denunciation of Manwaring, saying, "Every just King in a settled Kingdom, is bound to observe the Paction made to his People by his Laws, in framing his Government agreeable thereunto." [109]

Statements like these certainly indicate that the men making them were coming to emphasize the place of the people and to minimize the place of the king in the state; but there is no sure evidence that the men whose thinking was moving in that direction had pushed the king out of the commonwealth or had conceived of an organized nation setting itself up against its ruler. They primarily believed in contract within the state of which the king was a part, but not in contract between the state and the king outside and above it.

Nor did they in the twenties believe in resisting the king. When in 1626 Mr. More, a member of the commons, made a speech "by way of supposicion of a tyranny," [110] saying in effect "That we were born free and must continue free, if the King would keep his Kingdom," [111] the other members of the commons took him to task and ordered him sent to the tower.[112] They did not fear tyranny, for, in the language of Eliot, "our King is a pious prince, and "noe act of the King can make him unworthy of his Kingdome: it is against the tenet of our Religion." [113]

In the twenties, leaders in the commons still wished to bring back the unity between king and people which they regarded as so essential for the proper functioning of their government.[114]

[108] Rushworth, I, 503.
[109] *Ibid.*, 602.
[110] Gros., 6/3/26. Eliot used these words in reference to More's speech.
[111] C. J., I, 866.
[112] *Ibid.*
[113] *Ibid.*
[114] Outside of parliament, however, there are hints of possible resistance in the twenties. See *Cal. St. P. Domestic,* 1629–31, p. 17. Howell Jones of Rilth, stated that Evans said the "King was the 'poolingest' King that ever reigned, and that the end of it would be that he would be hunted out of the land, and that the Palsgrave would be crowned in his stead."

To achieve this unity, aggressive leaders in the commons were willing in 1628 to drop their proposed bill to restrict legally the king's power and work for a Petition of Right upon which all in the state—king, lords, and commons—could agree. To them the king was still a vital part—in fact, the head of the body politic—joined with the other members by living organic ties which could not be severed without the dissolution and death of the whole. To them "Prince and Republic were not yet incompatible." [115] The term "republic" could still be applied to their commonwealth whose head was an hereditary monarch and not an elective official. Although Pym and other aggressive leaders were inclined at times to push the king aside in their zeal for parliament and the nation, they were not yet ready to deny that he was the head of their commonwealth.

The great emphasis put by leaders of the parliamentary opposition during the critical twenties upon parliament's responsibility for the general welfare of the nation may be interpreted from the theoretical point of view as a last reminder to the king by leaders in the commons that the king as head of the body politic must take account of the nation— in particular, of the nation represented and embodied in parliament. If they had viewed the situation as the modern historian does, they might have penned a declaration on the subject in this fashion:

The kings of this realm have generally ruled with respect for the rights of their people and with their co-operation. They have been mindful of the "community of the realm." The Tudors secured the consent of their people in parliament when they dealt with great matters affecting the whole realm: with England's relation to Rome, with the form of religion to be established in the land, with the question of wages and enclosures, with the problem of the poor. Now in 1621 or 1629 we are telling you, our king, that we, the members of parliament and particularly of the commons, are vitally concerned with more adequate protection of our rights and also with questions of foreign policy, monopolies,

[115] F. W. Maitland, *Collected Papers*, ed. H. A. L. Fisher, 3 vols., (Cambridge University Press, Cambridge 1911), III, 253.

religion, and appointments to high office. In the Middle Ages such matters were naturally accepted as belonging properly within the sphere of your government, but now these questions concern us as well as you. We are, therefore, asking that you carry on the government in those realms with our co-operation and consent.

To state the point of view of parliamentary leaders in some such terms helps to clarify the problem of whether those men who advanced the concept of parliament's responsibility to the nation were following sound legal and constitutional precedents or were putting forth a revolutionary idea. In the sense that there existed an old tradition and established belief, reaching back into the Middle Ages and beyond, concerning the necessary co-operation between a true king and his people in a true commonwealth, Pym, Phelips, Eliot, and their running mates can be called conservative followers of tradition and precedent. On the other hand, the realms of government to which they were insisting the king must secure their assent, were realms which in the Middle Ages, in the Tudor period, and even during most of the reign of the first Stuart, had been generally accepted as belonging within the king's absolute prerogative, where any consent of parliament or people was not required. In insisting that new realms of government were the concern of the nation as well as the king's, leaders in the commons were setting forth an idea which could lead only to a political revolution.

Such an idea was the most effective answer the parliamentary leaders could have given to the royalist concept of the king's responsibility for the general welfare.[116] In the past the king had exercised that responsibility sometimes in parliament and sometimes outside. In the first decades of the seventeenth century, the royalists were more and more forgetting parliament and the nation, as they exalted the king's absolute power to provide for the general welfare. The parliamentarians replied by insisting that in all matters the king must secure the consent

[116] See chapter IV.

of that body which represented the nation. In the twenties, they seldom asked for more, but, in the forties, they proclaimed the right of the two houses without the king to govern the country.

The concept of parliament's responsibility to the commonwealth was not only an answer to royalist judges and councillors, but also to divine-right theorists. Some clerical writers [117] had lifted the king clear out of the state, while others had identified the king and state so completely that to them he was the state. These ideas, constituting a real departure from earlier legal precedents and political concepts, must consciously or unconsciously have been in the minds of parliamentmen who in the twenties set forth their own reply to divine-right theorists. In this decade and until the civil war, the parliamentarians never completely forgot the king as they exalted themselves and the nation. In this decade, however, the concept of parliament's responsibility to the nation developed so rapidly that by 1641 some leaders in parliament and some pamphleteers came to deny to the king all rights and any real share in the government. Such a complete departure on their part from earlier precedents and ideas might well not have come so quickly if the divine-right clergy had not in the same years gone to such extreme lengths. Their extreme views hastened the development of a radical, revolutionary theory which finally resulted in the execution of a divine-right king.

When, therefore, the concept which has been the subject of this chapter is viewed from many points of view, its real significance can hardly be overemphasized. As the Petition of Right drawn up in 1628 restated at a critical time in history the age-old idea of the absoluteness of men's rights against the sway of government, so also, the idea of parliament's responsibility to the nation, never proclaimed in a single document, but set forth boldly and convincingly during the ten years between 1620 and 1630, brought to life and shaped into new, almost revolutionary form, the age-old idea of the partnership between king and people in a true commonwealth and the necessary

[117] See chapter V.

consent of men to government. The two basic ingredients of modern democracy, consent of the governed and constitutional guarantees for certain rights, owe much to a group of determined leaders in the English house of commons who challenged their king on the basis of their rights and in the name of their nation. If today we remember and honor John Locke who wrote so convincingly on consent in government and the rights of the governed, we should also remember and honor John Pym, Robert Phelips, John Eliot, Edward Alford, Edward Coke, and Thomas Wentworth, as well as a score of other men who, more than fifty years before Locke wrote, spoke out boldly in the house of commons on behalf of both the rights of man and his necessary consent to government.

CHAPTER VIII

THE PURITAN CLERGY PLAY
THEIR PART

BETWEEN 1603 and 1630, the leaders of the opposition had set forth their interpretation of the constitution, which sharply limited the king, strictly proclaimed the rule of law, surely established certain basic rights of Englishmen, and aggressively demanded for parliament a large share in the government of the country. These men had stated and developed their views within the walls of parliament, in the give and take of debate on the many controversial issues of those years. In each parliament they had stood firm against the views of royalist councillors and lawyers, and at times had attacked the political views of royalist clergy. In each parliament they had advanced their own claims to deal with all matters of concern to Englishmen. In parliament the victory had been won by them and not by their opponents.

Was their growing opposition to the crown and to the royalist interpretation of the constitution supported and supplemented in the press and pulpit? Did the Puritan clergy rally to their side and assert the divine right of parliament, as the royalist clergy proclaimed the divine right of kings? Since the royalists controlled the press and pulpit, with varying degrees of strictness and effectiveness during the period from 1603 to 1640, the printed views of any opposition are of course less complete than the published ideas of the royalists. In the words of John Everarde, *"The liberty of the* Pulpit *is too little, but that of the* Press, *in our affaires, is much* less." [1]

Despite royalist censorship of press and pulpit, there are scattered hints that ideas which the government did not like

[1] John Everarde, *The Arriereban*, (London, 1618), Dedicatory letter.

were being expressed concerning kings and political questions. Professors Gooch and Davies [2] have collected and directed our attention to many of these scattered references revealing that some men were discussing questions regarded as dangerous by the government. They have shown us that some students and professors in the universities held political ideas in England in the early seventeenth century as well as in the twentieth. In 1613 the king was "angry with the Cambridge men for a disputation whether elective or hereditary sovereignties are preferable." [3] In the same year on a "Sonday" at "Paules Crosse" in London, "divers positions of Jesuites (specially of Suarez the Spaniard) were read and discussed . . . very derogatorie to the authoritie of Princes, and after the Sermon a goode number of his bookes were there publickely burnt." [4] By 1618 preachers and writers were frankly and boldly criticizing governmental policies, so bitter and determined had the opposition against James's pro-Spanish policy become. [5] In a series of proclamations and decrees, the government attempted to stop such criticism; [6] but was not completely successful, for during the rest of James's reign and until about 1630, sermons and tracts were preached and printed in England and Holland, and questions were raised in the universities which alarmed the government.

At Oxford in 1622 a young student of divinity, named Knight, came upon the writings of Paraeus, the famous Calvinist professor at Heidelberg, who had broken with the teachings of Calvin and advocated forcible resistance to kings who

[2] G. Davies, "English Political Sermons 1603–1640." See also his "Arminian versus Puritan in England, ca. 1620–1640," *Huntington Library Bulletin*, no. 5 (1934), pp. 157–81; and G. P. Gooch, *English Democratic Ideas in the Seventeenth Century*, (Cambridge University Press, Cambridge, 1927), ch. III.

[3] *Cal. St. P. Domestic 1611–1618*, p. 177.

[4] *The Letters of John Chamberlain*, ed. N. E. McClure, 2 vols., (The American Philosophical Society, Philadelphia, 1939), I, 488.

[5] See L. B. Wright, "Propaganda against James I's 'Appeasement' of Spain," *Huntington Library Quarterly* VI (1943), pp. 149–73.

[6] G. Davies, "English Political Sermons."

became tyrants. The ideas of Paraeus fascinated Knight as the ideas of Marx charm some students today, and this "unadvised young man," [7] who had been chosen to preach at St. Mary's, delivered a sermon there in which he proclaimed that under certain conditions "subordinate Magistrates might lawfully make use of Force, and defend Themselves, the Commonwealth, and the true Religion, in the field, against the chief magistrate." [8] The vice chancellor of the university, shocked at such views, summoned Knight and discovered that only two other students besides Knight had seen the manuscript of his sermon.[9] All three went to prison, and Knight was later committed by Laud to the Gate house. The University of Oxford condemned the views expressed by Paraeus and Knight, and insisted that everyone taking a degree in the future should take an oath "that he doth from his heart not only condemn the said doctrine of Paraeus, but that he will neither preach, teach, nor maintain the same, or any of them, at any time in the future." [10] The authorities at Cambridge took similar action, and the works of Paraeus were ordered burnt at Regents Walk in Cambridge, St. Mary's Church at Oxford, and Paul's Cross in London.[11]

The burning of books and the official condemnation of ideas seldom suppresses them. Again, in 1627, there is evidence that views unfavorable to kings were being expressed at Oxford. Nathaneal Carpenter, fellow of Exeter, preached three sermons very critical of kings, which "were very much applauded by all the scholars that heard them, and therefore were by them most eagerly desired to be printed." [12] In the same year at Cam-

---

[7] *Acts of the Privy Council, 1621–1623*, p. 237 as quoted by G. Davies, "English Political Sermons," p. 10.

[8] D. Neal, *The History of the Puritans*, 4 vols., (London, 1732–38), II, 135.

[9] A. Wood, *The History and Antiquities of the University of Oxford*, ed. John Gutch, 2 vols., (Oxford, 1796), II, 341–42.

[10] B. Brook, *The Lives of the Puritans . . .*, 3 vols., (London, 1813), II, 295. Brook's authority for this is MS. Chronology, II, 697.

[11] J. B. Mullinger, *The University of Cambridge*, (Cambridge, 1873–1911), II, 566.

[12] A. Wood, *Athenae Oxonienses*, ed. P. Bliss, 4 vols., (London, 1813–20),

bridge, Dorislaus, a professor of history, "in lecturing on Tacitus, selected for attention 'such dangerous passages, and so applicable to the exasperation of these villainous times' that Bishop Wren persuaded the Heads of Houses to censure the audacious pedagogue." [13]

If enough material can ever be discovered to enable the historian to tell a full story of the role played by Oxford and Cambridge in the growing opposition to the crown, the part played by Puritan preachers in and near the universities should prove very revealing. Several of the leading Puritan clergy were connected with one of the universities at some time—Carpenter with Oxford, John Preston, Arthur Hildersham, William Gouge, and Thomas Gataker (before 1600) with Cambridge. With the exception of Carpenter, however, there seem to be no significant political or rebellious ideas expressed by the above preachers in their sermons delivered at the universities.

Other leading Puritan clergy were connected with the London inns of court: Gataker preached at Lincoln's Inn between 1601 and 1611, and Richard Sibbes was at Gray's Inn for a time. Did these men and others play a part in shaping the ideas of lawyers who stood out against the crown in court and parliament? Here is another field of investigation for some future historian. That the government was not altogether happy about the situation is revealed in a letter of Archbishop Laud in 1633 to the inns of court. The king, so Laud explained, believes it of great importance "that such men as serve there should be . . . discreet and very obedient to those ecclesiastical laws which are settled by authority in this church and kingdom, forseeing that almost all young gentlemen spend part of their time in one or other of the Inns of Court, and afterwards, when they return to live in their several countries, steer themselves according to such principles as in those places are preached unto them." Accordingly, although "he [i.e., the king] will not

II, 422. Nathanael Carpenter was an ardent Calvinist, and also a poet, mathematician, and geographer. He became chaplain to Usher in Ireland.

[13] G. P. Gooch, *op. cit.*, pp. 61–62. Gooch cited *Cal. St. P. Domestic, 1627*, p. 470.

infringe any of their just and ancient privileges," yet the minister in their inn of court is instructed to read the "whole entire service" in the Book of Common Prayer, "for his Majesty is resolved that no one of those places shall use any pretence of privilege against government civil or ecclesastical." [14]

During the first part of the decade between 1630 and 1640 when no parliament was called in England, the government seems to have been fairly successful in preventing or suppressing hostile views.[15] "We learn from a letter of Selden that discussion of public affairs had to be carried on under the shelter of anagrams." [16] Beginning in 1636, however, with Burton's attack on prelates, criticism of church and government again became vocal, until by 1640 public opinion was thoroughly aroused against certain constitutional and ecclesiastical policies of the crown.

By far the most significant role in arousing public opinion outside of parliament and the law courts was played by the Puritan clergy. They preached in the universities, in the inns of court, in many churches in London, and in their parishes throughout England, particularly in the south and east. Not content with the opportunity afforded them for a sermon in the morning service, many preached again in the evening, and lectured on week days as well. Some were summoned before their bishops, and some before high commission, but the government never completely silenced them. Their sermons were printed and reprinted in the first forty years of the sevententh

[14] *Cal. St. P. Domestic, 1633–1634,* pp. 340–41. On the subject of dangerous views expressed in the inns of court, an unknown author wrote: "Would it not greive any true Subject to see how the Kings authority was of late despised in that outrage in Fleetestreete, backed by the Templers? wherein som observed a just judgment of God, that as the King suffered divines, who are, or should be, Gods lawiers and Souldiers, to tread Gods authority & law under foote, by slighting som proofs of Scripture, and sophisticating others; so God suffered Souldiers, Templers and other Innes of court men to spurn against his lawes and authority." A. Ar., *The Practise of Princes,* 1630, p. 19.

[15] This conclusion is based upon my own research and upon G. Davies, "English Political Sermons," p. 19.

[16] G. P. Gooch, *op. cit.,* p. 62.

century, sometimes abroad, but most frequently in England, particularly in London.[17] Some left or were forced out of the church and became separatists, but the great majority who remained in England stayed within the church.

Many of these zealous Puritan preachers, probably most of them, were uninterested in constitutional and political questions, according to the evidence of the sermons from this period I have read. They were primarily concerned with things of the spirit, with God and holiness, with human frailty and sin; and many of the political and constitutional views some of them did express are strikingly similar to many of the ideas of the royalist Anglican clergy.[18] The more one reads the sermons of English preachers in the period prior to 1640, the more difficult it becomes to label and define a Puritan in terms applying only to him and excluding all who were not Puritan.

Thomas Bell, for example, wrote that only God was above a king,[19] and cited Ambrose's remark that "Kings being freed by royall prerogatives of imperiall power, are not punishable by the lawes of man." [20] To Henry Burton, Charles was "their

[17] For the most recent studies of Puritan preachers, their sermons, and their activities in England, see, in addition to the works of Davies and Gooch already cited, W. Haller, *The Rise of Puritanism;* M. Knappen, *Tudor Puritanism* . . . (University of Chicago Press, Chicago, 1939); E. W. Kirby, "The Lay Feoffees: A Study in Militant Puritanism," *Journal of Modern History* XIV (1942), pp. 1–26; L. B. Wright, "Propaganda against James I's 'Appeasement' of Spain," *Huntington Library Quarterly* VI (1943), pp. 149–73; L. B. Wright, *Religion and Empire,* (University of North Carolina Press, Chapel Hill, 1943); and L. B. Wright, "William Perkins: Elizabethan Apostle of 'Practical Divinity,'" *Huntington Library Quarterly,* III (1939), pp. 171–97. Indispensable also for an understanding of the Puritans is W. K. Jordan, *op. cit.*

[18] Since most of the Puritans remained within the Anglican church before 1640, they were, of course, Anglicans. In this chapter, however, when reference is made to Anglican clergy, those who were not Puritan are meant.

[19] Thomas Bell, *Motives Concerning Romish Faith and Religion,* (Cambridge, 1605), p. 81. According to the Index of the Catalogue of the McAlpin Collection, Bell was an "anti-romanist writer; became romanist; recanted."

[20] Thomas Bell, *The Downefall of Popery,* (London, 1605), p. 3.

rightfull, and only Soveraigne King over them upon earth, next under God." [21] Bell asserted that kings might not be resisted,[22] while Burton concluded his *Baiting of the Popes Bull* with the prayer from the liturgy of King Edward VI, part of which reads: "From sedition, and privie Conspiracie, . . . from false and Hereticall opinions . . . Good Lord deliver us." To this litany Burton added, "And let all *England* say Amen." [23] Burton even reminded his readers that Christ paid tribute to Caesar.[24]

In 1636 the same Burton began a violent pulpit-press campaign against prelates, charging that "these Innovators" were the "Kings enemies" working against the kings laws.[25] The same note had been sounded earlier in 1628 by Alexander Leighton who wrote, "The loyaltie of obedience to the Kings Majestie and his lawes, cannot possiblie stand with the obedience to the Hierarchie" of the prelates.[26] "The Lord Bishops, and their appurtenances are manifestlie proved . . . to be intruders upon the Priviledges of Christ, of the King, and of the Common-weal." [27]

Puritans not only claimed that prelates intruded upon the king, but argued that the particular form of church government or toleration which they sought was not derogatory to the authority of kings. In *An assertion for true and christian church-policie,* William Stoughton, a professor of civil law and one of the most interesting and politically minded Puritan

[21] Henry Burton, *The Baiting of the Popes Bull,* (London, 1627), p. 60. Burton, a graduate of St. John's, Cambridge, and rector of St. Matthews, London, was one of the famous Puritans sought out and persecuted by the government at intervals between 1627 and 1640. He became an Independent, transforming St. Matthew's in 1642 into an Independent church.

[22] T. Bell, *The Catholique Triumphe,* (London, 1610), p. 108.

[23] H. Burton, *The Baiting of the Popes Bull,* p. 73.

[24] *Ibid.,* p. 51.

[25] Henry Burton, *An Apology of an Appeale,* (1636), p. 10.

[26] Alexander Leighton, *An Appeal to the Parliament* . . . , [1628], p. 5. Leighton, one of the most aggressive and bold of the Puritan writers, was not a member of the clergy, but a physician.

[27] *Ibid.,* title page.

writers under James, set out to show "how the Discipline by Pastors and Elders may be planted, without any derogation to the Kings Royal prerogative." [28]

Some Puritan preachers also took pains to demonstrate, as the royalist clergy did, the value of kings to the commonwealth. Nicholas Byfield wrote:

> Now the ends why humane societies became subject to Kings and to superiour Powers, were the Common-weale and the benefit of the people so united: for power was given to Kings, that so men might bee protected in the practice of vertue, that peace might be preserved among the Inhabitants, that the common priviledges might be maintained, that courses for raising of riches and trades might be held. Each man did looke to his owne wealth, but the King was to looke to the Common-wealth.[29]

Both James and Charles were praised by name by leading Puritan preachers. Robert Bolton, lecturing at Kettering in Northhamptonshire in 1625, asserted that "the child unborne will blesse King James for his premonition to all the Princes and free States of Christendome . . . his Golden pen hath given such a blow to that Beast of Rome, that he will never

[28] Published in 1604. The quotation is from the subtitle of the tract. A similar point of view was set forth in *English Puritanisme Containening. The maine opinions of the rigidest sort of those that are called Puritanes In the Realme of England* (1605). This tract is attributed to William Bradshaw by the D. N. B. English Puritans "hould and beleeve," Bradshaw wrote, "that the equalitie in Ecclesiastical Jurisdiction & authoritie, of Churches and Church Ministers, is no more derogatorie and repugnant to the State and glorie of a Monarche, then the Paritie or equalitie, of Schoolmasters, of severall Schooles, Captaines of severall camps, Shepheards of severall flocks of Sheep, or Masters of severall Families." pp. 11–12. In an anonymous tract *To the right High and mightie Prince, James . . . An humble Supplication for Toleration and libertie to enjoy and observe the ordinances of Christ Jesus in th' administration of his churches in lieu of humane constitutions . . .* (1609), the argument is set forth *"That the Church government* sollicited by us doth better sute with your Imperiall Scepter, and is of greater advantage thereto, then that of the Prelats" (p. 8).

[29] Nicholas Byfield, *A Commentary upon the first three chapters of the first epistle of Peter . . .*, (London, 1637), pp. 441–42. Byfield, a popular preacher and writer, became vicar of Isleworth in Middlesex.

be able to stand upon his foure legs againe." [30] Burton dedicated his *Baiting of the Popes Bull* to Charles, saying to him,
"one . . . whose naturall disposition also, like the Sunne un-
eclipsed, is freely to impart light and heate to the inferiour
Creatures; yea whose owne deare Person and crowne is em-
barked in the same adventure of God's people and His . . ." [31]
John Bastwick, who with Burton and Prynne suffered in the
pillory in 1636, also praised Charles, asserting "that never was
there any nation more happy in a King, then this our Nation
is in ours." [32]

For Puritan preachers to express such ideas is perfectly understandable in view of the past history and tradition of Puritanism and the particular circumstances in which they were
placed in the first forty years of the seventeenth century. Since
the Puritans' hatred of Rome was more intense and bitter than
that of other Anglicans, they would join naturally with the
Anglicans, and, if possible, outdo them in expressing fury
toward the pope and Roman Catholics. Since the most effective
way in the late sixteenth and early seventeenth century to meet
the challenge of Catholicism was to exalt a king, and since a
king could best be exalted against a pope by making the king
immediately dependent upon God, than whom there was no
higher, Puritans again naturally joined with Anglicans in proclaiming the divine right of kings against all papal authority.
This concept was no new idea in England, but one which had
been actively preached and proclaimed ever since Henry VIII
had broken all ties with Rome. Puritans, more completely
than Anglicans, approved of the independent policy followed
by Henry VIII, Edward VI, and Elizabeth. The Puritans
wanted further steps towards more complete Protestantism to

[30] Robert Bolton, *Some generall directions for a comfortable walking
with God* . . . , (London, 1625), p. 18. Bolton, a scholar and popular
writer, became rector of Broughton, Northhamptonshire, in 1611.

[31] Dedication.

[32] John Bastwick, *A More Full Answer of John Bastwick, Dr. of Phis-
ick* . . . , (1937), p. 4. Bastwick was a physician, not a member of the
clergy. He was persecuted by Laud along with Burton and Prynne.

be taken, and still looked to the monarch to carry out the final Reformation. Even after James disappointed those Puritan ministers who presented the Millenary Petition to him, many of them still looked to him to perfect the work earlier begun. And with good reason. Was not James, their king and earthly head of the church, the great champion of England's complete independence from Rome? Was he not a good Calvinist, and his daughter married to a leading Calvinist prince of Germany? Did he not support Calvinist theology at the Synod of Dort? Would it not be perfectly possible and natural for him to approve of the few final changes in the church desired by the Puritans? When Charles began to favor the Arminian clergy, and when Laud set out to make the church holy in ways the Puritans believed were opposed to the word of God, the Puritans had less reason to believe that the king would favor their cause, but they still hoped that all would be well once his evil councillors, the prelates, were removed.

For Puritans to look to the king for a reformation in the church was in line with English monarchical tradition and also with good Calvinist teaching. Calvin dedicated his first edition of the *Institutes* to Francis I of France, and, with some loopholes and exceptions, counselled nonresistance to earthly kings. It is true that his followers, Beza, Knox, Paraeus, and the Huguenot authors of the *Vindiciae* broke from the master's teaching and came to advocate resistance to bad rulers. Such views, however, were generally advanced when a particular Calvinist group was a minority one, with little hope of ever establishing a Calvinist form of worship, unless the ruling Roman Catholic authority could first be overthrown. In England the situation of the Calvinists was different from their position in Scotland under Mary Guise, in France under the last Valois kings, in the Netherlands under Philip II, or in the Empire under the Catholic Emperors. In England the Puritans were members of a national established church which had broken all ties with Rome; the thirty-nine articles of the church sounded good Calvinist doctrine; and many of its bishops under Elizabeth and James were staunch Calvinists in their theology. The Puritans might naturally hope that sooner or later the Anglican church would become truly Puritan and completely Calvinist. Their views would then prevail as the practices and policies of the dominant established church. A Calvinist theocracy would be achieved without forcible resistance, and such a theocracy, since it represented God's perfect plan for man on this earth, could allow of no deviation from it or resistance to it. The situation, then, in which English Puritans within the Anglican church found themselvesin the first half of the seventeenth century was one in which tradition and farsighted prudence consciously or unconsciously fostered cautious political views. It is true also that the government's censorship of press and pulpit served as a check upon too radical ideas.

There is nothing particularly new or original in the constitutional and political ideas which most English Puritans set forth in the period between 1603 and 1640. There is no Puritan writer whose thought can be compared in its originality and comprehensiveness with the thought of the *Vindiciae*. Nor is there a Puritan preacher or writer in this period whose political theory ranks with Ponet's.[33] In any general history of political thought, no Puritan writing or preaching in England prior to 1640 deserves a place; but in the history of the slow development of public opinion to the point where part of the nation finally took arms against the king and his supporters, the ideas contributed by many Puritan preachers are both interesting and significant.

The first and perhaps the greatest contribution made by Puritan preachers to the opposition against the crown was the way in which they linked their cause with God. Royalist preachers served the crown well by pointing out that, in exalting and obeying the king, man was acting in accord with God's will and plan for mankind. Puritan preachers also rested their

---

[33] *A Shorte Treatise of Politike Power*, 1556. It is significant that Ponet's treatise was republished in 1639 and again in 1642.

cause on God—His will and His plan—as they interpreted them, and thereby prevented the royalists from securing a monopoly on God. Many Puritans agreed with the royalists that the king held his authority only of God, but the Puritans took greater pains than most other Anglicans to point out that God and his laws were, after all, above even kings. To the Puritan it was really God and not the king who reigned supreme on earth. As Thomas Gataker said, "The mightiest Monarchs Territories are but a small patch of Gods footpace." [34] ". . . the life of the mightiest Monarch is but as a *nip of his naile*." [35] "Let us reverence them [i.e., princes] in God, and God in them; but not equalize them with God, nor preferre them before him. Let us beware how wee offend God for the pleasing of them . . . God is able to shield us against man: Man is not able to shelter us against God." [36] The laws of princes must "be grounded upon and agreeable to Gods Law, or else they are no Lawes, or as good as none." [37]

The Puritan believed that God had revealed His will to man in divine Scripture and had also given man a conscience to discern His wishes. Consequently man should, in general, obey kings who were ordained of God, but obedience to God had priority over obedience to kings. Nathanael Carpenter, whose sermon the Oxford students applauded, made it perfectly clear why God came first:

> But the sacred image of God, stampt in the reasonable soule of man, is to us both law and libertie, as well to preserve

[34] Thomas Gataker, *Certaine Sermons* . . . , (London, 1637). The title of this sermon is *An Appeale to the Prince of Princes* (p. 100). Gataker, a moderate Puritan, preached in the area near Cambridge and in London. He lectured at Lincoln's Inn and in 1611 became rector of Redrith, Surrey. He was a member of the Westminster Assembly.

[35] *Ibid.*, From *Gods Parley with Princes*, p. 89.

[36] *Ibid.*, From *Gods Parley with Princes*, p. 93.

[37] *Ibid.*, From *An Appeale to the Prince of Princes*, p. 97. The anonymous author of *The Fall of Babylon in Usurping Ecclesiasticall Power and Offices* (1634) wrote: "The Lord is our Judge, the Lord is our Lawgiver, the Lord is our King; *and that therefore it were a happy thing, if Princes and States would be pleased, to consider, that they are onely Lords over men properly and directly, as they are theire subjects and not as they are Christs Disciples, Christians and spiritually his subjects*" (Preface to the Reader).

the rights of Magistrates, as our owne priviledge. An obedience we justly owe to our superiors both *active* and *passive*, so farre forth as it may stand with the right of nature, and Gods honour, as that which God expresly commands, and no communitie can want. But when the sword of the Magistrate pretends a title to any part of divine prerogative, it findes alwaies, in the way of resistance, the right of the cause, or sinceritie of a good conscience, whereon, as on a rocke of Adamant, it may sooner hacke it selfe to pieces, than make a breach for entrie. Hence wise Magistrates may be taught to exact no more of their inferiours, than their commission from God dares to countenance, or their duty to him commands.[38]

Henry Burton expressed the same sentiment in these words:

That all our obedience to Kings and Princes, and other Superiors, must be regulated by our obedience to God. Wee must so obey man, as wee doe not therein trench or dash upon Gods Commandement. God must first be served. Therefore in all Commandements of man, wee must consult with Gods Commandements or Law, that it be not repugnant unto it. . . . the King is Gods Minister and Viceregent, and commands as for God, so from God, and in God. So as it is his office to command nothing against God. . . . If Princes shall commaund any thing against God, and his Law, then we must remember, that we are Gods servants too, and therefore must obey man in nothing, that stands not with our obedience, first to God. For this cause the same word of God is a rule both for the King, how to cary himselfe in governing, and for every Subject, how to cary himselfe to the King, and first unto God.[39]

If the Emperour commaund one thing, and God another: what thinkest thou? The greater power is God. Pardon O Emperour: Thou threatenest a prison, He hell.[40]

In these words of Burton lay the strength of the Puritan position. Although he, like most Puritans, advocated only passive

[38] Nathanael Carpenter, *Achitophel, or the Picture of a Wicked Politician*, (1629), pp. 50–51.
[39] Henry Burton, *For God, and the King. The Summe of Two Sermons Preached on the fifth of November last in St. Matthews Friday-Streete, 1636*, (1636), p. 76.
[40] *Ibid.*, p. 79.

resistance, he firmly and unequivocally placed God and conscience above kings. Subjects who actively obeyed kings against
God sinned, and so did kings who forced "any Christian to doe
any act of religion or divine service, that cannot evidently be
warranted by the same." [41]

The Puritan also linked his cause with God by reminding
kings that God expected them, whom He had ordained, to do
His work in this world:

> . . . they are not set in the throne, to doe and require the
> doeing of theire owne will, but Gods. [42]

> The Magistrate is *Ensifer Dei, Gods Swordbearer*: saith the
> Apostle, and that not to beare, or weare the sword for a
> shew; . . . but to draw it out, and to make use of it accord-
> ing to such directions as from God himselfe he hath re-
> ceived. [43]

> By reason of their office, they stand in Gods roome, and
> beare Gods Image; and in that respect are called, *Gods
> Sonnes*, yea Gods. [44]

> *Princes must provide for their peoples protection.* As they
> who are under government must be subject, so it becommeth
> Governours and Princes to be watchfull for the good of those
> that are under their charge. . . . That dignity and authority
> which the Governours have over their people, is not simply

[41] William Bradshaw, *English Puritanisme*, p. 3. Bradshaw also wrote
concerning the Puritan view of the civil magistrate: ". . . they hould that
as he is a Christian he is a Member of some one perticular Congregation,
and ought to be as subject to the Spirituall Regiment thereof prescribed
by Christ in his word, as the meanest subject in the Kingdome, & they
hould that this Subjection is not more derogatory to his Supremacie, then
the Subjection of his bodie in sicknes to Physitions, can be said to be
derogatorie thereunto" (pp. 32–33).

[42] *The Fall of Babylon in Usurping Ecclesiasticall Power and Offices*,
p. 19.

[43] Thomas Gataker, *Certaine Sermons*, From *Gods Parley with Princes*,
p. 75.

[44] William Gouge, *The Whole Armour of God* . . . , (London, 1627),
p. 188. Gouge became rector of St. Anne's, Blackfriars, London, where he
was a popular preacher. He took part in the plan for buying up impropria-
tions and was a member of the Westminster Assembly.

and onely for their owne exaltation, but for the preservation and protection of them over whom they are set. *They are Ministers of God to them for good, Rom. 13. 4.* . . . They must therefore *feed* their people, and *fight* for them: . . . Happy are those people and polities that have such Princes; that like *Mordecai, seeke the wealth of their people, (Est. 10.3.)* that preserve them in peace, that protect them from perill. Pray for such. Be thankfull for such. Be subject and obedient to such. Give to such their due. Such are worthy of double honour: and the double honour of maintenance and reverence is to be yeelded to such.[45]

Princes should care for their people and rule well:

What is better than *government?* The verie *Life* of a *State*. Yet if the *Scepter* be not swaied aright, if it rule not according to *justice* and *right; Regiment without righteousnesse degenerateth,* and turneth into *Tyrannie,* it is but *Robberie with authoritie.*[46]

O that a Prince might see a Tyrants mind,
What Monsters, what Chimeraes therein are.
What horrours in his Soule, hee still doth find,
How much him-selfe is with himselfe at warre,
Ever divided, full of thoughtful Care.
  What Pistols, Ponyards, Poysons he conceites,
  And thinks each one for his destruction waites.[47]

God waited to punish tyrants and judge kings.

Know King, how great-soever that thou be,
The King of Kings still ruleth over thee.[48]

[45] William Gouge, *Gods Three Arrowes: Plague, Famine, Sword* . . . , (London, 1631), pp. 203–5.
[46] Thomas Gataker, *Certaine Sermons.* From the sermon *The Christian Man's Care,* pp. 44–45.
[47] [Sir Francis Hubert], *History of Edward the Second . . . To-gether with the Fatall downs-fall of his two unfortunate Favorites Gaveston and Spencer. . . .* With the Additions of some other Observations both of use and Ornament. By F. H. Knight, (London, 1629), p. 104. According to the D. N. B. this historical poem by F. H. was probably writted by Francis Hubert, a clerk in chancery, in the reign of Elizabeth. It was not allowed to be published then. In 1628 an incorrect edition was printed, and in 1629, the correct one cited here. It is noteworthy that opposition to Charles and particularly to Buckingham was very great in 1628 and 1629.
[48] *Ibid.,* p. 5.

Forbeare to Sinne: There is a day of Doome,
There are Records, where thy sinnes are Inrol'd,
There is a just and fearefull Judge, from whom
Lyes no appeale: Who cannot bee control'd
    Whom teares almes, prayers may here to mercy move
    But then there is no place for peace or love.[49]

Forbeare to Sinne: Because there is a Hell,
Where cease-lesse, ease-lesse, Endlesse torments be,
Where Div'ls, & all the damned Soules doe dwell,
Whom Millions of yeares shall never free.
    Where to remaine, Is grievous past Conceit,
    And whence, not any hope to make retreat.[50]

Most Puritans in this period were willing to leave the king's punishment to God, but they wanted kings and their people to be reminded frequently of the surety and awfulness of God's final decree. No royalist preacher set forth God's judgment as vividly as Thomas Beard did. Beard's views are particularly significant because he was the master of the Huntington grammar school in which Oliver Cromwell was educated. As early as 1597 Beard wrote the *Theatre of Gods Judgments*[51] in order to show "the admirable justice of God against all notorious sinners, both great and small, but especially against the most eminent persons of the world."[52] Beard carried out admirably the purpose announced in the title of his book, devoting one whole chapter to showing "How rare . . . good princes have beene at all times"[53] and another to pointing out "That the greatest punishments are reserved and laid up for the wicked in the world to come."[54]

---

[49] *Ibid.*, p. 168.   [50] *Ibid.*

[51] I have used the third edition, published in London in 1631. A second edition came out in 1612, and a fourth in 1648. According to Brook, *op. cit.* Thomas Taylor wrote the *Theatre of Gods Judgments* with Beard. On the title page of the first edition it reads, "Translated out of French, and augmented by more than three hundred Examples, by Th. Beard." The third edition is dedicated to the mayor, aldermen, and burgesses of Huntington. Beard preached in Huntington, and in 1630 was made a justice of the peace.

[52] *Ibid.*, title page.   [53] Ch. 49.   [54] Ch. 52.

If you be mightie, puissant, and fearfull, know that the Lord
is greater than you, for he is almightie, all-terrible, and all
feareful: in what place soever you are, he is alwayes above
you, readye to hurle you downe and overturne you, to
breake, quash, and crush you in pieces as pots of earth: he
is armed with thunder, fire, and a bloudye sword, to destroy,
consume, and cut you in peeces. . . . it is a horrible thing
to fall into the hands of the Lord.[55]

By sounding stern warnings of God's awful judgment, by
subordinating the king and obedience to him to God and His
will, Puritan preachers never allowed their congregations or
readers to forget that God was truly king in England. Many
an English Puritan preacher made a king so subordinate to
God that it would not be difficult for men listening to his ideas
to wonder and raise questions in their own minds concerning
the divine right of King James or King Charles. If Puritan
preachers had made no other contribution than this to the
growing opposition to the crown, theirs would have been a
great one.

A goodly number of them did more, for they preached and
wrote, not only of a king in relation to God and his laws, but
also of a king in relation to human laws and rights, to the
commonwealth, to people in general, and to parliament in
particular. In subtle ways they conveyed the idea that God
sometimes expected man to act, that He would not do all His
work alone.[56] When the Puritans talked in such terms, they
were expressing ideas similar to those upon which the parliamentary opposition rested its case against the crown, and they
were supplementing and strengthening those ideas by all the
fervor and conviction which Puritans brought to any cause or
idea they sponsored.

The parliamentarians had tried to limit the king more and
more by the law of the land. Some Puritan clergy also talked of
the law of the land. God, Beard wrote, "enjoineth" kings "to
have alwaies with them the book of his Law," [57] and to observe

[55] *Ibid.*, pp. 541–42.   [56] See pages 340–41 and 346–47.
[57] Thomas Beard, *op. cit.*, p. 12.

"all the precepts that are contained in that booke. As for civill and naturall Lawes, in so much as they are founded upon equitie and right (for otherwise they were no Lawes) therein they are agreeable to, and as it were dependents on the law of God, as is well declared by *Cicero* in the first and second booke of his Lawes: . . . If then Princes be subject to the law of God, . . . there is no doubt, but that they are likewise subject to those Civill lawes, by reason of the equitie and justice which therein is commended unto us. And if (as *Plato* saith) the Lawes ought to be above the prince, not the Prince above the Lawes, it is then most manifest, that the prince is tyed unto the Lawes, even in such sort, that without the same, the government which he swaieth can never be lawfull and commendable." [58] Beard agreed with Aristotle that if a perfect king could be found he would need no law over him; but he asked "where is it possible to find such a Prince so excellent and so vertuous, that standeth not in need of some law to be ruled by?" [59]

Thomas Scott, the bold and prolific preacher and pamphleteer against James's policy of appeasing Spain, also pointed out that the law limited the king:

> Gods Law is *Caesars* verge, which *Caesar* must neither *transgresse,* nor suffer to bee transgrest. Where God hath set no Lawe, there Caesars Lawe (I *meane the Lawe of the Land, which is the hedge to this high-way of the King)* must stand. And this must agree with the equity of the Lawe of God from whence it originally takes life and strength. . . . as the Lawes of God must guide our consciences in our religious duties, so the positive Lawes of the Kingdome must be the *high-way* wherein every one must walke in active obedience.[60]

To Puritan preachers, kings were limited by laws, and also limited in taking taxes from their people. Preachers found

[58] *Ibid.*, p. 13.   [59] *Ibid.*, p. 15.
[60] Thomas Scott, *The Workes* . . . , (Urick, 1624). From the *High-Wayes of God and the King,* (1623), pp. 70–71. For an excellent discussion of Scott and his significance, see L. B. Wright, "Propaganda against *James I's* 'Appeasement of Spain.'"

different ways of expressing the idea that princes could not take taxes arbitrarily. Beard used the favorite text of the royalists, Romans 13:7, to make a telling point on that question:

> Marke how he [i.e., Paul] saith *Give unto all men* their due: and therein observe, that kings and princes ought of their good and just disposition to be content with their due, and not seek to load and overcharge their subjects with unnecessarie exactions . . . it is most unlawful for them to exact that above measure upon their commons, which beeing in mediocritie is not condemned. I say it is unlawful both by the law of God and man.[61]

According to holy scripture (Deut. 18) kings should not hoard gold and silver, nor heap up treasure.[62] As for the laws of man:

> truely, there is nothing more rightfull and just in mans societie, than that every one should possese and injoy that which is his own, in peace and quietnesse, without disturbance or violence, in which respect also, rules of justice are established, called lawes, which no good kings will ever seeke to stand against. They are indeed Lords of the earth, as some say, and truely; but so, that their Lordships stretch no further than right, and passe not the rule of equitie: and not withstanding, the proprietie of goods and possession, remaineth untouched. To kings (saith *Seneca*) pertaineth the soveraigntie over all things, but to privat men the proprietie.[63]

Paul Baynes, another Puritan preacher, did not talk of property as openly as Beard did, but subtly and cleverly conveyed the idea that God expected a king to respect property. "God useth" the king, Baynes wrote, *"as his instrument for our peace and prosperity* . . . All our tranquility, all our prosperity, our wealth, our conveniences, that wee sit in our Chambers, every one keeping peace under his own Vine and figgetree, all this is by the King. . . . Seeing Kings are the instruments whereby peace and prosperity is granted, as you love your wives and children, lands, goods, houses, pray for the welfare of your

[61] Thomas Beard, *op. cit.*, p. 448.
[62] *Ibid.*, p. 449.
[63] *Ibid.*, p. 451.

King, for his peace is your peace." [64] He might well have added, "As you love and wish to retain your own possessions, pray for the king, for he guards and protects them but leaves them to you."

Puritan preachers, like speakers in parliament, pointed out that the king was bound by his coronation oath to respect the laws and the rights of his people. In discussing this subject, Beard compared a Hebrew and a Christian king, saying:

> David did never assume so much to himselfe, as to desire to have libertie to doe what he listed in his Kingdome, but willingly submitted himselfe to that which his office and dutie required; making . . . a Covenant of peace with the Princes and Deputies of the people: and we know, that in everie Covenant and bargaine both parties are bound to each other, by a mutual bond to performe the conditions which they are agreed upon. The like is used at the coronation of Christian Kings, whereas the people is bound and sworne to do their allegeance to their Kings; so the Kings are also solemnely sworne to maintaine and defend true Religion, the estate of Justice, the peace and tranquilitie of their subjects, and the right and priviledges (which are nothing but the Lawes) of the Realme. [65]

Henry Burton discussed the "mutuall stipulation or Covenant which the King and his Subjects make at his Coronation." [66] By it the king took "an explicit solemne oath to maintaine the ancient Lawes and Liberties of the Kingdome, and so to rule and governe all his people according to those Lawes established: So consequently, and implicitly, all the people of the Land doe sweare fealty, allegiance, subjection and obedience to their King, and that according to his just Lawes." [67] Subjects should "yeeld all feare, honour, obedience to their

---

[64] Paul Baynes, *A Commentarie Upon the First and Second Chapters of St. Paul to the Colossians* . . . , (London, 1634), pp. 245–49. Baynes followed the popular William Perkins as lecturer at St. Andrew's Cambridge. He became a nonconformist when Bancroft stopped his lectures.

[65] Thomas Beard, *op. cit.*, p. 13.

[66] Henry Burton, *For God and the King*, p. 38.

[67] *Ibid.*, p. 39.

Soveraigne, . . . considering in speciall, how our Gracious Soveraigne hath entered [in the Petition of Right] into Solemne and sacred Covenant with all his people, to bee their King and Protector, and to governe them according to his good and just lawes, and to maintaine all their just Rights and Liberties, and according to the Patterne of God himselfe, whose viceregent he is, to demaund of them no other obedience, but what the good lawes of the Kingdome prescribe, and require." [68] In Burton's opinion the king was bound to his people by a solemn compact.

The royalist clergy accused the Puritans of subscribing to the belief that the consent of man rather than the will of God was the basis upon which the authority of kings rested. Royalist preachers denounced, by name, Buchanan and Paraeus for holding such damnable views, but never to my knowledge especially named in their sermons or writings prior to 1640 any contemporary English Puritan. It is true that Puritan preachers appear to have been conservative and cautious on this subject, and I have not found one who, before 1642, rested all the king's authority upon the people or proclaimed outright republican views. Nevertheless, several of them discussed the king's relation to his people or the people's part in government with more democratic leanings than the royalists could possibly approve of.

Early in James's reign, William Stoughton [69] gave a very frank and interesting answer to a charge which had been earlier made by Bishop Cooper in his *Admonition*.[70] Cooper had claimed, so Stoughton explained, that if the democratic or aristocratic principles desired by Puritans in their church government "be made once by experience familiar to the minds of the common people . . . it is greatly to be feared, that they will very easely transferre the same to the government of the

[68] *Ibid.*, pp. 41–42.

[69] *An assertion for true and christian church-policie*, (1604).

[70] T. Cooper, *An Admonition to the People of England . . .* , (London, 1589).

common weale." [71] "This reason," Stoughton replied, "might seeme to carrie some shewe of affrighting a Monarch, if the same were insinuated unto a king, whose people were never acquainted with the principles and reasons of Democracie, or Aristocracie: but this feare being insinuated unto our late Soveraigne Ladie the Queene, whose people ever since the time they first began to be a people, have had their witts long exercised, with the sence and feeling, of the reasons and principles, as well of *Democracie,* as also of Aristocracie," [72] is groundless. Stoughton illustrated the meaning of his statement by giving a very penetrating and exceptional analysis of the democratic and aristocratic features of the government of England in his own day. The people, he explained, took part in criminal and civil justice.[73] By many statutes it was clear "that the Administration of publike affaires, in the common weale, hath never bene usually committed, to the advisement, discretion, or definitive sentence, of anyone man alone." [74] The privy council helped the king with matters pertaining to "his Kingly estate," and the parliament assisted him in matters concerning the "Church, the King and the common weale." [75] "And is not their consultation in Parleament, a mere Democraticall consultation?" [76] Stoughton never referred to the English government as a mixed monarchy, but he clearly and frankly explained its nature and functioning in terms to which the adjective "mixed" might be applied by a more philosophically minded person.

Thomas Gataker was a second Puritan preacher who discussed the people in relation to government. Gataker admitted that God ordained kings, but boldly added:

> Againe, Princes receive power from their people. *The might of a Prince consisteth in the multitude of his people.* And

[71] William Stoughton, *op. cit.,* p. 349, quoting T. Cooper, *An Admonition,* p. 82.
[72] *Ibid.,* pp. 361–62.
[73] *Ibid.,* p. 362.
[74] *Ibid.,* p. 377.
[75] *Ibid.,* p. 378.
[76] *Ibid.,* p. 362.

the throne is supported by the Ploughmans paines. It is their subjects shoulders that beare them up; as the lower stones in the wall doe those that lye aloft over them: take these supporters away, and they will lie as low as the lowest. . . . The Prince hath as much need of his people, as the people have need of their Prince: and the Prince can no more be without his people, than the people can be without their Prince.[77]

In another passage Gataker reminded a king that fundamentally he was of the same mortal clay as his people:

He shall not lift himselfe up above his Brethren; saith God by Moses of the King himselfe. . . . You are the *first-borne,* as he saith of our Saviour, *but amongst many Brethren.* . . . Though you be now above them, yet there is no difference betweene you and them, either in birth or in death: you were both alike before death; you shall be both againe alike after death: It is but in the *interim* of this short life only, that you are somewhat in some things unlike. It is with men as with Counters: howsoever while the account lasteth, one standeth for a penny, and another for a pound, yet are they all Counters alike before and after the account, when they are together in the bag, *aut in utero, aut in urna, either in the wombe, or in the tombe.*[78]

Thomas Scott made a contribution to the question of the people's relation to the king from another angle. Like Gataker he spoke of God ordaining kings, but he also referred to the special spirit God had given kings to enable them to rule well.[79] To Scott that spirit was not something mysterious, not that realm wherein the king was admitted to be absolute in order that he might provide for emergencies and for the general welfare. On the contrary, that spirit was the law of the land and the public voice of the people. In Scott's own words: ". . . this Spirit whilst it continues with them [i.e. kings] doth never contradict the publique voice, that is, the Lawe of the State, but joynes with it and speaks the same language, from whence per-

[77] Thomas Gataker, *Certaine Sermons.* From *An Appeale to the Prince of Princes,* pp. 99–100.

[78] *Ibid.* From *Gods Parley with Princes,* p. 90.

[79] Thomas Scott, *The Workes.* From *High-Waies of God and the King,* pp. 67–68. This tract was first published in 1623.

haps that common speech arose, that the *voice of the people is the voice of God,* if it bee joyned with the voice of the King; and this voice is to be heard and obeyed for conscience sake, being heere opposed to the Spirit of privacie, which will rule, though without reason; and the more weake it is, is for that the more wilfull." [80] A king, Scott contended, should rule in accord with law, and carry out his work publicly, not privately. "And thus much the crowne that a King weares testifieth, which is a type of the love, and acknowledgement, and consent of the people in his government." [81] In his pamphlet *Vox Regis,*[82] Scott made another extreme statement concerning the relation between king and people. He believed that the king should have parliament's consent for his marriage, for, he explained, "Princes are maried to the commonwealth; & the wife hath power of the husbands body as the *husband* of hers. The Commonwealth then hath power of the Prince in this Point." [83] In this same pamphlet Scott also said that one could not really serve the king well if he did not truly serve the kingdom, so inextricably joined together were the two.[84]

Scott was not primarily a philosophically minded political theorist but a skillful political pamphleteer, yet, in the way he linked king and people, he revealed a keen understanding of the growing part which the people in parliament were coming to play in the sixteen-twenties in the government of the country. He may well have been the inspiration for some parliamen-

---

[80] *Ibid.,* p. 68.   [81] *Ibid.,* p. 70.   [82] First published in 1623.
[83] T. Scott, *The Workes.* From *Vox Regis,* pp. 13–14.
[84] *Ibid.,* p. 67. The importance of placing the public welfare above private interest was pointed out by Samuel Ward of Ipswich in *A Peace-Offering to God for the blessings wee enjoy under his Majesties Reigne;* . . . on Sunday the 5. of October, 1623 . . . , (London, 1635). Ward wrote: "It's not onely selfe-love, but want of judgement, that makes fooles prize a Domesticall and private welfare before the Common wealth, and the good of the Kingdome, which is in it selfe the greater, and would in the long runne be greater to the particular man. Is any cost bestowed on the private Cabbin, comparable to the saving of the whole Ship? The very Heathens rejoyced more in their Countries good then in their owne" (p. 486). Ward served as town preacher of Ipswich for over thirty years. In 1635 he was brought before high commission and suspended.

tary leaders to look to the commonwealth, as many of them did in this decade, for support against the claims of the king.

The most interesting and complete attempt to justify the limitation of the king by the laws of the land and the rights and consent of the people seems to have been made by the un-known author of a long manuscript tract entitled "The Lawes of England."[85] The author was probably a Puritan, whether a member of the clergy or not it is impossible to tell, but cer-tainly a keen observer of the great constitutional controversy going on in England between 1620 and 1640. Like other writers in this period, he emphasized the similarity between Israel and England. In this tract, his main thesis was that English laws were based on the laws of God. To sustain this contention he first entered into a detailed discussion of Hebrew laws. God, so this author explained, allowed patriarchal government prior to Moses, but then "In this Regiment of Moses, God now began to establish a Commonwealth amongst his People, and gave them Lawes of his own making wch were of 2 sorts."[86] The first were the ten commandments for worship.[87]

> The other were certaine Politique Lawes, for the Govern-mn't of their Commonwealth, consisting Chiefly upon these 3 heads. First Concerning God, and his Religion, in for-bidding all Idolatry, and superstition, and Commanding his pure Worshipp. The second concerning the p[er]sons of his people, in forbidding all wronge to be done to them; and Commanding all right and Justice to be done by them. And the Third was Concerning the Law of Property in their Goods and possessions, wch he strictly commanded to be ob-served and held from any manner of Theft, Rapine and violence, or any other injury. . . . And it is very observable, that Although God, holy and Righteous, needed not in ye delivery of both these Lawes the Consent of the people to them, yet to teach all Governours in the world, that in the

[85] Ellesmere MSS. 34/C/17, Hunt. Lib. The MSS. number given on the inside of the tract is El/35/C/17. The tract seems to have been written sometime between 1625 and 1640, but I have not been able to date it more specifically.
[86] *Ibid.*, p. 5.
[87] *Ibid.*

making of Lawes the consent of the People is requisite: He
sent for Moses to Come to him to try the People, whether
they would yeild their consent to all these Lawes, wch they
most readily did. For these are the words in the 3ᵈ verse,
[24 Ex.], And Moses came and told the People all the words
of the Lord, and all the Judgments: And all the People
answered wth one voyce and said (wch implyes a question
precedent) All the words wch the Lord hath said will wee
doe; which answere doth strongly inferre this Conclusion;
that by the Consent of the People unto Lawes two things are
asserted, First an approbation by them of those Lawes; and
then a secret paction to observe them: And when the People
had thus Assented to these Lawes of God, then was there a
Record made of them, and not before; For it was said in the
4ᵗʰ verse And Moses wrott all the words of the Lord.[88]

The author next proceeded to trace Hebrew history in the
period after Moses, and concluded that throughout their history there were "Nine fundamentall rights and Liberties, wch
that people was lawfully intituled unto, and enjoyed, and wch
their Kings and Princes could not by Law take from them
against their Wills." [89] These nine rights and liberties were as
follows:

I. Their Right and Interest in God, [and] in his pure wor-
shipp: When Kgs commanded things against true worship
people not have to obey for it was a sound Ground in reason
as well as in Religion, It is better to obey God then man.
. . . II. *The second* Right belonging to the People, is a
Right in their King, One as he is a man taken to Regallity
from among themselves; The other as hee is their Governour,
the King. . . . From the first Consideration the People are
greatly interested in the Love of their Prince. From the
second, in his Justice, and Protection. . . . III. The Third
Right, which the People had, was to the Lawes of the Kingdome; not only those Lawes, which Concerned themselves,
but likewise those Lawes, wch concerned their King: for
both were to be knowne by the people, and in both they had
an Inheritance, as well as in their King. . . . IV. The Fourth

[88] Ibid., pp. 5–6. In the margin of the tract, at this point the author
cites 24 Exo. 1. 2. 3 and 5 Deut. 27.
[89] *Ibid.*, p. 18.

Interest of the People was the Liberty of their Persons, God had delivered his people from the slavery of Egypt, and thereupon could not endure that his people should ever after be in Bondage. . . . V. The Five next Rights, which ye people, and all people in the world besides, may by the Lawes of God and nature Challenge to themselves are those Jura Familiae, consisting in Wives, Children, servants, Goods, and Lands, in which all Lawes in the World have given to the Father of the Family a king of Supreame power, making them Lords and Kings in their owne houses. All these Five are reduced to that Lawe of property, wch the Master of the family was, by the Lawe of nature, intituled unto long before any Lawes were written. . . . For it is a solid and a true Conceit of M. Hooker, that there was no impossibility in nature, but that men might have lived in private Families without any publique regiment; And that the Choyce of our Supreame Governour for the ordering of those families, did arise from deliberate advise and Composicion betweene men to have it otherwise.[90]

The rights of property contained in the ten commandments were "nothing else, but the writing out of the Lawe of Nature by the Finger of God in great Letters what he had written before in the hearts of men." [91] According to the clear teaching of Scripture, kings might not rightfully take their subjects' property. If Naboath had yielded his vineyard to Ahab he would have sinned against God.[92]

The similarity between these rights of the Hebrews and the rights Englishmen were asking for in the seventeenth century is striking, but the author of this pamphlet wanted to leave no doubt that these rights of the Hebrews still prevailed in England. ". . . though the Jewes be dispersed, and gone, yet there is still an Israell of God remayning upon Earth." [93] He never explicitly said England was the fortunate land, but he implied that it was in many ways. The first English laws, for example, came from King Lucius who was advised by a Christian bishop,

[90] *Ibid.*, pp. 18–25.
[91] *Ibid.*, p. 26.
[92] *Ibid.*, p. 27.
[93] *Ibid.*, p. 34.

Eleutherius, to reject the Roman laws as corrupt and to rule by the laws of God: [94]

> According to those directions of Eleutherius, so agreeable to the Lawes of God, . . . was this our Kingdome governed, and by such Lawes of it, as are the nearest to the Lawes of God of any in the world. . . . the same Government, Customes, Liberties, and Lawes have continued in this Land from the dayes of Lucius to this very day, being now almost 1500 yeares . . .[95]

Many close similarities between English and Hebrew laws were pointed out and discussed by the author. The rights of the English people consisted in "1. The Liberty and Freedome of his person. 2. The Property of his Goods. 3. The Property of his Lands and possessions." [96] Laws in England, as among the Hebrews, were also made with the consent of the people:

> This assent of the people unto Lawes, hath its ground from the very frame and Constitution of a Commonwealth, for there are but two foundations, wch beare up publique Societies, The one a Naturall inclination, whereby all men desire sociable life and fellowship; The other an Order, Agreed upon the manner of their Union in Living together, which is no other then the Lawe of a Commonwealth, the very soule of a Politique body, the parts whereof are by Law animated, and set on worke for the Common good. For though I hold it true, which that great Master of Phylosophy teacheth, that there is a kind of Naturall right in the more Noble and vertuous to governe them wch are of a servile disposition; nevertheless, for the manifestation of the right of yre people, and mens more peaceable living, the assent of them, who are to be governed, hath alwaies been thought necessary; for we see by experience, that mens stomachs do naturally rise at restraint, yet when you tell them of a law in it, they presently yeild as to a Conclusion issuing from their owne wills.[97]

[94] *Ibid.*, pp. 39–40.   [95] *Ibid.*, p. 41.

[96] *Ibid.*, p. 60. In discussing this point, the author points out that in Domesday Book the lands of subjects were set down separately from the kings "to the end that neither of their possessions might be interrupted" (p. 60).

[97] *Ibid.*, pp. 61–62. It is obvious that this unknown writer was familiar with Aristotle's *Politics*.

It is quite understandable why this tract remained in manuscript, for in it the author put forth very great claims for the English people. He proclaimed that God had given them a share in the foundation of their government, and had Himself provided that the king was limited by their fundamental rights. Those fundamental rights included not only their property and personal rights, but a right to their king and a right to consent to laws. This unknown author was claiming for the English people all that leaders of the parliamentary opposition and the more extreme Puritan clergy were asking for in the period between 1620 and 1640, and he was resting his demands upon God's plan and established government for His chosen people in Israel and in England. Here was a complete answer to any divine-right claims of the royalist clergy, for here was divine sanction for the traditional rights and the new demands many Englishmen were making in the decades prior to the civil war. The ideas this author set forth were not original with him, but he cleverly wove together all the constitutional rights and powers Englishmen were claiming and gave their demands the backing of Almighty God. He spoke a language which the seventeenth-century Englishman, particularly the Puritan, well understood. To him the sanction of God, when clearly evidenced and demonstrated by concrete passages of Scripture, was the final appeal, higher and more conclusive than any sanction that can be invoked today. When political opinions in our own time are supported by appeals to science or to economic facts and statistics, they often become more convincing, but such appeals have not yet claimed the allegiance of western man in the twentieth century as completely as God claimed the English Puritan's in the seventeenth. Whoever the author of the *Lawes of England* may have been, he deserves a place of honor alongside of Coke, Pym, Phelips and Eliot, Beard, Gataker, Burton, and Scott, for with them he played a notable part in setting forth ideas concerning the basic rights and necessary participation of men in government.

However firmly and boldly the Puritan preacher or writer

might proclaim the supremacy of God and his laws, the rights of man, and his necessary consent to laws and acts of government, the king and the royalists were in control of the administration of the central government between 1603 and 1642, and were pursuing policies often diametrically opposed to the principles of government set forth by the Puritans. In the face of this stubborn constitutional fact, the Puritan outside of parliament faced a dilemma similar to the one constantly challenging the leaders within parliament, namely, the problem of persuading or coercing the king to change his policies to agree with theirs.

In facing this problem, the Puritan preacher, unlike the parliamentary politician, could not check the king and indirectly shape his policies by refusing to grant him taxes; he could only preach and write, and, when he was silenced and punished, endure the loss of his livings, the loss of his ears, and the ignominy of the pillory. With the means at his disposal, the Puritan preacher tackled the problem, bringing to it all the determination and stubbornness, all the zeal and impudence, and all the courage of his convictions. Because he was doing God's work, endeavoring to bring God's truth into the commonwealth of England, he knew he was sustained by God. "So the godly being in league with God," Thomas Gataker wrote, "may have all his forces, and armies for their helpe, and assistance, whensoever need shall be . . . Even the *Angels* themselves (saith the *Psalmist*) *pitch their tents about those that feare God, etc. they lye in garrison, about the godly, to defend and deliver them;* they lie *in campe* against *their enemies* to *offend,* and to *destroy* them" [98] "Gods Children" must never be "dismayed" "if the enemies of *Gods Church* seeme sometime to *prevaile* against it. For they shall never be able to root it out for all that." [99]

With God and His holy angels supporting him, the Puritan

[98] Thomas Gataker, *Certaine Sermons.* From *An Anniversarie Memoriall of Englands Delivery from Spanish Invasion,* pp. 33–34. First published in London in 1626.

[99] *Ibid.,* p. 38.

set out upon his task. Believing in the supremacy of the king, he did not desire in these years to resist him, only to convince him. A king must still be obeyed if he sin, Thomas Bell wrote, but "He may be admonished by God's true Ministers in the pulpit and court of Conscience." [100] He may even be censured. When subjects perform such an act, they are, William Bradshaw explained, to "kneele downe before him, and in the humblest manner to Censure his faultes, So that he may see apparently that they are not carried with the least spice of mallice against his Person, but onely with zeale of the health & Salvation of his soule." [101]

It was the Puritans' responsibility at all times to reveal the truth to king and people. The king might have the power to appoint bishops, but neither he nor his people must ever be allowed to forget, the more radical Puritans believed, that prelates were the creation of the devil, not of God, and that they were truly in alliance with the pope and his Catholic minions, who were God's and England's great enemies on this earth. Despite the royalist control and censorship of pulpit and press, Charles and his supporters were frequently reminded that, in maintaining and favoring an episcopal hierarchy, they were playing into the hands of their Catholic adversaries, strengthening the hope of both the pope and the English Catholics that England could easily and quickly be brought back to the fold.

For the Puritan preacher or writer to talk in such language was good political propaganda. From the middle of Elizabeth's reign until at least the end of the seventeenth century, most Englishmen had a fear of Catholicism and could be aroused when this fear was stirred up. The royalist clergy tried to condemn the Puritans by pointing out that their political views were akin to those of the Jesuits, whereas the Puritans retaliated by maintaining that the English prelates were really the pope's conscious or unconscious accomplices in England. The effectiveness of both arguments lay in the appeal they made to

[100] Thomas Bell, *The Catholique Triumph,* p. 108.
[101] William Bradshaw, *English Puritanisme,* p. 27.

Englishmen who feared Catholicism. By using such arguments, which aroused peoples' fears and emotions, both sides intensified the differences dividing them, thereby making it more difficult for the moderates to work out a compromise agreeable to both.

The Puritan preacher was ever vigilant in searching out the enemy. He was also alert to recognize the "voice of God" in any form God might choose to speak. God, so Thomas Scott pointed out in *Vox Dei*,[102] usually worked by ordinary means, but sometimes he used extraordinary. He normally worked through kings, his lieutenants on earth, but he did on occasion raise up David "to quicken his [i.e., Saul's] zeale."[103] In nature one member was sometimes called upon to "supply the defect" of another; ". . . when the eye waxeth blynd, the hand, grope's, the foote beat's for way, and the eare, by listening, seeke's to guide the body right, and to supplie the place of an eye."[104] Thus extraordinary actions were sometimes proper. Although rebellion was unlawful, nevertheless it was proper for Abraham to join with the King of Sodom in his rebellion against the King of Elan, because the King of Elan held Abraham's brother Lot a prisoner. Under such circumstances "nature byndes him [i.e., Abraham] to it, and if hee should neglect his duty in this case he were worse than an infidell."[105] "For in the case of necessity, *God* himselfe dispenseth with his written law; Because the law of Nature, which he hath written in every mans hart, subjects him thereunto."[106] By those bold statements Scott did not suggest that Englishmen rise up against their king. He stated only that God had chosen to use Prince Charles and Buckingham, who had just returned from Spain without Charles's marrying the Infanta, as His extraordinary means of "quickening" the king. It is highly significant, however, that Scott as early as 1623 talked of the extraordinary

[102] First published in 1623.
[103] Thomas Scott, *The Workes.* From *Vox Dei*, p. 16.
[104] *Ibid.*, p. 25.
[105] *Ibid.*, p. 28.
[106] *Ibid.*, p. 34

means which God sometimes used and of the law of nature written in every man's heart, for such radical suggestions could be used to justify more radical actions than Scott contemplated at this time. By the sixteen-forties many Puritans and other members of the opposition came to employ arguments of the same nature as Scott used in *Vox Dei* in 1623.

Another potentially dangerous note was sounded by A. Ar in his *Practice of Princes*.[107] The author of this tract turned to the Old Testament for those general principles laid down by God for princes, "whereby they ought to square all their actions and government." [108] According to the wisdom of the Bible:

> . . . *in the multitude of the people is the honour of a Kinge, and for the want of people cometh the destruction of the Prince.* . . . Here therefore questionles, they can not be excused who incensed the King against his subjects in Parliament." [109]

A King and his people are a body politik, and the Parliament his representative body: Now as in a body, if the faculty of the braine in one side be stopped, that it can not descend through the sinewes to the senses of moveing in the limbes and the members, then those parts have the dead palsie, and the man becomes as it were halfe dead, and as unable to doe any service effectually, as our men were at the Palatinate, Cales, Ree, Rochel and in the Parliament howse: so is it with the body politick of great Britain, through the practise of som Jesuited Spirits, who, beeing disguised in the sheepes clothing of a protestant outside, & gotten into the place of favourits & counsellors, have cuningly infected many; both Bishops and others; In whom and by whom, the braine for the most part, is ill affected and the reciprocall passages betweene the head and the members are stopped; so that the right facultie can not descend, through the sinewes, the peeres, Judges and Bishops, to the senses of moveing in the Kings body the Parliament; and so his Ma[jes]tie giveing no life and strength to that body and the best members thereof, nor they meanes to him, the whole

107 Published in 1630. (It has not been possible to identify A. Ar.)
108 A. Ar, *Practice of Princes*, p. 4.
109 *Ibid.*, p. 7.

body is halfe dead, & so unable to offend adversaries, that it can not defend it selfe, but must needes perish, if those ill humours in the braine of counsell be not by his majestie purged and removed, whereas if he did agree with the Parliament, and had a counsell favouring the moveing indeavours of the same, he must needes grow dreadfull to them, who now hope to see his kingdom (by these continued divisions) easely conquered.[110]

This long passage has been given in full, because in it the argument used so effectively against Strafford, Laud, and other ministers of the crown eleven years later was so clearly set forth. No one in parliament, to my knowledge, voiced such a radical argument prior to 1640.

In another passage this unknown writer suggested the possibility of rebellion—a very radical note in 1630: [111]

. . . God that oft payes by retaliation, suffers people to deale so with Princes, as they deale with him, and theire Servants to bee alike faithfull to them in theire service, as they are to him in his. If people see theire Princes cast away the word of the Lord in divers things, they wickedly grow as careles of Gods word, which enjoines subjection to Princes, and which otherwise *stilleth the madnes of the people,* and keepes them in aw, God causeth the Prince that feares him, and sincerely furthers his word preached, to be by his people reverenced, loved, feared and enriched with presents and gifts, as *Jehoshaphat* was: he therefore that doth it not, but rather the contrary, he must needes finde the contrary; him he suffers to be molested with enemies, and the rebellions of his owne vassals, as were *Solomon, Rehoboam, Jeroboam, Joram* and others, wherein that is fulfilled, which the Lord

[110] *Ibid.,* p. 12. This same writer spoke out boldly against the king's advisers and servants, saying: "Wisdom saith of a true king *The pleasure of a King is in a Wise servant* (this wise man is one truly religious not an Achitophel. . . . A wise *King scattereth the Wicked, and causeth the Wheele to turne over them.* . . . Wisdom also sheweth that it is for a Kings honour and safety to have wicked men sifted out, and cut off or expelled . . ." (pp. 13–14).

[111] In 1636, Henry Burton spoke of the "paction" made by a king to his people and added: "And therefore a King governing in a setled Kingdome leaves to be a King, and degenerates into a Tyrant, as soone as hee leaves off to rule according to his lawes." *For God and the King,* p. 40.

saith, *Those that honour me, I will honour, and those that despise me shall be lightly esteemed. . . .*[112]

The idea suggested by A. Ar, that king and people were bound together so indissolubly that he who sought to separate the two was hurting the king, was an idea both Burton and Prynne found useful. Burton wrote, ". . . the King and his people make one politicke body; and hee cannot love the Head, who seekes to hurt the members; or who setts the Head against the members, or who for advancing the Head, destroyes the members; or who maketh a Schisme and rent betweene the Head and the members." [113] Prynne advanced this same argument another step, claiming in his *Lord Bishops none of the Lord Bishops* that prelates had become "bad wens" in the body, and should therefore be cut out in order to save the life of the whole body.[114] The prelates having "flown off from under the protection of Royall Prerogative and Law" "lye naked and exposed to this Parliament" [115]—a point of view St. John made telling use of in his case against Strafford in 1641.

Much of this more radical talk by Puritan writers and preachers had been made without specific reference to parliament, but some Puritans recognized that parliament was opposing the crown, that parliament espoused Puritan policies, and that parliament was the best means by which effective action could be initiated and carried out.[116] They remembered that parliament had passed the great laws on religion in the sixteenth century, severing all ties with Rome and setting up the form of worship and doctrine of the church.

[112] A. Ar, *Practice of Princes*, p. 19.
[113] Henry Burton, *An Epistle to the true-hearted nobility*, (1636), pp. 28–29.
[114] Published in 1640, p. 77.
[115] *Ibid.*
[116] Thomas Scott wrote concerning parliament: "In the Parliament then (which is the whole State representative) these high-wayes are made; and the fundamentall customes of our State, makes every Freeholder a way-maker in this case, not binding any man before he hath bound himselfe by the Knights and Burgesses who are his Spokesmen." *The Workes, op. cit.* From *The High-Wayes of God and the King*, p. 86.

In 1628, Alexander Leighton [117] wrote his stirring Appeale to the Parliament to rise up and act:

> *As God hath set you forth (right Honourable) for this great worke of reformation;* so your choyce and place requireth *you to bee* men of activitie. . . . *Joshua did well to pray, but he must up and doe.* . . . *let every man gird the sword of justice upon his thigh, and doe execution according to desert . . . Make way then for religion and righteousnesse, . . . And God will be with you . . . hee is an unworthy man that preferreth his owne particular safetie to the savinge of the common weale.*[118]

The matter is no lesse weight than the *Kingdome of Christ;* in the suppressing, or advancing whereoff, standeth the ruine, or reviving of our Kingdomes. . . .[119]

The Parliament hath in it the power of the whole Kingdome, yea both of the head and of the body. Then power must be put in use, or it looseth the *power.* You are the *Elders of Israell;* you are an *armie* of *Generals;* that supreame Court, that may call any place, or person to an account, whether they be for the glorie of God, the good of the King and State, or no; you are the *Physicians* of State; up and doe your cure; In a word, it were happie for our King and us, if you knew your power *practicallie.*[120]

Except ye keep the *ship,* till ye have beaten the Dunkirkers of State; neither *King, you* nor *we* can be saved. . . . Your Honours know, that everie dissolution of a Parliament, without reall reformation, is against *right, reason,* and *record.* Is it not the right of the State, to be disburdened of *Caterpillars, moathes,* & *Cankerwormes;* and of such *Lions,* & *Beares,* as devour *Religion,* & *State Policie?* What reason is it, that the State assembled from all the parts of the Kingdome, should waste *time* and *meanes;* and when they pitch upon the point, they should be blowen up with the Romish breath of the enimie? [121]

[117] *An Appeale to the Parliament.*
[118] *Ibid,* A2 r-v.
[119] *Ibid.,* Epistle to reader.
[120] *Ibid.,* p. 174. In the margin of this passage, Leighton cites *Smith de Reip. Angl.*
[121] *Ibid.,* p. 337–38.

Leighton did not specifically admonish them to rebel, "But Gods people, with all, must labour to be of one minde, and of one heart; and by entering covenant with *God*, against his *enemies*, and all that is *enmitie* to God, resolve to hould them, at staves end, till God give the victorie." [122] These were ringing words—a forecast in 1628 of the way twelve years later Puritan preachers would inspire the commons, listening to the many sermons delivered before them,[123] to push forward with God's work in the world.

Two months before the Long Parliament met, Calybute Downing [124] preached a sermon in which he called upon parliament to act. It was all very well, he explained, for Christians just to pray and suffer in countries under pagan kings, but there was a difference in a country "where the Religion is *Lex terrae*, settled and protected by the Civil Laws, and power." [125] In such a case parliament should act:

> . . . consider that the States of a Kingdome, either actually assembled in a representative body, or virtually concurring in a common resolution, for the common good, and only hindred from assembling by the common Enemy; it is affirmed, by the greatest Assertors of Regall Royalty, that they may goe very far, before they can be counted Rebels, or be mistaken.[126]

Downing went to even greater lengths in the advice he gave. He actually sounded the note of rebellion:

> . . . consider that when a party by power breaks the Laws of the Land, that they may break the Laws of God, and thereby force you to goe along as their friends, or put you to make a stand, and so conclude you the States Enemies, where the Laws of the Land are thus by them made too short for your security, the Laws of Nations come in for reliefe, till it can

[122] *Ibid.*, p. 333.
[123] See chapter IX.
[124] *A Sermon preached to the Renowned Company of Artillery*, 1 Sept. 1640, (London, 1641). Downing had earlier exalted the king's power. See pages 190, 201.
[125] *Ibid.*, p. 38.
[126] *Ibid.*, pp. 37-8.

be otherwise provided: for twas never intended by Lawmakers to lay them on, with so rigid a will, but that still,
salus populi should be *sola, et suprema lex;* and no State did
ever intend, to cast itselfe into a desperate Case, by good
Lawes; so that as for the good of the person of a Prince, they
are not only allowed, *jura dominationis,* but also *arcana
dominationis*: so for the safety of the body of the State, there
are *arcana,* Latitudes allowed for security; especially when
the Enemies (who are not true Instruments but Tools of
State, *Dominationum Provisores,* Purveyers of usurpation,
that work through *Alps,* or Conscience) have concluded, they
lose not reputation, nor abuse Religion, if they get their
Ends: In such a Case Rational *Grotius* is cleer, that in
*gravissimo et certissimo discrimine, lex de non resistendo,
non obligat;* but I hope he meant it tenderly.[127]

Thus, by 1640, the way had been prepared in pulpit and
press, as well as in parliament, for the great role the new parliament was about to play in the affairs of England. The ideas
had been set forth by which the king was made subject to God
and His laws, to man and his rights, and to man's necessary
consent to government. The need for action—and drastic action—had been stressed, and often the necessity as a last resort
of armed resistance had been suggested. By 1640, some men were
ready with God's help to move forward and effect a reformation in church and state. In bringing about this quickened and
aroused public opinion upon which much of the success of the
early work of the Long Parliament depended, the Puritan
preachers and writers had played their full part. They had
contributed ideas of their own, they had supplemented and
strengthened those advanced within the walls of parliament,
and above all they had given the opposition that zeal and courage without which no force arrayed against an established authority can have great chance of ultimate success.

[127] *Ibid.,* pp. 36–37.

CHAPTER IX

PARLIAMENT FORCES THE ISSUE

BETWEEN 1629 and 1640, the royalists had carried out their policies and their ideas with considerable success. Under the legal absolutism advocated by councillors and lawyers, England had been efficiently and progressively ruled. The finances of the government had been soundly administered, and the new revenues raised had been sanctioned by a majority decision of the judges in the common law courts. In the church, bishops and royalist clergy were bringing about order and uniformity and even beauty and "holiness" in the church services. In council and court, in pulpit and press, the views of the royalists had been proclaimed to the people. As for the opposition, they had had no opportunity to announce their views in a parliament; they had failed in the ship-money case to prevent a great victory for legal absolutism; and although they had not been completely silenced in pulpit and press, some of the more ardent Puritan clergy had chosen to leave England, and some who remained were in prison. An impartial observer taking stock in 1639 of the relative success of the royalists and of their opponents would certainly give the victory to the royalists, and might easily predict that within another ten years the English king would become an absolute monarch. Since he now had control over the common law courts and the church, his absolutism could be challenged only in parliament, and, according to the existing constitution, parliament could meet only when the king chose to call it.

By the nature and magnitude of their success, however, the royalists had immeasurably strengthened the forces arrayed against them. Men of property who had been unwilling to take more drastic action against the crown in 1628 than a Petition of Right were thoroughly aroused and angered by the legal decision in ship money in favor of the king's prerogative against their property. Should the king ever need to call parliament again, both parliamentary extremists and moderates were agreed that concerted action must be taken to stop legal absolutism before it won its final victory. They were also agreed that something should be done to modify or change a church whose leaders carried out ecclesiastical policies distasteful to many Anglicans and abominable to most Puritans, and some of whose clergy preached political doctrines contrary to the basic views of most Englishmen.

When in November, 1640, Charles called parliament, the real weakness of the royalist cause was immediately revealed. The king had been forced to summon parliament because his clergy had involved England in war with Scotland by trying to carry out their policies in that land, and because his councillors and lawyers could discover no new means of raising money legally to meet the increased expenses of the war. His supporters, both clerical and legal, had failed him, and he was left alone to meet the pent-up antagonism of men in parliament and throughout England who were now ready to take full advantage of the opportunity which was finally theirs. For them the long period of preparation and waiting was over. In less then nine months the royalist case for legal absolutism, built up so carefully and successfully for thirty-five years, collapsed without having enough adherents to put up a strong defense of it in parliament or press. In less than nine months, not only the work of the Stuarts but much of the work the Tudors had done in strengthening the institutions of government, was swept away. Instead of talk, there was action. Instead of criticism of the king's ministers, there were impeachments, often ending in attainders effectively removing those councillors and judges who had been carrying on the government. Instead of a minority decision in favor of the subject, a statute was passed declaring the complete illegality of ship money. Instead of a Petiton of Right, now there were statutes: one abolishing the court of star chamber, the judicial power of the privy council, and the regional prerogative courts in the north and the west; and another, the court of high commission. Instead of parliament's existence being dependent upon the pleasure of the king, provision was made for the continuance of the present parliament and for the summoning of future ones without the king's sanction. The speed and thoroughness with which the parliamentary opposition swept away the personnel and institutions of prerogative government is one of the most remarkable achievements in English constitutional history.

This book is concerned with the arguments and the ideas upon which the parliamentary attack was based. The most important conclusion emerging from a study of the speeches and debates is the fact that the old arguments are again brought forth and employed. Whenever possible in 1640 and 1641, as in 1610 or 1628, parliamentary leaders rested their actions and their arguments on the law, the constitution, and the legally recognized authority of parliament. And again at this time, when the law and constitution failed them, the more aggressive leaders were not daunted but pushed on, justifying their more illegal and aggressive actions by appeals to the nation at large for whose welfare parliament again claimed full responsibility. Theirs was a double responsibility, as Sir John Wray clearly demonstrated when he said in a speech against Strafford: ". . . let us remember what we now are, not only Parliament-men, but Publick-men, and English-men: As Parliament-men, let us follow the steps of our Ancestors, and be constant to that rule of Law which was their guide, and Should be ours. As Publick men, forget not whom we here represent, and by how many chosen and trusted." [1]

During the first nine months of the Long Parliament old arguments based on law and right were most common. It was natural and possible to employ such arguments, because at this time parliament's main concern was to attack the encroachments upon the law and their rights which royalist councillors and judges had been making for the past decade. To stop those

[1] Nalson I, 786.

infringements was the immediate and all-important task of the parliamentary leaders. Their plans and their actions focused upon this major objective. Consequently, they could present their case against the illegal encroachments of the monarch by turning to the concepts of law and right with which they had been battling the crown for forty years. Arguments based on law were familiar and therefore convincing, and they were also in line with a theory of government for which law and precedent afforded partial sanction at least. It was the solemn task of parliamentary leaders to reestablish a rule of law under which the subjects' rights would be truly secure against the actions of government.

It was also their solemn responsibility to use to the utmost the authority of parliament, the highest human authority in England. The full power of parliament was desperately needed, for the nation was suffering with distempers, and, as the speaker of the commons said in his speech to the king, "this great Councell is most Soveraign against the distempers of this Nation." [2] Only parliament was powerful enough to right the wrongs, for it was the great "physician" of the state, possessing a greater power to heal than the king alone.[3] "The King out of *Parliament* hath a limited Power, a circumscribed Jurisdiction, but waited on by his *Parliament,* no Monarch of the East is so absolute in dispelling *Greviances.*" [4]

If any member of the commons felt too insignificant to perform his part in this great task of healing the state, he should have discarded all doubt and humility after listening to the sermon preached by Stephen Marshall before the commons

[2] *Master Speaker his Speech to his Majestie in Parliament,* Nov. 5, 1640, (London, 1660), p. 6.

[3] *Pax Vobis* . . . Dec.   , 1641, p. 17. In a number of the pamphlets cited in this chapter, no place of publication can be given. Information concerning them can be found, by the date given, in the *Catalogue of the pamphlets, books, newspapers, and manuscripts relating to the civil war* . . . collected by George Thomason, 1640–1661, 2 vols., (London, 1908).

[4] *Speeche of the Lord Digby in Parliament concerning grievances and the Triennial Parliament,* Jan. 19, 1640–1, p. 24.

November 17.[5] Marshall chose as his text 2 Chronicles 15, 2 "The Lord is with you while yee bee with him, and if yee seeke him hee will be found of you." This eloquent Puritan preacher showed that God was watching England and parliament in their great work now beginning. Members of the commons had been summoned "to beare the iniquitie of the whole King-dome." [6] You are called, he said, "to be the Repairers of our breach, to heale, and prevent our ruine." [7] "You that are the flower of your Tribes, the chief of the Thousands of *England*: You that are lifted up above your Brethren, whom God had made the Head, and not the Taile of the places where you live! . . ." [8] *"Up and be doing,* and the *Lord be with you* in his cause." [9] The Lord will truly remain at your side if you do your part, for in England, Marshall implied, He has entered into a special covenant of grace with His people, revealing clearly to them "like the Sunne shining in his strength" what should be done.[10] Englishmen in the past have failed lamen-tably to do their full part, but God remains with them in His covenant of grace—England has still been "kept as another Land of Goshen." [11] If, however, God is to continue to stay in England, men must now actively assist Him in His work.[12]

Marshall would have liked the commons to embark im-mediately upon the task of establishing God's church and wor-ship on earth, but the commons turned first with true religious fervor towards the task of re-establishing and strengthening the rule of law which they believed the royalists had overthrown or perverted during the past eleven years. Again in 1640, as in 1628, they proclaimed that law was their great inheritance, guaranteeing them property and liberty, and establishing cer-tain forms of action by which those fundamentals were pro-tected. ". . . Propriety of Goods," Waller said, "is the Mother

[5] London, 1641. See the article by E. Kirby, "Sermons before the Com-mons, 1640–42," *American Historical Review* XLIV, (1938–39), pp. 528–48.

[6] *Ibid.*, p. 29.   [7] *Ibid.*, p. 36.   [8] *Ibid.*   [9] *Ibid.*, p. 48.

[10] *Ibid.*, p. 10. See also p. 35.

[11] *Ibid.*, p. 19.

[12] *Ibid.*, p. 28 and p. 42.

of Courage and the Nurse of Industry; it makes us valiant in War, and industrious in Peace." Therefore, "Let us give new force to the old Laws, which have been heretofore for the maintaining of our Rights and Privileges, and endeavor to restore this Nation to the fundamental and vital Liberties, the propriety of our Goods and the freedom of our persons . . ." [13] An "end of government," Pym declared, was "To preserve Men in their Estates, to secure them in their Lives and Liberties"; [14] while St. John asserted that without its "Polity and Government" England was nothing "but a piece of Earth, wherein so many men have their Commarancy and abode, without ranks or distinction of men, without property in anything further than Possession." [15]

Holding such exalted views concerning the nature of their polity and the perfection of their laws, parliamentarians naturally insisted that the law was completely the basis of the king's rule—that he had no power in any realm whatsoever to rule without or against it. In Pym's words, "The Lawes of this Kingdome have invested the Royall Crowne with Power sufficient for the manifestation of his goodnesse and his greatnesse." [16] Consequently to the parliamentarians, the king's prerogative was so completely legal in its nature and so vitally active in its functioning that it could nullify those acts of the king not truly manifestations of his legal prerogative. Leaders in the commons now proclaimed that the law was sufficient to settle any conflict between prerogative and liberty, for it was the law which defined the bounds of each. The prerogative of the king could not be dangerous to the liberty of the subject, "so long as both of them admit the Temperament of Law and Justice." [17] As Smith of the Middle Temple said,

> Prerogative and Liberty are both necessary to this Kingdome: and like the Sunne and Moone, give a lustre to this benighted Nation, so long as they walk at their equall dis-

---

[13] Rushworth, III, 1141.   [14] *Ibid.*, VIII, 666.   [15] *Ibid.*, VIII, 699.
[16] *Two Speeches made by John Pym* . . . 25 Nov., 1640, p. 4.
[17] Nalson, I, 315.

tances: but when one of them shall venture into the others Orbe, like those Planets in conjunction, they then cause a deeper Eclipse. What shall be the compasse then, by which the two must steere? Why nothing but the same by which they are, The Law: which if it might runne in the free current of its purity, without being poysoned by the venemous spirits of ill-affected Dispositions, would so fix the King to his Crowne; that it would make him stand like a Star in the Firmament, for the Neighbor-world to behold and tremble at.[18]

A statement like this was the parliamentary answer in 1641 to the distinction Fleming had made in 1606 between the absolute and the ordinary prerogative of the crown. Because of the way absolute prerogative had been used to encroach upon their property and liberty, the parliamentarians had come finally to deny its existence in law. In 1628 they had still accepted some absolute prerogatives, but in 1640 they would accept only those prerogatives which were embedded in the law, and they were determined that none of these should encroach upon their rights.

In so extending the sphere of law, they could not always be too careful or exact in defining clearly the law they exalted. Law guaranteeing their rights and checking the king was proclaimed to be fundamental law. It was even regarded as the binding principle in society and in the universe. Pym delivered the most famous eulogy of law made by a parliamentarian at this time. He said:

The law is that which puts a difference betwixt good and evil, betwixt just and unjust; if you take away the Law, all things will fall into confusion, every man will become a Law to himself, which in the depraved condition of humane nature, must needs produce many great enormities, Lust will become a Law, and Envy will become a Law, Covetness and Ambition will become Laws; . . . The Law hath a Power to prevent, to restrain, to repair evils; without this, all kind of mischief and distempers will break in upon a State.

[18] *An Honourable and worthy speech spoken in Parliament by Mr. Smith of the Middle Temple* Oct. 28, 1641, (London, 1641), pp. 3–4.

It is the Law that doth entitle the King to the Allegiance and Service of his People; it entitles the People to the Protection and Justice of the King. It is God alone who subsists by himself, all other things subsist in a mutual dependence, and relation . . .

The Law is the boundary, the measure betwixt the King's Prerogative, and the Peoples Liberty; whilst these move in their own Orbs, they are a support and a security to one another; the Prerogative a cover and defence to the Liberty of the People; and the People by their Liberty are enabled to be a foundation to the Prerogative, but if these bounds be so removed, that they enter into contestation and conflict, one of these mischiefs must ensue: If the Prerogative of the King overwhelme the Liberty of the People, it will be turned into Tyranny; if Liberty undermine the Prerogative, it will grow into Anarchy.[19]

Here was the answer to the royalist clergy who had tried to demonstrate that the king was all important, that he bound society together, and that he put a difference between good and evil and between just and unjust. To Pym it was the law, not the king, which was all-pervading. Exactly which law produced all good and prevented all harm Pym did not make clear and probably did not know. Nevertheless, in this eulogy he raised the concept of law, which had always been a basic belief with the parliamentarians and with most Englishmen, to the point where he expressed the hope that government rested entirely on legal foundations.

His eulogy of law was the parliamentary way at this time of expressing the need for unity in government. That need had been a driving principle with both royalist councillors and judges and also with the royalist clergy, the one looking for unity in legal absolutism, the other in divine right; and now, in 1640 and 1641, the parliamentarians made their supreme attempt to discover a unifying foundation in law. They too wanted a unified government and hoped to demonstrate that the law provided one.

Since leaders in parliament believed that law was the bind-

[19] Rushworth, VIII, 662.

ing cohesive force in government and society, they naturally insisted that law must be able to settle and remedy all that was amiss. "The Laws, whereby all other parts of a Kingdom are preserved, should be very vain and defective, if they had not a power to secure and preserve themselves." [20] Law could, if properly interpreted and applied, overthrow councillors and judges who had twisted it to their own illegal purposes. If judges and councillors, Bagshaw declared, "pervert the meaning of the laws, or contract their power when they ought to extend it, or make them speak more loudly, or softly, as they themselves are tuned for it, the blame should fall heavily on those trusted ministers. . . . What now remains but that we should use the law as an ally, which, because it has been turned against us contrary to its plain disposition, should now right us and itself against our adversaries? Surely the law is not so weak as to take care for the safety of others and never provide for its own defense against those, be they peers or people, that have abused it?" [21] Law must, parliamentary leaders were claiming, possess the necessary sanction to defend itself.

Judges, who had been entrusted with the care of the laws safeguarding the subjects' liberty and restraining the king's prerogative, had betrayed their trust. They had done more: they had used the law itself to deprive subjects of their liberty in the ship-money case. "For now the Law doth not onely not defend us, but the law itselfe is made the instrument of taking all away," St. John declared in a speech concerning ship money.[22] Falkland in a speech against Finch expressed a similar view, saying that he "turned our Guard into a destruction, making Law the ground of illegalitie: that he used this Law not only against us, but against it self, making it, as I may say, *Felo de Se*, making the pretence (for I can scarce say, the appearance of it) so to contribute the utter ruine of it self." [23]

[20] *Ibid.*, p. 669.
[21] *Cal. St. P. Domestic, 1640–1641*, p. 260.
[22] Mr. St.-John's Speech to the Lords . . . concerning Ship-Money, (1640), p. 31.
[23] Nalson, I, 726.

The judges' action was worse in one way than Strafford's, Falkland contended, for "my lord Strafford is accused of high Treason for being supposed to have endeavoured to supplant the fundamentall lawes of this kingdome; these have done it openly." [24] ". . . by these opinions there is a Surrender made of all Legall defence of propriety, that which hath been Preached is now judged that there is no *meum* and *tuum* between the King and the People . . ." [25]

The law proved to be the basis of the parliamentary attack upon the king's judges, and it was the law to which the leaders turned in their attack upon Strafford, the king's great minister. It could not fail them now, so they believed, if they searched hard and long enough. And search they did. The attempt to condemn Strafford on a legal basis "caused the most Learned of the Long Robe to tumble over their Law-Books, and to apply their minds to look into the bowels of our antient Laws, and the reason of them, from whence they had their Being." [26] Yet this search did not reveal concrete laws which could correctly be cited against Strafford. In fact Pym unconsciously admitted that the law had failed them when he said that Strafford's treason against law was especially wicked, because it was against the "being of the Law," rather than the "Rule" or concrete embodiment of it. For forty years, leaders in parliament had talked of the rules or concrete embodiments of law, and now Strafford successfully defended himself on that conservative basis, forcing the opposition to turn from the law to other more drastic remedies and more radical ideas.

[24] *D'Ewes (Long Parl.)*, ed. W. Notestein, p. 117, n. 28.

[25] Nalson, I, 714. Clarendon wrote in his *History of the Rebellion*, (I, 108), that after the legal judgment in ship money had been given, men "no *longer* more looked upon it as the case of one man, but the case of the kingdom." According to Waller, "these sons of the law have torn out the bowels of their mother." S. T. III, 1301. Holles said: "It is no wonder if the knights, citizens, and burgesses assembled in parliament, have sent up some of their members to stand upon mount Ebal to curse these judges; to denounce a curse upon them who have removed our land-marks, have taken away the boundstones of the propriety of the subject, have left us no *meum and tuum* . . ." S. T. III, 1297.

[26] Rushworth, VIII, Preface.

Before these more revolutionary ideas are considered, the views expressed in the early months of the Long Parliament concerning the great legal and constitutional authority of parliament must be considered. Now, for the first time in the long parliamentary struggle against the crown, there seems to be the proper respect paid by parliament to its own great authority. In 1610, Whitelocke had clearly demonstrated the legal supremacy of the king-in-parliament over the king-out-of-parliament,[27] but his clear analysis had seldom been the foundation of the parliaments' claims. This concept depended upon the co-operation of the king, who had, in the years between 1603 and 1629, generally disagreed with the lords and commons, his partners in his parliamentary supremacy. In 1640 and 1641, the king was, by the political pressure and strength of the forces arrayed against him, forced to agree. Against his political desires but with his legal consent, he now co-operated with the two houses; and king, lords, and commons rose to their full parliamentary omnipotence, passing statutes as far-reaching and sovereign in their nature as those earlier passed in the Reformation Parliament between 1531 and 1536. It was, therefore, natural that arguments and ideas advanced by parliamentary leaders at this time should stress more than ever before the supremacy of parliament.

Many speakers jealously exalted parliamentary acts above the acts of any other individual or group in the state. A feeling of parliamentary superiority emerged in their attack on the canons recently set forth by the clergy. "Doth not," Digby asked, "every Parliament-Man's heart rise to see the *Prelates thus to usurp to themselves* the grand preeminence of Parliaments?" [28] Statute law, made by parliament, was also appealed to in order to justify or denounce certain actions. D'Ewes, for example, stated emphatically (but unhistorically) that "all the power" of the star chamber court "tooke its first originall and beginning by the statute of a.° 3.° H.7." [29] Men were deter-

---

[27] See page 86. [28] Rushworth, IV, 31.
[29] *D'Ewes, (Long Parl.)* ed. W. Notestein, p. 276.

mined that the king's supporters should realize the great potentialities of acts of parliament. Crawley, a justice of the bench of common pleas, had declared "That the King's Right to Ship-money was so inherent a Right in the Crowne, as an Act of Parliament could not take it away," [30] and this statement was cited against him by the house of commons. St. John objected to ship money primarily because of the "opinions of the Judges and the reasons of the Judgments." If those judgments are accepted, he said, "Parliaments have noe power, for this is a Judgment of Parliament overthrowne by the Judges. Whereas Judges have come to the Parliament to know what Law was." [31] The alleged statement of Strafford that "He would make an Act of State equal to an Act of Parliament" [32] was bitterly condemned.

Parliament also asserted its authority at this time by maintaining that the consent of all in parliament was essential for action within the state. The belief that the consent of all was necessary for direct taxation had long been an established cornerstone of parliament's position, and in 1641 the act granting tunnage and poundage to the king relied upon the "common consent in Parliament" [33] to assert its control over indirect taxation. This same notion of consent played a most important role in the controversy over the canons. The Erastians denouncing the canons argued that "nothing can binde the laitie without consent of parliament." [34] As St. John said, ". . . wee are now all one bodie, and must bee all bound by consent in Parliament." [35] Glynne put it this way: "There must bee conjunction off all the state to binde themselves. As the lords cannot binde themselves without consent [of the King and Commons] nor the commons [without consent of the Lords

[30] *Articles of Accusation exhibited by the Commons against Sir John Bramston, . . . Sir Francis Crawley,* [July], 1641, p. 24.
[31] *D'Ewes (Long Parl.),* ed. W. Notestein, p. 74, n. 9.
[32] Rushworth, VIII, 512.
[33] *Statutes of the Realm,* 16 Charles I, c. 8.
[34] *D'Ewes (Long Parl.),* ed. W. Notestein, p. 21.
[35] *Ibid.,* p. 155.

and King]. So there cannons cannot binde without consent [of the King and Parliament]." [36] On December 15, 1640, it was resolved in the House of Commons "That the Clergy of *England,* convented in any Convocation, or Synod, or otherwise, have no Power to make any Constitutions, Canons, or Acts, whatsoever, in Matter of Doctrine, Discipline, or otherwise, to bind the Clergy, or the Laity, of this Land, without common Consent of Parliament." [37] This resolution well typifies the Erastian spirit of the commons who were demanding common consent in matters ecclesiastical as well as secular.

In all of the ways considered up to this point, in its stress upon consent, in its jealousy of its own acts, and in its assertion of authority over the most fundamental things in the state, parliament was really asserting its legislative power. In this period too, parliament definitely attacked instruments of government whose legislative activities had encroached upon its own position. Nevertheless, there is less talk than might be expected about the nature of the legislative power, perhaps because men were too busy legislating to talk much about the great power they were exercising.

There was no speaker in parliament in 1640 or 1641 who gave as clear and analytical a statement concerning parliament's supremacy as James Whitelocke had given in 1610. Nathanael Fiennes came closest to it in his attack upon the recent canons of the clergy. In the first canon, he explained:

> . . . the framers of these Canons have assumed unto themselves a Parliamentary power, and that too in a very high degree, for they have taken upon them to define what is the power of the King, what the libertie of the Subjects, and what propriety he hath in his goods. If this bee not proper to a Parliament, I know not what is. Nay it is the highest matter that can fall under the consideration of a Parliament, and such a point as wherein they would have walked with more tendernesse and circumspection, than these bold Divines have done. . . . Another thing in this first Canon,

[36] *Ibid.,* p. 70, n. 13.
[37] C. J., II, 51.

wherein they have assumed unto themselves a *Parliamentary power* is in that they have taken upon them to define what is treason, besides what is determined in the statute of treasons.[38]

In the sixth canon:

> . . . these Canonists have assumed to themselves a *Parliamentary* power and that in a very high degree, in that they have taken upon them to impose new Oathes, upon the King's Subjects. . . . to impose an Oath, if it bee not an higher power, then to make a Law, it is a power of making a Law of a most high Nature, and of higher and farther consequence than any other Law, and I should much rather chuse that the convocation should have a power to make Lawes, to bind my person and my estate, then that they should have a power to make Oathes to bind my conscience: a Law binds me no longer then till another Law be made to alter it, but my Oath bindes mee as long as I live.[39]

In these remarks Fiennes stated clearly that only parliament had jurisdiction over certain basic essentials. Whether he would have extended his list to include all powers of the king is impossible to tell.

Great as parliament's full authority was recognized to be, and extensive as the sanction of law was believed to be, neither proved to be an adequate and convincing basis for justifying the attack upon the king's ministers. Leaders pushing that attack were confronted with the old constitutional dilemma: since the appointing power belonged legally to the king, the

---

[38] *A Second Speech of the Honourable Nathanael Fiennes . . . in the Commons House of Parliament touching the Subjects Liberty against the late Canons and the New Oath*, 1641, p. 2 and pp. 5–6.

[39] *Ibid.*, p. 11. See also the speech of William Pierrepont at the impeachment of Sir Robert Berkeley, July 6, 1641. Pierrepont said: "Unlimited power must be in some to make and repeal Laws to fit the dispositions of Times and Persons, Nature placeth this in common consent onely; and where all cannot conveniently meet, instructeth them to give their consents to some they know or believe so well of, as to be bound to what they agree on. His Majesty, your Lordships and the Commons are thus met in Parliament, and so long as we are often reduced to this main Foundation, our King and we shall prosper." Nalson, II, 334.

opposition could legally remove his ministers only if they could prove that they had committed treason against the king. There was no constitutional way of removing them on grounds of policy. To meet this problem parliamentary leaders resorted to the same arguments which had occasionally been used in the twenties against unpopular servants of the crown. Their arguments against Strafford ran in this fashion: it was the law which was the basis of the king's rule and which held the government together. Strafford had broken the law by destroying the unity between the king and his people. That unity rested on law, and the king's rule rested on law. Therefore Strafford's action against unity was likewise against law, and consequently against the king. In a famous speech against Strafford, Pym said:

> Other Treasons are against the Rule of the Law, this is against the being of the Law: It is the Law that unites the King and his People; and the Author of this Treason hath endeavoured to dissolve that Union; even to breake the mutuall, reversall, indissoluble band of protection and Allegiance, whereby they are, and I hope ever will bee bound together.[40]

Pym claimed that the unity between king and people was a basic law, whereas in reality it was a desirable political objective which did not exist at this time when king and people were so sorely torn asunder. His attempt to condemn Strafford on a legal basis failed because the legal argument he presented was easily recognized as essentially political in its nature.

St. John was another in parliament who also spoke clearly of treason against the commonwealth. In explaining to the lords the reasons for the commons' attainder of Strafford, he said:

> My Lords, in Judgment of greatest Moment, there are but two ways of satisfying those, that are to give them; either the *Lex lata,* the Law already established, or else the use of the

[40] *Two Speeches made by John Pym,* p. 2.

same Power for making new Laws, whereby the old at first received life.[41]

Concerning the use of the legislative power, he pointed out that the

> . . . same Law gives Power to the Parliament to make new Lawes, that enables the inferiour Court to Judge according to the old. The Rules that guide the Conscience of the inferiour Court is from without, the Prescripts of the Parliament, and of the Common-Law; in the other the Rule is from within, That *Salus Populi* be concerned; that there be no Wilfull Oppression of any of the Fellow Members, that no more Blood be taken than what is necessary for the Cure, the Laws and Customes of the Realme as well enable the Exercise of this, as of the Ordinary and Judiciall Power.[42]

Later in the same speech he added the remark that the parliament is

> . . . both the Physician and the Patient; If the Body be distempered, it hath power to open a Vein, to let out the corrupt blood, for curing it self; if one Member be Poysoned or Gangred, it hath power to cut it off for the preservation of the rest.[43]

Here was the dangerous doctrine of necessity on behalf of the general welfare which the parliamentarians had for years accused the royalists of employing, and which they were still denouncing. "My Lords, for many years by-past," Glyn declared, "your Lordships know an evil spirit hath moved amongst us, which in truth hath been made the Author and ground of all our distracions, and that is *necessity* and *danger*." [44] Parliamentarians, like St. John, however, now found the argument useful and necessary. Their justification of it was the same as the royalists' had earlier been, except that they made parliament, and not the king, responsible for the welfare

[41] Rushworth, VIII, 676.
[42] *Ibid.*
[43] *Ibid.,* p. 702.
[44] *Ibid.,* p. 731.

of all. In April, 1641, one speaker argued that parliament could employ drastic action in case of necessity, for "to deny unto that representative Body, the High Court of the Kingdome a liberty to doe anything not unjust in itselfe (though not as yet legally declared to be just) for the preservation of that greater body it represents, . . . is neither agreeable to the Law of Nature, nor of the Land, nor of God, nor to a rule of his Lordships owne." [45]

The same argument of necessity in order to preserve the whole was used to explain or justify the unprecedented claims or actions of parliament in the first year of the Long Parliament. Earlier in the twenties, as new parliamentary procedure developed, the argument most frequently used to justify the new or questionable steps taken by parliament had been the plea that such action was good or necessary for the commonwealth; and now in 1641 the same argument was used to justify parliament's grasp of new powers. On February 20, 1641, for example, Pym suggested that the citizens of London might be called upon to lend money, for "in case of necessitie and in pursuance of the truste that is imposed in us for the safety of the commonwealthe wee may assume a Legislative power to compell suche as bee noted riche men to lend ther moneyes by Act to bee passed here." [46] Another problem facing parliament at this time, solution of which required that new powers be exercised by the houses, was the question of the Catholic recusants. Parliamentary leaders still regarded them as dangerous and were no longer content merely to petition the king, as they had in the twenties, that something be done about them. In 1641 parliament suggested that the dangerous recusants be rounded up, that commissioners be appointed to handle the matter, and insisted that no recusant escape because of his parliamentary privilege. The question then arose of the grounds

[45] *An Answer to the Lord Digbies Speech to the Bill of Attainder of the Earle of Strafford, April 21, 1641*, p. 17.

[46] *D'Ewes (Long Parl.)*, ed. W. Notestein, p. 382, n. 2. See the article by W. Coates "Some Observations on the Grand Remonstrance," *Journal of Modern History* IV, (1932), pp. 1–18.

on which privilege of parliament could be denied a recusant. In their answer, the commons said, "Privilege of Parliament is granted in regard to the Service of the Commonwealth, and is not to be used to the Danger of the commonwealth." [47] The question came up again in November, Pym then advocating that the authority of parliament was sufficient to seize "persons suspected to bee dangerous or likely to bee disturbers of the publike peace." [48] D'Ewes cautioned that only a few recusants should be taken in custody, but in the course of his remarks said ". . . wee for the publike safetie weere willing to take from the freeman of England who weere Commoners a parte of ther libertie. . . ." [49]

Thus, even in the earlier period of the Long Parliament, when great constructive measures were passed and legal constitutional arguments often sufficed to win a victory, there were times when more radical ideas were proclaimed to justify unprecedented illegal actions or claims on the part of parliament. The concept that parliament was responsible to the people was used in 1640 and 1641, as in earlier years, to justify unprecedented actions and demands of the two houses upon the king.

No theorist sprang up in these early months to justify the great power wielded by parliament by asserting a full theory of popular sovereignty; but Nathanael Fiennes, who had proclaimed parliament's great supremacy, also made far-reaching claims for the final authority of the people in the English government. In attacking the divine-right ideas of the clergy, he said:

> Mr. *Speaker,* We all know that Kings, and States, and Judges, and all Magistrates are the Ordinances of God, but (Sir) give me leave to say they were the Ordinances of men before they were the Ordinances of God. . . . (Sir) it is worthie noting, that they are Ordinances of men, but that they are to be submitted unto for the Lords sake, and truely their power is

[47] L. J., IV, 369.
[48] D'Ewes, (Long Parl.), ed. W. Coates, p. 162.
[49] Ibid., 172.

as just, and their subjects alleageance as due unto them, though we suppose them to be first ordinances of men, and then confirmed, and established by Gods Ordinance, as if wee suppose them to be immediate ordinances of God, and so received by men.[50]

Within the walls of the commons Fiennes made the most extensive claims for parliament and people. Outside the commons it was Henry Parker, the ablest writer supporting the cause of parliament during the period from 1641 to 1650, who made the clearest analysis of the situation during these early months. In his pamphlet on ship money,[51] Parker tackled this problem in the same practical way as Wentworth had handled the problem of arbitrary imprisonment in 1628. If the law was doubtful on the point, as Parker half implied it was, the matter should be cleared up in parliament.[52] The prerogative, he wrote, "ought to be deduced out of the written and knowne Lawes of the Kingdome, . . . wee ought not to presume a Prerogative, and thence conclude it to be a Law, but we ought to cite the Law, and thence prove it to be Prerogative." [53] The laws he was primarily interested in were laws made in parliament, for there "National Laws are made by consent of Prince and people both, and so cannot be conceived to be prejudiciall to either side." [54] Parliament was, in his opinion, a body possessed of great authority. It might alter statute law and common law. In fact,

[50] *A Second Speech of the Honourable Nathanael Fiennes*, pp. 3–4. On this subject Mr. Glynne said: "No canon can bind without common consent. . . . Henry the Eigth would not have prayed the aid of an act of Parliament if by law he could have done it of himself." *Note Book of Sir John Northcote*, (J. Murray, London, 1877), p. 8.

[51] [Henry Parker], *The Case of Shipmony briefly discoursed*, (London (?), 1640).

[52] *Ibid.*, p. 47.

[53] *Ibid.*, p. 14. At this date, however, Parker did not claim that all the king's prerogatives were legal. He wrote that "Prerogative, except that which is essentiall to al Kings, without which they cannot bee Kings, is alterable, and it ought to be deduced out of the written and knowne Lawes of the Kingdome" (p. 14).

[54] *Ibid.*, p. 5.

What the Common Law was, this court can best determine; but it is obvious to all men that no Prerogative can be at the Common Law, but it had some beginning, and that must bee from either King or Subject or both: and in this, it is not superior to our Statute Law, and by consequence, not unalterable.[55]

Parker admitted that our laws "do not by special mention restrain extraordinary impositions in time of extraordinary danger," [56] but he tried to show that the general intent of the law was against unparliamentary exactions of money at all times. Certainly whenever doubt existed, parliament's advice was the best to follow, for it was safer than the advice of the king's private councillors. "That an inconsiderable number of Privadoes should see or know more than whole Kingdomes, is incredible: *vox populi* was ever reverenced as *vox Dei,* and Parliaments are infallible, and their acts indisputable to all but Parliaments. It is a just law, that no private man must bee wiser than Law publickly made." [57] Parliament "can affect nothing but the common good." [58] "No advice can be so fit, so forcible, so effectuall for the publike welfare, as that which is given in Parliament . . ." [59]

In the remarks of Parker, of Fiennes, of St. John, even at times of Pym, there is clear indication that these men had reached the point where they were beginning to think in terms of full parliamentary control of the king.

Yet for nine months they worked with the moderates with remarkable harmony, and by their agreement and by the legal consent of the king to their bills, far-reaching statutes were passed which remained as a permanent constitutional heritage from this period. Since the king no longer possessed institutions through which he could rule by means of his absolute prerogative, the subjects' rights and the law of the land safe-

[55] *Ibid.,* p. 15.
[56] *Ibid.,* p. 30.
[57] *Ibid.,* p. 35.
[58] *Ibid.,* p. 36.
[59] *Ibid.,* p. 38.

guarding them were made more secure, and the legislative supremacy of parliament more complete. A great legal victory for the subjects' rights and for the law of the land was won.

The king, however, still possessed important prerogatives through which he could exercise absolute power in certain realms. He possessed the appointing power in church and state, and the control of the army and of foreign affairs. His prerogatives were still great, but so were the established rights of the subject. For government to function harmoniously (or even adequately) it was still necessary that the subject give the king taxes and not encroach further upon the absolute powers remaining to him; it was still necessary that the king ask for money, and not try to overthrow the subjects' rights nor challenge the great legal authority of parliament; and above all, it was still necessary that king and subjects agree in parliament upon legislation necessary for the common welfare.

By the summer of 1641 a balanced government, so dear to the hearts of Englishmen, had been restored; but a balanced government was by its very nature one where authority was divided between king and subject. To the more conservative members of parliament, that balanced government now restored after years of more absolute rule, was a final goal—an ideal which they wished to maintain without further change. To the more aggressive members of parliament, that balanced government posed several problems. Did it really afford adequate security for the subjects' rights and the great authority of parliament? Since the king still possessed the appointing power, could they trust the way he might use it? If, for example, he should appoint bishops with the views of Laud, then their work in ridding themselves of Laud and high commission might be undone. If he appointed subservient judges, might they not in the future render legal decisions harmful to the subject? [60] The king still possessed the power as head of the

[60] See *D'Ewes, (Long Parl.)*, ed. W. Coates, p. 44. "Robert Goodwin moved [Oct. 28, 1641] touching ill Counsellors that if wee did not take a course to remove such as now remained and to prevent others from coming in heere-

militia and might use it to raise an army and turn against them. The aggressive parliamentary leaders felt far from secure with the balanced constitutional government existing in the latter half of 1641. They also did not wish to lose those new powers which they had illegally acquired, for the king still possessed sufficient power to turn against them and charge them with illegal actions—perhaps even treason.

The parliamentary leaders felt insecure and fearful and at the same time greedy for more power. Such a combination of feelings is hardly conducive to maintaining a balanced set-up requiring for its functioning harmony and trust between the king and his parliamentary partners. The actions and desires of the leaders in the commons were not trusted by the king, nor his by them, and on good and sufficient grounds in both cases. In the existing situation each partner profoundly distrusted the other, and thus the balance they had achieved through law rested on unstable political foundations.

Urged on by their feeling of insecurity and their desire for greater power, the more aggressive parliamentary leaders, who had always been willing when necessary to act and argue illegally, began in the latter part of 1641 to demand more and greater powers for parliament. The more security they demanded, the more they encroached upon the law and thereby widened the gap between themselves and the king, whose legal stand increasingly began to win the support of many moderates. Their pursuit of security ended finally, as such pursuits so often do, with war as the only remaining means left them to achieve this ever-vanishing goal.

The thinking of some of the leaders was also conditioned by their conviction that God's kingdom must be made secure in England. In November, 1640, the majority in the commons were agreed that something should be done to reform the church. But what! On that question moderate Anglicans, mod-

after all wee had done this Parliament would come to nothing, and wee should never be free from danger." See also the discussion by W. Coates, *Ibid.*, Introduction, pp. XXX, XXXI.

erate Presbyterians, and more radical sects could not agree. By the fall of 1641 a great reformation of the government had been accomplished, but how could they stop now with God's work undone? Jeremiah Burroughs reminded them of their responsibility in a sermon preached before the House of Commons September seventh, 1641.[61] "Ye are engaged," he said, "in as Honorable service for God and his people as ever any Assembly was since the world began; you have a blessed opportunity to lift up the Name of the great God, to make godlinesse to be honoured in the world . . ."[62] On the same day Stephen Marshall reminded the commons that they still had "great works to do, the planting of a new heaven and a new earth amongst us;"[63] "as yet the Lord's Temple is not builded, nor the Scepter of Christ thoroughly set up."[64] The conviction that God's work still remained to be done played an important part in leading the more aggressive leaders on to more drastic demands.[65]

With the reconvening of parliament on October 20, they set out on their program of further reform in church and state. Again the aggressive group was in control, again they pushed forward, and again they justified their new claims and demands on the basis of the welfare of the nation at large. Because they were responsible for a great trust—the welfare of the people of England—all irregular and unprecedented actions on their part were correct and necessary. When, for example, the question of helping the king to suppress the Irish rebellion arose, the suggestion was made that parliament would help only if the king would let them choose his councillors. Pym justified this encroachment upon the appointing power

[61] *Sions Joy . . . A Sermon Preached to the Honourable House of Commons Sept 7, 1641,* (London, 1641).
[62] *Ibid.,* A2v.
[63] *A Peace Offering to God . . . Sept 7, 1641,* (London, 1641), p. 22.
[64] *Ibid.,* p. 50.
[65] In speaking against episcopal government as early as June 11, 1641, Sir Henry Vane said: "For hath not this Parliament been called, continued, preserved, and secured by the immediate Finger of God, as it were for this work (i.e., reforming church government)? Nalson, II, 278.

of the king by saying, "In the publik Councells off the king, publik interest." [66] The welfare of the people was again used as an argument for the unprecedented procedure followed in addressing the Grand Remonstrance to the people and not to the king. Culpepper, Hyde, and Falkland called attention to this innovation, reminding the commons "That it was sans president, nor by the power given us by the words of the Writt for election could wee make a remonstrance to the people." [67] Pym replied to this objection in these words, "The Honour off the King is the safty off his people." [68]

As the distrust of the king grew in the early part of 1642, parliament began to demand for itself more and more control of those powers which had been accepted, even as late as 1640, as part of the king's prerogative. Again in the name of the nation, their claim was put forward. On May 3, the lords and commons issued a statement justifying their stand on the militia question. They being "intrusted with Safety of the Kingdom, and Peace of the People . . . can never be discharged before God or Man, if they should suffer the Safety of the Kingdom, and Peace of the People, to be exposed to the Malice of the malignant Party at home, or the Fury of Enemies from abroad; . . . do resolve to put their said Ordinance in present Execution; and do require all Persons in Authority . . . to put the same in Execution; and all others to obey it, . . . as they tender the upholding of the true Protestant Religion, the Safety of his Majesty's Person and his Royal Posterity, the Peace of the Kingdom, and the Being of this Commonwealth. . . ." [69] In another declaration of May 19, the lords and commons again justified their stand on the basis of the safety of the commonwealth. In normal times and according to the law and constitution, they explained, king and parliament should act together to preserve; "yet since the Prince being but one person, is more subject to accidents of nature and chance, whereby the Commonwealth may be deprived of the

[66] *D'Ewes, (Long Parl.)*, ed. W. Coates, p. 105, n. 20.
[67] *Ibid.*, p. 184.   [68] *Ibid.*, n. 14.   [69] C. J., II, 560.

fruit of that trust which was in part reposed in him, in cases of such necessity, that the Kingdome may not be inforced presently to returne to its first principles, and every man left to doe what is right in his own eyes, without either guide or rule, the Wisedome of this State hath intrusted the Houses of Parliament with a power to supply what shall bee wanting on the part of the Prince." [70]

In the declaration of November 2, the lords and commons explained why it was better that they, and not the king, should decide in case of danger. "There must be a Judge of that Question wherein the safety of the Kingdom depends (for it must not lye undetermined)." [71] If agreement could not be secured, either the king or parliament must judge. If judgment were permitted to the king, his judgment would be out of court. Moreover, "if the Kingdom best knows what is for its own good and preservation; and the Parliament be the Representative Body of the Kingdom, it is easie to judge who in this case should be the Judge." [72] Parliament must judge, must interpret the law, and must supply anything personally missing on the king's part, because parliament was responsible for the welfare and safety of the commonwealth of England. So ran the official declarations of parliament, and so ran the arguments of the growing number of pamphleteers springing to parliament's defense when war began.

John Marsh, for example, was a writer who aimed to prove that parliament had acted correctly in the militia question. He believed that, when matters concerning private individuals were involved, parliament should exercise its power of judging according to definite laws and precedents.

Otherwise it is where it concerneth the Common-wealth, for there I conceive, under favour, (especially, as in this case, in

[70] *An exact Collection of the Remonstrances, Declarations . . . between the Kings most Excellent Majesty and his High Court of Parliament . . . Dec. 1641 . . . Mar. 21, 1643*, pr. for E. Husband, (London, 1643), pp. 207–8.
[71] *Ibid.*, p. 697.
[72] *Ibid.*

time of imminent danger) they are not tied to any legall way of proceeding, but they may, and are bound, as well by their Oaths of Allegeance, Supremacy, and their late Protestation, as by their Writ, by which they are called to Parliament, to take notice of all things, which may be obnoxious and prejudiciall to the Common-wealth: and to debate, determine, and declare the Law concerning them, though they have nothing judicially before them; for if they should, in this case, expect a complainant, the Common-wealth might perish, before they could yeeld any ayd or assistance, for the securing of it.[73]

If parliament should not in such a case be able without the king to declare the common law, "this great Court, which so farre transcends all others, in other things, should be lesse in power, in this particular, then any other, Which ought not to be conceived, or imagined." [74] Marsh insisted that parliament's action in the militia question was only a declaration of the law, yet his own statement actually went far beyond mere interpretation.

During the same months when the lords and commons and pamphleteers were justifying their stand against the king on the basis of their responsibility to the nation, they were also denying that the king possessed any rights or prerogatives belonging absolutely to him. According to their interpretation, all rights of the king were his only in trust, even "the very Jewels of the Crown are not the Kings proper goods, but are onely intrusted to Him for the use and Ornament thereof." [75] They now declared that "calling and dissolving Parliaments" was only "a trust reposed in the Kings of this Realme, and never intended as a Prerogative, wherein they might use their pleasure, whatever the exigence of the Kingdome should bee." [76] "The question between his Majesty and Parliament is not," declared the two houses to the Netherlands, "whether hee

[73] [John Marsh], *An Argument, or Debate in Law: of the great Question concerning the Militia* . . . , (London, 1642), p. 39.
[74] *Ibid.*, p. 40.
[75] *An exact Collection* . . . , pr. for Husband, p. 266.
[76] *Ibid.*, p. 701.

shall enjoy the same prerogative and power which hath belonged to our former Kings, his Majesties Royall predecessours, but whether that prerogative and power should be employed to our defence, or to our ruine." [77]

As parliament talked of the use and purpose of the prerogative, at the same time it stressed its own control over it. On May 26, 1642, the houses proclaimed that everything entrusted to the king should "be managed by the advice of the Houses of Parliament." [78] On November 2, 1642, they declared "That we did and do say, That a Parliament may dispose of any thing wherein the King or any Subject hath a right, in such a way as that the Kingdome may not be in danger thereby." [79] One pamphleteer argued that in obeying parliament, one really obeyed the king, for parliament stood for the king's "Soule," for his "Person," for "his *State, Wealth, Honour,* and *reputation,*" even for his "Posterity." [80] By parliament's own declarations and by pamphlets justifying its actions, the rights of the king were argued away. His rights were his only in trust, parliament should reduce all of the prerogative to law, and parliament should manage that trust. Parliament seldom attacked the prerogative directly; but since it stressed the use to be made of it, it actually undermined its original nature as an inherent right and claimed for itself responsibility for the general welfare, so long an essential part of the king's authority as head of the state.

Parliament and its supporters also stressed the importance of parliament in its relation to the liberties of the land. For years they had talked of the liberties of Englishmen, and now they proclaimed that these liberties depended absolutely upon parliament and that all could safely trust parliament to deal with them as it thought fit. Even the moderate D'Ewes reminded the

[77] *Ibid.,* p. 637.
[78] *Ibid.,* p. 266.
[79] *Ibid.,* p. 726.
[80] *The Vindication of the Parliament and their proceedings,* [Oct. 15], 1642, pp. 23–25. When he spoke of parliament, this writer really meant the two houses.

commons that "there is a great deale of difference where our liberties are taken from us without law and where wee shall for a time upon urgent necessitie receede from them by our owne common consent in Parliament." [81] One remonstrance in favor of the parliament spoke of "our true and undoubted Religion, Laws, Properties and Liberties, which are deposited for our use and avail in that great and wise Councell." [82]

In many of the quotations just given, the lords and commons or the pamphleteers did not bother to justify the power they claimed. As they encroached upon the rights of king or subject, they became more confident and less disposed to justify and theorize. Yet it must never be forgotten that these illegal and unprecedented powers were taken over by parliament in the name of the nation—as trustees for its welfare.

The actions, arguments, and justifications of parliament in the months just before and after the outbreak of war may be summarized as follows. In the first place, the two houses definitely assumed the offensive, claiming more and more of the king's own power, which in the early seventeenth century, and as late as the summer of 1641, had been generally accepted as part of his kingly prerogative. In the second place, the most common and the most basic argument used by parliament and its supporters to justify this aggressive encroachment upon the king, and to justify the war beginning in July, 1642, was the argument that all irregular actions taken by parliament were necessary because it was responsible for a great trust, the welfare and safety of the people of England. Finally, as the two houses aggressively encroached upon the king in the name of the nation, they actually took over greater and greater power for themselves, with little real concern for the nation at all. It was the two houses, not the nation, who became the protector of the peoples' and the king's rights, the interpreter

[81] *D'Ewes, (Long Parl.)*, ed. W. Coates, p. 245. D'Ewes made this remark on Dec. 7, 1641, in a discussion of a proposed bill giving great power to a lord general.

[82] *The Remonstrance or Declaration of . . . the County Palatine of Chester,* (London, Aug. 12, 1642).

of the law, and the only judge of the nature and extent of their own authority. The two houses actually claimed sovereign power for themselves and exercised it in the part of the nation under their control.

Why, therefore, the modern scholar asks, did not they and their supporters frankly admit the realities of the situation? Was not the basic issue whether England should be ruled by an absolute king possessing complete power to choose his advisors and interpret and control the law, or by the lords and commons possessing final authority to make laws, to control public policy, and to govern with the king as a mere figurehead? Since the issue of sovereignty could no longer be postponed, was it not high time Englishmen decide whether they preferred a sovereign king or a sovereign lords and commons? No such frank questions were raised by parliament or by most of the pamphleteers during the first civil war.

On the contrary, although parliament assumed power and justified it on the basis of their responsibility to the nation at large, the two houses did not rest all their case on that argument. They never entirely abandoned the idea that they were fighting for law and the old balanced constitution.[83] In their declarations and speeches and in the writings of the pamphleteers, there was considerable talk of law and right, which the king and his wicked party had attacked and the parliament was defending. When, for example, parliament began to raise and commission forces, it claimed that it was preserving the old state of affairs against a king and party who would destroy them. Not the actions of parliament, but the actions of the forces raised by the king, would cause "the whole Frame of the antient and well-tempered Government of this Realm to be

[83] On Feb. 8, 1642, Thomas Smith wrote to Sir John Pennington concerning those who were leaving parliament at that time to support the king, and said: "When this rubbish is removed, the building will go on bravely, and then the King and his people will come to a right understanding one of the other, so firmly united in mutual affection that the head shall love and cherish the members, [and] they give due honour and obedience to their head; and we may see happy days, and all things rectified both in Church and State." *Cal. St. P. Domestic (1641–1643)*, p. 278.

dissolved and destroyed, and the English Nation inthrälled in their persons and Estates to an arbitrary Power." [84] To prevent this sad condition of affairs, parliament claimed that it had "lawfully" taken up arms, and that therefore all subsequent exercise of unprecedented power necessitated by the initial step, was likewise "lawful." County assessments in the fall of 1642 were "most necessary," but also based upon the "established Laws, and fundamental Constitution of this Kingdom." [85] Early in 1643 a parliamentary ordinance providing for weekly assessments reasserted that the two houses were "fully satisfied and resolved in their consciences, that they have lawfully taken up Armes, and may and ought to continue the same for the necessary defence of themselves and the Parliament from violence and destruction, and of this Kingdome from foreign invasion." [86] They were defending the true king and the true law from the violence of those who would overthrow them. If the person of the king was surrounded by evil and wicked counsellors, they must free him from the malignant party. If the law was doubtful and needed an interpreter, they should interpret it; but in their interpretation, it was law and not policy they were declaring. If force was necessary to achieve these objectives, it was essentially in 1642, as in 1215, the last legal means by which they could rightly coerce the king.

Such thinking actuated the minds of Englishmen in and out of parliament who fought against the king. Their theoretical justification was never based on a single concept, nor was it clear cut. It is somewhat confusing to the modern reader of their declarations, and one decidedly mixed in its ideology, including legal as well as political arguments, and bundling together many strange bedfellows. Because of the mixture of their arguments, their justification of their position may be called confused,[87] but that confusion can be explained and

[84] C. T. Firth, and R. S. Rait, *Acts and Ordinances of the Interregnum 1642–1660*, 2 vols., (London, 1911), I, 14.
[85] C. J., II, 868.   [86] Firth and Rait, I, 85.
[87] See J. W. Allen, *English Political Thought 1603–1660*, p. 415.

understood on the basis of the nature of the arguments parliament had been using against the crown for at least forty years. During all of this period they had employed two types of arguments. Whenever possible, as when the royalists had broken or encroached upon the law, they had rested their own case upon it; but when they themselves had encroached upon the king's legal powers, they had turned to the political argument that they were responsible to the nation at large for its welfare. Increasingly this second argument had come to be used, as more and more they had encroached upon the king's traditional powers. Nevertheless, appeal to law had been a great bulwark in the past and could hardly be forgotten or ignored by Pym, Holles, or Hampden. These men had advanced step by step to the point where they were resisting the king by force of arms, but armed resistance to their lawful sovereign was not their creed. They attacked the king, but not the institution of monarchy. They might in their more extreme demands reduce the king to a figurehead, but they still accepted him as an integral part of the state—as the head of their body politic. When in January, 1649, the full cycle of their resistance was reached in the execution of Charles I, many of the leaders still alive who had brought on the civil war disapproved of and denounced this illegal action of the Rump Parliament. In the years before 1660 they turned again to monarchy as the best means of restoring the rule of law. In view of their later as well as their earlier emphasis on law, it is but fair to credit them with some sincerity when, at times in 1642 and subsequent war-years, they talked as if they were the true guardians of the law and constitution.

To suggest the naturalness and sincerity of such arguments is not to deny that parliament must have continued to insist that its case was legal. Although Hyde's straightforward declarations presenting the king's case had made it all too evident that the king had now become the guardian of the law and constitution which parliament had broken, to have admitted the legality of the king's cause would have been political suicide for parliamentary leaders in an age when a legal argument was more convincing than any other to Englishmen in the upper classes.

Consequently, leaders in the commons never presented in their speeches or declarations a simple, straightforward case for parliament. During the years of war, as in the earlier years of peace, they talked of law and right, of security, and of their responsibility to the nation, but never set forth an entirely consistent justification for their actions. It is only a few of the leading pamphleteers during the war period who saw the issue clearly and set forth consistent and incisive political theories to explain or justify the great issues which Englishmen had debated for forty years, and over which they were now fighting a civil war.

CHAPTER X

THE ISSUES BECOME CLEAR

THE APPEAL to arms in the summer of 1642 brought an end
to the great controversy which had been waged for so
long within the framework of the constitution between the
proponents of strong kingly rule and strong parliamentary
rule. The civil war, however, did not end the constitutional
and political debates which had been carried on with mounting intensity ever since the accession of the first Stuart. On
the contrary, the resort to arms increased the quantity and
improved the quality of the constitutional and political thinking on both sides. A modern scholar reading through the
tracts, long and short, significant and insignificant, which
poured from the press in the war years, might well conclude
that the pen-and-ink army of both the royalists and parliamentarians was mightier and more effective than the military
forces of either side.

With the coming of war the floodgates were down, and
Englishmen, who had never been leaders in political thought,
quickly brought forth political ideas so challenging and significant that they won for their country a high, if not the leading place, in the political thought of the seventeenth century.
It was during the eighteen years between the outbreak of civil
war and the Restoration, that Thomas Hobbes, one of the
greatest of all political theorists, wrote his *Leviathan*, and
James Harrington, one of the most influential thinkers in
shaping American institutions, produced his *Oceana*. In these
same years also came the first great outburst of democratic
thought in history, with John Lilburne and Richard Overton
leading the way. These were the years when Gerald Win-
stanley, perhaps the most significant of earlier communist
thinkers, wrote; it was also in this period that Robert Filmer,

the leading exponent of divine right in seventeenth-century England, set forth his theories. The issues these men raised, the answers they gave to them, and the streams of thought they initiated or developed during less than twenty years are still vital and have become woven into the permanent texture of our thinking today.

Each of these theorists, it is hoped, can be better understood if he is read and interpreted in relation to the constitutional and political problems which Englishmen had faced and the ideas they had been expressing about them for forty years prior to the war. Hobbes's political philosophy is related not only to his ethics, psychology, and metaphysics, but also to the events through which he lived and the constitutional and political thinking which was his heritage. Hobbes desired passionately a unified state, but so had many English thinkers earlier in the century. Consciously and unconsciously they had striven to achieve unity in their polity—unity in the king through his general-welfare power or his divine right, or unity in the law cementing all parts of the polity together. Many of these earlier thinkers were not as blind to the need for unity in their polity as Hobbes implied they were in the *Behemouth;* [1] but they certainly could not have accepted the kind of unity which Hobbes believed to be the only answer to the eternal problem of authority and freedom in human affairs. Nor would Hobbes's *Leviathan* have been such an austere and dominating sovereign had not its creator been over-aware of the harm society experienced from lack of unity. Hobbes set forth his theory of sovereignty when England was torn wide apart by civil war, and when other thinkers, as well as he, were beginning to believe that only absolute sovereignty, resting either in the king or in parliament, could provide the unity their country so sorely needed. There are good historical reasons why Hobbes should have attributed more absolute power to his sovereign than Bodin had earlier given to his. Harrington desired a properly balanced government and worked out

---

[1] T. Hobbes, *The English workes of Thomas Hobbes*, ed. Sir W. Molesworth, 11 vols., (London, 1839–1845), VI, 319.

the means, both political and economic, by which he hoped
this balance would be achieved, thereby making a significant
contribution to political thought; but the ideal of balance was
his heritage from the past, for a properly balanced polity had
long been one of the most cherished beliefs of Englishmen.

If Harrington and Hobbes, the two giants in political
thought of this period, can better be understood by relating
their ideas to past streams of thought in England, in greater
measure is this true of the lesser thinkers. Lilburne's and Win-
stanley's thought grew out of the ferment of parliamentary
and Puritan thought developing in the years before and after
1642. The importance of rights, of fundamental laws and
liberties, of parliament's responsibility for the welfare of the
commonwealth, of the consent of man as the basis of government, had all been proclaimed long before Lilburne wrote.
In some ways it was he and the other Levellers, and not the
parliamentary theorists like Parker and Herle, who carried to
their logical conclusion those political ideas with which the
Parliamentary-Puritan opposition had long battled the king.
On the royalist side, Robert Filmer could have learned most
of his divine-right ideas from James or the Anglican clergy,
who had earlier expounded them; and he may well have
learned of the concept of sovereignty, which he linked with
divine right, from Manwaring, or even from his parliamentary
opponent, Henry Parker. The thought of all these men is in
great or small measure a product of the issues Englishmen had
long debated and the ideas they had long expressed.

It is not, however, these well-known leaders in thought, but
a few other thinkers writing in the first two or three years after
war began, who will be considered in this concluding chapter.
Representing the royalists, Henry Ferne and Dudley Digges
have been chosen, and speaking for the parliamentarians,
Philip Hunton, Henry Parker, and Charles Herle. These
theorists have been selected from many because, in their basic
concepts and arguments, the ideas which have been followed
so far in this book reach a point where their story can properly
be concluded. These writers recognized more clearly during

the troubled years of war than anyone had done in the earlier
days of peace the different problems and concepts of government which had long divided Englishmen. Moreover, some of
them, in particular those making the most complete claims for
parliament, reached the point in their thinking where their
ideas clearly reveal the great change in basic political assumptions which had come about between the early and mid-
seventeenth century as a result of the constitutional struggles.
These men definitely abandoned the constitutional idealism so
characteristic of thinking in an earlier period and turned to
political realism so characteristic of thinking in later ages.

Although each of these writers was well known and his intellectual stature appreciated by his most worthy partners and
opponents in the pamphlet war so fiercely waged, no one of
them won the recognition from his own party merited by his
intellectual contribution to the cause. The essential clarity
and moderation of Hunton's thought could hardly have been
appreciated in the midst of war; but neither Parker nor Herle,
who championed the cause of parliament so vigorously, was
fully appreciated by parliamentary leaders, nor Ferne nor
Digges by the royalists.[2] No one of these men can be regarded
as typical of the average pamphleteer defending the king's or

[2] Parker perhaps won the greatest recognition, for in 1645 he was made
a secretary to the commons, and in 1649 he secured the position he had
asked for in 1643, the registrarship of the prerogative office. Under the
Commonwealth, until his death in 1652, his valuable services won him
more material rewards.

Herle, rector of Winwick in Lancashire, preached frequently before
parliament and was an important member of the assembly of divines,
serving on several of its committees. Disapproving of the execution of
Charles I, he was even examined by the government in 1651 for giving
help to the royalists.

Hunton's support of Cromwell secured him a rich living at Sedgefield
in Durham in 1657, but his earlier support of the parliamentary cause
seems to have been unrewarded.

Ferne became chaplain to Charles I in 1643 and seems to have worked
closely with him for several years. He preached before the king in the
Isle of Wight on Nov. 29, 1648, just before Charles's death. In 1662, five
weeks before he died, he became Bishop of Chester.

Digges, the third son of Sir Dudley Digges, parliamentary leader and

parliament's cause through the civil war period. Each was unique in the clarity and penetration of his thought.

Until recent years these five theorists have been largely neglected by historians, but within the past fifteen years their intellectual stature and their contribution to the history of ideas in seventeenth-century England have been increasingly realized. Proefssor McIlwain [3] has rescued Hunton from obscurity and the unfair interpretation put upon his thought by Filmer in the seventeenth century. Professor Jordan has given us an account of Parker as a "Man of Substance," and I have discussed Parker's concept of parliamentary sovereignty.[4] Professors Gooch and Pease, and more recently Allen and Haller, have included some consideration of one or more of these thinkers in their works.[5] Consequently, it would be superfluous to consider again all phases of their thought; but it is important to present those aspects of it relevant to the central problems and ideas with which this book is primarily concerned.

Turning first to the royalists, the reader of this book will recall the fact that during the period from 1603 to 1640 royalist policy and thought had been aggressive. Exponents of the king's absolute prerogative and of his divine right had linked their ideas with older laws or traditional concepts, but in their thinking both groups had also exalted the king to the point

writer, was a mathematician and an ardent supporter of Charles. In 1643, when he was only thirty years old this brilliant young man died of fever at the royalist camp at Oxford.

[3] C. H. McIlwain, *Constitutionalism and the Changing World*, (Cambridge University Press, Cambridge, 1939), pp. 196–231.

[4] W. K. Jordan, *Men of Substance*, (University of Chicago Press, Chicago, 1942); and M. A. Judson, "Henry Parker and the Theory of Parliamentary Sovereignty," in *Essays in History and Political Theory in honor of Charles H. McIlwain*, (Harvard University Press, Cambridge, Mass., 1936).

[5] G. P. Gooch and H. J. Laski, op. cit.; T. C. Pease, *The Leveller Movement*, (American Historical Association, Washington, 1916); J. W. Allen, *English Political Thought 1603–1660*, (Methuen and Co., London, 1938); W. Haller, ed., *Tracts on Liberty in the Puritan Revolution 1638–1647*, 3 vols., (Columbia University Press, New York, 1934).

where they had claimed more absolute power for him than had ever in previous centuries been accorded the English monarch.

Their ideas of absolute prerogative and of divine right, however, had never risen to their full potentialities during those years before 1640 when there had been the closest connection between such ideas and royalist policy, and the greatest chance of those ideas being completely realized in the structure and functioning of the English government. With the possible exception of Dickinson, Manwaring, and James himself, no theorist had attributed complete sovereignty to the king. In the critical years between 1640 and 1642, the king had been shorn of many of his absolute prerogatives, and little respect had been paid to his divine right. During those two years, exponents of the theory of absolute prerogative or of divine right had kept silent. The theory of absolute prerogative had died in 1640 along with the great authority wielded by the king's councillors and judges who had championed it, and never again to my knowledge was it advanced as a serious theory of government in England. Pamphleteers supporting the king after the first civil war broke out did not base their case on the theory of an overriding prerogative, but some of them [6] did turn to divine right to justify their support of the king. Thus the theory of divine right lived on, finding in Filmer its greatest English advocate and, after the "martyrdom" of Charles, coming to play an important part in English policy and ideas. The royalist cause and the most significant royalist thought, however, between 1642 and 1645, did not rest on divine right or the absolute prerogative, but on the law. This legal-constitutional stand was possible because the civil war came in 1642 and not in 1640, that is, after the parliamentary opposition had become patently aggressive, claiming and exercising powers which law and precedent clearly gave the king. Consequently the royalists could correctly rest their case

[6] See especially, John Maxwell, *Sacro-sancta Regum Majestas: or, the Sacred and Royall Prerogative of Christian kings,* (Oxford, 1644); and Michael Hudson, *The Divine Right of Government, natural and politique* . . . Sept. 9, 1647.

on the law and constitution, and for once Charles was wise
enough to do so. He listened to Clarendon and allowed him
to present a justification of the king which, in its simple clear
enunciation of known laws and loyalties, had a great advantage over the confused and mixed arguments put forth in the
official parliamentary declarations.

Important royalist pamphleteers followed the lead given by
official royalist declarations. Now, for the first time in the long
struggle of ideas, royalist writers presented a clear-cut, well-
rounded, and complete picture of the king's position based on
the law of the land and established precedents. Such a theory
was set forth most clearly by Henry Ferne and Dudley Digges.
If Ferne had written during the earlier period, he certainly
would have been chosen in this book as the best exponent of
the ideas most Englishmen held concerning the position and
authority of an English king, even though there are some parts
of Ferne's thought with which parliamentarians would not
have agreed. It must have been the shock of war—the final
failure of Englishmen to settle their differences constitutionally—that led Ferne and Digges to see and analyze more clearly
than men had done before the true nature and position of
their king. Their thinking was also clarified by the shock these
believers in true monarchy suffered when they read the arguments of opponents, like Parker and Herle, whose claims for
the two houses of parliament relegated the monarch to an
insignificant position in the English polity. As Ferne and
Digges carried on a bitter pamphlet debate with Parker and
Herle and also with the more moderate and constitutional
Hunton, they achieved a truer insight and understanding of
the real nature and authority of the English king than had
ever been set forth in earlier ages when his position had not
been so directly challenged and openly menaced.

Both Ferne and Digges rested their case on the fact that, in
form, the English government was monarchical, that according to English law and precedent the king was the head and
supreme authority in the government. The king is, Ferne

claimed, "in all Causes and over all persons supreme." [7] According to *24.H.8.c.12,* "He was declared in Parliament to be *Supream Head of the body politique . . . with plenary, whole entire power . . . and Jurisdiction, to render and yeeld Justice . . . to all manner of Subjects."* [8] Petitions are addressed to him, and parliament is called and dissolved at his pleasure.[9] Let those rebelling against the king "prove that *England* is no monarchy; that they are not bound to beare true alleagiance by a necessary obligation flowing from the civill constitutions of this realme; that they may lawfully kill him, whose life they have sworne to defend with their utmost power." [10] The fact that the English government was a monarchy was a major argument used by both Ferne and Digges to prove parliament's action was unjustifiable rebellion.

Although these writers believed that the English monarch possessed real supremacy, they also agreed that he was a ruler whose power was legally limited in certain important respects: that there was a "Way of Legall, Morall, or Parliamentary prevention and Restraint, which is established by law for our security." [11] Their monarch was a king bound by oath to rule by law,[12] and a king many of whose actions were legal and binding only when performed through regular channels and according to prescribed legal forms. The higher ministers of the crown "ought to use all faire and Lawfull meanes for the restraining" [13] of illegal actions of the king or his agents. Their duty and parliament's was "to inform the King aright." [14]

[7] H. Ferne, *The Resolving of Conscience upon this Question . . . ,* (Cambridge, and re-printed at London, 1642), p. 10.

[8] H. Ferne, *Conscience Satisfied that there is no Warrant for the Armes now taken up by Subjects,* (Oxford, 1643), p. 15.

[9] H. Ferne, *The Resolving of Conscience,* p. 10.

[10] [Dudley Digges], *The Unlawfulnesse of Subjects taking up Armes against their Soveraigne in what case soever,* (Oxford, 1644), p. 114.

[11] H. Ferne, *A Reply unto severall Treatises pleading for the Armes now taken up by Subjects . . . ,* (Oxford, 1643), p. 32.

[12] *Ibid.,* p. 51.

[13] *Ibid.,* p. 11.

[14] *Ibid.,* p. 10.

Above all, the king was limited by parliament, and Ferne was more respectful of parliament's place in the English government than some councillors, lawyers, and clergymen had earlier been. "It is granted," he wrote, "that the two Houses of Parliament are in a sort Coordinate with His Majesty, *ad aliquid,* to some act or exercising of the supream power, that is to the making of Lawes, by yeelding their consent; and that they have this by a fundamentall Constitution." [15] Both Ferne and Digges believed parliament was so important that if the members used that "Legall restraining power, as they are bound in duty to doe, the Monarch cannot alter the established frame [of government]; he may perchance make some actuall invasions upon their Rights and Liberties (as they may often upon his Right and Prerogative) and runne a course in it selfe tending to subversion, but alter the frame or change the Lawes without their consent he cannot." [16]

The king possessed the actual power, but the two houses shared with him the exercise of it in certain realms, and this power exercised by them made "a large and reall difference in government." [17] The limitations upon the king provided by law were real. The fact that subjects could not resist him did not mean that his power was arbitrary. "For *Arbitrary* and *limited* power is distinguished by the *Restraint,* which the Law or Constitution of Government casts upon the governing power, not by the *abuse* of that power, which sometimes in the most limited Governments may break out into a licentious arbitrarynes; If force and not Law must tell us what Arbitrary power is, and releeve us against it in the Prince, I fear we should too often feel it from the hand of the Subjects." [18] These remarkable words of Ferne, written in 1642 when force and not law was dominant, express medieval thought and

[15] H. Ferne, *Conscience Satisfied*, p. 6.
[16] H. Ferne, *A Reply*, p. 39. In *Conscience Satisfied* Ferne wrote of the estates in parliament checking each other, pp. 36–37.
[17] *Ibid.*, p. 18.
[18] H. Ferne, *Conscience Satisfied*, p. 46.

English constitutionalism at their best. They are Ferne's most profound answer to his parliamentary opponents and also an answer to Hobbes before the *Leviathan* was written.

Ferne proved himself a great constitutionalist in another statement anticipating the idea later incorporated into the American constitution: that the constitution itself should be changed with more difficulty and require more agreement for any change than ordinary legislative matter. Ferne wrote:

> We should, conceive our selves in a surer condition, if such businesses, which nearly concern the Kingdom and the very Constitution of Government, were not carried by the major part of those that are present, but by a more unanimous consent, that is by the better halfe, at least, of the whole number, that belong to each house; such businesse, if need were, had better stay till the triall could be made by such a number, then to run the hazard of a watched opportunity, when few are present; and such resolutions would better sway with his Majestie, and better satisfie the whole Kingdome.[19]

A thinker writing these words can never be dismissed as a mere legalistic conservative. Ferne was a true conservative who wished to preserve the historical monarchical government of England; but he was also a creative constitutional theorist who recognized the need for new devices in the government of his country if the traditional constitution was to continue to bind king and people together in harmonious unity.

Digges also insisted that the limitations upon the king were real. To obtain supplies and to exercise his legislative power he must call parliament, and parliament would move against any agents of the king who had acted illegally. Moreover, "His interests are the same with the Subjects. They are not like two buckets, when one is lowest, the other is highest, but they

[19] *Ibid.*, p. 37. Ferne took over this suggestion from the Venetian constitution. Although he disapproved of that constitution, he approved of one feature of it. "Yet this meanes of security they have, Their resolutions of high concernments are not carried but by such a number of the whole Senate though many be absent; And let me take the boldnesse to say, We should conceive . . . [as given in text above]"

resemble the Head and rest of the Members, and the Head cannot thrive by a consumption of the Members." [20]

Though Digges and Ferne believed that the king was truly and effectively limited by the law and constitution, they also made it perfectly clear that all of his power was not so limited —"that his power or Soveraignty, wherein it is not limited by law, is not absolute and full." [21] The king still possessed regal power. In support of this point, Ferne ventured into the enemies' camp and made his own interpretation (the correct one) of Fortescue, whom his opponent Charles Herle had cited as supporting his own contention that the king's power was dependent upon the law and the people. It is true, Ferne wrote, that according to Fortescue, the king rules in part by a political power, "in as much as in the making of Laws the advice and consent of many is required, and his power regulated by such Law. But this *Principate of many* . . . so is it ill meant, to the excluding of His *Regalis potestas,* and so to make this government Democraticall, or Aristocraticall, rather than Monarchicall." [22] Herle, in other words, had neglected to mention that Fortescue wrote of the king ruling not by the political power alone, but by the regal *and* political power. This belief that the king still possessed regal power played a very important part in Ferne's thinking. The king, according to his interpretation, possessed the sole authority to make treaties, to control the militia, to appoint judges and other great officers of state, and to call and dissolve parliament.[23]

Digges was equally decisive on this point, insisting that "where Lawes cannot be produced to the contrary, there the King's power is absolute." [24] He admitted that a law must be made by the joint consent of king and both houses, and that

[20] D. Digges, *The Unlawfulnesse,* pp. 73–74.
[21] H. Ferne, *A Reply,* p. 31.
[22] H. Ferne, *Conscience Satisfied,* p. 19. See C. H. McIlwain, *The Growth of Political Thought in the West,* (The Macmillan Company, New York, 1932), pp. 360 ff.
[23] H. Ferne, *Conscience Satisfied,* p. 13 and pp. 25–26.
[24] D. Digges, *The Unlawfulnesse,* p. 118.

such a law "becomes absolute to those purposes, to which they passe their assent." [25] "To all other purposes (wherein Regall power is not expressly limited) the King is the whole people, and what he doth is legally their Act." [26] Except where parliament acts, "there he [the king] is Populus Anglicanus, legally the English nation." [27]

To Digges and Ferne this absolute power of the king, existing for and exercised on behalf of the people at large, was fundamental in all their thinking. To them this power was co-ordinate with, and not subordinate to, the legislative power of the king-in-parliament. In other words, they did not accept the supremacy of the legislative power over all other powers, and therefore they could not agree with Hunton who did. In refusing to accept that supremacy, they revealed that they were blind to the growing importance which legislation had come to have in the past one hundred and fifty years in England; but their conservatism was in line with earlier law and precedent, and, I venture to believe, their views would have found favor with more Englishmen than the ideas of Hunton in the first four decades of the seventeenth century.

Because Digges and Ferne maintained that the king possessed absolute power apart from parliament, and because they held that, according to law, he was head of the state and the head of parliament, they insisted that the two houses of parliament could not act legally against him. Any claim in 1642 that parliament was acting on behalf of the welfare of the state was ridiculous, for "The King is a part of the State." [28] "They cannot vindicate themselves from Treason and Rebellion, except they produce some Law of *England* which dispenses with their Allegiance in such cases, and shew that our civill constitutions are so framed, as to make *Bellum Civile, Bellum utrinque justum,* a Civill Warre, a *just* Warre of both

[25] *Ibid.,* p. 146.
[26] *Ibid.,* p. 151.
[27] *Ibid.,* p. 152.
[28] [Dudley Digges], *An Answer to a printed book [by Henry Parker] intituled Observations . . . ,* (Oxford, 1642), p. 43.

sides in the law notion which cannot be, except there be two supreme authorities to proclaime and manage it." [29] In England there is only one supreme authority, and that is the king.

According to Ferne, under the present circumstances, where the king and the two houses disagree, the only constitutional way of resolving the dilemma is for the king to govern by the extensive powers he possesses legally as king—through his independent powers not shared with parliament. Digges reasoned in a similar way, asserting in answer to Parker that if the "King and Parliament dissent, things must be at a stand, and the Subject must be obedient to the ordinary Law." [30] Apart from parliament, the king is supreme and possesses considerable absolute power. Until he and the two houses can agree, it is correct and legal that he rule by the legal power he possesses in his own right. Without the king, parliament can rightfully claim no legal authority at all, and therefore none of their actions can be legal; whereas many actions of the king are legal without the concurrence of his partners in parliament.

By such an analysis of the nature of the English government, Ferne and Digges set forth a very strong legal case for the king, thereby giving us the most clear and comprehensive defense of monarchy presented by the royalists in the whole first half of the seventeenth century. Moreover, this view of the monarchy was not merely royalist. For centuries before 1642 it had been quite generally accepted. No single person, however, before the civil war presented it as a whole, or discussed its real nature, strength, and weakness. This concept of monarchy had been so deeply embedded in law and practice that until it was challenged and denied, as the parliamentarians were frankly doing by 1642, it had been sufficient to assume and accept it, without presenting it in any formal or complete manner. Between 1642 and 1660 it was primarily the royalists who became the inheritors and guardi-

[29] D. Digges, *The Unlawfulnesse*, pp. 128–29.
[30] D. Digges, *An Answer*, p. 46.

ans of that traditional legal view of the constitution which again at the Restoration became the law of the land. As the best exponents of that view, Ferne and Digges deserve a more important place in the long history of constitutionalism than has been accorded them.

Neither of these writers confined his theories to the strictly legal and constitutional point of view he presented so well. Neither of them was content with the supremacy which the law allowed the king and which most Englishmen until quite recently had long accepted. Both of these theorists went beyond the law to history and to political thought to strengthen their arguments. Faced with the hard fact that the old law and constitution had failed to prevent Englishmen from fighting a civil war, Ferne and Digges instinctively craved real and basic unity in the English state, which they hoped to achieve by ascribing greater supremacy to the king than the law and constitution accorded him. Ferne sought this fuller supremacy by implication and perhaps unconsciously; Digges directly and very consciously.

Turning to early English history in order to refute the contention of some of his parliamentary opponents that the English government had been mixed and limited in its origins, Ferne maintained that the English monarch had possessed absolute power through the right of conquest until well after the Norman Conquest. In earlier ages the "Saxons made themselves masters of this Kingdome by Armes." [31] Theirs was a real conquest, not an expulsion. There is no proof that the Saxons in England continued to have that freedom which they might have had in Germany. The Saxons first set up seven kingdoms in England, and one of these eventually conquered the others. How then could you have an original mixture of government, as Hunton maintained, unless that mixture were in all seven? Throughout Saxon history, Ferne insisted, the government was monarchical, not popular or even mixed

[31] H. Ferne, *A Reply*, p. 22.

monarchy. The Saxon kingdom was finally subdued by William the Conqueror, a real conqueror who "disposed of the lands of the conquered, changed their tenure, and kept only what laws he pleased.[32] He did not, as Hunton maintained, succeed to the crown in the same right as the Saxon kings. After the Conquest, Ferne insisted, the king of England gradually "became a *Legall Monarch,* that is, bound himself to rule according to such Laws as he had graunted." [33] It was the monarch himself who granted the laws. Any limitation of his power came from his own will; and therefore, by implication at least, his will was sovereign. Ferne, however, was too ardent a constitutionalist to see clearly the full significance of his own remarks. He apparently failed to realize that the value of any legal limitations upon the king, in which he believed so sincerely, would tend to diminish and perhaps disappear if they proceeded only from the monarch's own will.

The brilliant young Digges, however, clearly grasped the concept of sovereignty which he may have learned from Hobbes's *De Cive* and injected it deliberately into many parts of his discussion. To Digges "That which makes a State one, is the union of supreame power, and this according as it is placed in one or more persons, gives determination to the forme." [34] In England the monarch possesses supreme power, as many acts of parliament testify, and therefore supremacy here is in the hands of one. His supremacy provides unity, and unified authority is absolutely essential in a state. If "there are divers supreame powers it is no longer one State." If subjects in a mixed monarchy may legally fight against the prince, as he interpreted (not too correctly) Hunton to assert, "this liberty makes two independent states, which are not compatible in one body, but would be as really distinct Kingdomes in *England,* as *Spaine* and *France* are . . ." [35] In order, therefore,

[32] *Ibid.,* p. 26.
[33] *Ibid.,* p. 27.
[34] D. Digges, *The Unlawfulnesse,* p. 65.
[35] Ibid., p. 68.

that England be recognized and preserved as one state, there should be no question concerning the complete supremacy of the king in government.

Thus, these two able royalist writers, who presented so well the legal and constitutional case for the king, did not consistently rest all of their case on the law and constitution. Although they are the outstanding exponents of constitutional ideals which they believed still shaped and determined the nature and functioning of the English government, they were not too sure that such ideals, which had served England well in the past, could entirely suffice to resolve the political realities England faced in the midst of civil war. Each found that the law and constitution were not entirely adequate for the present crisis, and each turned in part from constitutional to political arguments to justify the king's authority.

Digges at least was a keen enough thinker to see that in the last analysis it was rapidly becoming a question of sovereignty. If he had lived after 1643, this young, clear-headed champion of the king's cause, who loved the old and traditional but hated confusion and longed for unity, would probably have deserted the law and constitution entirely and advanced decisive political reasons for the complete sovereignty of the king. He died too soon for his thought to reach its full stature, yet he made a significant contribution to constitutional and political thought in these critical years. He merits a place with Ferne, his contemporary, for his clear presentation of the legal-constitutional authority of the king. He should also be grouped with Dickinson and Manwaring, his predecessors, and with Filmer, writing later, for all these men developed and advocated sovereignty of the king.

On the parliamentary side it was impossible for the cleverest pamphleteer or keenest thinker to present a completely legal case for parliament's resistance. Many legal arguments of Ferne and Digges and other royalists could not be answered on the basis of the law and constitution, and several of parliament's ablest supporters did not seriously attempt to do so. There was one man, however, who so analyzed and interpreted the English government on grounds for which there was strong legal and traditional support that he succeeded in demonstrating that parliament's powers were equal with the kings. Consequently, in his view, there could be no legal solution of the impasse. That writer was Philip Hunton, who, like Falkland and many others, was a moderate man hating civil war with all his heart. His hatred was not merely an emotion, for he saw the issue very clearly: "Engaged indeed I am to defend the Kings Supremacie against one part by my *Oath of Allegiance;* and engaged to defend the Priviledges of Parliament, and lawfull Liberties of the Subject, against the other part, by my *Protestation.*"[36]

Hunton is beginning to receive the recognition[37] he so justly deserves. He merits that recognition on three counts. It was he of all the writers in the sixteenth and seventeenth centuries who gave the best picture and keenest analysis of the English government as a true mixed monarchy; it was he who saw and explained more clearly than anyone else the constitutional and political dilemma into which this mixed monarchy had fallen in the civil war; and it was he who resolved that dilemma by ideas which Locke successfully employed forty-six years later. The clarity and penetration of Hunton's thought is particularly remarkable, since he wrote in the heat of conflict, not as a detached philosopher, but as one ardently loving the "liberty" of "his country."

Like most parliamentary supporters who theorized at all during the war years, Hunton gave some consideration to the origins of government, believing that God ordained that government should exist among men, but did not normally set up any one particular form of government. The institution of government often came about through the peoples' own action,

---

[36] [Philip Hunton], *A Vindication of the Treatise of Monarchy . . . ,* (London, 1644), Preface, A2v.

[37] See C. H. McIlwain, *Constitutionalism and the Changing World.*

receiving only indirectly the sanction and approval of God.[38] God did not bind men to a particular form of government "till they by their own Act bind themselves." [39] Hunton, however, was not primarily concerned with the condition of men before government existed. He did not explain how men established government but only stated that they possessed a *"virtuall radicall power* by publike consent and contract to constitute this or that forme of Government, and resigne up themselves to a condition of subjection on *Termes* and after a *form* of their owne constitution." [40] He believed that from the beginning the English government had been limited and mixed, but that a long process of development had gone on before its present form had been achieved. He recognized better than most of his contemporaries the part which development and change play in human institutions.

To him the essential fact about the English government was that it was both a limited and a mixed monarchy. As a limited ruler the king was a real monarch, yet he was truly limited, and limited in "the nature and measure of power," not just in the "exercise of it." The limitation of the king came from "outside" and was not, as Ferne and Digges maintained, a self-imposed limitation:

> He is then a limited Monarch, who hath a Law besides his owne will for the measure of his power. First, the supreme power of the State must be in him, so that his power must not be limited by any power above his; for then hee were not a Monarch, but a subordinate magistrate. Secondly, this supreme power must be restrained by some Law according to which this power was given, and by direction of which this power must act; else he were not a limited Monarch; i.e., a liege Soveraigne, or legall King.[41]

Moral limitation was not sufficient in a true limited monarchy. The limitation must be legal and civil.[42] Any acts of the mon-

[38] [Philip Hunton], *A Treatise of Monarchie*, (London, 1643), pp. 3–4.
[39] *Ibid.*, p. 3.   [40] P. Hunton, *A Vindication*, pp. 12–13.
[41] P. Hunton, *A Treatise of Monarchie*, p. 12.
[42] P. Hunton, *A Vindication*, p. 27.

arch within the real limits, i.e., within the "utmost extent of the Law of the Land" were binding and must not be resisted.[43]

In proving that the English monarch was limited, Hunton employed the usual arguments of the period, relying, for example, upon the king's oath to rule by law. Prescription was also cited as an excellent proof, for "In all ages, beyond record, the Lawes and Customes of the Kingdome have been the Rule of Government." [44] In the beginning "the Originall of the Subjects libertie was by those our forefathers brought out of *Germany*," [45] and according to Tacitus those early kings had limited power, though of a *"rude* and *unpolished"* form.[46] In Saxon times "this Limitation of Power and Libertie received some more *formall* and settled bounds afterwards by *customes* and *Lawes*." After the Norman Conquest, which was no real conquest, because the people voluntarily accepted William, the government "was perfected to this *Parliamentarie Forme;* and even this being at first but *rude,* grew to this *exactnesse* by length of Time, and infinite Contentions." [47] At the present time, he explained, the monarchy must act in a limited way because the king can judge only in courts of justice and can tax and make laws only with parliament's consent. Moreover, the monarchy is limited, because the king does not control the succession but is obliged to leave the crown "to whom the Fundamentall Law concerning that Succession hath designed it." [48]

In this discussion of limited monarchy, Hunton was essentially repeating with greater clarity than most writers the same ideas which Englishmen had long held concerning the nature of their government. Most of the royalists and all of the parliamentarians agreed that the monarch was limited, but they did not agree upon the source of the limitation. Hunton made

[43] P. Hunton, *A Treatise of Monarchie*, p. 14.
[44] *Ibid.*, p. 32.
[45] *Ibid.*, p. 35.
[46] P. Hunton, *A Vindication*, p. 36.
[47] *Ibid.*, p. 37.
[48] P. Hunton, *A Treatise of Monarchie*, p. 38.

it perfectly clear that true limitation must proceed from outside the monarch's will and thereby stated the case more clearly than most of his fellow parliamentarians either before or during the civil war.

Significant as Hunton's analysis of the nature of limitation in the English monarchy was, his contribution was greater when he analyzed the mixed nature of that monarchy. In England, he pointed out, the legislative power was not in the king alone, but in king, lords, and commons together; and "that Monarchy where the legislative power is in all three, is in the very Root and Essence of it compounded and mixed of those three; for that is the height of power, to which the other parts are subsequent and subservient." [49] It is, Hunton contended, perfectly possible for the supreme power to be mixed: ". . . to affirme severall *incomplete* independent powers concurring to make up one *integrall* mixt power, it is no absurdity at all." [50] Such a mixture is exactly the situation prevailing in the English government where laws can only be passed by the consent of all three partners in the mixed power. King, lords, and commons are truly co-ordinate partners. Each of them holds "equally from the fundamental Constitution; for if the power of one be originall, the other Derivative, it is no mixture." [51] No one of the three is supreme alone, but together the three are truly supreme, and therefore the supreme authority in England is mixed. The king-in-parliament is supreme over the king-out-of-parliament.

Hunton's contribution to constitutional and political thought was not that he was the first to assert the greater supremacy of the king-in-parliament over the king-out-of-parliament. Henry VIII is credited with stating that truth, and James Whitelocke had clearly proclaimed it in 1610.[52] Hunton, however, saw the full meaning of that supremacy as no one had earlier done. He recognized that if the king in parliament

[49] *Ibid.*, p. 40.
[50] P. Hunton, *A Vindication*, p. 15.
[51] P. Hunton, *A Treatise of Monarchie*, p. 25 and p. 40.
[52] See p. 86.

was supreme, then the supremacy was a mixed one, and the monarchy was in its nature mixed. He also perceived that the supremacy of king, lords, and commons was real supremacy, for to him legislation was the supreme act of government. He had read and understood Bodin. To him legislation included within its scope the power to make and to interpret the laws,[53] and also to deal with important matters concerning "the publike safety and weale." [54] Nor could any governing power of the king be independent of the legislative power, for "in the Governing Power, there is a confinement to the Fundamentall Common Lawes, and to the superstructive Statute Lawes, by the former concurrence of Powers enacted." [55]

Hunton's grasp of the all-pervading supremacy of legislation explains much of the uncertainty of earlier parliamentary thought. Unlike Hunton, most of the parliamentary leaders had not grasped the fact that legislation by its very nature was the supreme act of government, and that parliament, as the enacting body, possessed within itself ultimate control over the still-remaining absolute prerogatives of the crown. Since most parliamentarians failed to grasp the full meaning of legislative supremacy, so did naturally the more moderate royalists. Both Ferne and Digges made it a cardinal point in their theory that the king possessed considerable power outside of parliament, and consequently neither of them seems to have understood the nature of Hunton's mixed monarchy.

Whether Hunton or Ferne made the truer analysis of the nature of the English constitution is an important question, but one to which no categorical answer can be given. Support for the views of both can be found in English history and law. A main difference between Hunton and Ferne lies in the fact that Ferne did not grasp the fact that the legislative power was really supreme but insisted that it could exist alongside of other equally supreme powers not shared by the king with

[53] P. Hunton, *A Treatise of Monarchie*, p. 46.
[54] *Ibid.*, p. 48.
[55] *Ibid.*, p. 38.

parliament; whereas Hunton saw that the legislative power was truly supreme over all others. In the Middle Ages the supremacy of the legislative power had been growing, but it certainly had not been accepted as supreme over the independent rights of the king or subject. In the Tudor period that power had increased tremendously, but so had the independent prerogatives of the king and also some important rights of the subject. It may be argued that Ferne was stupid and old-fashioned in failing to admit the true legislative supremacy of the king-in-parliament, but he was in good company, as all the evidence shows that many thought like Ferne. There were few, if any, who seemed to see the situation as clearly as Hunton; but that fact only adds to his reputation, because it was high time that theory catch up with fact, that the legislative power of the king in parliament be understood in its true nature as really supreme. Hunton's grasp of that truth is one of his claims to greater recognition in English constitutional history and thought than is commonly accorded him.

He also deserves to be better known for a second, perhaps more important contribution: for his analysis of the dilemma which England faced in the civil war because of the nature of her limited and mixed monarchy. Normally that government, so Hunton argued, functioned excellently. The law restrained the king and, under most circumstances, the mixed legislative power adequately protected the subjects against the possible danger of a monarch becoming absolute.[56] In fact, to Hunton no better legal and structural devices could be worked out to resolve the insoluble problem of authority and liberty. He wanted no revolutionary change, only a preservation of the traditional and cherished form of government in his country.

Nevertheless, he clearly saw and frankly admitted that in this pattern of government there existed an important weakness which had resulted in civil war. In any form of government, he wrote, circumstances may arise for which no "legal" "remedy"

[56] *Ibid.*, p. 46.

exists. In a limited monarchy, it is impossible to erect a judge to determine whether or not the monarch has kept within his legal limits. If you make the king that judge, you make him absolute, "for to define a Power to a Law, and then to make him Judge of his Deviations from that Law, is to absolve him from all Law." That is what Dr. Ferne had done, according to Hunton, and on that theoretical basis he criticized Ferne. If you make the people that judge, you destroy the real meaning or essence of monarchy. If you make a foreigner that judge, you "lose the freedome of the State." For these reasons "I conceive in a limited legall Monarchy, there can be no stated internall Judge of the Monarchs actions, if there grow a fundamentall Variance betwixt him and the Community." It is impossible to constitute "a Judge to determine this last controversie, *viz*, the Soveraignes transgressing his fundamentall limits." [57] Likewise, in a mixed monarchy "there can be no Constituted, Legall, Authoritative Judge of the fundamentall Controversies arising betwixt the three Estates. . . . For the established being of such authority, would *ipso facto* overthrow the Frame, and turne it into absoluteness." [58]

In this dispute now raging in England the question really is "which of the three Estates hath the power of ultime and supreme judicature by Vote or sentence to determine it against the other; so that the People are bound to rest in that determination, and accordingly to give their assistance, *eo nomine*, because it is by such Power so noted and declared?" [59] To ask this question, i.e., "to demand which Estate may challenge this power of finall determination of Fundamental controversies arising betwixt them is to demand which of them shall be absolute." [60] Hunton condemned Ferne because Ferne, in giving final judgment to the king, had really made him absolute. He also condemned the solution reached by Herle in the *Fuller Answer*. Herle gave the final and sovereign judg-

[57] *Ibid.*, p. 17.
[58] *Ibid.*, pp. 28–29.
[59] *Ibid.*, p. 68.
[60] *Ibid.*, p. 69.

ment to the two houses, emphatically stating that their decision bound the people. "Good Lord!" Hunton ejaculated concerning both Ferne's and Herle's solution, "What extream opposition is between these two sorts of men? If the maintenance of these extremes be the ground of this warre, then our Kingdome is miserable, and our Government lost which side soever overcome." Herle had given to the two houses, Hunton showed, that power "which ere while they would not suffer, when the Judges in the case of Ship-money had given it to the King." [61] Moreover, "the reason of the two Houses divided from the King is not the reason of the Kingdome, for it is not the Kings reason, who is the head and chiefe in the Kingdome." A monarchical form of government had been established in England, and once established the people were "not at liberty to resolve againe: Or to assume a supreme power of judging, distructive to the frame of Government they have established, and restrained themselves unto . . . in this frame, the Houses could not be ordained a legall Tribunall to passe Judgement in this last case: for then the Architects by giving them that Judicature, had subordinated the King to them and so had constituted no Monarchie!" [62] To erect a judge was to establish an absolute government different in nature from the government England had long known. The judge, whether the king or the two houses, would be sovereign, and the supremacy would no longer rest in the mixed parliament composed of king, lords, and commons. In the clarity and steadfastness with which Hunton admitted the impossibility of any legal constitutional solution of the impasse which had been reached by king and parliament, he made his second great contribution to thought in these troubled years, for no one else either saw or dared to state the facts so dispassionately.

If Hunton was right in his claim that England was a true limited and mixed monarchy, then he was right that no legal judge could be constituted to pass legally upon the impasse when the king broke the law and the three partners in the

[61] *Ibid.*, p. 70.   [62] *Ibid.*, p. 71.

supremacy failed to agree. If he was right, then the royalists like Ferne and Digges were wrong in claiming that their actions in supporting the king were completely legal. Their actions were not legal, nor were those of the parliamentarians, since neither was justified by the constitution which made king, lords, and commons co-ordinate. Both were illegal, for both had forgotten the fundamental truth that king and people had always been joined insolubly together in the English polity. It is to Hunton's great credit that he recognized that the king was part of the state and also that the people were. The royalists tended to forget the people, and the more ardent parliamentarians, the king. After 1642 some of the latter did a good job in removing the king from the state altogether. Hunton steadfastly stood his ground, insisting that king and people together constituted the state of England. If that truth had not always been clearly written into English law, it certainly had been the assumption upon which the greatest of English monarchs had shaped their political policies. The fact that the Stuarts forgot that truth is one basic reason for the civil war.

Even though Hunton insisted that the constitution provided no legal way of resolving the issue, he himself supported parliament and urged others to do so. The judgment of the two houses, he said, is better than the judgment of private men, for it is made "by the best eyes of the Kingdom." [63] Private men should therefore be guided by that judgment. Although the militia ordinance "is not formally legall, yet it is eminently legall, justified by the very intent of the Architects of the Government, when for these uses they committed the Armes to the King." [64] Because the houses were acting to preserve and save, he justified their action and urged all to support it. Though he hated war, he was willing to fight, for "we may buy an immunity too deare, at the prize of a subversion of Religion, Lawes and Government, which is the case in dis-

[63] *Ibid.*, p. 73.
[64] *Ibid.*, pp. 62–63.

pute." [65] In his zeal for the parliament's cause, Hunton occasionally spoke as if its actions were legal.[66] Nevertheless, he always insisted that no "authoritative" judge could exist. Each person in deciding what course of action he was to follow was not exercising any "Formall Authoritative Power" but was following "the evidence of Truth in his own Soule." ". . . the fundamentall Lawes of that Monarchy must judge and pronounce the sentence in every mans conscience." [67] In theory it is as if the bands of society were dissolved, and a state of nature again existed. It actually is war because organized government has failed.[68]

In this simple but accurate picture of the individual moral judgment each man must make, Hunton made another significant contribution to thought—one which his fellow parliamentarians could not accept, and the royalists scorned. To Henry Parker and Charles Herle, thinking politically rather than constitutionally upon the problem, Hunton's solution of the dilemma was too judiciously moderate. To Robert Filmer his whole book was "a better piece of Poetry then Policy." [69] To John Locke, however, as Professor McIlwain has shown,[70] Hunton's analysis and solution of the dilemma

[65] P. Hunton, *A Vindication*, p. 9.
[66] P. Hunton, *A Treatise of Monarchie*, p. 67.
[67] *Ibid.*, p. 18.
[68] *A Vindication*, p. 69. Although Hunton did support the parliamentary cause, I cannot entirely agree with Mr. Fink who says that "In Hunton's hands, then, the theory of mixed government became a justification of resistance to the royal will." Z. S. Fink, *The Classical Republicans*, (Northwestern University Studies, Evanston), p. 26. Hunton's arguments in favor of resistance were, in my judgment, less convincing than many others set forth during these years of war because Hunton so carefully, as has been shown, denied the legality of resistance in a limited, mixed monarchy. The views of Charles Herle, similar on the surface to those of Hunton, did become "a justification of resistance to the royall will."
[69] R. Filmer, *The Anarchy of a Limited or Mixed Monarchy* . . . , 1648, p. 26. In 1683, when ideas of divine right were running strong at Oxford, the university decreed that Hunton's *Treatise of Monarchie* should be burned because the author claimed that the three estates of the realm were sovereign.
[70] C. H. McIlwain, *Constitutionalism and the Changing World.*

provided a key for his own thinking. Writing almost a half century later, in the midst of another revolution, Locke was quick to appreciate, and almost certainly to appropriate, Hunton's analysis of the way men and society must act when government fails. Perhaps Hunton, a modest man and a lover of his country's liberty, would ask no greater recognition than the tribute paid him when his idea was taken over by this later thinker so influential in shaping the constitutional and democratic ideas of men in the western world.

Philip Hunton was a brilliant constitutional thinker, ahead of his contemporaries in recognizing the true nature of mixed monarchy in England. Had James or Charles and their advisers accepted an analysis similar to his and fashioned their policies accordingly, England might have been spared a civil war, a Restoration, and a Revolution of 1688. It would have been a herculean achievement in political statesmanship to translate the legal supremacy of king, lords, and commons into an effective, harmonious, and co-operative government of these partners in the supremacy. There is little reason for believing that either James or Charles was capable of such leadership and co-operation. Whether their opponents in the lords and commons would have acted with true statesmanship is an unanswerable question, for they were never given the opportunity to co-operate as equal partners with the king.

On the other hand, before they had the chance to share supremacy with the king, their more aggressive leaders had actually gone beyond the point of asking for mere co-operation; they now desired to control the king and to be supreme themselves. In their struggle to keep the king within the limitations of the law, they had learned that the old sanctions of law were inadequate, (at least against James and Charles), that Hunton's limited monarch too often broke the legal bounds by which he was limited, and that new and more effective sanctions must be devised—in short, that legal limitation without political control did not work. They had also learned that they would really like to govern the country, not only to share in the making and administration of policy with the king, but to determine it themselves. The divergence between their own and the monarch's views on religion and foreign policy had made them desire, not to share government with him in a mixed monarchy such as Hunton's, but to shape the king's policies according to their own views. The more aggressive leaders had really gone beyond the limited and mixed monarchy described and prescribed by Hunton; they wanted the king controlled as well as limited; and they wanted to be the leaders, not mere partners, in the mixture.

None of the aggressive leaders ever stated their case in the above language. Most of them certainly did not comprehend the full meaning of the tactics and ideas with which they had battled the crown for forty years. Those who lived into the period after the death of Charles were glad to return to a limited balanced monarchy on the old pattern as the best security against dictatorship and military rule. Nevertheless, when in the sixteen-twenties, Coke and Phelips, and Eliot and Pym, began to push against the crown, aggressively seeking a greater share and control in government, they initiated a pattern of thought and policy which did not end with the civil war, or even with the Revolution of 1688, but went on until the house of commons finally came to govern the nation. Consequently, Hunton's legal and constitutional views were really outdated for the more aggressive politically minded parliamentary leaders before he wrote his *Treatise of Monarchie*. Although he was ahead of most Englishmen in recognizing the true supremacy of king, lords, and commons, already he could be classified as a moderate conservative by Henry Parker and Charles Herle. These political pamphleteers and a few others in the period of civil war put into words and worked out theories justifying the more extreme claims of aggressive parliamentary leaders. In the writings of Parker and Herle the full meaning of the arguments and ideas parliament had been developing so long became explicit and clear.

Hunton was a constitutional thinker, and a very good one. Parker and Herle were poor constitutionalists, but first-rate political thinkers. They justified the position parliament now claimed in the state in the only way it could rationally be supported by turning from constitutional to political thought. They grasped the basic political realities of their own age and constructed their political theories accordingly. With this realistic approach they made four outstanding contributions to the development of constitutional and political thought in England. In the first place, Parker and Herle understood the legal and constitutional problems parliament had faced in trying to limit the king and gave clear and decisive political answers to them. In the second place, they recognized that parliament had pushed its aggressive claims in government by claiming to speak for the nation, and they supported those claims by a mature and well-integrated theory of government resting on popular consent. In the third place, they were convinced that England needed a unified, not a divided government, and had the intelligence and courage to claim sovereign power for the lords and commons in parliament. Finally, they knew well the implications of the ideas they advanced and accepted their consequences, even though in so doing they had to abandon many age-old beliefs and assumptions and rest their case on new and untried forces and sanctions.

Of the two, Henry Parker was the greater thinker. He wrote first, and on many topics his views were more searching than Herle's. Herle, however, is worthy of recognition, and his views upon some problems more penetrating than Parker's. Although their ideas are not identical, they have enough in common to make it possible to discuss them together.

Their first great contribution to the thinking of this period lay in their analysis of the legal and constitutional problems parliament had faced in trying to limit the king, and in the way they resolved that constitutional impasse. Both of them clearly recognized and frankly admitted that the law had failed —had proved inadequate to limit the king and justify the claims of parliament. "Nothing," Parker wrote, "has done us more harme of late, then this opinion of adhering to Law only for our preservation." [71] "I wish we had not observed Law too farre, for they would never so farre recommend it to us, did they not know it might be sometimes unseasonable." [72] How ridiculous and futile it is when a royalist admits that we Englishmen "are Borne to liberty and safety as our right, yet grants no means to attaine to that right, nor remedy to recover it, except the King's grace. . . ." [73] Laws are not enough in and of themselves. They "may be imployed either to the benefit or prejudice of any Nation, . . . No Nation can be free without a three-fold priviledge: The first is in the framing and passing of Lawes. The second is in declaring and interpreting Lawes. And the third is in executing and preserving Laws in force . . ." [74] "No Nation can injoy any freedom but by the right and share which it has in the Lawes, and if that right and share does not extend to the preservation of Lawes in their true vigour and meaning, as well as to the Creation of them, t'is emptie and defeasible at the Kings meere pleasure . . ." [75] At this particular time, parliament desires and needs greater security than mere known laws.

Herle agreed that the law was not adequate. What good, he asked, are established laws and oaths? [76] "Can a Law never so well established tye those hands from tyranny, in which there is a power able to hinder its execution, nay finall declaration to be any Law at all." [77] If the king has power to break the law, there never can be any security. The only remedy can be to

[71] [H. Parker], *The Contra Replicant, his Complaint to His Majestie* . . . , (London, 1642), p. 19.
[72] *Ibid.*, p. 20.
[73] [Henry Parker], *The Cordiall of Mr. David Jenkins: or his Reply to H. P.* . . . answered, (London, 1647), pp. 8–9.
[74] H. Parker, *The Contra Replicant*, pp. 5–6.
[75] *Ibid.*, p. 7.
[76] [C. Herle], *A fuller Answer to a Treatise Written by Doctor Ferne, entituled The Resolving of Conscience upon this question* . . . , (London, 1642), p. 15.
[77] [Charles Herle], *Ahab's fall by his Prophets Flatteries* . . . , (London, 1644), p. 36.

place sufficient power in other hands to control him adequately.

According to Parker, the government must be constructed from the beginning with that objective in view. In his examination of the origins of government, he found that from the moment government and laws had been instituted among men the problem had arisen of how to handle magistrates who abused the laws. " 'Twas not difficult to invent Lawes, for the limitting of supreme governors, but to invent how those lawes should be executed or by whom interpreted was almost impossible, *nam quis custodiat ipsos custodes*: To place a superior above a supreme, was held unnaturall, yet what a livelesse fond thing would Law be without any Judge to determine it, or power to enforce it . . ." [78] In England the problem had been solved by constituting parliament as that determining judge and that sanctioning power. In normal times both king and parliament functioned according to law, but in extraordinary times like this one through which the country was passing there must be a final judge. Moreover, there must be a judge not only of law, but "In matters of Law and State both, where ambiguity is, some determination must be supreame." [79] Parker tried to show that the law gave that final determination to parliament,[80] but he was more convincing when he frankly abandoned legal arguments and resorted to political. A sovereign could only be effectively checked in governments where bodies like parliament had been "erected to poyze against the scale of Sovereignty." [81]

In *Jus Populi*, Parker's most philosophical pamphlet, written in 1644, this theorist again discussed the same great problem of effectively limiting kings. "Bounds are set," he wrote, "by God and Nature, to the greatest and most absolute Monarchs, as well as to the least, and most conditionate: but those

[78] [Henry Parker], *Observations upon some of his Majesties late Answers and Expresses*, (London, 1642), pp. 13–14. Reprinted in W. Haller, *Tracts on Liberty*, II, 165–215.
[79] *Ibid.*, p. 36.
[80] Ibid., pp. 43–44.   [81] *Ibid.*, p. 14.

Bounds seem but as imaginary Lines, or as meer stones, not reall Trenches, or Fortifications: They serve onely to discover to the Subject what his Right is, but they have no strength at all to protect him from wrong." [82] Human institutions, such as parliaments, are the only adequate protection. Human beings need more than law, even more than divine and natural law; they need human institutions, such as parliaments, to provide the necessary sanction behind law.

Herle reached the same conclusion as Parker concerning the place and power of parliament in the government if the limitation of the king was to be really effective, but he arrived at this belief by a somewhat different approach. Herle, like Hunton, stated that the English government was a mixed monarchy, and that "this mixture or Coordination is in the very supremacy of power itself." [83] The people were "a *coordinate part* in the *Monarchy,* or highest principle of power, in as much as they beare a *consenting* share in the *highest office* of it, the *making* of *Lawes.*" [84] The fact that the people today play such an important part in the English government constituted, in Herle's opinion, proof enough that they must have co-operated in setting up the form of government in the beginning. Because of the nature of the present government, it must have come into being in that form, and Herle stoutly maintained that it had. The fundamental law of that government was not something vague and general, but a thing of structure. It "is that originall *frame* of this coordinate government of the three *estates* in Parliament consented to, and contrived by the people in its first *constitution,* and since in every severall raigne confirm'd both by mutuall Oathes betweene King and people, and constant custome time (as we say) *out of mind,* which with us amounts to a *Law.*" [85]

[82] [H. Parker], *Jus Populi or a Discourse wherein clear satisfaction is given as well concerning the Right of Subjects, as the Right of Princes,* (London, 1644), p. 51.
[83] C. Herle, *A Fuller Answer,* p. 3.
[84] *Ibid.,* p. 14.
[85] *Ibid.,* p. 8.

In Herle's emphasis upon the co-ordination of king and people he resembled Hunton, but, unlike Hunton, he was not primarily interested in the constitutional meaning of this mixed co-ordinate supremacy. Herle was concerned with its political purpose. The co-ordination existed in order that the people might be safe against any arbitrary power of the king. "Now the end or purpose of this mixture of the three *estates* in this government, 'tis the *safety* of it's *safety,* as all government aymes at *safety,* so this temper in it at the making this *safety* more safe or sure: The common interest of the whole body of the Kingdome in Parliament, thus twisted with the Kings, makes the *Cable* of its *Anker* of safety, stronger." [86] On the basis of this concept Herle justified parliament's resistance to the king, but the discussion of that topic will be postponed until the views of a third pamphleteer on the question of how to limit the king effectively are examined.

Whoever the author of the short pamphlet *Touching the Fundamentall Lawes or Politique Constitution of this King-dome* [87] may be, he is one of the half dozen clearest and most profound thinkers supporting the claims of parliament during the years of civil war. On the basic question of adequate ways of limiting the king, his analysis and solution of the problem was more penetrating in some respects than Parker's or Herle's. He wrote:

> Fundamental lawes are not (or at least need not be) any written agreement like Meare stones, between King and People, the King himselfe being a part (not party) in those Laws, and the Commonwealth not being like a Corporation treated by Charter, but treating itselfe. But the fundamental Law or Laws is a setling of the laws of nature and common equity (by common consent) in such a *forme of Polity and Government,* as that they may be administered amongst us with honour and safety. For the first of which therefore, we are governed by a King: and for the second, by a Parliament, to oversee and take order that that honourable trust that is

[86] Ibid., pp. 7–8.
[87] London, 1643.

put into the hands of the King for the dignity of the Kingdome, be rightly executed, and not abused to the alteration
of the Politique Constitution taken up and approved, or to
the destruction of that, for whose preservation it was ordered and intended. . . . Fundamentall Lawes then are not
things of capitulation between King and people, as if they
were Forrainers and Strangers one to another (nor ought
they or any other Laws so to be, for then the King should
govern for himselfe, not for his people) but they are *things
of constitution,* treating such a relation, and giving such an
existence and being by an *externall polity* to King and Subjects, as Head and Members, which constitution in the very
being of it is a Law held forth with more evidence, and written in the very heart of the Republique, farre firmlyer than
can be by pen and paper . . .[88]

Thus in our government "there is not onely a common right,
but also a *particular and lawfull power* joyned with this right
for its maintenance and supportation."[89]

In these remarkable words an important transition from
medieval to modern thought was made. The medieval belief
that the law limited the king was proclaimed; but the medieval faith that law by its very nature could provide an effective
limitation was abandoned. The medieval language "fundamental law" was kept; but the fundamental law was defined
in terms of a "form of government" in which "lawful power"
was provided in order to keep the king within the bounds of
law.

This unknown pamphleteer, as well as Herle and Parker,
had come to see and admit that the law was not adequate to
guarantee the rights and liberties of the people—that power
was also essential. This power he gave to the people in parliament because the people were the source of power and their
welfare and safety was the supreme law. Englishmen could
only be secured against the king's misuse of authority when
parliament possessed the power to limit and control him. In

[88] *Ibid.,* pp. 3–4. The italics are my own, to emphasize the character of
the thought.
[89] *Ibid.,* p. 5. Italics are mine.

the constitutional conflict going on between 1603 and 1642, the parliamentary cause had at one time been argued on the basis of law, at another on the basis of parliament's responsibility to the nation for its welfare and safety. The first argument had been essentially legal, the second political. Until at least 1641, however, the legal arguments had been the most numerous, because they were the most convincing to Englishmen steeped in law and tradition, and never to my knowledge had parliamentarians before 1642 openly admitted that the law was inadequate, and that political as well as legal sanctions were necessary. It is to the credit of Parker, Herle, and this unknown pamphleteer that they admitted (reluctantly it is true) the inadequacy of the law and openly proposed political control by the nation in parliament as the only effective way to restrain monarchs who broke the law. They set forth this truth in 1642 and 1643, almost a half century before it became a historical reality as a result of the Revolution of 1688, but the time elapsing between the enunciation of the idea and its achievement as an historical fact serves only to increase the stature of these men who first clearly recognized the failure of legal and the necessity of political controls.

In exalting parliament's power, these writers, particularly Parker and Herle, turned to the people as the final authority justifying such great power. In the earlier decades of the century when parliamentary leaders had pushed their claims against the king, they had done it in the name of the nation and had occasionally talked of the power of the people; but these early leaders, who were men of action and politicians rather than writers and theorists, had never been interested (nor perhaps prepared) to support these claims by a real theory of government resting on popular consent. Puritan preachers and writers had also appealed to the people and their God-given conscience against the claims of kings, but they had not produced in the years of outward peace any well-developed theory of the place of the people in government. Only after all men knew that a civil war was upon them did such theories appear. On July 2, 1642, there was published Parker's *Observations upon some of his Majesties late Answers and Expresses*— a powerful tract in which the author rested the parliament's case squarely upon the power of the people. He was the first writer at this time to state a real theory of government based on popular consent, and consistently in his later writings he made the consent of the people a basic and organic part of his theories, thereby making a significant contribution to the development of democratic thought in England. Despite his early enunciation of the theory, Parker was not alone or in a small select company of men in advocating democratic ideas. During the years of civil war a large number of writers turned to the people as the final authority in government, and some of these theorists proved to be better democrats than Parker or Herle, for they did not assume that parliament spoke for the people. John Lilburne, Richard Overton, and other Levellers actually went from parliament to the people themselves for the final sanction in government. They are the writers in whose works the full meaning of parliament's earlier appeal to the nation is first truly realized. Because Parker detested and denounced Leveller ideas, he might not wish any credit for his own part in furthering democratic thought, but from a historical point of view he can not escape such recognition.

When in July, 1642, Parker made his bold appeal to the people, he sounded the most radical democratic note which had yet been uttered by a speaker or writer supporting parliament's cause.[90] "Power," he wrote at the beginning of his *Observations,* "is originally inherent in the people, and there is nothing else but that might and vigour which such or such a societie of men containes in itselfe, and when by such or such a Law of common consent and agreement it is derived into such and such hands, God confirmes that Law: and so man is the free and voluntary Author, the Law is the Instrument, and

[90] Parker himself had earlier in 1642 looked to the people as the basis for parliament's claims. See his *Some Few observations upon his Majesties late Answer to the Declaration or Remonstrance of the Lords and Commons* (London, 1642).

God is the establisher of both." [91] Both the king's and the parliament's authority rested on this power of the people. Since the king's authority depended upon the peoples', it should be used for their welfare and not for their harm.[92] The parliament's power also rested on the people; but since parliament was truly the "essence" [93] of the people, its actions, even against the king and law, could not be questioned, for it was acting for the welfare of all.

In Parker's later pamphlets, written between 1642 and 1644, he set forth a comprehensive and integrated theory of government resting on popular consent. Starting with the traditional concept of the fall of man because of Adam's sin, he painted a picture of man's existence before government arose which Hobbes himself might well have drawn, so dark, gloomy, and miserable was man's condition shown to be. Government, therefore, arose primarily because of sheer human need. "Necessitie," was the "main ground and end of Policie." [94] As human necessity was the main cause for the origin of government, so human consent was the most vital factor in its origin and continuance. Although Parker paid lip service to God's traditional part in setting up government among men, he insisted that "when wee are treating of worldly affaires, wee ought to be very tender how wee seek to reconcile that to God's law, which we cannot reconcile to man's equity: or how we make God the author of that constitution which man reaps inconvenience from." [95] To depend only upon the Scriptures "to discern what that supreme power is in all Countries" [96] was not recommended by this up-to-date theorist whose views took more account of man than of God.

Above all, Parker wished to show *"that Princes were created by the people, for the peoples sake, and so limited by ex-*

[91] H. Parker, *Observations*, p. 1.
[92] *Ibid.*, p. 3.
[93] *Ibid.*, p. 5.
[94] H. Parker, *Jus Populi*, p. 43.
[95] *Ibid.*, p. 57.
[96] *Ibid.*, p. 67.

presse Laws as that they might not violate the peoples liberty." [97] Princes, being created for the subjects' good, should act as servants of the people. Since their prince's power came from the people and was always conditioned by their needs, there could be no sound justification for absolute monarchy. ". . . no Nation yet ever did voluntarily or compulsorily embrace servitude." [98] In England, to be specific, it was the lords and commons in parliament who were "vertually the whole Nation" or people by whose "consent Royalty itselfe was first founded," and for whose ends "Royalty itselfe was so qualified and tempered as it is." In fact "both Kings and laws were first formed and created by such bodyes of men, as our Parliaments now are." [99] Government in England was established by the people (in parliament), and the people had never lost their basic authority. The Norman rule did not, Parker contended, rest merely upon conquest, but upon "the voluntary compliance of the English." At that time the English voluntarily transferred *"Heralts* right" to William.[100]

Parker's emphasis upon popular consent as the basis of government, and upon the welfare of the people as the guide for government's policies, provided him with ample justification for parliament's stand in 1642 and succeeding years. Charles's authority had come from the people and should always be directed towards their welfare. He had been trusted with much and had betrayed that great trust. In refusing to be guided by the advice of parliament he had deserted his people whose welfare was now guarded by the two houses of parliament. In normal times the people are best served when king, lords, and commons jointly rule, but "where this ordinary course cannot be taken for the preventing of publike mischiefs, any extraordinary course that is for that purpose the most

[97] *Ibid.,* p. 2.
[98] *Ibid.,* p. 66. In *Jus Populi* he cited Plato, Cicero, and Aquinas as leading authorities supporting his views of the importance of the people in government (pp. 26–29).
[99] H. Parker, *The Contra Replicant,* p. 16.
[100] *Jus Populi,* p. 14.

effectual may justly be taken." [101] Parliament's action in this crisis is correct, because it is in accord with the purpose of government: the welfare of the people. To Parker, essentially a realistic political thinker and not a constitutionalist, first things came first. The welfare of the people was the first consideration in any government, it was the "Paramount Law that shall give Law to all humane Laws whatsoever." [102]

When Charles Herle justified the action taken by parliament in the civil war, he did not approach the problem in as simple and straightforward a way as Parker did. Herle never set forth a clear-cut theory of government resting on popular consent. He did imply, however, that in England government had risen through the "consent of both King and People." [103] In the institution of government, therefore, king and people were co-ordinate. Such a concept might well have led Herle, as it did Hunton, to insist on the legal equality of the king, lords, and commons. Herle, however, was not primarily concerned with the mixed nature of government in England, but with the purpose of that mixture. Lords and commons had power co-ordinate with the king in order that they might limit him and prevent him from becoming arbitrary. Their action in the present crisis was correct because they were acting according to their original responsibility. Lords and commons had originally been made co-ordinate with the king, and that mixture originally set up lived on. So also "that *Reason* or *wisdome* of *State* that first *contriv'd* it dies not neither, it lives still in that which the Law calls the *Reason* of the *Kingdome*, the *Votes* and *Ordinances* of *Parliament,* which being the same (in the construction of the Law) with that which first *contriv'd* the *government,* must needs have still power to *apply* this *co-ordination* of the *government* to it's end *safety,* as well as it had at first to *introduce* it; otherwise it should not still continue in the *office* of a meane to it's *end.* Here in our present

[101] *Observations,* p. 16.
[102] *Ibid.,* p. 3.
[103] C. Herle, *A Fuller Answer,* p. 4.

case the necessity of applying this *coordination* or *mixture* of the government is *imminence of danger . . .*" [104] Since the king has refused to pass the militia bill which the two houses advise him is necessary to save the state, "the same ever-living *reason* of the State that first advis'd the government," must act.[105] Their present action was correct, Herle maintained, because it was in accord with the original purpose of government in England. In this emphasis upon purpose as justifying parliament's actions, Herle agreed with Parker, although he never set forth a complete theory of government resting on popular consent.

Herle even maintained that parliament's resistance was "legal," i.e., according to the original law and constitution. When the king would not act to save the state, then the people in parliament might act alone, against the king's personal wishes, because the constitution provided and allowed for resistance by parliament.[106] The people set up government and gave to parliament the legal constitutional right to resist the king.

Herle's emphasis upon resistance and upon the purpose of the co-ordination of king and people reveals the essentially political character of his thought in contrast to Hunton's. Herle set forth an analysis of the English government which resembled Hunton's in some respects. Hunton, however, remained a constitutionalist, accepting logically the legal consequences of his interpretation of the English government as a mixed monarchy; whereas Herle shifted his ground from the constitutional to the political, resting the constitution and structure of the government on the political power of the people and giving the people (in parliament) the power to resist the king in any crisis.

On this vital question of resistance, the anonymous author of the pamphlet *Touching the Fundamental Lawes* had some-

[104] *Ibid.*, p. 8.
[105] *Ibid.*, p. 9.
[106] *Ibid.*, p. 25.

thing significant to say. He maintained that it was part of the fundamental law itself, which he defined as a thing of structure, that the king assent at all times to laws enacted by parliament. He did not distinguish, as both Parker and Herle did, between normal and extraordinary times. The king did not have a negative voice in government. ". . . the King is juridically and according to the intention of the law in his Courts, so that what the Parliament consults for the publick good, That by oath, and the duty of his office, and nature of this polity, he is to consent unto, and in case he do deny it, yet in the construction and fundamentall law and constitution of this Kingdom, he is conceived to grant it . . ." [107] If he personally refuse to consent, "this hinders not but that they who have as fundamentally reserved a power of being and well being in their own handes by the concurrence of Parliamentary authority to the royall dignity, may thereby provide for their own subsistence, wherein is acted the Kings juridicall authority though his personall pleasure be withheld . . ." [108]

Because the author of this pamphlet defined so carefully the nature of fundamental law, he was able to present a more logical case than either Parker or Herle could for the actual legality of parliament's actions in the existing crisis, for in his definition of fundamental law he had included both the right and a power to maintain that right. Consequently, this pamphleteer, like Parker and Herle, actually rested his case upon the authority of the lords and commons in government, and not upon any traditional or accepted law.

The three theorists considered here had turned from the law to the people (in parliament) to justify parliament's actions. As their emphasis had shifted, so had their ideas concerning the nature of law and its place in the English polity. In the first decades of the century, Englishmen normally looked upon law as primary—as more basic than the actions of mere men in government. Very few had realized the im-

[107] *Touching the Fundamentall Lawes*, p. 9.
[108] *Ibid.*, p. 11.

portance of making law. Herle, however, clearly saw that the supremacy in government "consists not in *declaring* law, . . . 'tis the making of law the supremacy especially consists." [109] ". . . that is the highest Act of Government." [110] In the period before the civil war, Magna Carta had been regarded by the parliamentarians and by some royalists as the particular embodiment in England of an all pervading basic law. To Parker, however, Magna Carta was more human and earthly. It belongs "to us as we are living and sociable creatures." [111] To Parker also, in striking contrast to earlier English thinkers, law was not always the best guide for state life, requiring by its very foundations and nature, decision and discretion on the part of men guiding and controlling government. "Lawes ayme at *Justice,* Reason of state aymes at safety; . . . reason of State goes beyond all particular formes and pacts, and looks rather to the being, then well-being of a State. . . . Reason of State is something more sublime and imperiall then law: it may be rightly said that the Statesman begins where the lawyer ceaseth." [112]

With Parker and Herle the older medieval idea of law had gone, and the more modern one of man's human needs and his part in government had come to play a leading role in their thinking. As their ideas of man pushed older ideas of law into the background, so also their ideas of man removed God from the central place in human affairs so long accorded Him. The convenience of man and the equity of man were, so Parker maintained, more important in considering "worldly affaires" [113] than vague and general ideas of God's law. Although Herle was a clergyman, he, in common with some of his fellow Puritans, did not believe that God operated

[109] C. Herle, *An Answer to Doctor Ferne's Reply* . . . , (London, 1643), p. 20.
[110] C. Herle, *Ahab's Fall,* p. 40.
[111] [H. Parker], *Animadversions Animadverted* . . . , p. 2. It is not certain that Parker was the author of this tract. The tract was first published in London in 1642. I believe Parker was the author of it.
[112] H. Parker, *The Contra Replicant,* pp. 18–19.
[113] H. Parker, *Jus Populi,* p. 57.

directly in the institution of government. *"Divinity,"* he wrote, "gives onely generall rules of obedience to all lawful authority, tels us not where that authority is, as in its adaequat subject, or how tempered or qualified either in this of *England,* or any other government." [114] The "form and limitation" of government was an act of man, or, as he said, an "act of the will, and so Arbitrary." [115] Herle admitted that God's laws were unalterable, but he always interpreted those laws to suit the needs of man. He easily turned Romans 13, that oft-debated passage of scripture, to his own purpose. The power that is ordained by God to be obeyed, he insisted, is that to which man has consented, and in England that is the supreme power in parliament.[116] God did not interfere in the constitution or form of government. That institution was an act of man. Scripture came to Herle's assistance when he wished to demonstrate the value of many advisers in a kingdom. On the title page of his second pamphlet against Ferne is a citation from Proverbs 11, 14: "In the multitude of Councellours there is safety." That kings need many councillors and good councillors was the theme of his sermon on Ahab, whom he pictured as suffering from the wicked advice given by his bad councillors.

With both Herle and Parker, a real departure was made from those older ideas which had long conditioned and tempered Englishmen's views upon their polity and their politics. In the thoughts of these writers, the transition from the medieval to the modern became explicit. With them the pendulum definitely swung away from God and His law, reaching down and guiding man, towards man and his concerns and actions as the central and guiding force in state life.

In no respect was this change more apparent than in relation to their views upon the need for real sovereign power in government, and the arguments by which they demonstrated

[114] C. Herle, *An Answer,* p. 3.
[115] C. Herle, *A Fuller Answer,* p. 17.
[116] *Ibid.,* pp. 22–23. By parliament, he really means the two houses.

that such power could be exercised safely in human society. Among the many supporters of parliament's cause in the years between 1603 and 1649, it was Henry Parker who first clearly grasped and set forth the concept of parliamentary sovereignty. Herle also, but several months later than Parker, saw the need for sovereign power and gave it to parliament, explaining and justifying it by a well-integrated theory. During the years between 1642 and 1649, many men produced theories of government resting on popular consent, but comparatively few attributed real sovereignty either to parliament representing the people or to the people themselves.[117] By their frank realistic grasp and enunciation of this concept of parliamentary sovereignty, both Parker and Herle stood head and shoulders above most of the parliamentary theorists of the period. In setting forth this theory, they made their third significant contribution to the political thought of this period.

To proclaim a concept of sovereignty was desperately hard for most men, whether they were royalists or parliamentarians, during the whole first half of the seventeenth century. Among royalist supporters of the crown, both lay and clerical, the concept of sovereignty was rare; and among their parliamentary opponents it was never clearly stated, except possibly by Whitelocke, before Parker's *Observations*. To advance such a concept it was necessary, in the first place, that men recognize clearly and accept unequivocally the fact that England had become a united state, one in which political power was truly supreme over all competing feudal, regional, and ecclesiastical authorities within the land. Today it is natural for us, who so easily accept the supremacy of the political, to see that Tudor England had become a sovereign state. It was infinitely more difficult for men living in the first half of the seventeenth century to grasp this truth, for in their intellectual heritage there had been no common or complete acceptance of political forces and factors as all-pervading and controlling in hu-

[117] M. A. Judson, *The Development of the Theory of Parliamentary Sovereignty 1640–1649*. Radcliffe doctoral dissertation, 1932.

man affairs. To them the theoretical meaning and the implications of a sovereign political state were as vague and nebulous as are to some men today the real meaning and political significance of the economic and scientific forces which transcend the state's boundary and sovereignty. For Englishmen to grasp the concept of sovereignty in the early seventeenth century, it was actually necessary for them to recognize the essential unity of the state at a time when the government of the state was divided between the king-in-parliament and the king-out-of-parliament. To expect men in whose government authority was divided to go back of government to the state, a relatively new entity in the civilization of western Europe, would be asking them to be truly profound and creative political thinkers, which Englishmen were not in the early part of the seventeenth century.

Nevertheless, despite the difficulties, some English thinkers in the decades before the civil war began to understand the constitutional and political realities of their own age, and a few actually attributed sovereignty to the king. It was infinitely harder to attribute it to parliament, for, during the whole period between 1603 and 1642, the component parts of that body—king, lords, and commons—were struggling against each other. With the exception of Whitelocke's, no real theory of parliamentary sovereignty was set forth before the civil war. During the war Hunton developed to its logical conclusion the idea implicit in Whitelocke; but a year before Hunton's *Treatise of Monarchie* appeared, Parker wrote his *Observations* setting forth a theory of parliamentary sovereignty which, from the political point of view, outmoded Hunton's before it was enunciated. In this tract Parker gave sovereignty not to a parliament in which king, lords, and commons were co-ordinate members, but to lords and commons alone.

Only by reviewing and analyzing the obstacles blocking Englishmen's minds to an understanding of the concept of sovereignty, is it possible to appreciate fully the intellectual stature of Henry Parker. He saw, as few of his contemporaries did, that England had become a unified political state. He saw that such a state required a government in which the final determination of policy and of controversial questions was clearly understood and accepted. He saw that a parliament in which king, lords, and commons were co-ordinate in authority would be no real solution for a nation engaged in fighting a civil war to determine which among these partners in authority was truly supreme. While the struggle was just beginning, Parker denied any real sovereignty to the king, giving it instead to the lords and commons whom he called the "essence" of the people of England.

Henry Parker was able to think in such terms because in the first place, as Professor Jordan has so clearly demonstrated, he had a sure and realistic grasp of the working of political forces.[118] He understood before Harrington that the balance of power had already shifted from the king to the people arrayed against him, and that any stable government must reflect that underlying political fact. Parker recognized that legal sanctions against arbitrary monarchs had failed and that only human power, organized into governmental authority, could provide an effective sanction for truly limiting kings. He was enough of a democrat to make the people the source of political authority and their welfare its supreme goal, but his democratic ideas began and ended there. His classical conservative fear of mob rule and his instinctive feeling (almost passion) for the necessity of order in human affairs led him to attribute the sovereignty essential for order, not to the people themselves, but only to parliament by whom it could be safely wielded in an orderly way.

Of all the factors leading Parker to enunciate a theory of parliamentary sovereignty it was perhaps his feeling for order and unity which is most significant. In the years between 1640 and 1642, he proclaimed his belief in order and unity in three pamphlets [119] setting forth his Erastian views on the relation

[118] W. K. Jordan, *Men of Substance*, pp. 141 ff.
[119] The three pamphlets are: *A Discourse concerning Puritans* . . .

of church and of state. "Supream power," he wrote, "ought to be intire and undivided, and cannot else be sufficient for the protection of all, if it doe not extend over all: without any other equall power to controll, or diminish it." [120] The prince should be supreme in causes both ecclesiastical and civil. Otherwise, "humane nature must needs be destitute of those remedies which are necessary for its conservation, since power cannot be divided . . ." [121] Only where order and government exist can there be the sound foundation essential for the development of life in the ecclesiastical sphere.[122] Throughout human history, he asserted, kings have possessed more than temporal power. Their power has rightly extended over ecclesiastical things and persons, and most powers claimed and exercised by ecclesiastical persons have been sheer usurpations. Not only Catholics but Protestants as well have been guilty of that usurpation. Bishops, Presbyterians, and even Calvin "attribute" too much "to priests." [123] "This," he said concerning Calvin's view, "is a way to erect *regnum in regno*, and to maintaine such concurrent jurisdictions, as cannot possibly stand to-gether." [124]

Since Parker held such views, it is understandable that in the summer of 1642 he insisted upon the imperative necessity of a final supreme "determination" of authority. He had always championed parliament against the king and was now willing to give that body sovereign power. There was no need of calling another parliament to decide the issue, for why appeal " in *infinitum.*" Nor was there need of appealing to the people at large, for if we did that, "we do the same thing as to proclaim Civill Warre, and to blow the trumpet of general

(London, 1641); *The true grounds of Ecclesiastical Regiment* . . . , (London, 1641); and *The question concerning the Divine Right of Episcopacie truly stated,* (London, 1641).

[120] *The true grounds of Ecclesiastical Regiment*, p. 8.
[121] *A Discourse concerning Puritans*, p. 17.
[122] *The true grounds of Ecclesiastical Regiment*, p. 78.
[123] *A Discourse concerning Puritans*, p. 28.
[124] *Ibid.*, p. 31.

confusion." [125] Since parliament is "indeed the State it self" [126], it should and does possess the final authority. Parker's insistence upon the necessity for unity in state and government remained basic in all his later writings. In 1645 he wrote: ". . . the end of all government is the preservation of humane society, the meanes of doing whereof is by union and unity, and Authority is the effectual meanes of producing and propagating unity and therefore whensoever Authority is divided, Unitie may alwaies, and sometimes must admit of division which destroyes it, for unity and division are destructive one of another. . . ." [127] ". . . unity which is the preserver of humane society, must be provided for before any other duty that is required of man." [128]

Charles Herle also had a deep sense of the need for order and unity in human affairs. "Order," he wrote, " 'tis the *sinnew,* and *soule* of Nature," [129] and "if Order be the *soule,* Unity 'tis the center of Nature . . ." [130] Because Herle believed in unity and because he championed parliament's cause, he, like Parker, came to ascribe sovereignty to the two houses. There must be, he wrote, a "finall and casting resolution" of the "sence" of the law, "without which the *Record* is but the *Sheath* 'tis the sence is the *Sword* of the Law; such a power of faculty there must be in every legall Government, after all debatement, to give Lawes their Sence beyond all further debatement . . ." This "decisive faculty" should rest in the "two houses in whose *votes* the Law itselfe places that very same specifick *reason* of the Kingdome, that at first *contrived* and still *animates* the Government." [131] Men would go on forever searching for finality if there did not exist some last power

[125] H. Parker, *Observations,* p. 43.

[126] *Ibid.,* p. 34.

[127] [H. Parker], *Jus regum, Or, a vindication of the regall power: against all spirituall authority* . . . , (London, 1645), p. 17.

[128] *Ibid.,* p. 37.

[129] C. Herle, *The Independency on Scriptures of the Independency of Churches,* (London, 1644), p. 37.

[130] *Ibid.,* p. 38.

[131] C. Herle, *A Fuller Answer,* p. 14.

to declare the law. Since the houses of parliament are "the highest Court, from which there lies no appeale, [they] must needs have the *finall judgement* of what is *Law*, or els there must be no such *judgement*, and so the government destructively defective in that same *summum in eodem genere*, which must be *radix* et regula, the root, rule, or measure, of all inferiours . . ." [132] Not only must the two houses have the final judgment, but they must likewise have the power to act in support of any decision they make.

Their sovereign power included, according to Herle, the power to make law and also to perform other "acts of the supreme power," such as the choice of ministers, the making of treaties and wars, and even the assembling of parliament and the execution of laws. [133] Thus Herle, even more explicitly than Parker, claimed new and revolutionary powers for the lords and commons. Of all the supporters of parliament in these years, it was this country clergyman who first openly and unequivocally demanded and defended parliament's right to those prerogative powers of the king which Pym, Eliot, and other aggressive parliamentary leaders had first challenged but never clearly demanded for themselves in the earlier period.

Both Parker and Herle gave sovereign power to the two houses of parliament, and both emphatically denied that the people possessed such power out of parliament. To both men parliament and people were identical for all political purposes. Parker wrote in the *Observations,*

> The whole Kingdome is not so properly the Author as the essence it selfe of Parliaments . . . [134] [In *Jus Populi* he showed that] the parliament is indeed nothing else, but the very people it self artificially congregated, or reduced by an orderly election, and representation, into such a Senate, or proportionable body. Tis true, in my understanding, the Parliament differs many wayes from the rude bulk of the

[132] C. Herle, *Ahab's Fall*, p. 38.
[133] C. Herle, *An Answer*, pp. 22–32.
[134] H. Parker, *Observations*, p. 5.

universality, but in power, in honour, in majestie, in commission, it ought not at all to be divided, or accounted different as to any legall purpose.[135]

Herle also emphatically insisted that the people outside parliament had no right to resist. Parliament's decision was final: —"*In this final Resolution of the States judgement the people are to rest* . . ." [136] The idea that the people could resist king or parliament is a "position," Herle maintained, "which no man I know maintaines, that Parliament is the peoples own consent, which once pass'd they cannot revoke, he [i.e., Ferne] still pursues his own dreame of the peoples reassuming power, whereas we acknowledge no power can be imployed but what is reserved, and the people have reserved no power in themselves from themselves to Parliament." [137]

Both Parker and Herle admitted that the sovereign power they ascribed to parliament was, in the last analysis, arbitrary because of its very nature. On this point Parker wrote: "To have then an arbitrary power placed in the Peers and Commons is naturall and expedient at all times, but the very use of this arbitrary power, according to reason of State, and warlick policy in times of generall dangers and distresse is absolutely necessary and inevitable." [138] Herle admitted that if Parliament pronounced the last judgment, it was really exercising an arbitrary power:

> . . . it cannot be denyed, nor avoyded that as the Government in the forme or qualification of it was, at first an act of the will, and so Arbitrary; so it still remaining the same it must remaine some where arbitrary still, else our forefathers should not convey that same government to us which they began, they cannot bind us in that wherein they were themselves free: it is the priviledge of Gods laws only to bind unalterably, now where should the *Arbitrarines* of this faculty reside for the States use, but where it was at first in the *con-*

135 H. Parker, *Jus Populi*, pp. 18–19.
136 C. Herle, *A Fuller Answer*, p. 18.
137 *Ibid.*, p. 25.
138 H. Parker, *The Contra Replicant*, p. 30.

sent and *reason* of the state which as (we have seen) the Law places in the *Votes* of Parliament . . .[139]

Both writers made it clear that they recognized that there existed no theoretical restraint or limit upon such arbitrary sovereign power as they ascribed to the two houses. According to Parker *"all the right of King and people* depends upon their [i.e., Parliament's] pleasure." [140] The houses could limit and enlarge the king's prerogative and, more significant, "abridge the freedom of the Subject, . . . repeale our great Charter," repeal the petition of right, and even "subject the whole Kingdom for ever to the same arbitrary rule as *France* grones under." [141] According to Herle, parliament cannot be resisted, even if it should "enact Paganisme itselfe." [142] Could Herle, a clergyman in the church, have chosen a more striking example to illustrate the absolute sovereignty of parliament?

Although both men recognized that parliament's sovereign power might mean arbitrary rule, they were confident that their countrymen's lives, liberties, and properties were safe in the keeping of parliament. The remarkable modernity and political realism of their thought comes out in all their ideas, but nowhere so strikingly as in the reasons they gave why arbitrary sovereign power could safely be intrusted to parliament. Parker looked to the composition of parliament, believing it "so equally and geometrically proportionable," that it took "away all jealousies." [143] Power in the hands of one or a few men could be dangerous, but not, he insisted, in the hands of many, and parliament was "neither one nor few, it is indeed the State it self." [144] ". . . every man has an absolute power over himselfe, but because no man can hate himselfe, this power is not dangerous, nor need to be restrayned." [145]

[139] *Ibid.*, p. 17.
[140] H. Parker, *Observations*, p. 45.
[141] H. Parker, *Contra Replicant*, p. 30.
[142] C. Herle, *An Answer*, p. 14.
[143] H. Parker, *Observations*, p. 23.
[144] H. Parker, *Observations*, p. 34.
[145] *Ibid.*

Consequently, when those individuals constituting the state act together in parliament, they are not going to hurt themselves since they are the state. Because of the numbers in parliament, because its members are virtually the state, and because of "it's common interest joyned with its indirectness and integritie," absolute power may safely be entrusted to parliament. Though it is not infallible, there is less "probability" of its "erring" or being "deceived" than where one individual possesses such great power.[146]

Herle gave perhaps more penetrating answers to the same problem, maintaining that arbitrary power in a state was absolutely necessary, but "where this arbitraries [is] allayed and balanced by *number,* trust, *self interest,* 'tis best secured from doing hurt." [147] ". . . experience shows that most mens actions are swayed most what by their ends and interests: . . . The Members [of parliament] are all subjects themselves, not only *intrusted* with, but self *interested* in those very *priviledges* and *properties*" [148] of subjects, which kings pursuing their own interests often override. ". . . it was the wisdom of this government, considering mens aptnesse rather to warpe after their *interests,* and *ends,* then to be kept upright by their *skills* and *oathes,* to trust it rather to many independent mens *interests,* then a few dependent mens *oaths,* every dayes experience tels us that *interests* are better state security than oaths . . ." [149]

This striking remark by Herle (that interests are better security than oaths) well illustrates the great change which had occurred in constitutional and political thought in England between 1603 and 1643. When James became king, men

[146] *Animadversions Animadverted,* p. 7.
[147] C. Herle, *A Fuller Answer,* p. 17.
[148] *Ibid.,* p. 16.
[149] *Ibid.,* pp. 17–18. Such great power did not mean that men in parliament were infallible. ". . . they are not therein in themselves *infallible,* but to us inevetable: our own judgments are not enthralled, 'tis our interests are entrusted and so, subjected to their decisions: our judgments are not infallibly guided from either erring with them or differing from them, but bound up in, and superseded by theirs, from gaine-saying or resistance . . ." *A Fuller Answer* (p. 18).

still clung to the medieval belief that binding law and sacred oaths provided adequate security against arbitrary government. Forty years later a few thinkers had come to see that these were not enough. In the crisis of war they had turned to the organized power of the nation in parliament to give human sanction to the law and to provide that security which sacred oaths often failed to give. In calling upon the collective power of the nation in parliament and in giving it sovereignty, they now looked to the interests of men to guard them against the inherent dangers of arbitrary unlimited power.

In the years immediately after 1642 and 1643, when Parker and Herle set forth these newer ideas, there proved to be no real security as one arbitrary group after another took its turn in trying to govern England. The cycle of revolution had begun and was not to end until the Restoration cut it short in 1660. Even then it did not really end, for only with the Revolution of 1688 was there achieved a resolution of the constitutional and political problems which for over a century had divided Englishmen.

From the vantage point of that revolution it is possible to see in retrospect the full meaning of the ideas with which Englishmen had debated their great issues in the first half of the century. In the Revolution of 1688 the power of the English people who counted politically in the affairs of the nation triumphed, and never in the future was their power successfully overthrown by kings. This power of the people came nakedly into the open in the months elapsing between the time James fled the country and William and Mary were accepted as monarchs, but it was quickly clothed in constitutional forms which men understood and revered. Political might was thus tempered by its association with medieval rights and medieval concepts of limited authority. England now achieved her medieval constitutional ideals, but the victory was won by means of a modern political revolution. By that revolution certain constitutional ideals long cherished by Englishmen were transmitted to the future, and certain political realities came to be accepted both in the functioning of government and in men's ideas concerning it.

From the constitutional point of view, the Revolution of 1688 was, in the first place, a victory for rights—for those rights which parliamentarians had long claimed as the heritage of all Englishmen. As a victory for rights it was also, in the realm of ideas, a victory for the concept that the ruler was limited by the rights of his people and the law of the land. The earlier efforts of Stephen Langton, William Marshal, and the barons of thirteenth-century England, of Edward Coke, Edwin Sandys, Thomas Wentworth, and their compatriots in the first part of the seventeenth century lived on to become, through the medium of the Bill of Rights, the medieval and seventeenth-century contribution to our Anglo-American pattern of government and our fundamental beliefs concerning its nature and purpose.

The Revolution of 1688 was also a victory for parliament's supremacy in the English government, for the rights of Englishmen were no longer set forth in a petition of right, but in a statute accepted by king, lords, and commons. As a statute, the Bill of Rights was an agreement of all the realm and the highest act of the legislature of the realm—the institution of government finally accepted as the supreme legal authority in the land. Whitelocke's and Hunton's concept of a supreme mixed government—one legally co-ordinate of king, lords, and commons—had finally become a functioning reality. Because parliament was now the supreme authority, accepted as such by the nation and by the nation's new rulers, it could in the future protect rights more effectively than it had ever been able to do in earlier ages when its final authority had not been completely recognized or accepted by either the monarch or substantial parts of the nation. From the constitutional point of view, therefore, Coke, the champion of rights and of law, and also Hunton, the advocate of the co-operation of king and people in a supreme, mixed parliament, could well have regarded the Bill of Rights and the parliament enacting it as their own achievement.

But so too could Parker and Herle, and Pym, Phelips, and Eliot, for when the Revolution of 1688 is viewed from the political point of view, the real significance of the great contribution these men made to political policy and thought becomes clear. In their own age Parker and Herle were revolutionary thinkers who crossed over the line from the legal and constitutional to the political—a step which Hunton steadfastly and consistently refused to take. They, following along the path which Eliot, Phelips, and Pym had gone with hesitating steps, saw clearly that law and right could never be secure until they were guarded and maintained by the political strength of the nation, and true co-operation of king and people never prevail until the basic authority of one was achieved as a political reality. Parker and Herle turned boldly from God and the king to the people in parliament for the final sanction in government and were unafraid to give the people of England, represented in parliament, sovereign power. They were unafraid because they believed that the composition of parliament and the number and self-interest of its members would provide as much security against arbitrary rule as human institutions can afford to human beings.

These ideas contributed by Parker and Herle played a significant part in the political realities of the Revolution of 1688. That event was "glorious" and "bloodless," but it still was a revolution. In that revolution both Whigs and Tories rose up in their political might and agreed to change their ruler. Because they agreed, the revolution was "bloodless"; but that action by the "people" was truly revolutionary. It destroyed in England, for all practical purposes, the force of the concept that kings ruled by divine right. It demonstrated the fact that only when the political strength of the nation was united and organized could there be real security for law and right. It meant ultimately that, in the supreme parliament where king, lords, and commons were legally co-ordinate, the two latter, and eventually the commons alone, were truly sovereign, for the new rulers of England received their power at this time from the hands of their "people in parliament" and could never in the future free themselves completely from their democratic heritage.

INDEX OF NAMES